EXPORT/IMPORT TRENDS AND ECONOMIC DEVELOPMENT IN TRINIDAD, 1919-1939

EXPORT/IMPORT TRENDS AND ECONOMIC DEVELOPMENT IN TRINIDAD, 1919–1939

Doddridge H.N. Alleyne

Canoe Press
Jamaica • Barbados • Trinidad and Tobago

Sir Arthur Lewis Institute of Social and Economic Research
University of West Indies, St Augustine

Canoe Press
7A Gibraltar Hall Road Mona
Kingston 7 Jamaica
www.uwipress.com

CATALOGUING-IN-PUBLICATION DATA

Alleyne, D.H.N.

Export/import trends and economic development in Trinidad,
1919–1939 / D.H.N. Alleyne.

p. cm

Includes bibliographical references.

ISBN: 978-976-8125-91-0

1. Exports – Trinidad – History. 2. Imports – Trinidad – History.
3. Trinidad – Commerce – History. 4. Trinidad – Economic conditions. I. Title.

HF3365.Z5T493 2010 382'17'0972983

Cover design by Robert Harris.

Printed in the United States of America.

Contents

Foreword

Doddridge Alleyne, the author of this book, was born in Charlotteville, Tobago, in 1927. This fishing village on the north coast of the smaller "twin island" of the British colony of Trinidad and Tobago was remote and isolated at the time (and for long after); it was at a considerable distance from the little capital, Scarborough, and almost impossibly distant from the colonial capital, Port of Spain. Alleyne went to Charlotteville Methodist School; like many Tobagonians, he was brought up in the Methodist Church, a denomination traditionally of great influence in the island. He went to Trinidad for his secondary education, attending a private school, Osmond High School in Port of Spain. During this period, 1930–50, when secondary education in the prestigious boys' colleges was fee-paying (unless you won a College Exhibition, and these were few indeed), the private high schools played an important role in the social and educational mobility of hundreds of aspiring young people. At Osmond, Alleyne's academic promise was recognized, and he was able to attend Queen's Royal College, the premier boys' school, to study for his Higher School Certificate in the mid-1940s. Nearly sixty years later, in 2003, he was inducted into the Queen's Royal College Hall of Honour, a tribute bestowed on very eminent "Old Boys".

After working in the public service for some time, Alleyne received a Colonial Development and Welfare Scholarship, which allowed him to pursue tertiary education in the hallowed halls of Oxford University, taking the famous "PPE" – Philosophy, Politics and Economics – at Balliol College, acquiring the BA and MA degrees. In 1958, he submitted to Balliol a thesis of well over four hundred pages, which is now, more than fifty years later, being published. His alma mater recognized his distinguished career in 1999 by making him an honorary fellow of Balliol.

Straight out of school, the young Alleyne joined the colonial civil service, working through the era of decolonization and independence, giving forty years of selfless and distinguished service to his country. With the assumption of power by the People's National Movement led by Eric Williams in 1956, and especially after national independence in 1962, he became one of a small group of dedicated public servants who worked with the government to lay the foundations of the modern state and economy. Their salaries were small and their perks were few; they worked with a notoriously mercurial leader; their hours were long and irregular, and family life was often sacrificed to the demands of public service. Alleyne was one of the most outstanding members of this group. He rose to the top of the heap, serving as permanent secretary in the three crucial ministries of petroleum and mines, finance, planning and development, and then as permanent secretary to the prime minister and head of the public service. In all these positions, he was central to remaking Trinidad and Tobago in the 1960s and 1970s, and he worked very closely with Williams.

Alleyne was one of the founders of the nationally owned energy sector which has done so much to shape the modern economy. With little directly relevant training, and few blueprints to follow, he led the negotiations which led to the purchase of the gas stations belonging to British Petroleum, and the subsequent creation of the National Petroleum Marketing Company (NP). This was in 1968; with the start of the oil boom in 1973–74, Alleyne found himself leading negotiations for the purchase of Shell Trinidad and the creation of TRINTOC (Trinidad and Tobago Oil Company) to manage the former Shell assets. After Williams's death, he was at it again in 1985, when he participated in the purchase of TEXACO's assets in Trinidad – the largest oil producer and refiner in the country – and those of TESORO. It was entirely fitting that in the national commemoration of the hundredth anniversary of commercial oil production in Trinidad and Tobago (2009), Alleyne was recognized as a "Pioneering Hero" for his work in these negotiations, and more generally, in his efforts to bring about national control of the country's petroleum industry. He also led the discussions which led to the purchase of the local branch of the Bank of London and Montreal, and the subsequent creation of the National Commercial Bank, owned by the government, in 1970 – the forerunner of today's very successful First Citizens Bank. In carrying out these complex negotiations, and for other purposes, Alleyne travelled the world pursuing his country's interests, often in very difficult circumstances.

Working with Williams was never easy, and Alleyne was perhaps the most distinguished member of that coterie of senior public servants who surrounded him, to fall victim to his often inexplicable bouts of anger and vindictiveness. The story is told in some detail in the chapter entitled "Williams and His Mandarins" in Selwyn Ryan's *Eric Williams: The Myth and the Man*, published in 2009 by the University of the West Indies Press. This eminent and manifestly honourable man, head of the public service, was accused in 1975–76 of serious infractions of public service rules, interdicted by the Public Service Commission, put on three-quarters salary, and told to prepare for a formal hearing by a special tribunal. When the tribunal was finally convened, all the charges against him were suddenly dropped. Alleyne had been exonerated and returned to work; but Williams never spoke to him again, and he remained in the proverbial wilderness for several years to come.

In the last year of Williams's life, he gave permission for Alleyne to serve as a United Nations petroleum adviser to the Government of Kenya (1980–82). Here he drew on his experiences at home in establishing the framework and structure of the National Oil Company of Kenya. This international exposure helped to prepare him for the major assignment given to him after Williams had died, by the People's National Movement government of George Chambers: to serve as his country's ambassador and permanent representative to the United Nations (1983–88). Here he sat on the Security Council for a term and actually presided over that body for brief periods in 1985 and 1986. At the UN he also chaired the committee on the arms embargo against South Africa in the dying years of the apartheid regime. As chairman of the Committee of Non-Aligned Countries, he helped to craft a resolution on the Iraq–Iran war, which eventually led to the end of the conflict. His years at the UN representing his country certainly marked a fitting conclusion to his career in the public service. None could (or did) question his claims to one of the nation's highest award, the Chaconia Medal (gold), which he was awarded for "long and meritorious service to Trinidad and Tobago".

This book was originally researched and written as an Oxford thesis submitted in 1958. Yet it remains a valuable and pertinent study, by no means outdated by the passage of time. The fact is that the *economic* history of Trinidad and Tobago has been seriously under-researched, as compared with its political, social and cultural history. We still lack a scholarly account of the evolution of the country's economy, both overall, and for specific periods. What Alleyne has written is a detailed, empirically rich study of the economic (and social) history of the colony in the crucial twenty years between the two World Wars (1919–39), the period when the foundations for the modern, post-war economy were laid. (If only I had been able to read this work when I wrote my *History of Modern Trinidad* many years ago.) The study is based on meticulous research into a wide range of primary sources, especially official reports and papers, and statistical materials such as the colonial censuses and fiscal records. No other work, to my knowledge, provides us with this kind of basis for understanding the modern economy of Trinidad and Tobago.

Perhaps the central thesis of the book is that the oil industry came to maturity in the 1920s and especially the 1930s, and supplanted export agriculture as the colony's chief source of export income, a fateful shift for the country's future. In his detailed study of exports (chapter 1), Alleyne shows the steady rise of oil, and the decline of cocoa and sugar, as export earners. As early as 1930, oil represented 52 per cent of exports as compared to 36 per cent for sugar and cocoa combined; by 1939, oil accounted for 75 per cent of total value of exports, a domination more total than was ever enjoyed by King Sugar in his day or cocoa during its "golden age" (1890–1920). As Alleyne notes, oil "saved the economy from the depths of poverty", but the levels of spendable domestic income were still very low, both absolutely, and in relation to the total export incomes. A high proportion of oil's profits went to pay dividends, a low proportion was siphoned off for taxes and royalties, and for labour; there was an ominous, and growing, gap between total export values, and local disbursements of all kinds.

Chapter 2 subjects the colony's imports to the same kind of detailed scrutiny. Alleyne shows that there was a shift in the balance between imports of food and beverages, and imports of manufactured goods: while in 1919, 49 per cent of imports were food and drink and 40 per cent manufactures, by 1939 the percentages were 25 and 68, respectively, suggesting a society less preoccupied with basic food needs and with, perhaps, a higher standard of living, despite the Great Depression of the years after 1929. He gives an interesting example of what students of social history can do with imports data: in 1919 imports of shoes and boots amounted to 0.4 pairs per capita; by 1939 it was 1.8, a fourfold increase, reflecting an increase in the standard of living, fuelled partly by cheap Japanese and Chinese footwear.

In chapters 3, 4 and 5, Alleyne considers the fortunes of the agricultural sector in considerable detail. While sugar, cocoa and other products declined overall in terms of export values, they remained immensely important as employers of labour. He provides a detailed account of the fall of the cocoa industry in the 1920s and 1930s, carefully analysing the complex, interrelated causes of this secular decline, coming after a thirty-year period (1890–1920) when it was the colony's leading export industry. He also considers the local government's many efforts to rescue the industry, especially the plantation sector which was dominated by French Creole owners. Turning to sugar (chapter 4), he shows that by 1930 sugar had overtaken cocoa in terms of export values, but was itself undergoing difficulties; indeed, the whole agrarian economy was deteriorating. Alleyne analyses patterns of amalgamation and consolidation in the sugar industry, technical changes and new cultivation methods, attempts to control the world sugar market through international agreements and quotas, the cane-farming sector, and the local government's efforts to aid the plantations. Finally, in chapter 5, Alleyne concludes his discussion of the agrarian economy by looking at the rather limited efforts to diversify by cultivating coffee, citrus, bananas and coconuts.

But it was oil, not agriculture, which would dominate Trinidad's twentieth-century economy, and Alleyne gives us in chapter 6 a detailed history of the local oil industry in a period of dynamic growth. He shows that the key decisions on issues like leases of oil lands, fees, taxes and royalties were made, not in Port of Spain, but by an "inter-departmental committee" in London, driven by empire-wide policies and concerns. Both in terms of capital and technology, and in terms of governmental policies, the industry had its mainspring abroad. Its importance to Britain was huge: in 1929 Trinidad became the leading oil exporter in the empire, and this strategic role naturally assumed even greater significance as Europe drifted towards war in the late 1930s. Production increased very rapidly in the second half of the 1930s (and even more so once the war began), and refining was also greatly expanded, so that by the mid-1930s refining capacity had outstripped production and imported crude was becoming more and more important. In 1938 Trinidad had greater refining capacity than Venezuela. The next leap forward for the local oil industry would be marine production, which only got underway after the war.

Though this book is primarily an economic history, students of Trinidad's social history will find much of relevance in chapters 7 and 8, which deal, respectively, with population and labour. In chapter 7, Alleyne provides a thorough and interesting demographic analysis based mainly on the censuses of the period. The colony's population grew rapidly between the wars, even though Indian immigration had ceased in 1917; this was nearly all natural increase. Compared with other British Caribbean colonies between 1921 and 1946, Trinidad's rate of population growth was greater than that of any other colony. Birth rates were high, averaging 32 per thousand in the period; and, despite the Depression, death rates were steadily declining, from 24.46 per thousand in 1919 to 15.8 in 1938. Even infant mortality rates fell, from an appalling 154.75 per thousand in 1919 to 98.42 in 1938. These were years when the government made considerable efforts to improve public health and fight the major killer diseases of adults and children.

Using the census and other sources, Alleyne discusses the provision of social services, including education, and notes the rise in literacy rates in the period, although perhaps one-third of all school-age children were not enrolled between 1921 and 1931. In a careful and interesting analysis, the author looks at population density, urbanization and housing. The drift to the towns, especially the capital, began long before World War II, putting severe pressure on housing stocks and social services.

This excursion into social history continues in chapter 8 on labour; a chapter which provides the indispensable background to the strikes and riots of 1937. Alleyne analyses changes in the patterns of labour demand and supply, in relation especially to the sugar and cocoa industries, the main employers throughout the period, and the balance between wage labour on the estates and peasant production. Using a variety of sources, he provides much detailed data on wages and conditions of work, noting the vicious circle of depressed agriculture, an overstocked labour market, low wages and irregular employment, low labour efficiency because of malnutrition and disease. Typical of underdeveloped colonial economies, Alleyne shows the very large numbers employed in domestic service: about 8,000 in 1911, 18,600 in 1921; and also as shop assistants, a miserably paid job even if more socially acceptable than domestic service.

Of course, the 1930s saw considerable labour unrest, culminating in the "Butler Riots" of June 1937. Alleyne looks at the agitation for a minimum wage and the only partially successful efforts of Captain Cipriani and his Trinidad Workingmen's Association to secure decent minimum wages for a range of occupations. He concludes this chapter on labour with an account of the development of trade union legislation and the establishment of a labour adviser (1938), and the rapid formation of unions in the aftermath of the riots. Chapters 7 and 8 show clearly that Alleyne's concept of economic history is broad and that he grasps the complex links between economic and social developments (and, for that matter, political).

The last chapter returns to more classically economic history by providing an analysis of public finance: the structure of government revenues and expenditures, taxes and duties. Typical of a Caribbean colony, customs and excise duties were the largest source of government income all through the period (54 per cent in 1939), though revenues from internal sources, including income

Preface

This study is an attempt to make a contribution to the small but growing body of collected and analysed information on the economic development of the West Indies. It is concerned with only one of the former colonies, Trinidad and Tobago. However, from time to time it will be necessary to make references to, and comparisons with, some of the others.

It is hoped that, particularly at this time when the former colonies of the region are very much in the search of a workable integration framework, some new knowledge about the economic background of one of them would prove of some value. It is interesting to recall a remark once made at a seminar, namely, that *West Indian Federation was the brainchild of those who hoped, by the addition and multiplication of poverty, to produce wealth and a higher standard of living.* The federation did not long survive, but other forms of mutual collaboration were created to the benefit of the colonies, later independent nations. These include CARICOM and the Caribbean Development Bank, among others.

While this observation as regards the multiplication of poverty may be an exaggeration, it must be conceded that it contains a grain of truth. Many of the islands can still be described as "backward", "poor" or "underdeveloped" according to the school of thought on the subject to which one adheres. This study is concerned, however, with one of the less underdeveloped of the former colonies. It is hoped that this study will indicate the extent to which any economic contribution Trinidad and Tobago can make to Caribbean collaboration would have been conditioned by the economic forces which operated and developed in the inter-war years. If, in spite of the difficulties of the period, some progress was then possible, there is hope for the future.

The choice of the period was not difficult. There has already been done, for the islands as a whole, some very valuable work on the periods of slavery and the immediate post-emancipation and indentureship era. Some research is being done on the late nineteenth century and the first decade of the twentieth century for the three larger islands. In a thesis comparing the economic development in Puerto Rico, Trinidad and Tobago and Jamaica, J. O'Neil Lewis has treated the post–World War II period.

The inter-war years therefore selected themselves. The period has not yet been studied either for the West Indies as a whole or for Trinidad and Tobago, in particular. However, the researcher was soon convinced that a study of the inter-war period in the economic development of Trinidad and Tobago would do more than merely fill a gap. For in spite of its being a period characterized by two depressions (in the 1920s and 1930s), it provided a solid basis for the growth in Trinidad and Tobago in the post–World War II period.

It was in this period that the petroleum industry came to maturity and supplanted agriculture as the chief source of export incomes. It saw the growth of urban population and of trade unions and the accomplishment of many essential public works.

The study has also revealed information that would supplement and modify certain findings concerning the Trinidad and Tobago economy: for example, A.R. Prest's conclusion ("War Economics of Primary Producing Countries", p. 264) that "there is no question that American war demands in some form or other were entirely responsible" for the exodus of labour and cane farmers from the sugar industry. However, this claim would have to be somewhat modified once it is understood that in spite of rapid population growth the actual numbers engaged as cane farmers and as agricultural labourers had already been declining even in the inter-war years. There is no denying that American spending did contribute considerably. However, it gave a greater impetus to, but did not initiate, the flight from agriculture. The internal weaknesses of agriculture had already provided a motive for such flight.

The approach to the study was stimulated by the work of Professor and Mrs Hicks in their *Report on Finance and Taxation in Jamaica* (1955). In the absence of national income data it was necessary to use the trade statistics as indicators of economic development. One objective of the study would be to determine the impact on the trade of the islands of the world economic forces operating in the inter-war years.

However, as important as the analysis of the export/import situation might be, it was undertaken not merely as an end in itself but as a means of understanding the internal workings of the economy. This is a study of the interaction of external and internal forces in the economic development of Trinidad and Tobago in the inter-war years. For example, although the decline of the cocoa industry started with the fall in world cocoa prices after 1920, it required the basic internal and as yet concealed weaknesses of the industry to make the decline as absolute as it became by 1939. It therefore makes sense to begin with the export situation.

The study itself could not be done by a more qualified person. Doddridge Alleyne has been a practitioner with a decidedly scholarly orientation. His penchant for seeing connections where others did not, and his scrupulous attention to detail, have made him a most remarkable and unusual public servant. What is more, his ability to combine the passion of his national pride with sober thought and scholarship was equaled only by his ability to combine his sense of responsibility as a public servant with his commitment to document the truth as he saw it. The basic philosophy of this book, that *the quality of the legacy we now enjoy has been conditioned by the calibre of the heritage with which we have been endowed,* is as poignant today as it was yesterday and as it will be for many years to come

Karl Theodore
Department of Economics
University of the West Indies
St Augustine, Trinidad and Tobago

Introduction

This study examines for the inter-war period the development of the Trinidad and Tobago economy in which primarily two, sometimes easily distinguishable but closely related, influences were at work. The first concerns mainly the impact on the trade of an export-based economy, of the world economic forces operating in the inter-war years – a period of acute fluctuations in world trade and commodity prices; a period albeit in which only a few years can be regarded as even relatively prosperous; a period which was characterized by the sharp post-war depression of the early 1920s and the Great Depression of the 1930s. It is in this sense therefore a study (especially in the early phases of the period) of the struggles of a primarily agricultural economy in the context of world economic depression. The second influence concerns the reactions of the internal economy to the external trade factor and also the way in which purely internal factors influenced the trade statistics. The picture is therefore one of the interaction of external and internal forces on the economy.

Chapters 1 and 2 therefore analyse the export/import situation. In the absence of national income data the trade statistics are used as indicators or trends in the internal economy. Chapter 1 which analyses exports divides the period into five phases: two of depression and three of relative prosperity. It indicates the primacy of agriculture, chiefly cocoa, in the first phase (1919–21). At that time cocoa, the "economic barometer" of the country, accounted for 51 per cent of exports. In the second phase (1921–1926 to 1927) some new parity has been established between the three chief exports industries, cocoa, sugar and petroleum, with their contributions to exports standing in 1923 at 29 per cent, 26.1 per cent and 28.7 per cent, respectively. But this period of parity was short-lived and by 1925 the trend which was to become established for the rest of the period was clearly visible. Petroleum had become the chief contributor to the value of domestic exports. Cocoa fluctuated somewhat and after 1931 declined catastrophically both as regards total export values and its relative contribution to exports. In 1939 cocoa contributed 3.1 per cent and petroleum 74.6 per cent. The transformation of the economy was complete.

What happened to sugar meanwhile? In phase 1 it contributed between 20 per cent and 37 per cent of the total export values. This contribution fell somewhat (15–20 per cent) in the late 1920s; was more or less stable at say 20 per cent in the early and middle 1930s and then by 1938 was again contributing only 15 per cent of exports. The chapter therefore considers that the economy had experienced two major shifts, two major types of imbalances. In the first the economy had passed from an imbalance in which agriculture (largely cocoa) was predominant to one in which petroleum predominated. The period of balanced growth had been brief, that is, 1923–24. The second type of imbalance is that which saw the shift from domestic to foreign ownership of the industries chiefly responsible for export earnings. Petroleum was largely foreign owned and financed and even within agriculture sugar, which become superior to cocoa, was becoming increasingly foreign owned. The chapter then considers the distribution of export incomes between domestic and foreign income earners.

Chapter 2 analyses imports. Here the same sorts of trends as seen in chapter 1 are reflected. While in 1919 the contributions of "food and drink" and "manufactures" to total imports were 48.7 per cent and 39.9 per cent, respectively, by 1939 the situation was reversed and the contributions were 25.3 per cent and 67.7 per cent, respectively. In the latter period imports of machinery for mining and refining had become the largest single item. The petroleum industry had dominated both exports and imports. Per capita imports of certain food and clothing items were then demonstrated. In many cases (especially milk) these showed remarkable increases, especially as import prices fell in the 1930s.

The later section of the chapter considers in greater detail imports of machinery and other producer goods and examines the influence upon them of the prices of the exports they were used to produce.

Following on this picture of the trading position the study then examines the reactions in the internal economy to the external trade factors. Chapter 3 examines the cocoa industry: the "golden age" of the industry 1870–1920; the factors affecting the expansion in that period and then the factors contributing tax, first levied in 1918, did increase. In terms of expenditure we see a partial shift from the classic colonial policy of spending the minimum on social services and infrastructural projects. This was a new era of colonial thinking on "development", especially in the 1930s. Expenditure on social services, including health and education, rose steadily. The period after 1934 saw new, large infrastructural projects undertaken: the deep water harbour scheme for the capital, electrification and water developments, hospitals, schools, slum clearance and public housing – altogether considerable spending on social capital. In 1938–39 long-term planning was accepted by the colonial government, which drew up a five-year development programme including a fairly large expenditure based on buoyant oil revenues, but the outbreak of the war deflected this first foray into development planning. Alleyne notes that Trinidad and Tobago, more than most other colonies, had a policy of developing financial reserves, and this would be a strength in the post-war years.

The inter-war period was important, Alleyne concludes, because it marked the transition from an economy mainly dependent on agricultural exports to one dependent mainly on oil, from a situation in which the chief export industry was locally owned (cocoa) to one in which they were foreign owned (oil, sugar). The leading characteristic was the tendency of the economy to become increasingly orientated outwards; by 1939, both oil and sugar were overwhelmingly dominated by foreign capital. As oil extraction and refining, sugar cultivation and manufacturing, each became more capital intensive, these industries had to look to foreign sources of capital and technology; the internal capital market was weak or altogether absent. These developments, complicated by the somewhat contradictory consequences of World War II and the "American occupation" of the colony, would impact on the evolution of Trinidad and Tobago's economy after the war and into the modern period – an economy which, as we have seen, the author contributed significantly to shape between the 1960s and the 1980s.

This book provides us with a detailed economic history of Trinidad during an important period, which saw a boom just after the end of World War I, followed by a prolonged depression, and then partial recovery just before the start of World War II. It helps the reader to grasp the essential foundations of the modern, post-war economy which came into being in the era of decolonization and independence. Because the economic history of Trinidad and Tobago has been generally neglected both by the historians and the economists, it fills a significant gap in the literature. This book will be an important building block for a scholarly and comprehensive economic history of modern Trinidad and Tobago, and will thereby contribute to our understanding more generally of the evolution of Caribbean economies.

Moreover, this book can be read as a case study of a British colonial economy in the first half of the twentieth century. It will contribute to our knowledge of the evolution of Caribbean colonial economies in general, stimulating fruitful comparative work with Jamaica, Barbados and Guyana, especially, and more broadly with Puerto Rico, Cuba, Haiti and the Dominican Republic. And it will add to the literature on British colonial policy and practice in this period.

For these reasons, I welcome the appearance of this book, despite the long gap between its writing and its publication. It is a classic work that deserves a place in the library of every serious student of the economic and social history of Trinidad and Tobago and the Caribbean.

Bridget Brereton
University of the West Indies
St Augustine, Trinidad and Tobago

to the decline after 1921. Export prices falling in 1921 triggered off the decline. Thereafter internal weakness – indebtedness, over-expansion, neglect and disease – combined to cause the ruin of the industry. Government assistance was powerless to save the industry.

Chapter 4 then treats the sugar industry. It considers the process of amalgamation of estates; the attempts to improve efficiency in the field and in the factory. It was found, however, that on the whole the production methods employed in Trinidad were inferior to those in, say, Puerto Rico. The cane-farming section of the industry is then considered. It was responsible for more than 40 per cent of all cane crushed yet it had little say in the methods of determining the price paid by the manufacturers for farmers' canes. This was largely because cane-farmers were numerous and largely disorganized and regarded cane farming as a part-time activity. The latest formula then under review by which the price of cane was determined took into consideration all the costs of the manufacturer but not those of the cane farmer. It made even dividends a determinant of the equation with cane price the residual. Sucrose content of the canes which would have been a good means of determining the price to be paid was not considered at all. Government assistance to the industry was on a far more lavish scale than was assistance to cocoa. The terms of the loans made were also much more lenient. In addition government banned imports of sugar, divided the local market among the sugar manufacturers and fixed the local market retail price of sugar at a level much higher than the export price. In this way the local market was giving a subsidy to the industry. In exchange for this concession and the gains from imperial preference on sugar, the industry undertook to pay at least a minimum price for farmers' canes.

Chapter 5 examines the minor agricultural industries. They represented the search for an alternative, that is, peasant owned crops that could take the place of cocoa. These industries, however, also experienced fluctuating export prices. The most important characteristic of these industries is the shift from crop to crop as world prices and market conditions favoured now one and then the other. The grapefruit industry alone proved a success.

In fact the petroleum industry is the pivot of the study. Chapter 6 considers the early history of the industry, the conditions of leases; it finds that in certain important respects the arrangements were faulty. There operated, for example, a system of regressive royalty rates which were intended to encourage large-scale production. It would appear, however, that the charging of lower royalty rates for a higher output cannot be justified in terms of the finances of a poor country. These efforts were being made to attract capital to the industry when capital was already eager to come into that particular sector of the economy.

The chapter treats the rapid growth of production, especially after 1935. Already in 1926 Trinidad had overtaken India and had become the chief source of empire oil. The growth in technological innovation was rapid and sustained. Refinery capacity expanded rapidly. Although Venezuelan crude oil output far exceeded Trinidad's, her refinery capacity was much smaller. The stage was being set for large increases of crude petroleum imports to sustain Trinidad as a refining centre should her domestic supplies run out.

The contribution of the industry to domestic incomes is examined in considerable detail. A later section then considers the firms engaged in the industry and the degree of profitability experienced by them.

In chapter 7 it is seen that the population was growing at nearly 2 per cent per annum, thereby threatening to double itself in thirty-five years. The youthfulness of the population also indicated that, *ceteris paribus*, the rapid rate of growth was likely to continue and increase. Also considered are the questions of population densities and the decline and growth of towns with the shift in the economy from agriculture to petroleum mining. The chapter shows, for example, the decline of Arima, formerly the centre of the prosperous cocoa industry, and the rapid growth of San Fernando, flanked on the north and south by the oil mining and refining industry and the sugar industry.

This population question introduces in its train the questions of labour, employment and wages. Chapter 8 examines the supply of and the demand for labour; the impact upon the labour market of the cessation of the system of indenture; the seasonal demand for agricultural labour; and the relatively small numbers employed by the petroleum industry and the creation of trained cadres in this industry able to handle advanced machinery.

It then examines the question of wages and the cost of living. Labour in Port of Spain seemed to be somewhat better off in 1935 than pre-war and very much better off than in 1920. The position of agricultural labour, while much better than in 1920, was on the whole less favourable than before World War I. The chapter then considers the growth of trade union legislation and the number of trade unions. It was only after the conflicts of unorganized but dissatisfied labour led to the strikes and riots of 1937 that a labour department was established by the government.

Chapter 9 analyses public finance: the size and composition annually of revenues and expenditure; the development schemes undertaken; the national debt and debt policy. In each case is seen the influence of the external trade situation. Note, for example, the sharp setback of the early 1920s when payments into the sinking fund (normally the first charge on revenue) regarding the Imperial Treasury Loan had to be suspended (1923 and 1924) and when even the reserves became negative. These factors coming so soon after the prosperous fifty years of the "golden age of cocoa" had succeeded in destroying the earlier confidence; had imposed a restrictionist mentality and led to a complete cessation of loan issues for ten years, that is, until 1932.

It has been found also that government policy for the raising of loans was not in fact counter-cyclical. This point is essential to make, since the coincidence in time of new loan issues with depression periods can give the impression that the policies were counter-cyclical. Most of the expenditure on loan-financed schemes was curtailed, abandoned or postponed precisely at the time when it could have done most towards curbing unemployment. Instead only *ad hoc* and piecemeal measures were employed temporarily to reduce unemployment.

But these shortcomings were influenced largely by changes in the trading position of the economy. This adverse trading condition of the depression of the 1920s during which the reserves became negative resulted in an obsession with maintaining reserves, surplus balances and increasing them through budget surpluses.

One of the chief questions in this context, therefore, turns around the timing of the switch of emphasis; at what stage could it be decided that the policy of restraint and reserves build-up had succeeded and justified a policy of expansion and initiation of new public works? Of course our privileged position in time and the clarity of hindsight gives us an advantage over those who were actually responsible at the time for the decision. It would appear, however, that while the policy on reserves was on the whole correct, the relaxation was overly delayed by one or two years.

As stated above, the oil industry is the pivot of the study. The study therefore reverts to the question of this industry and compares the contribution of the industry to exports and to revenue and concludes that not enough use was made of this wasting asset in providing capital for new social overheads. It was not until 1938 that any plan was formulated (it failed because of World War II) for employing the oil revenues, not directly to finance particular schemes as this would have meant the continuation of the practice of piecemeal development, but to underwrite and service the long-term loans necessary for five-year development programmes. In the event the war supervened and the plan miscarried. Would the plan have succeeded if it had been undertaken two or three years previously?

There are four appendices. The first treats the terms of trade of certain sections of the cocoa and sugar industries. The second considers the question of domestic production of food, especially in view of the size of the bill for food imports, and the decline of the agricultural industries. The third considers the government policy of tariff protection for local industries. The fourth contains the statistical appendices.

1 Exports

Trinidad's three main export commodities were cocoa, sugar and petroleum. It is proposed, therefore, to indicate in each of the five phases into which the period is divided, the extent of the contribution of each of these industries to the total values of exports and later to see the trends in the export of each commodity for the whole period.

Phase I: 1919–1920 to 1921

In this period, the post-war boom, the chief contributors to the value of exports were cocoa and sugar:

		1919	1920	1921
Value ($M)	Cocoa	12.4	15.5	6.5
	Sugar products	5.0	13.1	7.3
	Petroleum	4.1	3.1	3.5
Per cent of total export	Cocoa	51.2%	43.4%	33.3%
	Sugar products	20.6%	36.8%	37.1%
	Petroleum	16.7%	8.7%	17.7%

As yet the petroleum industry had not made a considerable impact on the total exports. The industry was still trying to find its feet. It should be observed, however, that whereas the fall in the values both of cocoa and sugar were quite large, that is, $15.5 million to $6.5 million and $13.1 million to $7.3 million, respectively, the value of petroleum exports rose from $3.1 million in 1920 to $3.5 million in 1921 and that although the 1921 figures followed the general trend of being lower than those for 1919, the drop in the case of petroleum products was very small compared with that in either of the two main agricultural products.

Taking the two agricultural industries it is seen that the export values of sugar products increased between 1919 and 1920 by 162 per cent while cocoa export values increased by only 25 per cent. This difference in the rates of increase in export values is explained largely in terms of price movements. The price of cocoa had since 1870 been high relative to all other agricultural products – the period 1870–1920 being regarded as the "Golden Age" of the Trinidad cocoa industry. The effect of the post-war boom upon cocoa prices was therefore much less than upon sugar prices which had been relatively low in the pre–World War II years.[1]

The upsurge of demand for sugar in the immediate post-war years encountered, not a fully expanded industry as was the case with cocoa,[2] but one in which European beet sugar production had been eliminated by war while cane sugar production had not yet increased sufficiently to make good the deficit. There was therefore a large increase in sugar prices, followed by an expansion of output in every sugarcane producing country. But this expansion of output (and export) in the case of Trinidad was significant compared with the upward movement of prices.[3] For cocoa, export values had increased by 25 per cent and quantity by only 3 per cent.

In 1919–20, therefore, in both commodities the factors, price and quantity of exports, reinforced each other – in sugar more so than in cocoa. In 1920–21, however, in the case of cocoa the two factors diverged. While the quantity of exports rose by 20 per cent[4] to 75.2 million tons (the peak of production in the entire history of the industry), the value of exports fell from $15.5 million to $6.5 million (that is, by 58 per cent). The situation in sugar was different. Both price and quantity reinforced each other but in a downward direction, the fall in export values from $13.1 million to $7.3 million (45 per cent) being greater than the drop in the quantity exported from 48,000 tons to 46,100 tons (4 per cent).

Phase II: 1921–1922 to 1926–1927

The export figures for the period 1921–27 are of twofold importance: firstly, in so far as they show the sharpness of the depression of the 1920s, and secondly, in so far as they show a significant shift in the composition of exports.

While petroleum held its own, both cocoa and sugar have fallen swiftly in value. The fall in the case of sugar products being $1.7 million (that is, from $7.3 million in 1921 to $5.6 million in 1922) and cocoa about $1 million (that is, from $6.5 million in 1921 to $5.6 million in 1922). The year 1923 confirmed this trend: a decline in the absolute and relative values of agricultural exports and an increase in the values of petroleum products exported.[5]

		1921	1922	1923	1924	1925	1926	1927
Value ($M)	Cocoa	6.5	5.6	6.2	5.6	6.0	6.1	8.0
	Sugar products	7.3	5.6	5.4	6.1	5.4	4.9	3.8
	Petroleum products	3.5	3.7	5.9	6.6	7.5	9.0	11.2
Per cent of total exports	Cocoa	33.3	32.3	29.9	25.8	26.9	25.4	29.9
	Sugar products	37.1	31.3	26.1	28.2	24.1	20.5	14.0
	Petroleum products	17.7	20.5	28.7	30.2	33.4	37.3	41.6

The years 1923 to 1925 were the critical period for the composition of Trinidad and Tobago exports. In that period the contribution of each of the three staples to total exports was almost the same: cocoa, 29.9 per cent; petroleum products, 28.7 per cent; sugar products, 26.1 per cent. After 1925 the dependence on petroleum became more and more marked. Further, until 1939, by making the total export figures appear respectably large (especially in the Great Depression of the 1930s), it masked the very sorry plight into which the rest of the economy had fallen. In the early 1920s the contribution of petroleum to exports was small. In the 1930s this contribution was large. But in the 1920s the amount of export income accruing to domestic producers (omitting petroleum) was larger than in the 1930s.

Pre-1923, therefore, saw prosperity, the dominance of the agricultural industries. Post-1923 saw the partial ending of that dominance; the emergence of petroleum on a level of equality with each of the agricultural industries in terms of export values and this trend continues up to 1926 and after. In 1924 petroleum products became the largest single contributor to exports (that is, 30.2 per cent). But after 1926–27 its contribution became increasingly larger and must be examined at greater length in the subsequent phases.

Within the agricultural sector, however, the struggle for dominance continued, alternating between sugar and cocoa. In the case of cocoa there were severe fluctuations in output accounted for largely by weather conditions, disease and neglect, consequent on the low prices. The trend, however, was increasingly downward. Price and quantity therefore can be said to have reinforced each other in a downward trend for most of the period 1921–22 to 1926–27.

In the case of sugar, however, although there were fluctuations in output, the dominant trend was upward – so that although prices, except in 1923–24, were falling steadily the values of exports were more or less maintained. The growth in production and exports largely offset the falling trend in prices.

Certain factors which are analysed in greater detail in the following chapters (3 and 4) account for this. Here it is essential to bear in mind this difference between the industries, for it sprang largely from an attitude on the part of the respective producers, partly from the disparity in the inherited financial bases of the industries, partly from the then existing weaker financial position of cocoa peasantry compared with sugar plantocracy in times of depression especially, partly from disease and partly from the inherent capacity of sugar productivity to increase with great rapidity as opposed to cocoa where the elasticity of supply is rather low and where an aging plantation can have very adverse effects on production. The important thing, however, is that while cocoa producers were despondent

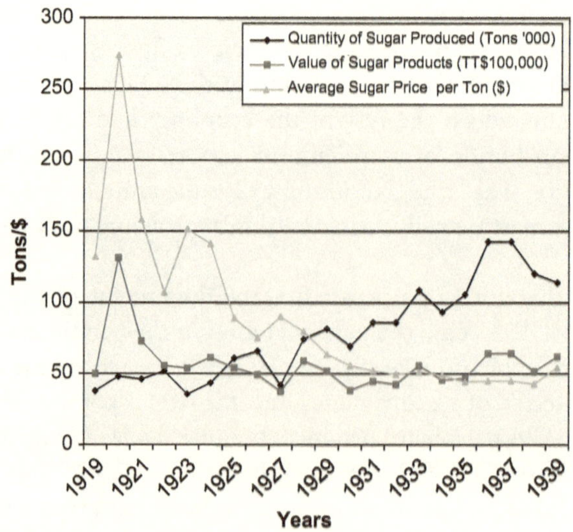

Figure 1: Sugar production/exports 1919–1939.

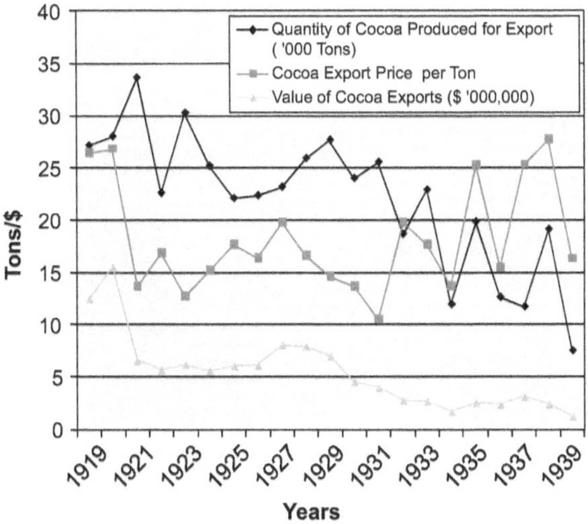

Figure 2: Cocoa production/exports 1919–1939.

and neglected their estates and cocoa holdings, sugar producers were less so and were expanding output, so that increases in production offset the decline in prices (figures 1 and 2).

Phase III: 1926–1927 to 1928–1929

In terms of total export values this period saw a revival. In 1929, for the first time since 1920, exports rose above the $30 million level (figure 3a). In a sense this represented a major advance because, if the "artificial" year 1920 is omitted, exports before the period of study and up to 1929 only once approached $20 million. The 1913 figure was $11 million.

The composition of trade shows that the growth of petroleum exports (in absolute and relative terms), which was seen in the earlier period was accelerated in this later period. In 1930 they accounted for more than one-half of total exports.

	1926	1927	1928	1929	1930
Petroleum (%)	37.3	41.6	40.3	46.7	51.9
Cocoa (%)	25.4	29.9	26.7	22.1	21.4
Sugar products (%)	20.5	14.0	19.9	16.5	4.9

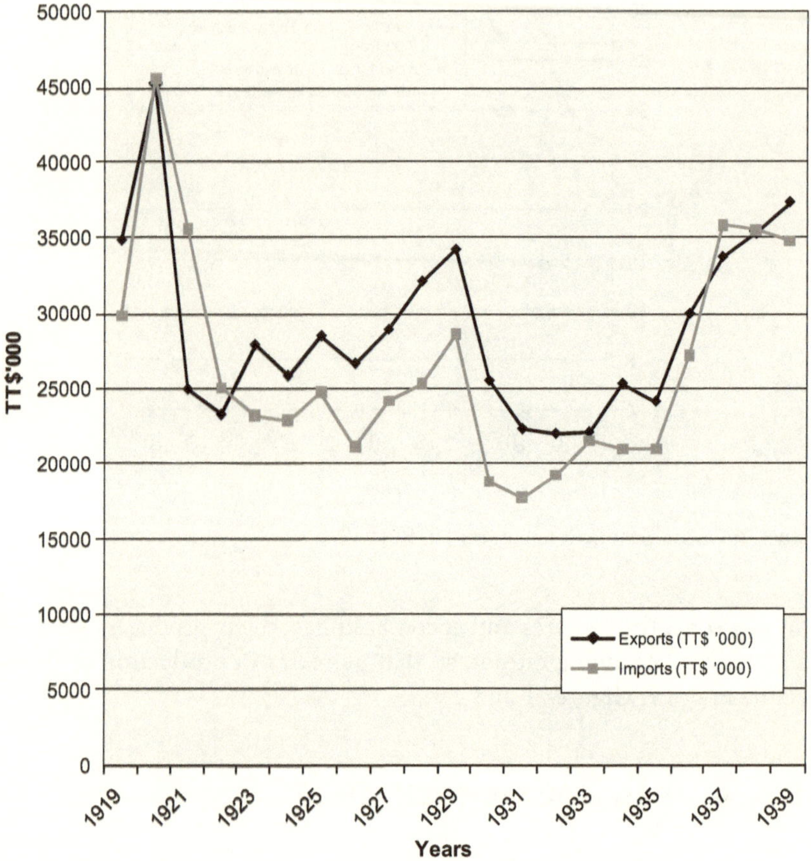

Figure 3a: Exports/imports trends 1919–1939.

The growth in total exports during the period was due almost entirely to the growth in the petroleum sector (note the sharp upward trend in petroleum exports in the figure 3b). On the whole the trend in the agricultural sector was downward. Cocoa experienced relative prosperity. Both output and prices turned up, the latter slightly. But in sugar, apart from a slight upturn in 1927, the price trend was downward. In that year, however, output and exports fell steeply, thus offsetting the favourable price movements. In spite of this, however, the general trend in sugar output and exports was upward, if erratically so. The fluctuations are therefore reflected in export values, but on the whole the most general conclusion seems to be that the advance in export values was negligible.

The economy had now shifted from a position in which agriculture dominated to one in which petroleum was dominant. The economy had passed

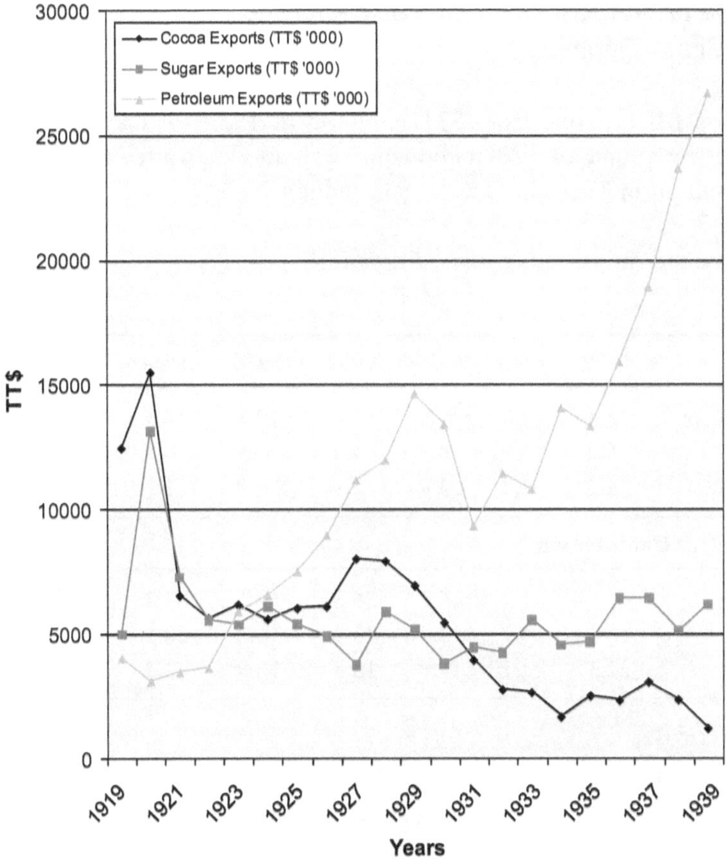

Figure 3b: Three main exports 1919–1939.

from the stage of being dependent for exports on one pillar (that is, agriculture) through that in which the twin pillars of petroleum and agriculture supported exports (1923–24) and incomes, to that which because of the two divergent trends (the shrinking or stagnation of agriculture and the expansion of petroleum) the export economy had once more reverted to a dependence on one industry only. It is not as though both sectors were growing with the one (petroleum) growing faster than the other. The advantages of this sort of growth would have been obvious and great. The dominance of petroleum, though due to its own absolute growth, was accentuated by the stagnation and shrinking of the other sector.

A position of imbalance was therefore restored; a closer examination and comparison of these two periods of imbalance will be undertaken later.[6]

Phase IV: 1930–1931 to 1935–1936: The Great Depression

Exports fell in value from $31.4 million in 1929 to their lowest Great Depression point of $20 million in 1931 and thereafter rose slowly to $27 million in 1936. In fact the $30 million level was only reached again in 1937.

How did the various commodities fare?

($M)	1929	1930	1931	1932	1933	1934	1935	1936
Petroleum	14.6	13.4	9.4	11.4	10.8	14.1	13.3	15.9
Sugar	5.2	3.8	4.5	4.3	5.6	4.6	4.7	6.4
Cocoa	6.9	5.4	4.0	2.8	2.7	1.7	2.5	2.3
Percentage Contribution								
Petroleum	46.7	51.9	46.7	56.8	52.1	63.2	58.5	59.1
Sugar	16.5	14.9	22.4	21.2	26.8	20.5	20.6	23.9
Cocoa	22.1	21.1	19.8	13.8	12.9	7.5	11.1	8.7

As the figures for 1931–33 indicate, the petroleum industry did not escape the general downward trend in prices[7] brought about by the Great Depression. There was a slight drop in production and exports in 1930 but thereafter both production and export picked up again. In spite of the fact that the 1929 value figure for exports was not again attained until 1936, the percentage contribution of the commodity to total exports rose almost steadily (with some little fluctuations). The reason is to be seen in the maintenance of the export values of sugar (with a slight upturn in 1935–36) and the absolute and relative decline of cocoa.

The dominance of petroleum having been established, how did these two major agricultural industries compare and what factors affected the trends? Mention has already been made of the factors which stimulated the expansion of output in sugar and the contraction in the case of cocoa.

It is fair to say that these same factors continued to operate during the Depression. But there was one new important consideration – imperial preference. In 1932, sugar was given a considerable measure of preferential treatment in the British and Canadian markets.[8] In the former market, the preference was large. In the latter it was large and assured for about ten years. This fact of preferential treatment therefore assisted the industry not only in terms of price and so the value of exports, but also in terms of the renewed confidence in the future. The expansion of production after 1932 is evidence of this new confidence (see figure 3b for sugar exports).

The preference received by cocoa was negligible and necessarily so as the competition was intra-empire (West African) and world demand was low. Cocoa, which had for nearly every year of the early twentieth century and much of the late nineteenth century held a superior position to sugar, was in 1930–31 superseded by the latter and has never since challenged it.

In chapter 5 treating the internal development in these two industries, the causes of decline and so on are elaborated. In the case of cocoa, low prices, the unsatisfactory financial basis of the industry, absentee though local ownership, disease, neglect, reinforced each other in a cumulative process which led to the demise of the industry. Though the unsound financial basis of the industry was in a sense one of the chief factors making for failure, price was the factor that triggered off the decline. It can therefore be asked, but without much chance of a definite answer, whether the granting to cocoa of assistance on a scale similar to sugar (if this were practicable) could have saved the industry.[9]

In the event, export values fell to a low level of $1.7 million in 1934. The 1920 figure was $15.5 million. But this was a freak year; a better comparison would be with 1921 and 1922: $6.5 million and $5.6 million, respectively, or the war years (World War I) of between $7.5 million and $9 million. Seen in another light, this industry which at the beginning of the period accounted for over 50 per cent of exports was in 1934 contributing 7.5 per cent and in 1936, 8.7 per cent. As will be seen in the examination of Phase V: 1935, 1936 to 1939: The Revival, the decline was complete, well-nigh irreversible.

The export graph for cocoa shows violent fluctuations which are not only the result of weather, but also due to neglect and disease. Many of the upturns are reflections of spasmodic attempts to profit temporarily from slight improvements in prices. The main trend, however, is downward.

Phase V: 1935, 1936 to 1939: The Revival

In what respects, and in what sense, was this period a revival? There were no spectacular price increases. Sugar prices were steady at about $42.5 per ton under imperial preference. Cocoa prices did have a slight upturn in

($M)	1935	1936	1937	1938	1939
Petroleum products	13.3	15.9	18.9	23.7	26.7
Sugar products	4.7	6.4	6.4	5.2	6.6
Cocoa	2.5	2.3	3.1	2.4	1.2
Percentages of Exports					
Petroleum	58.5	59.1	59.9	70.1	74.6
Sugar	20.6	23.9	20.4	15.3	18.4
Cocoa	11.1	8.7	9.8	7	3.1

1936 and 1937. In petroleum only kerosene and motor spirit prices showed slight increases.

In spite of this, total country export values increased from $22.8 million (1935) to $35.7 million in 1939. The contributors were neither sugar nor cocoa. It was nearly all due to an explosive expansion of production, refining and exports in the petroleum industry, where between 1935 and 1939 exports doubled their value, increasing from 13.3 million to $26.7 million. This industry had by now dominated the economy as no other industry had done so far – not even cocoa during its Golden Age could account for much more than 50 per cent of exports. In 1939, petroleum products contributed 74.6 per cent in value of domestic exports.

In the agricultural sector, cocoa continued to decline. Sugar was established as the second largest contributor. These twin factors – the dominance of petroleum over the whole economy and the dominance of sugar within the agricultural sector – point to the twofold nature of the imbalance in the economy. In the first sense the imbalance is in the dependence on a single type of industry to the exclusion of others. In the second it is in the maldistribution of the proceeds of export incomes. Both petroleum and, to a lesser extent, sugar are owned by expatriate entrepreneurs and the profits of both industries flow abroad. Insofar as the economy becomes more and more dependent on either or both of these industries to the exclusion of cocoa, to that extent therefore is the percentage of export incomes accruing to domestic producers reduced. In the case of sugar this is less so than in petroleum as profits were much smaller in the former and as the numbers employed were much larger.

The following section goes on to treat the question of the distribution of export/incomes between domestic and foreign recipients.

The Distribution of Export Incomes

Any analysis of the distribution of export incomes between domestic and foreign or expatriate recipients is necessarily open to question. The absence of precise data sees to that. But it is possible, by using the available data, to form some picture and a not entirely inaccurate picture of this distribution.

Under the heading spendable domestic incomes from exports items such as the export values of cocoa, coconuts, rubber, agricultural industries which are almost entirely owned by persons resident in Trinidad, could safely be included. There is another of the agricultural industries (sugar) that is much more difficult to place in this category because a part of the proceeds of this industry must have gone abroad in the form of profits. But profits in sugar in the 1920s and 1930s could not have been very high or high for many years running. In fact there were many years in which no profits were made at all. It is therefore proposed to include all of sugar under this heading, bearing in mind all the time that domestic incomes are thereby exaggerated to some extent.

Petroleum and asphalt export values are at once more difficult to handle and yet easier. More difficult because a larger percentage of these more prosperous industries goes abroad in the form of profits, because the sums going to capital equipment and depreciation and the writing off of wells are sometimes considerable, difficult to assign to a particular scheme and often so linked with depreciation and other items of account in the United Kingdom part of the enterprise that it is impossible to determine what part accrued to Trinidad and Tobago alone. But for the moment consideration is not being given to that part of export values which goes to gross or net additions to the capital potential of the economy, but only to that part of spendable export incomes which accrue to domestic recipients. This means that, for one thing, the difference between total incomes and domestic incomes as here interpreted does not necessarily equal exported profits. It may be found that the amount of imported equipment and so on is greater in terms of money than the value of total exports minus incomes to domestic recipients. This may be the case where, for instance, loan or share capital (of United Kingdom or other origin) financed the oil industry. In view of the fact that there is nearly always an export surplus on current account, however, the last possibility does not seem to arise except for the two periods when there was an import surplus.[10] In any case the size and steadiness over time of the export surpluses which correspond with the surplus, that is, exports – (imports + local disbursements) of the petroleum industry indicate *ceteris paribus* that although certain units may have been financing their development from external capital, the industry as a whole was either self financed or was in a position to repay its external commercial debts fairly promptly.

To revert, however, to the question of export incomes accruing to domestic recipients – the Petroleum Association of Trinidad published annually for the period 1927–35 inclusive a statement[11] of the amounts spent locally by the oil companies both in terms of the revenue to the government, wages to employees, royalties to private individuals and other items. This study takes issue with the statement on a number of grounds and has attempted so to modify it as to make it more realistic.[12] The data have been set out in two series which represented an upper and a lower limit of oil industry contributions to spendable domestic incomes from exports.

Since cocoa accounted for about 50 per cent of exports at the beginning of the period and petroleum for upwards of 70 per cent at the end of the period and it is known what their contributions to local incomes were, the picture should be fairly accurate. Even where it may be somewhat unclear with regard to the level of domestic incomes from exports, it is accurate with regard to the classification of agricultural incomes versus the rest, that is, the first type of imbalance referred to earlier. In table 1, therefore, the value of agricultural exports is taken as the basis. To this is added domestic incomes distributed by the petroleum and asphalt industries. As stated earlier the data are set out in two series. Series I exaggerates the total of domestic incomes in relation to series II. Whichever of the series is more accurate, they differ only in a matter of degree, the nature of the problem is the same: a continuing reduction in the proportion of total export values accruing as spendable incomes and savings to domestic recipients.

In phase I which saw the highest point of total export values (actually the 1920 figure is the same as that for 1939), nearly the whole of the value of exports went to domestic producers. In phase II, however, with the growth of the petroleum industry and the decline in the values of agricultural products the gap between total exports and the level of domestic incomes from exports widens. This trend continues for the whole of the period with the high points in 1929 and post-1935 – the periods of greatest prosperity of the oil industry. Correspondingly the per capita value of spendable domestic incomes from exports falls with the decline of the agricultural sector and the growth of the population (see table 2).

Table 1 Distribution of Export Incomes ($M)

	1919	1920	1921	1922	1923	1924	1925	1926	1927	1928	1929	1930	1931	1932	1933	1934	1935	1936	1937	1938	1939
Total exports	24.3	35.7	19.6	17.8	20.6	21.7	22.5	24.0	26.8	29.7	31.4	25.8	20.0	20.1	20.8	22.2	22.8	27.0	31.5	33.7	35.7
Petroleum exports	4.1	3.1	3.5	3.7	5.9	6.6	7.5	9.0	11.2	12.0	14.6	13.4	9.4	11.4	10.9	14.1	13.3	15.9	18.9	23.7	26.7
Domestic incomes from exports – series I																					
Total agricultural exports	19.6	31.3	15.0	12.5	12.9	13.2	13.3	12.8	13.4	15.8	14.7	10.9	9.5	8.1	9.2	7.3	8.4	10.1	11.4	8.9	7.8
Petroleum industry contribution[a] series I	?	?	?	?	?	?	?	?	7.6	7.0	7.7	8.1	5.6	6.2	6.3	6.6	6.8	9.5	13.0	16.8	16.7
Asphalt industry[b] series	?	?	?	?	?	?	?	?	1.17	0.96	19.7	0.85	0.76	0.48	0.46	0.52	0.68	0.5	0.6	0.5	0.6
Total spendable incomes from exports[c] – series I	19.6	31.3	15.0	12.5	12.9	13.2	13.3	12.8	22.17	23.76	23.37	18.85	16.86	14.78	15.96	14.42	15.88	20.1	25.0	26.2	25.1
Domestic incomes from exports – series II																					
Total agricultural exports	19.6	31.3	15.0	12.5	12.9	13.2	13.3	12.8	13.4	15.8	14.7	10.9	9.5	8.1	9.2	7.3	8.4	10.1	11.4	8.9	7.8
Petroleum industry contribution series II[d]	?	?	?	?	?	?	?	?	5.78	5.48	6.1	6.43	4.77	5.17	5.1	5.39	5.74	7.76	10.39	13.77	13.93
Asphalt industry contribution series II	?	?	?	?	?	?	?	?	1.06	0.89	0.87	0.73	0.56	0.39	0.38	0.43	0.52	0.4	0.5	0.4	0.5
Total domestic income from exports series II	19.6	31.3	15.0	12.5	12.9	13.2	13.3	12.8	20.24	22.17	21.67	18.06	14.83	13.66	14.68	13.12	14.66	18.26	22.29	23.07	22.23
Series II as per cent of exports	80%				62.6				75.5				74.1				64.3				62.3
Petroleum exports contribution to domestic incomes + capital goods imports																					
Petroleum contribution to income series I									7.6	7.0	7.7	8.1	5.6	6.2	6.3	6.6	6.8	9.5	13.0	16.8	16.7
Petroleum contribution to import									4.98	2.99	4.3	4.4	1.4	1.7	2.5	2.7	3.1	4.6	8.2	8.5	6.0
Total									12.6	10.0	12.0	12.5	7.0	7.9	8.8	9.3	9.9	14.1	21.16	25.3	22.7
Petroleum exports									11.2	12.0	14.6	13.4	9.4	11.4	10.9	14.1	13.3	15.9	18.9	23.7	26.7
Balance									–1.4	2.0	2.6	0.9	2.4	3.5	2.1	4.8	3.4	1.8	–3.7	–1.6	4.0

[a] Petroleum industries contribution series I is the sum of items 8 and 17 on pp. 171–72 (table 53a).
[b] The figures for asphalt after 1935 are estimates only.
[c] Between 1919 and 1926 the petroleum and asphalt industries must have made some contribution – perhaps 50 per cent or 30 per cent or the export values of those industries. But the data have only been available since 1927. For the period 1936–39 no published data were available. They were obtained after great difficulty in Trinidad. Note the post-1935 increase in petroleum industry contributions corresponding to the growth of the industry and especially refining capacity after that date.
[d] Petroleum contribution series II is the sum of items 8 and 18 in table 53a, pp. 171–72.

Table 2 Per Capita Domestic Incomes from Exports

Year	Per Capita Value of Agricultural Exports ($)	Total Domestic Incomes (Series I) from Export Industries (per capita) ($)	Total Domestic Incomes (Series II) from Export Industries (per capita) ($)
1919	50.69	–	–
1920	80.19	–	–
1921	40.66	–	–
1922	33.36	–	–
1923	34.11	–	–
1924	34.57	–	–
1925	34.54	–	–
1926	33.29	–	–
1927	34.21	56.46	51.66
1928	39.79	59.88	55.71
1929	36.45	57.82	53.74
1930	26.38	48.05	43.71
1931	23.01	38.43	35.93
1932	19.31	35.23	32.56
1933	21.66	37.58	34.56
1934	16.90	33.37	30.36
1935	19.19	36.10	33.33
1936	22.53	44.84	40.73
1937	25.00	54.82	48.88
1938	19.14	56.36	49.62
1939	16.47	53.00	46.95

The lowest curve on figure 4 indicates the level of agricultural incomes. It indicates further what the position of the economy would have been had there been no petroleum industry to relieve the situation. The possibility of there being no alternative industry to relieve the economic distress must not be overlooked or discounted. Chapter 5, for example, deals with the abortive attempts to find alternative agricultural industries to take the place of the declining industries, especially cocoa. Had there been no petroleum industry, therefore, the level of export incomes in 1938 and 1939 would have been but a small fraction of the export incomes earned not only in 1920, an exceptional year, but in 1919 or even in the sharp depression year 1921. They would have been little above the level of such incomes of the

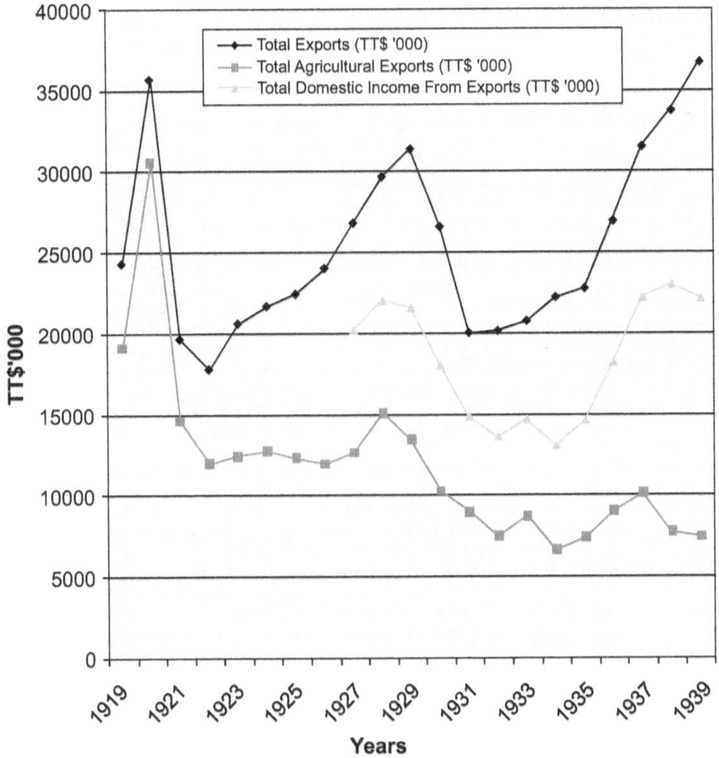

Figure 4: Total domestic income from main exports.

Great Depression period of the early 1930s. The other West Indian islands (Jamaica, Barbados, St Kitts and so on) received the full blast of the ill-effects that resulted from dependence on a single-crop economy which is exposed to continued low prices. Trinidad and Tobago escaped, at least she suffered relatively less than the others and this entirely on account of her petroleum industry. The upper curve indicates to what extent the petroleum industry saved the situation.

Table 2 showing the per capita level of export incomes from agriculture and all sources makes the position clearer. In 1927 per capita export income from agriculture alone was $34.21 million. The petroleum industry contribution brought the figure to $56.46 (series I) and $51.66 (series II). The corresponding figures for 1935 were $19.19, $36.10 (series I) and $33.33 (series II). But compare the per capita values of spendable domestic incomes from exports in 1919 and 1930 when the total value of exports was about the same. It is seen that per capita income for 1919 (agriculture alone) was $50.69 versus $48.05 (series I) and $43.71 (series II) in 1930.

It is evident, therefore, that the petroleum industry saved the economy from the depths of poverty. But the level of spendable incomes even after this help was still very low, both absolutely and in terms of the total of export incomes. Why is it that this prosperous industry contributed relatively so little to spendable domestic incomes from exports; so little compared with the depressed agricultural industries? In a later chapter the whole of the oil industry is treated in greater detail. It is not proposed therefore to anticipate that chapter. Briefly, however, and strictly from the point of view of the export/import situation, the following points should throw some light on the reasons for this disparity between the industry's contribution to total and to domestic incomes from trade.

Firstly, the industry is very capital intensive. Large sums have therefore to be spent on renewing and expanding the equipment required to maintain the industry at a high level of efficiency. The sums spent on depreciation and especially those spent on imports of machinery should therefore be taken into account in assessing the contribution of the industry to domestic incomes.[13] (The range is now widened from purely spendable incomes accruing to domestic recipients and now includes investment items.)

It is the view taken in this study that, in part at least, the difference between the high per capita income figures for 1919 as compared with say 1930 or 1935 is due to the over-weighting of the former – over-weighting in the following sense. All of the incomes from agriculture or rather cocoa and most of that part from sugar that went to labour and the cane farmers was re-spent on consumption goods (largely imported). In the case of cocoa which was the chief contributor at the time little or none of these export incomes went to repaying debt and relieving the estates from encumbrances.[14] Senile areas were not replanted. This failure to utilize part of the proceeds of export incomes to disencumber the estates and replant old areas leaves a high gross figure for the contribution of the industry to domestic incomes. One of the results of this neglect was the ruin of the industry when prices fell. The oil industry, however, was renewing and expanding its capital base. Comparison should therefore be between per capita value of agricultural exports and series I to which has been added the total oil industry imports. The result is given in table 2.

But even after account is taken of these imports of machinery and other equipment, there is still a considerable gap for some years (except for one of the years for which complete data are available – 1927) when the industry appears to have a deficit. In addition to the fact that for most of the period there is still a considerable gap, the problem still remains of a small contribution to local incomes relative to total exports.

The chief factor operating is profits. It can be argued that the riskiness of the initial ventures and the capital intensity of the enterprise warrant high levels of profits. The industry must continue to appear attractive to those who had the courage and the financial resources to undertake the development in the first place, and who lost considerable sums in the initial stages of development when knowledge of the geology of the island was scanty indeed.

However, as will be seen in the chapters 6 and 9, the levels of taxation and the method adopted of assessing royalties were inadequate. The former was very low and the latter was regressive rather than progressive. As the industry's output expanded rapidly in the 1930s, therefore, its contribution to total exports increased relative to the other industries; further, as the refining part (that is, the more profitable part)[15] of the industry expanded, the industry became even more capital intensive, the proportion of total revenue going to labour was reduced, and the gap between total export values and local disbursements of all kinds was increased. These points are elaborated in the chapters 6 and 9. For the moment, therefore, it is necessary to draw the strands of this chapter together.

Firstly, the period shows five distinct phases. There are three periods of prosperity and two of depression. The immediate post-war boom was sharp but short. It was overtaken in the midst of its prosperity by the depression of the 1920s. The upturn at the end of the 1920s was neither considerable nor particularly long-lived. It also was overtaken by the Great Depression of the 1930s. Relief came in 1935–36. At the peak in 1937, however, there is evidence of a slight downturn to 1939 and one wonders whether the spectacle of upturn and recession would have continued had it not been for the advent of World War II. On the whole, therefore, the period was nearly always affected by depressions. The plateaux of prosperity appear as mere interludes in a long period of depression.

Secondly, the composition of exports changed. Except for a short period in the early 1920s when sugar, cocoa, and petroleum made more or less equal contributions to exports, the economy suffered from an imbalance of one kind or another. In the early period, cocoa was the predominant industry. In the final years it was petroleum. There was another sort of imbalance also. In the former period the dominant industry was locally owned. In the latter period both in agriculture (sugar) and in mining (oil), the owners were expatriate. The result was that most of the profits from these industries flowed abroad.

Which of these periods of imbalance was better or worse for Trinidad and Tobago? In the latter a smaller proportion of export incomes accrued to domestic recipients, but the chief industry was rapidly strengthening the productive capital of the island, putting it as it were beyond the ill effects of the vagaries of world primary produce prices. Further, as the cocoa industry was more compact than the peasant industry, it could be more easily taxed. With the same level of exports in 1920 as in 1935, for example, government revenue from income taxes was much larger in the latter period than in the former.[16]

In addition, the high level of export incomes in the early period when cocoa predominated, did not lead to a real strengthening of the financial basis of that industry with the result that it collapsed at the first blast of the Depression. Old areas were not replanted. With but few exceptions all the earnings from cocoa went to consumption goods.

On the whole, therefore, while it can be argued that the imbalance of the second period had its disadvantage in the amount of profits flowing abroad, its advantages, direct and indirect, to the economy outweighed the disadvantages. Further the imbalance of the second period (as of the first) was not a matter of choice. That is to say the switch from agriculture to oil was not a voluntary choice; it was brought about by the decline of the one and the expansion of the other in a process of world market changes. The situation could have been worse if there had been no petroleum industry. It would have been better, however, if a different system of taxation and royalty rates had been devised from the inception of the industry.

2 Imports

The total of imports into Trinidad and Tobago has been classified under five heads in the Blue Books and other government publications, as follows:

1. Food and drink
2. Raw materials
3. Manufactures
4. Miscellaneous
5. Bullion

The classifications bullion and miscellaneous are rather small contributors to imports and can, for the purpose of this analysis, be treated accordingly.

The stability of raw materials (composed largely of coal imports) might give the impression that industrial activity was stagnant. This is somewhat misleading. The industrial sector, such as it was, relied upon domestically produced oil for electricity and power. Coal was used mainly for the railways and the bunker trade before trains and ships were connected to oil burners (see also chapter 6).

The two largest and most significant classifications are food and drink and manufactures. Together they accounted for 88.6 per cent of imports at the beginning of the period and 93.0 per cent at the end of the period. It is interesting to note that while in 1919 the contributions of food and drink and manufactures to total imports were 48.7 per cent and 39.9 per cent, respectively, by the end of the period the situation was reversed and the contributions were 25.3 per cent and 67.7 per cent, respectively.

In one sense at least this was a healthy sign. It indicated a society that was becoming relatively less concerned with the basic problem of filling its stomach. Before any attempt is made to analyse the more positive implications of this shift, it is necessary to see what the per capita movements of food imports were and, more importantly, what were the significant items included under the wide umbrella of the classification "manufactured goods".

Food and Drink

A proper appreciation of the importance of the item or category "food and drink" in the imports of Trinidad and Tobago requires an understanding of the pattern of economic development that the colony had inherited and the pattern of consumption that went hand in hand with that pattern of development. Before the first decades of the twentieth century (the domestic oil industry being of comparatively recent origin), the economic activities were purely agricultural. Sugar and cocoa were the chief crops and all energies were devoted to their development. An export economy was developed, the produce of the plantations being exported and all items of food and clothing imported. The following quotation gives an idea of what the situation was in the seventeenth to nineteenth centuries.

> "Men are so intent upon planting sugar," a correspondent wrote to Governor Winthrop in 1647 about the West Indies, "that they had rather buy foods at very dear rates than produce it by labour, so infinite is the profit of sugar workers after once accomplished." And Samuel Vetch in 1708, "there is no island the British possess in the West Indies that is capable of subsisting without the assistance of the Continent, for to them we transport their bread, drink, and all the necessaries of human life . . . in so much that their being much more their well being depends entirely upon the Continent."[1]

And lest the impression be conveyed that this pattern of development was a thing of the past, note the report of the director of agriculture in 1931 where he sought to isolate the factors which contribute to the "reluctance to grow food crops".

> For more than 50 years prior to 1920 cocoa averaged more than $20.00 per bag in value and it was sound business during this period to neglect food crops in favour of an export crop the returns from which allowed an ample margin for the purchase abroad of relatively less valuable articles. Today the position is altered for cocoa is worth half what it used to be.[2]

It is in this context, therefore, that the food and drink imports of the islands should be considered. The specialization and trade emphasis pervades the whole economy and it will have to be considered at a later stage how far this pattern of development can be justified in view of changing world prices and demand and supply conditions. A later section therefore analyses the movements in terms of trade. The following section analyses the trend in the imports of the important individual items relative to population growth and to price changes.

Earlier, it was shown that the category "food and drink" accounted for 48.7 per cent of all imports in 1919 and that this figure declined steadily throughout the period until by 1939 the contribution to total imports was only 25.3 per cent. This is the sort of shift in the composition of imports that may indicate a country improving its standard of living, especially if the total imports are increasing so that the smaller percentage in the latter years indicates (given the increase in population) not a smaller but a larger amount of food imports. Or better yet if domestic food production had increased. Such a country is becoming less concerned with the business of filling its stomach and is devoting more of its resources, or rather a larger proportion of its resources, to other commodities such as capital goods or durable consumer goods.

Within the category food and drink, however, another type of analysis can be undertaken. It should be possible to find out how different items within the group moved relative to each other; whether there are new items within the group and how fast was the growth or decline or fluctuations in the case of each. Also, it may be possible to find out to what extent these movements in imports were determined by shifts in local incomes or in prices of the imported articles.

Cereals (Rice and Flour)

These two items are clearly the most important in terms of value among the food items imported. In the year 1919 when total food and drink imports (net) were $9.5 million, the imports of flour were valued at $3.6 million and rice at $1.09 million, that is, together about 50 per cent of the total. In terms of volume, flour shows a remarkable steadiness over the period (see statistical data, appendix 4). Firstly, the sudden increases which are evident in other import items for the year 1920 are absent in the case of flour although the same income changes due to cocoa prices must have operated. Actually, there was a drop in the volume of imports in that year (a fall from 59.7 million pounds to 52.86 million pounds). Price per pound had moved meanwhile from 6.11¢ (BWI) to 6.84¢. It would appear, however, that imports of flour and consumption of flour are not greatly affected by price considerations. Lest it be concluded that the fall in the imports in 1920 was necessarily due to the increase in price of 0.7¢, see what happened in 1921 the when the price had fallen to 5.49¢ per pound. Imports fell even more to 50.51 million pounds.

Both price and income[3] elasticities of demand appear to have been very low. As can be seen from the statistical table, while there were great fluctuations in the price of flour there were relatively small changes in the amounts of flour imported. Indeed, it would appear that the increases in flour imports were no more than enough to offset the rise in population that took place over the period. While price influences cannot be ruled out altogether, it would appear that in the case of flour they were not important; that people wanted a certain amount of flour which they bought at the high or low price at high or low incomes. There are no indications that a fall in prices led to anything like a corresponding rise in imports and vice versa. Also, there are no close substitutes which would affect the imports of flour. The consumption pattern in terms of flour was set. Per capita imports are about 150 pounds per annum during the period.

In the case of rice, however, there are possible substitutes such as vegetables locally grown or imported as well as from locally grown rice. In spite of this, however, volume imports have risen from 15.4 million pounds in 1919 to 46.3 million in 1939. If 1938 were taken as 100, then quantity imports for 1919 would be 36. This upward trend has been steady and sustained throughout the period. Prices, on the other hand, fell steadily and rapidly throughout the period and this factor which operated very little in the case of flour is perhaps almost wholly responsible for the increase in imports. If the 1938 price index were taken as 100, then 1921 would be 201, 1924 would be 160, 1931 would be 96, and so on (see statistical table).

In the case of flour, the price/income elasticity of demand was much less than unity. In the case of rice it is the opposite and this for two reasons. (1) Rice is a food which increases its bulk considerably upon being cooked. To those with small incomes and large families, therefore (and Trinidad and Tobago was a land of large families), rice is the food that commends itself readily.[4] Any fall in the price of rice means that for the same outlay the family can be fed so much more adequately. (2) There is another consideration and this affected most people in Trinidad and Tobago during this period. As the price of rice fell relative to vegetables imported or domestically grown, there was a tendency to shift away from such vegetables to rice. There was a substitution effect as a result of relative price changes.

Per capita annual consumption, which was 40 pounds in 1919, was 55 pounds in 1921, and 70 pounds in 1927. By 1939 it had risen to 94 pounds.

Prices, however, had moved from 7.1¢ per pound to 2.1¢ per pound. While making these comparisons between flour and rice, however, and in spite of the vast increases in the per capita consumption of the latter, it should be borne in mind that the per capita consumption of the former has always been very much greater than the latter, that the per capita consumption of flour in 1921 was about 2.5 times that of rice and that in 1939 it was about 1.6 times as great.[5]

Milk

The growth in the import of milk (condensed) is even more remarkable than that of rice: from 1.27 million pounds in 1919 to 9.4 million pounds in 1939. Taking 1938 as 100, then 1919 would be 14.68. As in rice the per capita annual imports rose swiftly from 3.3 pounds (1919) to 19.7 pounds, a sixfold increase, in spite of the rate of population growth. This increase is largely explained in terms of price reductions: that is, from 19.2¢ per pound in 1919 to 9.2¢ per pound in 1939. But price effects may well have been supported by income effects especially after 1935 when per capital imports rose rapidly.[6] Compare, for example, 1933 and 1938 when price was almost the same. The 1933 per capita imports were 10.9 as against 19.1 for 1938. In 1933 (depression) incomes must have been much below those for 1938. The period after 1935 saw the rapid expansion of the oil industry, a slight revival in cocoa, and the initiation by government of certain major public works, the net results of which could not have failed to have beneficent effects on incomes. It is difficult to determine the relative influences of these two factors, price and income, on the quantities imported. In the prosperous year of 1920, with price at 6.4¢ (1919 = 19.2¢) per pound, per capita imports were very high – 15.4 pounds (1919–1933).

Why did demand for milk in contrast to, say, flour react so sharply to improvements either in price or income? Firstly, there was the absence of anything but a rudimentary dairy farming industry in the colony, so that supplies of fresh milk were difficult to obtain. Even where it was produced it could not be accepted as being really free from infection. There were no milk processing or cold storage plants for handling milk in bulk under sanitary conditions. But this fact alone does not answer the question. One has to look to a second factor – price. The prices of the 1930s were, on the whole, about one half of those of the 1920s. This reduction brought milk within the range of large numbers whose incomes were very small. There had been, therefore, a large potential demand which was left unsatisfied because of price/income effects. The price reductions of the 1930s together with income increases, especially of the late 1930s, led to the rapid increase in imports seen in the statistical table.[7]

Fish (Salted Cod)

It is easy to see the old established items, the cornerstone of consumption patterns established since the seventeenth century. Flour of whatever sort and now fish – salted cod. The latter thought to be fit for no other use but for slaves.[8]

In both the per capita imports vary but little in spite of price or income changes. Total salted fish imports moved from 5.0 million pounds in 1919 to only 6.8 million pounds in 1939 in spite of population growth; so that per capita imports moved from 13 pounds to 14.4 pounds in the same period – the fact that price in the former year was double that of the latter year made no difference.

Manufactured Goods

This broad classification given in the trade statistics includes so wide a range of commodities that it is extremely difficult to make any worthwhile deductions based on total figures given in this category. What it is proposed to do is to extract the chief items comprising each of the following sub-divisions and continue the analysis from that point.

1. Consumer goods other than food and drink, for example, cotton goods, boots, shoes and so on
2. Producer goods, for example,
   a. Machinery
   b. Others, such as cement, timber, fertilizers, manures and so on

The first sub-division will supplement the consumption goods analysis carried out earlier. The latter will give some indication of the addition through imports of the productive capacity of the colony.

Consumer Goods (Other Than Food and Drink)

Cotton Goods

P.T. Bauer[9] used this item of imports as his chief indicator of the trend in the terms of trade of the West African cocoa producers. In his case, cotton goods accounted for about 25 per cent of imports in Nigeria and 21.3 per cent in the Gold Coast for the period 1949–51. In Trinidad and Tobago during the inter-war period, cotton goods could only be regarded as one of the possible indicators. The contribution of cotton goods of all kinds to total imports was about 8 per cent in 1919 and about 3.6 per cent in 1939; in money terms $1.56 million and $1.19 million. By comparison the contribution of flour was much larger: $3.65 million (19 per cent) in 1919 and $1.56 million (4.7 per cent) in 1939. More importantly, the other capital goods items such as machinery (overwhelmingly for the oil industry) quite dwarfed the consumption items.

Quantity imports (gross) of cotton piece goods (as opposed to all cotton goods mentioned earlier) were 7.8 million square yards in 1919 and varying with frequent but slight fluctuations throughout the period were 9.6 million square yards in 1939. Incidentally, the per capita consumption in 1919 and 1939 are the same: 20 square yards; 1921 was 30 square yards; 1927 was 26.5 square yards; and 1935 was 26 square yards. On the whole, therefore, there was no spectacular increase in imports, c.i.f. average value per yard varied between 18¢ and 12.3¢ per yard in the 1920s, but fell in the 1930s to about 9¢ to 10¢ per yard. In spite of the relative cheapness of the prices of the 1930s, however, imports did not increase considerably.

The failure of cotton piece goods imports to increase rapidly (for example, compared with certain food items) can be largely explained in terms of a substitution effect. Imports of made-up apparel increased much faster than imports of cotton goods. In addition, the introduction of cheap artificial silk in 1930 (and the rapid increase in its imports after 1935) must have affected the growth of cotton imports. The value of imports of apparel increased from $307,200 in 1919 to $982,200 in 1939; all silk goods from $58,300 to $574,700. The breakdown of these categories from 1935 (when there was a change of classification) shows that gross imports of silk piece goods increased as follows:

		In square yards (millions)
1935	....	0.91
1936	....	1.36
1937	....	2.28
1938	....	2.05
1939	....	2.15

On the whole, therefore, while a consideration of cotton goods imports alone may give the impression that there was very little progress, a glance at the complete picture of clothing imports shows a different story. There was a substitution effect influenced largely by the low prices and enormous out-turn of textiles during the United Kingdom, Japan, India, Hong Kong struggle for the world textile markets in the 1930s.

Boots and shoes indicate the same trend. The value figure for boots and shoes imports rose from $283,200 in 1919 to $644,800 in 1939; the quantity figure from 14,300 dozen pairs to 69,700 pairs, a more than sixfold increase. What is even more interesting, however, is the fact that whereas in 1919 imports were 0.4 pairs per capita, in 1939 they were 1.8 pairs per capita, a fourfold per capita increase. In the late 1920s to early 1930s, it was just about one pair per head.

The chief factor in this increase was price. Even in the boom year of 1920 when imports were double those of 1919, the per capita imports were 0.9 pairs. Once again it was the inflow of cheap Japanese boots and shoes in the 1930s, later replaced by Hong Kong shoes, that increased the per capita imports. Of course the United Kingdom retained her share of a better quality, more expensive shoe. Japanese supplies, however, reached down to a poorer, previously untapped, market. It was for this reason that the imposition of high tariffs to exclude Japanese shoes met resistance in Trinidad and Tobago.[10]

Producer Goods

Cement

The quantity of cement imported increased from 5,100 tons to 42,500 (1919–39). If 1938 is taken as 100, the quantity index for 1919 is 11, a ninefold increase. In spite of the rapid increase in population, the per capita imports increased correspondingly from 0.26 cwt in 1919 to 1.8 cwt in 1938. The two best years were 1937 (1.9 cwt) and 1939 (2.06 cwt). But the whole of the period 1935–39 showed per capita imports of cement above the 1 cwt level. Up to 1931 it was hardly up to 0.9 cwt per capita.

To some extent, this increase in cement imports was due to fall in prices from $24.9 and $32.9 per ton in 1919 and 1920, respectively, to about $13 to $14 per ton, during and after the Great Depression of the 1930s. The years 1938 and 1939 saw another upward movement in price to $15.7 and $17 per ton, respectively. With 1938 = 100, the average import value index of 1919 stands at 160 and at 210 for 1920. The lowest year was 1935 when the index stood at 80.

But price was not alone responsible for the increase in imports. The increased imports of cement were required either for house-building or for other capital works. In chapter 7, "Population",[11] it is shown that the amount of room-space built in Port of Spain in the period of 1931–41 was lower than that for the earlier decade. How, therefore, does one account for the rapid increases in imports in the 1930s?

Firstly, it should be observed that the period of greatest increase coincided with the post-1935 revival in trade, a revival characterized by the expansion of the petroleum industry. The second factor must have been the major capital works undertaken by the central government after 1935, that is, the Deepwater Harbour Scheme, the Housing Scheme, Central Water Scheme, and School Building Programme. Each of these (especially the first-named) would have required considerable quantities of cement.

Machinery

Before analysing this item of imports, it is necessary to make certain reservations about the trade statistics. C.P. Kindleberger[12] refers to some of the difficulties of handling the item machinery. In addition to these universal difficulties, the trade figures of Trinidad and Tobago further complicate matters, especially after 1935 when there was a change of classification. Even in the Statistical Abstract of the British Empire the warning is given that the change of classification makes comparison with previous years difficult.

The Statistical Abstract, the Blue Book and the Colonial Reports agree more or less until 1934. (The Customs Report itself does not help matters. The total of all items under machinery [1935], for example, gives a different figure $1.8 million from that given under the heading Machinery $2.8 million without breakdown.) Thereafter, there is wide divergence; the Statistical Abstract figure for machinery imports being much lower than those in the Blue Book or the Colonial Reports. Judging from the expansion of the exploration, drilling, and especially the refining sectors of the petroleum industry (the chief importer of machinery) it would appear at first sight that the Statistical Abstract figures are somewhat on the low side. The Blue Book figures may perhaps be somewhat exaggerated on account of the change of classification. But they approximate much more closely to what one would expect from the expansion of the industries and new public works mentioned earlier. Incidentally, the imports of the oil industry, the chief component of which is machinery and which are also largely responsible for the island's imports of machinery, show the same sharp upturn after 1935. Note the following:

	1933	1934	1935	1936	1937	1938	1939
Blue Book/ Colonial Reports	2.4	2.6	2.8	4.3	7.7	7.4	–
Total oil companies (imports composed largely of machinery)	2.5	2.7	3.1	4.6	8.2	8.5	6.0

The Blue Book and Colonial Report figures appear to have the support both of the oil companies' import figures, the total customs figures (without breakdown) and the level of import and general economic activity in the island for and after 1935. It is proposed therefore to accept the Blue Book or Colonial Report figures as representative of machinery imports for the period.

Having disposed of that difficulty about the trade statistics, it is necessary to face the other, that is, the difficulty of assessing the meaning in real or quantity terms of the money value in which the commodity is given in the trade statistics. The problem is one of determining average values. The authority quoted by Kindleberger[13] maintains that the money value of a given weight of machinery above a certain size (whatever its use) varies, if at all, within narrow limits so that determining average value per ton should be fairly easy. This contention is not at all supported by some of the data available from the Trinidad and Tobago trade figures. In any case one wonders how much reliability can be placed upon it.

In the absence of average value figures, total value figures are employed in the following analysis as indicators of the addition to the country's economic potential. This approach has its obvious limitations. It assumes that prices are constant and even more so it assumes that $1 million of agricultural machinery imports (whatever its weight or function) is equal in its productive capacity to $1 million of, say, oil mining or refining machinery. Since there appears to be no way out of this difficulty, the value figures will be used while the fact of their relative inaccuracy will always be borne in mind.

As can be seen from table 3, the petroleum and sugar industries were chiefly responsible for the growth in machinery imports, the former playing the major role. Together, these two industries accounted for about 76 per cent of the total machinery imports in 1920 and 87.6 per cent in 1921.

Table 3 Imports of Machinery ($'000) – Chief Components

Year	Total	Other Agricultural	Sugar and Accessory	Oil Industry
1919	1,776.5	–	–	–
1920	5,174.4	35.0	604.8	3,320.0
1921	5,716.8	30.2	774.5	4,234.1
1922	1,549.4	10.8	138.7	944.6
1923	1,835.0	62.2	275.5	1,026.2
1924	1,843.2	20.6	390.2	1,217.7
1925	1,852.8	38.4	306.0	1,235.5
1926	2,462.4	34.4	154.5	2,028.9
1927	3,859.2	22.5	184.3	3,227.0
1928	3,004.8	60.9	216.5	2,300.6
1929	4,291.2	72.9	162.2	3,634.1
1930	4,200.0	36.9	168.5	3,326.9
1931	1,555.2	30.2	169.5	924.5
1932	1,766.4	66.7	221.2	1,192.3
1933	2,424.0	45.1	195.8	1,746.7
1934	2,683.2	81.1	197.3	2,017.9
1935	2,840.6	45.3	220.7	2,450.0*
1936	4,329.2	61.3	175.8	4,000.0*
1937	7,667.9	69.6	153.9	6,950.0*
1938	7,373.1	102.2	135.1	6,960.0*
1939	–	130.8	364.4	–

*Rough approximation only. For total oil companies' import composed largely of machinery, see chapter 6

It is proposed to deal mainly with these two items, touching upon others only where the import figures show the need for some explanation.

Petroleum Industry Machinery Imports

The high level of mining industry machinery imports in 1920–21 was due to the following causes. Firstly, in 1920 certainly and 1921 perhaps also, the high level of imports was the result of a sudden easing of the supply position consequent on the cessation of war and the reconversion of factories in the United Kingdom and United States from a wartime to a peacetime footing.

Table 4 Petroleum Exports – Average Values

Year	Crude (¢ per gallon)	Fuel Oil (¢ per gallon)	Kerosene (¢ per gallon)	Motor Spirit (¢ per gallon)
1919	8.0	4.8	33.4	29.2
1920	8.8	6.0	20.4	28.0
1921	8.2	5.6	21.6	30.2
1922	3.6	5.0	15.0	19.4
1923	5.0	5.6	17.6	16.2
1924	3.2	5.0	14.2	13.0
1925	3.0	5.2	10.6	12.2
1926	3.6	5.2	19.0	14.2
1927	3.6	5.2	21.0	16.0
1928	2.8	4.2	15.8	11.6
1929	3.2	4.0	10.0	11.0
1930	2.8	3.6	13.4	10.8
1931	2.2	2.2	13.8	5.8
1932	2.8	2.2	10.8	7.0
1933	2.2	2.0	13.6	6.2
1934	2.3	3.1	16.0	6.4
1935	2.4	2.5	10.6	5.9
1936	2.4	2.5	8.6	6.9
1937	2.3	2.8	10.0	7.4
1938	2.5	3.1	9.7	7.4
1939	–	–	–	–

The 1919 Mines Department Report remarks on the shortage of drilling equipment which was holding up development while the 1920 report speaks of an easing of the supply position. Further, one company report[14] refers to the embarrassment experienced when, having planned in terms of receiving certain equipment over a three-year period, it found that delivery was made in one year and payment had to be made promptly. This freeing of a backlog in addition to the telescoping into one year of a three-year import programme was therefore partly responsible for the 1920 imports. The 1921 imports may have been similarly affected. It seems, however, that the other factor, high export prices, also operated.

Table 4, giving average prices of petroleum exports, indicates that the high imports of machinery coincide with high prices for exports for 1919–21.

The immediate post-war shortage of equipment must have been particularly galling to companies that had spent large sums in exploration and drilling that was not always successful. The easing of the supply position coming therefore on top of the favourable market situation must have influenced imports of machinery. Under the stimulus of high prices there was a considerable increase in the number of new wells started and in the footage drilled.

As soon as export prices fell in the depression of the 1920s, imports of machinery also fell. It is quite possible that one factor, unconnected with export prices, was that, as indicated earlier, the removing of the supply bottle neck had caused 1922 and 1923 import targets to be fulfilled in 1920–21, thus reducing the need for imports in the 1920s.

But the drop in imports from $4.2 million to $0.9 million needs further explanation. The Mines Department Report (1923) states that

> the financial conditions prevailing during the period under review have been unfavorable to any large expansion of the petroleum industry of the colony, with the result that development has been chiefly confined to those companies already operating in the colony, which have in most cases concentrated their energies on the extension of the proven fields so that no great amount of prospecting work has been undertaken in the new areas.

There was, however, a continuation of an active drilling programme, carried out in the early years of the period, mainly with the equipment imported during 1920 and 1921 and before. Actual crude oil production was the "largest yet known", that is, 21 million gallons more than in 1922.

So far reference has been made to mining machinery imports. However, petroleum refining had been proceeding and increasing from before 1919. In 1922 Trinidad Leaseholds Limited (TLL) completed its refinery at Pointe-a-Pierre. In 1926 the company added a Dubbs Cracking Plant for the treatment of its fuel oil (see chapter 6). United British Oilfields of Trinidad (UBOT) also had its refinery at Point Fortin and increased its capacity from time to time as funds permitted. Virtual tea kettles were put up here and there in south Trinidad, often providing spectacular but dangerous explosions from time to time.

What seems to be the case, therefore, is that the petroleum industry, having started its expansion on the crest of the post-war boom and considerably increased its imports of heavy quantities of machinery, even perhaps in spite of great increases in the price of that machinery, was convinced by 1922 that the boom was not likely to continue and immediately curtailed its investment in imported machinery. At the same time, it seems to have attempted the maximum use of the material already imported to minimize its losses if prices fell disastrously or to maximize its profits in the other event.

Imports of petroleum machinery turned upwards again in 1926 when they were $2.03 million out of total machinery imports of $2.46 million (82.5 per cent). Although there was some increase in petroleum products prices, it was not considerable and did not occur in the chief export product, fuel oil. Either, therefore, the upturn of the late 1920s was ably anticipated or the view must be confirmed that investment in the industry though sensitive to price changes in the export products was also largely influenced by longer term policies of exploration drilling and refining which had as their driving force the continued efficiency of the industry.[15]

The Mines Department reports[16] (1926–30) indicate the expansion of operations in spite of low prices. Imports grew steadily overtaking the 1920 figure in 1927, until 1931 when for the first time continued low prices had their effect and once again machinery imports slumped to $0.9 million from $3.3 million of 1930.

After 1934, imports of machinery increased rapidly again. Both mining and refining were responsible. See chapter 6 on oil for an indication of the rapid increase in refining throughput capacity made possible by new imports.

Agricultural Machinery

The sugar industry was the one mainly responsible for imports of agricultural machinery. As in mining, there were in 1920 and 1921 heavy imports of machinery. The question of an easing of the machinery supply position may have operated here also. But much more important were the high prices and the prospect of continued prosperity in the industry as world demand exceeded supply. "In 1920, sugar production to meet market demand amounted to only17.5m short tons, while before the war consumption had already attained 21.0m short tons. Markets reacted automatically with a sudden bound which created a barrier that could not be gone over by everybody."[17]

It would appear that it was in the atmosphere of such speculative international trends that decisions were taken to increase output of canes and refining capacity. The reports of the director of agriculture point to increased activity on the plantations and also to attempts to improve both the strains of canes grown and the manner of tilling the soil (1919). It is shown that in implemental tillage the cost is lower; fewer labourers per acre are required, especially where mules are used; the kind of labour necessary is more easily obtainable and with sufficient animals and implements a larger area can be dealt with in a given time; "in all cases implemental tillage resulted in lower cost and increased crop".

This was a conscious effort to reduce the cost of tillage which may have gone up for the reason given by Professor Shephard,[18] that is, after the end of the indenture system (1917) there was a shortage of labour for both cocoa and sugar and that as a result there were increases in wages which led to increased costs of running plantations. The following factors can therefore be isolated as influencing the import of machinery for the sugar and other agricultural industries for the years 1920–21:

1. The increase in world price and optimistic speculation as to the continuation of the trend.
2. The gap between demand and supply of sugar and the prospect of gain if output could be increased both by increasing the yield of canes through better tillage and strains and more effective factory processes.
3. Attempts to mechanize in the field, substituting the factory machinery for scarce factory labour which had become expensive and perhaps very unmanageable because of this very fact of scarcity.
4. Cane farmers were becoming increasingly restless and dissatisfied with the price paid for their cane and with the manner of determining that price.[19] At the beginning of the period, their canes were producing about 48.5 per cent of all sugar. There were indications that the cane farmers were reducing the area of cultivation. Further, the supply from that source was often irregular, and the plantations wished to make up for any shortages from the farmers by increasing their own acreages correspondingly and employing mechanical tillage. Large refining units can only be run efficiently at full or near full capacity. The year 1923, though a somewhat isolated case, illustrates this. The director of agriculture in 1922 reports, "The low price of sugar caused many farmers to be very disappointed, leading to neglect of cultivation and reduction in planting for 1923. The exports of sugar were 35,523 tons less than in 1922." In the very next year there was this great increase in the importation of agricultural machinery.
5. The amalgamation of estates and the establishment of central factories. The process of amalgamation had started in the nineteenth century. "The reduction in the number of sugar estates in Trinidad was from 110 in 1865 to 58 by the end of the century."[20] In 1919 when the

> period under study begins the number was 15. In 1936 there were only 11. By 1937–38 there was further amalgamation with the advent of Tate and Lyle to the Trinidad sugar scene.

The net result of these amalgamations was greater efficiency through larger crushing and refining units (see, for example, the lowering of the conversion ratio of cane to sugar). These amalgamations and improvements were largely responsible for the imports of machinery.

But the question of the effect of sugar prices on machinery imports requires further elaboration. There was an interesting connection between prices or prosperity in the industry and amalgamation. "Most amalgamation and reduction in the number of sugar estates in Trinidad was largely a process of natural selection." Whenever the industry suffered from world price conditions, only the fittest could survive. These bought up the less fortunate and expanded the size of the manufacturing unit. But rising prices also gave to the large survivors the wherewithal to purchase the larger and more modern factory machinery. Table 5 shows the trends in prices and agricultural sugar machinery imports.

As can be seen from table 5, the price of sugar continued its fall from the boom of the immediate post–World War I era. As a matter of fact, it would be seen that prices after 1930 level off at approximately $49 per ton with the introduction of imperial preference. When we look at imports both of agricultural machinery (mostly tractors) and sugar-making and refining machinery, however, there is really no comparable downward trend. In the case of the former there has been a tendency for imports of machinery to continue buoyant in spite of the decline in the price of sugar. Similarly, there has been no drastic drop in the imports of refining machinery and parts.

It does appear that there is a case of rationalization of the industry. In one sense, it can be regarded as taking place in spite of the fall in price of the product. In another sense it can be taken as necessitated by the fall in prices. Insofar as one would expect a firm to be better placed financially in times of rising prices to expand its plant and increase its fixed capital and insofar as one could expect the reverse when prices fall, then it can be said that imports have been rising in spite of a fall in product prices. However, the table for quantity and value of sugar exports shows that while prices have been falling, output and exports have been rising steadily with the result that the actual revenue has either been maintained or has risen slightly.

Earlier, when comparing the exports of the sugar and cocoa industries, mention was made of this difference in attitude towards falling prices in

Table 5 Relation between Price of Sugar and Value of Agricultural Machinery Imports

Year	Sugar Export Price ($ per ton)	Sugar Machinery Imports Value ($'000)	Agricultural Machinery Imports Value ($'000)
1919	–	–	–
1920	–	604.8	35.0
1921	–	774.5	30.2
1922	–	138.7	10.8
1923	132.0	275.5	62.2
1924	123.6	390.2	20.6
1925	71.2	154.5	38.4
1926	66.0	184.3	34.3
1927	82.2	216.5	22.5
1928	72.8	162.2	60.9
1929	56.7	168.5	72.9
1930	49.0	169.5	36.9
1931	43.9	211.2	30.2
1932	46.6	195.8	66.7
1933	45.6	197.3	45.1
1934	40.0	220.7	81.1
1935	36.6	175.8	45.1
1936	37.1	153.9	61.3
1937	43.6	135.1	69.6
1938	37.6	364.4	102.2
1939	–	–	130.8

both industries. In the case of cocoa, a fall in price when it appeared to be permanent or long lasting, led to immediate foreclosures on mortgages, neglect of holdings, and a general deterioration of the industry. In such cases it has never recovered.

However, in the case of sugar the fall in price resulted in every effort being made to expand production and it is in this context that one should consider these somewhat "perverse" movements of imports of machinery. To get a further insight into the picture, one should see the international situation as far as sugar was concerned. There was a renewal of the struggle between beet sugar (which had received a severe knock during World War I) and cane sugar. As Enrico Romolini put it, "while all merchandise as a rule are faced with the same fundamental problems which must be solved to maintain their position in world trade, sugar must meet the additional problem of the competition between beet and cane on account of the difference of their net cost".[21]

Quite apart from considerations of cost of production and the need to maintain employment at home, however, the production of beet sugar was maintained for the simple reason that in time of war external sources of supply of sugar may be cut off. In such a situation of conflict between beet and cane, the need in the case of Trinidad and Tobago as with any other sugar-producing country was not only to produce more sugar but to produce more sugar more cheaply.[22]

After the boom period of the 1920s, however, the industry could not really afford very large imports of machinery. It could do no more than maintain imports at a level consistent with *maintaining efficiency*, even its very survival.

The upturn in 1939 could perhaps be seen in terms of new machinery for the Tate and Lyle factory.

3

The Cocoa Industry[*]

The Golden Age of the Trinidad and Tobago Cocoa Industry

To understand the developments and changes in the cocoa industry of Trinidad and Tobago in the inter-war years and to grasp fully the consequences for the economy of such changes, it is essential to start the analysis some time before the period of study. The proper perspective would be achieved if the analysis were carried, but not in detail, into the years 1870–1920, the "golden age" of the Trinidad and Tobago cocoa industry.

The following features characterized the period: high prices in the world market for cocoa; high yields per acre on the cocoa estates; an expansion of the acreage under cocoa, and low wages in the home market for labour. What were the causes and consequences of these factors operating in the cocoa industry?

High World Price of Cocoa

Between 1870 and 1920 the average price of cocoa on the world market was approximately $14 per fanega (110 pounds). Although Trinidad and Tobago's contribution to total world trade in cocoa was quite substantial, it can quite safely be said that these high prices were caused almost entirely by

[*] We are indebted to Professor C.Y. Shephard of the Imperial College of Tropical Agriculture, who has written a number of very interesting and informative articles on agriculture in Trinidad, for a considerable part of the information that went into this chapter.

forces external to that economy such as the development of new methods of processing the cocoa beans and the emergence of new cocoa products which caused a new demand to develop, and the rise of living standards and per capita income in the chief importing countries of Europe and America (table 6).

These new products included cocoa-powderized in drinking chocolate which was beginning to compete with tea as a beverage; and eating chocolate in which cocoa butter, an extract from the cocoa bean, was used. Cocoa butter was also used in the manufacture of cosmetics and pharmaceutical preparations. On the question of the demand for cocoa by the confectionery trade, Paul Bareau observed: "It is worthwhile taking a closer look at the increase in confectionery consumption between the wars to discover if possible what were the main reasons for this development. One basic fact is that this expansion took place mainly in countries where living standards were high and rising."[1]

There was, for example, "a very close correlation between the increase in confectionery sales and the national income in the US". It was also true for the period 1870 to the beginning of World War I that the per capita and total cocoa imports were greatest in those countries, for example, the United Kingdom, France, Germany, United States, Switzerland and the Netherlands, in which the standard of living was high and rising.[2]

The Premium on Trinidad and Tobago Cocoa

Trinidad and Tobago, Venezuela, and Ecuador were the chief producers of the "fine"[3] types of cacao. The new producing countries, Gold Coast, Nigeria and so on, were producers of "ordinary" types, although by 1920 production of the latter type greatly exceeded that of the former type. The former because of its superior variety and better methods of preparation enjoyed a premium over the ordinary types. The margin varied considerably. Table 7, however, gives an indication of how the prices of both varieties compared for the period 1918–31. The same sort of margin obtained for the earlier period.

On the demand side, therefore, prices were maintained because of the rising standard of living in consumer countries – and also because of the premium placed on fine cocoa. On the supply side there was also an important contributor to rising prices – the inelasticity of supply of cocoa. The main cause of the inelasticity is the length of time needed to bring a new cocoa estate into bearing, that is, five years. Not even after five years, however, does the cocoa tree attain its highest output. This position is not reached

Table 6 Output of Main Cocoa Producers, 1894–1944

'000 metric tons / Main Producers	1894–95 to 1898–99	1919–20 to 1923–24	1924–25 to 1928–29	1929–30 to 1933–34	1934–35 to 1938–39	1939–40 to 1943–44
Ecuador	19.8	36.2	20.7	14.6	17.6	13.6
Brazil	12.6	57.3	68.1	91.6	129.9	126.8
Trinidad and Tobago	12.0	28.4	24.6	21.0	14.3	6.6
São Tomé and Príncipe	9.4	20.8	16.7	11.0	10.2	6.7
Venezuela	8.2	20.8	19.2	15.9	16.8	14.3
Gold Coast and Togo	0.1	166.5	224.5	232.3	282.6	230.2
Nigeria and the Cameroons	0.1	27.4	46.0	62.7	99.9	99.4
Total	**88.1**	**431.4**	**513.2**	**568.8**	**748.2**	**640.6**

Source: Extracted from "Cacao: A Review of Current Trends in Production, Price and Consumption", FAO Commodity Series, Bulletin no. 27, November 1955.

Notes: By 1934–35 to 1938–39 such countries as the Dominican Republic and the French Cameroons, in which production was insignificant in the late nineteenth century, had also outstripped Trinidad and Tobago.

Trinidad and Tobago production had fallen from 13.6 per cent of world total in 1894–95 to 1898–99 to 6.6 per cent in 1919–20 to 1923–24; a little under 2 per cent in 1934–35 to 1938–39; and to just a little under 1.0 per cent in 1939–40 to 1943–44. She had slipped from third place in world production in 1894–98 to ninth in 1935–39.

Table 7 The Relation between the Average Prices of Gold Coast and Trinidad and Tobago Cacao 1919–1931

Year	Trinidad	Gold Coast	Gold Coast Price (Per Cent of Trinidad Price)
	Price per cwt		
1918–19	90s. 0d	65s. 0d	72.2
1919	110s. 0d	84s. 0d	76.4
1920	112s. 0d	81s. 6d	72.8
1921	57s. 0d	43s. 6d	76.3
1922	70s. 0d	45s. 0d	64.3
1923	53s. 0d	36s. 0d	67.9
1924	63s. 4d	38s. 11d	61.5
1925	73s. 6d	43s. 10d	59.6
1926	68s. 2d	52s. 2d	76.5
1927	82s. 4d	71s. 11d	87.3
1928	69s. 2d	59s. 7d	86.1
1929	60s. 11d	46s. 10d	76.9
1930	57s. 2d	37s. 5d	65.5
1931	43s. 10d	25s. 11d	59.1

Source: Shephard, *The Cacao Industry of Trinidad* (quotations supplied by Messrs Woodhouse, Carey and Browne).

until the tree is fifteen years old.[4] It is therefore easy to see why supplies proved to be in the short run unresponsive to the pull of demand and why prices remained buoyant.

Although in the period 1870–1920 world supply of cocoa did not keep pace with demand, investment in the industry was taking place in every country which now contributes to world trade in cocoa. The Gold Coast and Nigeria, for example, which had exported no cocoa until, say, 1896–97 and then only 100 metric tons each, had by 1920 increased their exports of cocoa to 126,800 and 17,400 metric tons, respectively. In Trinidad and Tobago exports had increased almost threefold, from 10,300 metric tons in 1894 to 28,500 metric tons in 1920.

What were the factors internal to the Trinidad and Tobago economy and relevant to a study of the inter-war period that were responsible for this increase in production?

Expansion of the Industry

Before the actual question of expansion of the Trinidad and Tobago cocoa industry is analysed, however, it is necessary to look at another external factor which closely affected the pattern of agricultural development in the islands: that is, tariffs and bounties.

The reduction of import duties in the United Kingdom and the absence of such duties in the United States of America and in Holland, two of the chief importers of cocoa, played their part. For sixty years after 1853 both British and foreign cocoa paid only 9/4 per cwt in the United Kingdom. Subsequently, during World War I the duty was raised steeply and by 1916 was £2.16.0 per cwt. In 1919, preference on British cocoa was reintroduced with the result that the colonies paid £1.15.0 and foreign countries £2.2.0 per cwt.

The relevance of the tariffs question emerges when one realizes that in Trinidad and Tobago cocoa and sugar were rival industries. While cocoa was enjoying favourable price and tariff conditions, sugar was experiencing just the opposite. Cane sugar and beet sugar were in competition and the countries that were the chief importers of sugar were also producers of beet sugar. To protect their beet sugar production, therefore, these countries assisted their sugar industries both by means of subsidies and by tariffs. If cane sugar was to compete with beet sugar in such a situation productivity in the cane sugar industry had to be stepped up, not only in terms of yield per acre but also in yield per unit of labour employed, to lower unit costs. The factory process also needed to be improved. It also meant that only the largest and most efficient companies with sufficient financial backing could compete with beet sugar. In Trinidad two trends emerged: The former French owners of sugar estates sold out to large British companies who were mostly absentee owners. There was also a tendency towards integration of estates. This second trend concerns the sugar industry, however, and will be treated later. The first point, that is, the French owners selling out their sugar estates, is most important for the cocoa industry; for it was with the proceeds of sale of their sugar estates that the French purchased and developed cocoa estates at a time when high prices and world demand for cocoa indicated that cocoa was the best crop to be invested in.

Perhaps it will be useful to insert at this point a note on the position of the French in Trinidad that was never owned nor occupied by France. The following quotation sheds some light on the matter.

> Although under Spanish rule in the 18th century, the island was dominated not so much by the Spanish as by the French. The island was an undeveloped and sparsely populated one under its Spanish rulers. They were, however, anxious to develop the island by immigration and made special concessions of land of remission of taxes to those settlers of the Catholic faith who decided to settle in the island. As a result, towards the end of the eighteenth century there was a flow of Frenchmen from the surrounding islands into Trinidad. They came with their French speaking slaves and at the end of the century and in the early part of the 19th, were reinforced by a further flow of refugees from the French possessions of the Caribbean. The uprisings of the "Black Jacobins" of Haiti were only the outstanding evidence of an unrest which swept through all the French West Indian islands where the same struggle between slaves, members of the French revolutionary assembly . . . and the planter class in the Caribbean took place.[5]

and again, "In this island whose total population never exceeded 50,000 at any time in slavery (1828 was the peak year) there were two rival slave 'industries', cacao and sugar cane, in the hands significantly of the rival Spanish and French who eventually each retreated before the other, and both before the British, not only in sugar cane but also in cacao."[6]

One sees, therefore, the French as the planter class interested in the first place in sugar and who, under the pressures mentioned earlier, sold out their estates to the British who could perhaps more readily get financial assistance from a then expanding Great Britain. The proceeds of these sales went to purchasing the cocoa estates of the Spaniards. The most important district in which the French bought out the Spanish estates was the Montserrat area.

The Montserrat "Experiment" was at the base of the expansion. Actually, the line of analysis which treats the source of the capital responsible for the expansion of the cocoa industry before treating the case of the Montserrat "Experiment" reverses the time sequence of these occurrences. For it was the Montserrat "Experiment" which made possible the creation of the estates for the purchase of which the French used the capital retrieved from sale of the sugar estates.

The Monsterrat "Experiment" was a system of land settlement employed by Governor Sir Arthur Gordon as a solution to the problem of the squatters, some 400 in number, who settled in the Monsterrat area. His plan was not to get the squatters off the land, but to give them ownership of the land and so give them some incentive to cultivate it more intensively. The land was to be sold to the squatters at the upset price of £1 for ordinary, 10/- for lagoon Crown lands per acre. For those who did not have the whole of the purchase price of £1 there was a system of deferred payments which resulted in the payment of £2 in four equal annual installments. When these new peasant proprietors wanted money either to pay their installments or to expand their cultivation, the merchants advanced them loans on mortgage. The experiment was a success and so the system spread to other parts of the island. "These measures proved of the greatest consequence for they not only gave the first real impetus to the development of a living body of peasant cacao proprietors but also greatly facilitated the formation of the large cacao estates."[7]

The Contract System

Another factor which operated in the development of the cocoa industry of Trinidad and Tobago was the contract system,[8] under which the owners of land suitable for growing cocoa made an agreement with another person that the latter should cultivate a certain area of land in cocoa according to certain agreed specifications as to spacing of plants, drainage and so on. The contractor was free during the early years of the cocoa plantation or estate to plant food crops which he could dispose of as he thought fit. Actually these food crops acted as further shade for the cocoa trees. After a number of years the owner of the land took over the area planted by the contractor paying him on the basis of an agreed schedule of prices for the cocoa trees which had been grown.

The expansion of cultivation was further assisted by a system of mortgage-financing which will be analysed in greater detail in a later section.[9] One can get an idea of the confidence that was placed in the cocoa industry from the following extract from the Colonial Report on Trinidad, 1928:

Opening for the Investment of Capital

> "Of the industries which offer inducements to investors of capital, the cultivation of cocoa is perhaps the most attractive and profitable investments are to be secured either in:
>
> a. the formation of an estate
> b. the purchase of an established estate, or
> c. the investment of capital on the security of an established estate.

> "Investment on mortgage can usually be obtained for sums under $1,000 (£208.6.8) at 10 per cent; from $1,000 up to $6,000 (£1,250) at 8 per cent and over $6,000 at 6 or 7 per cent."

By the twentieth century, therefore, cocoa had become gilt-edged security. It was the chief absorber of domestic credit in the island.

The other factor mentioned earlier that played an important part in the growth of the industry was cheap labour. In cocoa, as in sugar, the most important single cause of cheap labour was the system of indenture which until its termination in 1917 provided Trinidad with hundreds of thousands[10] of obedient labourers whose wages were 25¢ (1/0½) per day compared with the general rate of 35¢ (1/5½) to 50¢ (2/1) for men and 25¢ (1/0½) to 35¢ (15½) for women.

Communications

Another factor that made its contribution was the development of roads and, in Trinidad, railways which made it possible to bring the produce of the interior to the port. It has not been possible to obtain specific data on the growth of road mileage before 1919 (table 8).

By 1914 there were 111 miles of railway open to traffic compared with 116 miles in 1951. The railway network had been established by the first decade of the twentieth century.

The high yield per acre obtained is explained largely in terms of the relative youthfulness of the industry and the fact of new plantings. An estate reaches its maximum productivity for five years or so. Thereafter the decline is very gradual and reasonably high production can be obtained even when the trees are twenty-five to thirty years old. Continued expansion of the area under cultivation maintains the average youthfulness of an estate and so maintains a high average yield.

To sum up, therefore, the following are the factors which were most influential in the development of the Trinidad and Tobago cocoa industry:

1. The high world price of cocoa, influenced largely by rising living standards in consumer countries.
2. The decline of the sugar industry which released French planters' skill and capital for cocoa development.
3. The Montserrat "Experiment".
4. The contract system.

Table 8 Growth in Road Mileage 1919–1938

Year	Main Roads (miles)			Local Roads
	Total	Oiled or Metalled	Gravel or Burnt Clay	
1919	1,051.4	518.8	287.3	683.3
1923	1,084.6[a]	556.5	291.6	664.0
1927	1,073.7	616.2	258.7	642.9
1931	1,077.0	639.0	226.0	691.0
1935	1,080.0	695.0	223.0	753.0
1938	1,080.6	724.5	207.0	764.4

Source: Compiled from data in Colonial Reports.
Notes: The figure for 1923 is suspect. It is even greater than that for 1938.
"In 1910 a road scheme to cost £588.7 thousand was adopted and it provided for completion of the works estimated for within 10 years from 1st April 1911."
World War I completely upset the finance of the scheme owing to the difficulty of raising the loan necessary to cover a proportion of the cost. According to the arranged programme, £530,000 should have been expended by 1919, but only £298,000 was available (see Colonial Report, 1922).

5. The mortgage system.
6. Indenture.
7. Road and railway development.

Each of these factors played its part, sometimes singly, sometimes in conjunction with others to bring about the type of cocoa industry with which it is intended to deal for the period under study.

The Trinidad and Tobago Cocoa Industry 1919–1939

The foregoing analysis points to the factors which were responsible for the development and expansion of the cocoa industry. From this point on it is necessary to consider in greater detail the characteristics of the industry for the period under study.

The beginning of the period found the industry prosperous and expanding. It was the largest contributor in terms of value to the exports of the colony. In 1919 cocoa exports were 60.74 million pounds valued at $12.4 million, that is, 51 per cent of total exports. In 1920 the export figures were 63.75 million pounds valued at $15.48 million, that is, 43.4 percent of total exports in value terms. As can be seen on the figure showing the exports of the colony,[11] the value of cocoa exports reached their zenith in 1920. Thereafter, the decline was swift and almost unchecked. As was shown in chapter 1, cocoa exports fell in value from $12.4 million in 1919 to $1.2 million in 1939. While in 1919 cocoa represented 51 per cent of total exports, it represented only 3.3 per cent of the exports in 1939.

This decline could not be foreseen at the time, however, and as the expectations of planters are no less important in determining the course of agricultural industries than are the expectations of entrepreneurs in manufacturing industries, it should be interesting to form an estimate of what were the expectations of the Trinidad and Tobago cocoa planters; what factors influenced these expectations; how these expectations were given expression (in economic terms) and what were the consequences when these expectations proved groundless.

From the report of the director of agriculture for the years 1919 and 1920 comes the following extract: "The price of cocoa jumped rapidly about the middle of 1919 from 90/- per cwt to about 130/- at the close of the year. During 1920 it reached about 140/- in March, April and May and then fell rapidly, the year closing at 75/- to 80/- (all London prices)." Prosperity had lasted so long that planters must have regarded this further rise in prices as an indication of still greater prosperity to come.

To understand what were the forms in which these expectations found expression one must turn again to the period 1870–1920. In the earlier part of this chapter, the expansion of the industry and the systems of mortgages were mentioned. This process of expansion on the basis of mortgages in which cocoa estates were regarded as "gilt-edged security" continued and was accelerated by what could afterwards, and only afterwards, be regarded as the freak conditions of the post–World War I period. Thereafter there was a decline and it is reasonable to assume that the greater the shock of this disaster was for the planters, the greater was their optimism and the more ambitious their plan of expansion.

When consideration is being given to the causes and consequences of the decline, however, we must note the importance of the industry to the whole economy. The whole economic and social patterns of the society were influenced by cocoa. A reference to the earlier period shows that the industry started among peasant proprietors both in Trinidad and in Tobago. It never ceased to be a peasant crop although large estates emerged. At a time of prosperity, therefore, the export earnings of the cocoa industry were distributed throughout the economy, with every social stratum benefiting. Similarly, when the depression came to the industry, every section of society was affected. Although in the case of a plantation economy it is possible to draw a distinction somewhat clearly between the owners (especially where these are absentee) and the employees on the one hand and on the other the rest of the society which is dependent for its livelihood on other economic activities, it is not possible to do the same for the cocoa industry of Trinidad and Tobago at the time when this study commences. The whole economy was so closely tied up with cocoa that the term "economic barometer" as applied to cocoa was amply justified. This last point will be elaborated when the causes and consequences of the decline are being considered. For the moment it would suffice to say that over 235,000 acres (two-thirds of the cultivatable acreage of the islands) were at one time devoted to cocoa and that between 25,000 and 40,000 persons including small-holders were employed in the industry.

The Causes of the Decline of Cocoa in Trinidad and Tobago

Factors External to the Economy

World Production and Demand

Dr Eric Williams, in an article treating the precarious position of the West Indian islands' dependence on agriculture for their well-being, said that in the case of Trinidad, when she attempted to break away from the instability characteristic of a mono-culture (sugar) and turned to cocoa, the West African colonies turned her back.[12] The statement is in a sense true; but it can be misleading. There was no straight and declared competition between these two, not even on the question of the premium of "fine" over "ordinary" cocoa. African production of cocoa expanded at a remarkable rate and as world demand was not such as to absorb the increased production at the then existing high prices, prices fell.

> World cacao production increased by more than 600% between 1900 and 1939 from 102,000 tons to about 750,000 in the last pre-war years. During this long period, production rose annually by 16,000 tons or by an average of 5.1% per annum. No other crop except rubber underwent such rapid growth. Although the rate

> of increase diminished during the inter-war years 1920-39 as compared with the previous period, the 87% rise in total output (or 3.3% annually) was sufficient to support continued expansion in the industry.

and

> Africans were quick to realize the economic advantages of this crop in an otherwise subsistence economy. But less happy were the final economic results. The impact of the massive African supplies on the world markets depressed prices which fell continuously from 1900 to 1939 and contributed to the ruin of the industry in the original producing countries of Latin America.[13]

There are other important factors in the decline of the Trinidad and Tobago cocoa industry but if it is at all meaningful to speak of a prime cause, then the low prices which were paid for most of the period qualify for the title. For it destroyed that optimism which was seen as characteristic of the outlook of the planters; by destroying confidence it unmasked the weakness of the mortgage system; it hindered cultivations; and made it impossible to fight disease and pests when they broke out. In short it set in train a number of subsequent factors acting and interacting upon one another and culminating in the destruction of the industry.

Mortgages

The brief analysis of the period 1870–1920 showed that mortgage arrangements were to a large extent responsible for the development of the cocoa industry. In a country where there was no established money market and where the nature of the banking system[14] made it impossible for the ordinary peasant to qualify for bank advances with which to cultivate his holdings, mortgages became the only answer to the problem of finding capital for development. On the question of the sources of this capital used in these mortgage arrangements, Professor Shephard observed: "The sale of the small sugar estates to English companies, the profits of other industries, the savings of individuals in varied occupations, and the wealth derived from the cocoa industry itself rendered large sums of money available for investment in cacao mortgages."[15]

The loans were easy to obtain. For as long as there was full confidence that the price of cocoa would remain high, the moneylenders placed no restraint on their debtors, and the latter were prepared to pay the high rates of interest because the returns from their investment were more than adequate to meet these expenses. It was an era of easy, if not so cheap, money.

Duration of Loans

Once again the question of creditworthiness combined with that of length of period required for repayment of the loans to make it impossible for the established commercial banks to play a useful part in the development of the industry. For the small peasant proprietors and all except the largest ones needed credit for purposes and in conditions which, in the words of Ida Greaves, were "outside the proper scope of commercial bank operations".[16] The local moneylenders made loans available for a period of five years. Since a cocoa plantation takes at least five years to come into bearing, a loan for a shorter period would hardly be of much use.

But these money lending arrangements were not governed by the same strict rules that are observed in the commercial world. While, therefore, the system made money available for development, which the banking system did not, it also left loopholes for practices which in the end defeated the very purpose for which the system was started. Mortgagors were allowed and in some cases even encouraged to extend the period for the repayment of the loan without definite formal renewal. In other words, although at the time of the original loan agreement there were definite written undertakings to repay the principal at the end of five years, creditors allowed their debtors to continue paying them handsome interest on the old loan without liquidating it and without fixing another period at the end of which the capital would become due and payable. This meant that in law the debtors were at the mercy of the creditors who could foreclose at any time after the expiry of the first five years.

As long as prices continued to be buoyant there was no immediate problem. However, as soon as prices slumped and continued their downward trend creditors became anxious about their capital. They could foreclose, and many of them did foreclose before the government introduced legislation to prevent further foreclosure. But to the creditor who was perhaps ignorant of the methods of cultivating cocoa, of what use was it to him that he had suddenly become the owner of large areas of cocoa lands, the produce of which would no longer repay the cost of cultivation?[17]

With the fall in cocoa prices it can therefore be said that the bottom had fallen out of the local money market and a number of adverse factors were set in motion. But it is evident that one cannot blame only the fall in prices or the extraordinary growth of West African production for the critical situation in Trinidad and Tobago. The boom had continued long enough to have allowed most of the planters and proprietors to pay off their mortgages. They did not; instead they had spent heavily on imported consumer goods. "The reports issued by Committees instituted in the Islands have confirmed the evidence given in an inquiry as to the ill-effect of improvidence and non-resident ownership."[18]

This interpretation of the pre-1920 situation has not gone unchallenged, however. In the Legislative Council debate of 9 December 1921 on the bill providing for assistance to the cocoa industry it was claimed that there was considerable misunderstanding of this question. "Why almost all cocoa estates are mortgaged"? It was not evidence of extravagances and waste, but evidence of the energy and enterprise of the owner. "But for that enterprise and wise use of credit this Colony would not have been developed as it has."[19] It was also claimed that mortgages were considerably reduced in the three to four years when prices were high.

There is no denying the energy and enterprise shown by owners in developing the industry. Without that wise use of credit in the first place the industry and the economy would indeed have lagged behind. What cannot be denied, however, is that in spite of high prices, estates were not disencumbered; cocoa proprietors indulged in high living and they were overtaken at the height of their optimism by the fall in cocoa prices. "The most important (cause of the decline) is the fact that in times of high prices planters were improvident and thriftless."[20]

Unsuitable Land

Here is another reason why the blame for the decline should not be ascribed unduly to external forces and why internal mismanagement or over-optimism must be held partly responsible.

During the period of expansion, cultivation was carried on beyond the limits of marginal land into areas which were so unsuitable for cocoa that cultivation could only be justified in terms of high prices and a continuation for a long period of high prices (table 9).

It may be argued that this conclusion is unjustified; what is marginal land depends a great deal on what the world price of the product is or is likely to be within a given time, and what is sub-marginal land today may be yielding huge profits in a year's time, and that contention will be amply borne

Table 9 Estimated Division of Land on Basis of Suitability for Cocoa

Class	Suitable		Unsuitable	
	No.	Acres	No.	Acres
50 acres or under				
Resident proprietor	3,500	24,869	3,500	24,869
Non-resident	1,450	18,359	2,550	32,181
Over 50 acres				
Large proprietors	352	56,772	180	27,950
		100,000		85,000

Source: Report of committee appointed to inquire into the needs of the cocoa industry, Council Paper 61/1940.

out by the history of cocoa prices in the period since World War II. For "the demand for cocoa has expanded sufficiently to cause the dollar price of the commodity to rise by nearly 600 per cent compared with pre-war quotations, and the sterling price to rise by 750 per cent".[21] It is with this sort of reservation in mind, therefore, that one should consider the question whether cultivation was in fact pushed too far into unproductive areas. The Imperial Economic Committee on Cocoa Marketing, in its report in 1932, commenting on the cocoa industry in Trinidad and Tobago remarked that "on certain soil it is impossible to make cocoa pay and these will have to be given up to a more suitable crop or abandoned". This point is further supported by the following comment: "The Economic Survey carried out by the Government in 1930 has shown that probably one-fifth of the area under cocoa is uneconomic. Existing low prices considerably increase this fraction." It is evident that these comments spring from two considerations: firstly, the ideal conditions for the productions of cocoa; and secondly, the average price which it would be prudent to expect the market to pay at any given period.

On the basis of these two considerations, therefore, the Trinidad and Tobago cocoa industry had expanded into areas where the low output per acre and per unit cost could only be maintained at high world prices. As soon as world prices fell below that high level then only the most productive areas, the least-cost areas, could be depended on to give suitable reward for effort and expense (table 10a, 10b, and 10c).

Table 10a Average Cost of Management and Supervision on the "Best Estimates" and "Worst Estates", 1923–1924 to 1929–1930

	Per Acre ($)	Per Cent of Total Expenses	Per Bag of Cocoa ($)
Best estates	4.82	25	2.29
All estates	4.91	22	3.11
Worst estates	4.63	19	4.57

Table 10b Average Cost of Management and Supervision etc. on Estates with Different Yields

Yield in Bags per 1,000 trees	Cost of Management – Supervision		
	Per Acre ($)	Per Cent of Total	Per Bag of Cocoa ($)
Less than 3	3.04	13	3.70
3–5	4.40	23	3.91
Over 5–7	4.75	23	2.96
Over 7–9	6.58	24	3.02
Over 9–11	5.68	23	2.31
Over 11	6.81	18	2.25

Table 10c Average Cost of Management and Supervision etc. on Estates of Various Sizes

Sizes (Acres)	Per Acre ($)	Per Cent of Total	Per Bag of Cocoa ($)
Less than 150	6.02	23	3.53
151–250	5.45	22	3.36
251–350	4.99	26	2.91
351–550	4.92	22	2.97
551-750	3.11	21	2.72
75 and over	3.59	16	2.90

Source: Shephard, *The Cacao Industry of Trinidad*, part 5.

Non-resident Owners

In the case of the sugar estates, the term "non-resident owners" refers to persons who owned the estates but were living in, say, Great Britain. In the case of the cocoa estates the non-resident owners may have lived no more than 50 or 100 miles away from their estates which they rarely visited. They could not be bothered with the actual supervision of the estates. Either they had inherited these estates and would not spare the time to learn anything about cocoa cultivation or they had acquired the estates by foreclosure, or in the case of some professional men they may have bought cocoa estates because at the time when cocoa was profitable it was a mark of prestige to own a cocoa estate.[22] In many cases as they expanded their estates, most often by the contract system, they found their own capital inadequate. They therefore borrowed from the merchants and "as the peasant proprietor becomes tied to the local store keeper so the estate proprietor becomes tied to the merchant exporter and ownership of the estate becomes doubly removed from cultivation".[23]

The result very often has been that the merchants foreclosed and appointed managers and overseers to run the estates.

> Of some 17,000 proprietors, only some 5,000 or less than 1 in 3 live on their estates, and of these 5,000 resident owners 4,000 are owners of property of not more than 50 acres. Most of the overseers are underpaid and therefore not very interested in giving their best. The conduct of a cocoa plantation . . . is a business, and needs skills, hard work, proper equipment, close and efficient supervision, cheap working capital and strict records.[24]

Some or all of these were lacking on the Trinidad and Tobago holdings.

The Number of Family Estates

The malady here was not the more common one of fragmentation consequent on the death of the head of the family. Professor Shephard saw the trouble rather in an eagerness to maintain incomes for a number of heirs who did nothing on the estates. The result was therefore a curtailment of investment and cultural practices.

Costs

In the period after World War I there was a tendency for costs to rise. The cessation of indenture coinciding with fairly high export prices was chiefly responsible for the rise in labour costs especially.

For a comparison of wages in various cocoa producing countries, see the following extract from the report of a committee which in 1940 investigated the needs of the cocoa industry:

> From one cause or another the Cocoa Industry has paid to labourers during the period of the depression an uneconomically high rate of wage in relation to the world price of cocoa and the yields obtaining in Trinidad or in comparison with those in other countries competing with our product, as will be seen from the following statement:

Gold Coast	18–20¢ per day
Brazil	18–20¢ per day
Ecuador	12–18¢ per day
Grenada	30¢ per day
Trinidad	45–50¢ per day

> With a knowledge of the cost of living in this Colony and of the wages paid in other industries, we cannot recommend relief of the financial difficulties of the cocoa growers by reductions in the rate of wages.[25]

Diseases and Pests

In the period under study, many types of diseases and pests attacked the cocoa industry in Trinidad and Tobago and contributed to the worsening of conditions in the industry. This section does not seek to analyse in detail the diseases and pests of the cocoa industry, it seeks only to examine the effects upon exports of the incidence of disease in the industry. The aim is not to enter into the technical details of pest eradication but to see how after market conditions had affected the industry, price and disease combined in influencing the course of the industry.

The director of agriculture in his report for the year 1919 referred to the special campaign launched in 1919 to deal with the cacao beetle which had attacked the southern part of Trinidad. Also there was a report of the presence of *Rosellinia* root disease of cocoa found in the colony where it had not been previously reported. In 1923 for the first time his report established a link between diseases of cocoa and the price of the commodity: "As a result of low prices for the crop many cacao cultivations have received less attention than usual, which is unfortunate, as it leads to an increase in disease, particularly black pod."[26]

In 1924 when the crop had fallen to 56.5 million pounds, that is, about 6 million pounds below the average of the previous five years and 11 million pounds below the 1923 total, the director of agriculture reported:

> The drop is doubtless due partly to the cultural work on many estates having been reduced to a minimum owing to the long prevailing low prices, and partly to the abnormally heavy rains in some districts towards the end of the year which ruined much of the young crop. It becomes increasingly evident that the reduction of cultivation makes the trees more liable to be adversely affected by any abnormalities in the weather.[27]

Before further evidence is adduced to show how the fall in the price of cocoa facilitated the spread of disease in the cocoa industry, it should be useful to make the point that the low price of cocoa was instrumental only in aggravating the situation. Diseases had started to take their toll before the fall in price. The low prices only made fighting the diseases more difficult or, in some cases, impossible. The government had set up at River Estate in North Trinidad an experimental station for cocoa which was fairly well provided with money and facilities for treating infected trees. Even here, however, there was some considerable difficulty in curbing the diseases. The 1925 report of the director of agriculture on the River Estate, for example, states

> The steady increase in the amount of diseased or black cacao reaped during the last few years calls for attention as it indicates the persistent increase in disease not only on very young but on half fully developed fruit. When it is borne in mind that this 10,099 lbs (of spoilt fruit) represents only the small proportion that has been matured sufficiently to be reaped, the quantity of fruit lost in the younger stages must be much larger. This condition exists at River Estate in spite of constant reduction of shade, good cultivation and sanitation and fairly low rainfall. It will therefore seem reasonable to conclude that in some of the wetter districts of the colony where conditions are not equally good, the poor crops of the past few years are not entirely due to lack of cultivation, soil conditions or the

> other factors which are often blamed, as to the actual incidence of the particular disease or diseases affecting the cocoa pod in its various stages of growth and development.[28]

The other disease which was of importance was the witchbroom disease which made its appearance in 1928. Within one year of its discovery, witchbroom (*Marasmius perniciosus*) had made its presence felt in no uncertain terms. In spite of the efforts of the government and of the planters, the disease continued to spread. "At the end of 1928 some 600 acres were actually infected and the area suspected to harbour represented about 6,000 acres." After one year, that is, at the end of 1929, the affected and suspected areas totalled upwards of 44,000 acres, "and when it is remembered that 100 acres carry approximately 30,000 trees, some idea is gained of the magnitude of the task". Here, however, a few modifications must be made. The disease did not affect every tree in a given area. The acreage figure therefore distorts the incidence of the disease. This is borne out by the director of agriculture's comment: "It is frequently the case that several thousands of acres planted in cacao have only two or three hundred trees infected with the disease, but for the purpose of keeping a check by the Department such areas are classed as infected districts."[29]

To what extent did the disease affect production both in the early stages and afterwards? In its early stages the infection was "practically confined to vegetative tissues" and losses from infection were very small, but "it is reasonable to assume that if the vegetative phase of the disease is not thoroughly controlled, subsequently crop losses will begin to increase".[30]

In the low-lying areas where humidity is high, the estates were more vulnerable and diseased pods were found very early in the campaign.

In its later stages the disease could be very destructive. "It is the testimony of Ecuador that in 10 or 12 years witchbroom together with monilla has reduced their crop by fully 50 per cent."[31] In the case of Trinidad and Tobago the damage was not so spectacular. The following extract gives an idea of what happened in, say, nine years.

> As an indication of crop losses sustained on account of witchbroom in the most highly affected areas it may be mentioned that detailed records kept on 11 properties during the 1937-38 season showed an average loss of crop of 37.5 per cent; the range being from 22.5 per cent to 51 per cent. At Marper Estate, where regular control measures are practised, crop losses during the same period amounted to less than 9 per cent.[32]

The following table gives the damage done to cocoa on the Marper Estate which was relatively well equipped for fighting the disease. Note the steadily increasing ill effects of the disease.

Year	1932	1933	1934	1935	1936	1937
Per cent loss of mature witchbroom pods	0.87	1.25	1.33	1.31	3.84	8.67

So far consideration has been centred mainly on the question of the incidence of the disease and the destruction which resulted. Now, it is proposed to show how the economic factors, for example, prices and export income changes, affected the industry and, later, what were the consequences.

The important thing to note about the figures quoted in the table is that they concern an experimental station financially well provided for. It is essential to bear this point in mind when an attempt is made to analyse what happened in that section of the industry which is at once responsible for the exports of cocoa of the colony and which, as it can depend on no secure income, must have its cultural activities governed by considerations of prices, export incomes and expectations of what world market conditions will be. What can be seen immediately is the fact that on the Marper Estate it was possible to keep losses from witchbroom to a level approximately three times below that of the average estate. Why was this possible or rather what is the explanation for this difference between experimental station and the average cocoa estate? The director of agriculture reports showed that there had been considerable difficulty in getting the peasants and even some of the estates to follow the advice of the agricultural advisers on questions of culture and so on. But there was another more important reason: the price of cocoa was so low that proprietors had neither the money nor the incentive to maintain or improve cultural practices.

In 1925, three years before the outbreak of the witchbroom disease, but three to four years after the first severe drop of the world price, the Agronomist reported on "the falling off in condition of many cocoa properties due to the long period of low prices and some unfavourable seasons. The result has been in many cases the cessation or reduction of cultural work and of attention to pests and diseases."[33] There was some recovery in production in 1927–28 and "better prices, at any rate in the early part of the year (1928), also encouraged more activity, and the cocoa crop exceeded that of the previous year by approximately 6 million lb and was the largest since 1923".[34] There is need for caution here, however; because of the importance of the weather[35] in determining output in any one year, and also because of the basic inelasticity of the supply of cocoa, it must be only after great care that stress should be placed on the importance of short run price changes on production directly. If this is borne in mind, however, it will be possible to draw some conclusions about the importance of price in determining effort and money expended in cultural operations which will, with or without a longish time-lag, determine or influence output and so exports.

Turn first to the cost of controlling the disease. "It is probable that effective control work could be done in medium to high infected areas at a cost of between $3 and $3.50 per acre. It will be seen therefore that the control of the disease is largely a question of economics."[36]

In 1932, Professor Shephard had come to a similar conclusion:

> The cocoa planters in general have neither the means nor the credit facilities to combat the disease by more intensive methods of cultivation and strict methods of control. One third of the area is so unprofitable that it cannot survive even if prices rise to unexpectedly high levels. The great majority of the cacao properties could not survive with present prices. There is reason to believe that a large section of the industry will remain profitable despite the presence of witchbroom, provided that more intensive methods are pursued, that prices rise to about $15.00 a bag and that the disease can be kept in reasonable check in the meantime.[37]

He also made the following statement, however, which seems to be the crux of the whole problem: "The financial condition of the industry and the Colony imposes strict limitations upon the measures which can be adopted to control the disease."[38]

The achievement of the Marper Estate must be taken only as an indication of what can happen in a special case:

> It is interesting and informative to note the crops of cacao at Marper since the Government purchased it. There have been seven completed years and in spite of witchbroom and other diseases and pests, the average crop has been two and a half (2½) bags (165lbs each) per acre. This rate of cropping is probably twice that of the average of the Colony.[39]

Marper's cultural efforts were not determined by price per bag was is the case with the rest of the industry. Both Professor Shephard and the mycologist seem to agree on the per acre cost of controlling the disease, that is, $3.00 to $3.50 per acre. (For the prices of Trinidad and Tobago cocoa at store, Port of Spain, see table 11.) For the period 1931–32, when Shephard made his recommendations about the minimum price consistent with the industry remaining profitable, the price in Trinidad and Tobago was about $11.00 per bag.

But Shephard's comment about the financial position is important in that it concerns itself not only with the industry but with the whole economy. For if the industry could not, out of its own resources, provide the capital to

Table 11 Price of Trinidad and Tobago Cocoa at Store – Port of Spain

Year	Per Bag (165 lb, $)
1918–19	30.45
1919–20	35.88
1920–21	15.00
1921–22	16.20
1922–23	14.28
1923–24	14.25
1924–25	19.50
1925–26	18.75
1926–27	22.88
1927–28	21.75
1928–29	17.32
1929–30	16.17
1930–31	11.40
1931–32	11.40
1932–33	7.87
1933–34	8.61
1934–35	9.00
1935–36	10.50
1936–37	15.99
1937–38	10.86
1938–39	9.75

Source: Data supplied by the Cocoa Planters' Association of Trinidad.

fight the disease the only other source of help was the government. At this time of worldwide financial stress, the government was in no better financial position and the measures which it was able to recommend and about which it legislated were of necessity severely handicapped by the financial stringency.

The Weather

As indicated earlier, the weather was another factor which hampered the industry. The director of agriculture blamed the poor crop of 1922, "the smallest in nine years", on the unfavourable weather towards the end of the year but the price effect on the supply of cocoa is negligible in the short run.[40]

Similarly the low crop of 1924 which was "about 6 million lbs. below the average of the last five years and 11 million lbs. below 1923" was attributed partly to "the abnormally heavy rains in some districts towards the end of the year, which ruined much of the young crop".

Abnormal weather of any kind affects the cocoa crop adversely. Although in the previous examples the trouble was with over-abundant rain, the trouble in 1926 was drought.

From experiments carried out on the Marper Estate the Agricultural Department arrived at a theory on the effects of the weather on cocoa crops: "An interesting correlation has come to light connecting rainfall (or lack of rainfall) with the crop of the following calendar year. On both occasions where the graph of yield shows a peak the rainfall in the preceding year was abnormally low."[41]

That there is such a correlation one cannot doubt but surely it would require more than two such instances of the conjunction of a certain type of weather and good or bad crops to warrant the conclusion that a correlation does exist.

Consequences of the Decline

The first and most important consequences of the fall in prices and the consequent decline of the industry was the collapse of credit facilities. It must be remembered that in the absence of an established money market, cocoa was the backbone of the credit system. Cocoa was gilt-edged security. Overnight, almost, people found that their creditworthiness had disappeared completely. This destruction of confidence was crucial. It affected the whole economy. As will be seen later it affected even government's fiscal policy.[42]

To follow this train of events note the remarks of the acting governor when he introduced the bill to render assistance to the industry in 1921: "as a consequence of the existing conditions employment has been stopped or at all events curtailed to a very great extent . . . The agricultural community in general has no liquid assets – no balances at the banks to draw upon . . . Agriculture being in the state in which it is today the entire trade of the community suffers."[43]

It is essential to remember that petroleum had as yet, in 1921, made very little contribution to domestic incomes from exports (see chapter 1 on exports). Since export incomes from cocoa had declined imports also declined. Since import duties were the chief source of government revenue this latter also declined.

Earlier it was shown that one of the factors which contributed to the collapse of the industry when the price of cocoa slumped was the fact that in the period of high prices cocoa cultivation had been pushed into areas which were unsuitable for that crop. The result was that there were many high cost areas in production. One of the immediate consequences of the slump in prices was the shift in some areas from cocoa to sugar. "Not inconsiderable areas of cocoa have been felled and sugar cane substituted, and this with the running out of estates or fields with poor soils or otherwise unfavourably situated, is no longer offset to the same extent as hitherto by the production from new plantations" (1925).[44]

This last point emphasizes the difference between Trinidad and Tobago and, say, West Africa. In the latter the output of cocoa could be increased over a much longer period as new lands were brought into bearing so that the effects of ageing on production could be offset. In the case of Trinidad and Tobago, the physical size of the islands at once placed limits to any such expansion and after a point, reached in the early twentieth century, the area under cocoa could only be expanded at the cost of decreasing returns as the more unsuitable areas were cultivated.

The 1926 report of the director of agriculture, while re-emphasizing the shift into sugar, noted also a shift into coconuts and mentioned "that other areas are the scences of actual or prospective oil operations". In the Caroni district and in the Caparo Valley the shift to sugar was quite considerable. But since the Caroni area was in fact already a sugar-growing area it would seem that the transition was both easy and in a sense justified. The expansion of cocoa into this area could not in the first place have taken place except in conditions of very high prices. The sugar companies also helped the transition: "The Ste Madeleine Co. is putting down a light railway to tap very fertile lands at the back of the Oropouche lagoon" (1927).

But it would be unwise to conclude that there was a drastic reduction of the area under cocoa (see table 12). Perhaps the greatest reliance should not be placed upon the acreage figures given there: but they can be used as approximations of the actual area under cocoa. It is surprising to find, for example, that the 1932 figure is larger than that for 1920 after the reported cutting down of trees in 1925. The 1926 figure is perhaps more accurate.

It is significant that in spite of the reported reductions in cocoa acreage, disease, pests and neglect, there was not, until after 1933, any considerable permanent fall in the quantity of cocoa exported: "It may be noted that

Table 12 Productivity per Acre

Year	Acreage '000 Acres	Production cwt.	Productivity per Acre
1919	206.5	542.4[a]	295 lb
1920	202.3	429.1	–
1921	202.0	671.8[a]	–
1922	202.0	452.2	–
1923	202.1	463.0	253
1924	202.0	503.5	–
1925	202.0	441.8	–
1926	189.7	447.0[a]	265
1927	*	463.7[a]	–
1928	*	517.9[a]	–
1929	209.0	552.6[a]	216
1930	*	480.6[a]	–
1931	*	510.6[a]	–
1932	225.0	373.4[a]	–
1933	220.0	458.1[a]	234
1934	220.0	239.3[a]	–
1935	210.0	396.3[a]	–
1936	205.0	253.0[a]	–
1937	205.0	234.4[a]	128
1938	–	–	–
1939	185.0[b]	–	–

Source: The Statistical Abstract of the British Empire.
*Not available.
[a]Figures for exports.
[b]Estimate obtained in Trinidad Council Paper 61/1940.

notwithstanding all its trials and setbacks, the Colony crop has remained fairly stationery in the vicinity of 24,000 tons during the last ten years."[45]

The reason for the high level of the cocoa crop, in spite of the difficulties mentioned earlier, may very well be the basic inelasticity of supply. Once the cocoa estate has come into bearing then unless it is completely destroyed or very badly damaged it will continue to produce and the fall in output will not be swift but gradual. As Professor Shephard observed, "The effect of the neglect of cacao cultivation, is not an immediate or heavy reduction of yield but a steady decline over a number of years." The more permanent effects are brought about by ageing.

It would appear that although there was some reduction of the acreage the more important factor affecting output was the fall in the population of prime trees per acre. That is to say that in the late 1930s the acreage figures are largely nominal; that either from disease or neglect or ageing or inter-planting of coffee or all of these factors together, one acre of cocoa in, say, 1936–37 did not have as many healthy heavy bearers as one acre in 1919. In 1940 it was estimated that over 50 per cent of pickets should be replanted with better yielding material.[46] This is revealed in the decline in per acre productivity from 293.4 pounds in 1919 to 127.7 pounds in 1937. Compare these, however, with 412.5 pounds per acre, the average for 1929–36 on the government-run Marper Estate.[47]

But perhaps another point should be noted on the question of productivity per acre in cocoa. It can be most misleading to judge per acre productivity merely by quantity reaped and more so by quantity exported. As Professor Shephard stated earlier the decline in yield is usually very slow. If the estate is thoroughly cropped every year the graph of output after the peak has been reached descends but slowly. But the important thing is that the estate must be thoroughly cropped.

Where prices are low, not only are cultural practices neglected but harvesting is sometimes not undertaken at all. In such cases to use total crop as an indication of productivity per acre can be misleading. This explains in fact why total production and per acre productivity often rise considerably in response to rising prices and this in spite of the basic long run inelasticity of supply of cocoa.

Population Shifts

With the decline of the cocoa industry there was a corresponding shift of population from certain cocoa areas to the towns and to the areas around the growing oil industry. For example, Arima, in the northern part of Trinidad, and the centre of the cocoa industry, had its population considerably reduced by the decline of cocoa. This point is further developed in chapter 7.

Government Measures of Assistance to the Industry

The cocoa industry was so important to the economy of Trinidad and Tobago that when prices fell in 1921 there was an immediate desire on the part of the government to do something to preserve the industry. It has already been shown how insecure was the financial basis on which the industry rested. As soon as confidence in the "economic barometer" had waned there was a rush to foreclose on mortgages. Since the industry had been over-expanded in its time of prosperity and debtors had neither saved nor paid off their debts but had continued their indebtedness without legal contract, many of the proprietors were at the mercy of the moneylenders who would in any case have been quite incapable of looking after the estates that they were to receive on foreclosure.

The government therefore passed the Mortgages Extension Ordinance of 1921 which suspended until 30 June 1923 the powers of mortgagees:

1. To demand payment of the sum secured;
2. To exercise a power of sale over, or right of entering into possession of or appointing a receiver over, a plantation;
3. To commence or continue an action for breach of covenant to pay the sum secured, or an action for any penal rate of interest.

   Provided that any time after 30th June, 1922, the Supreme Court may grant leave for the exercise of any such powers if interest is unpaid for more than six months.[48]

The ordinance came into force on 9 December 1921 and was originally due to expire on 30 June 1923. It is interesting to note that whereas the severity of the price fall was appreciated by all there was still the belief that it would be temporary. In the event the Mortgages Extension Ordinance had to be twice extended before it was allowed to expire on 31 March 1925.

But the government measures were not as weighted against the mortgagees as might appear at first glance. Recognizing the inadequacy of the Mortgages Extension Ordinance, the government at the same time passed the Agricultural Relief Ordinance under which the Relief Committee was empowered to make advances from government funds to the owners of cocoa properties for the purpose of carrying on the cultivation, reaping and marketing of the produce, paying interest on mortgages and other encumbrances and meeting other necessary personal expenses. It is obvious that the government was attempting to satisfy all parties. Having first protected the debtor, it then sought to protect the interest payments to the creditor. Finally to safeguard its own funds it empowered the Relief Committee to assume prior charge on the crops and property without necessarily requiring the consent of existing encumbrances.

It was an effective safeguard against unscrupulous debtors. But it did not find favour with the large mass of cocoa producers. Compared with the loan that was to be made in 1930 to the sugar industry these conditions were most ungenerous. For in the case of loans to the sugar industry the rights of prior encumbrances were respected. The Hon. L.A.P. O'Reilly ably summed up the government's action on the matter thus: "That a mortgagee with a perfectly fixed right of property, with a fixed asset passing to him by virtue of his mortgage, should find himself ousted by a subsequent advance and without his permission! That was the vice."[49]

But the government could not seal all the exits. The expectation was that the crisis though sharp would be short. Add to this the fact that the government wished to reduce to an absolute minimum the amount expended on these schemes. The result was that no government machinery was set up to inspect and value the properties on which loans were to be made. It was felt that after a couple of years, at most, all would be well again with the industry and all sums owing to government would be repaid or at least collectible. In the event all that was demanded from persons seeking loans was a sworn statement about the value and condition of the property. Many of these statements proved unreliable, and some of the loans were misapplied. There were, therefore, cases of prosecution and the stopping of advances after a system of inspection and valuation was instituted.

Applications for loans were made in respect of 305 properties and granted in 186 cases.[50] The sum advanced up to 31 December 1924 by the committee was £160,802 ($772,000), and the amount received was £108,817 ($522,200). In some cases properties were sold by public auction or transferred to mortgagees on payment of all sums due to government under the ordinance.

How is one to assess the government's measures outlined earlier? If one considers that there were at least 16,000 properties of various sizes producing cocoa in Trinidad and Tobago at the time when the total of 186 cases of assistance were given, it shows how inadequate the provisions were. Judging from the fact that there were only 305 applications for assistance in an industry which from all accounts was experiencing difficult conditions, the conclusion must be either that the terms were not attractive enough or that confidence in the industry had evaporated completely overnight, and proprietors were not prepared to involve themselves in any further indebtedness. Whatever the reasons it is clear, however, that as a means of restoring the industry the Agricultural Relief Ordinance was not successful. Professor Shephard comments, however, that the experience gained by the administration of the ordinance was put to good use in organizing the Agricultural Bank which was set up in 1924.

It must be conceded, however, that the government, by entering into the field normally reserved for private enterprise, was acting quite in advance of many administrations which were much better equipped financially and with personnel to perform the task. Also it was filling the gap caused by the absence of a banking system geared to financing this type of enterprise. If the total amount loaned to 186 estates was approximately £160,802, that is, $772,000, then the average loan must have been approximately $4,000. Judging from the following table showing the number of estates of different sizes which comprised the Trinidad and Tobago cocoa industry, it is obvious that not many, if any, of the smaller units would qualify for such a large sum. If any of the small units did receive loans then the average for the remaining units must be even greater. It would appear, therefore, that the scheme worked more for the benefit of the large than for the small proprietor. The larger the number of small loans paid out the larger the amount of the loans received by the larger units.

Relation of Cocoa Estates of Various Sizes (Visited) to Total Area in Trinidad and Tobago (1930)

Gross Acreage	Number of Estates	Total Gross Acreage	Total Cocoa Acreage
0–10	10,038	62,744	36,270
11–50	5,009	99,229	58,575
51–100	456	32,162	19,140
101–200	288	41,822	25,174
201–500	65	48,629	22,364
501–1,000	221	71,045	39,965
More than 1,000	11	23,437	7,466
Total	**16,088**	**379,068**	**208,954**

Source: Shephard, *The Cacao Industry of Trinidad*, part 1.

The Agricultural Bank was set up in 1924, taking the place of the Relief Committee referred to earlier. The bank was established, "with the primary object of providing for the redemption of mortgages".[51] Although this was perhaps the most urgent task it intended to undertake its scope was wider, that is, fostering and encouraging agriculture in the colony and aiding in the development, maintenance and improvement of agricultural lands. It had an authorized capital of £250,000, of which £25,000 was originally held in reserve. Later, this reserve was made available for investment subject to a minimum of £10,000 being available for temporary advances.

It soon became obvious that the amount of money available for loans was inadequate. The Waterworks and Agricultural Bank Loan Bill was therefore passed in 1932 to provide for the raising of a loan for the bank. There were delays and uncertainties which resulted in no effect being given to the ordinance and initially the bank had to be financed from surplus funds of the colony, on which the bank paid interest at 5 per cent per annum. As in the case of the Relief Committee, loans were secured by a first mortgage on the property and on the personal covenant of the owner.

An elaborate system of repayment of loans was evolved. The borrower was required to repay each year by equal half-yearly instalments, a sum equivalent to 8 per cent of the original loan. Interest was charged on the outstanding balance at 7 per cent per annum. Each instalment consisted partly of principal and partly of interest, with the proportion of the instalment that went into interest becoming progressively smaller and that going to repaying principal becoming progressively larger. Table 13 gives some idea of the manner in which the system worked.

To safeguard government funds and prevent the granting of disproportionately large loans, the bank restricted the size of loans to 50 per cent of the estimated value of the property. The value of the property was determined by capitalizing the profits of the property at 8 per cent; 8 per cent being the proportion of the original principal which had to be repaid at each instalment and being also somewhat above the interest rate charged. It was, however, most difficult to establish what were the profits of the properties. For no books were kept by most of the estates, and valuations based on acreage and yields varied considerably from estate to estate and from year to year. Also any conclusions as to the amount invested in any property was nothing but guesswork. Table 14 indicates the number and amount of loans granted by the bank up to December 1931.

The rate of interest on loans at 7 per cent was just one half of 1 per cent higher than that charged by the Kenya Land Bank when it commenced operations in 1931.[52] It would appear, judging from the fact of the

Table 13 Prescribed Half-Yearly Instalment for Every Hundred Dollars of the Loan

Half Year	Prescribed Half-yearly Instalments ($)	Apportioned		Balance of Principal Owing
		On Account of Interest at 7% ($)	On Account of Principal ($)	
First	4.00	3.50	0.50	99.50
Second	4.00	3.48	0.52	98.98
Third	4.00	3.46	0.54	98.44
Fourth	4.00	3.44	0.56	97.88
Fifth	4.00	3.42	0.58	97.30
Sixth	4.00	3.40	0.60	96.70
Seventh	4.00	3.38	0.62	96.08
Eighth	4.00	3.36	0.64	95.44
Ninth	4.00	3.34	0.66	94.78
Tenth	4.00	3.32	0.68	94.10
Twentieth	4.00	3.04	0.96	85.82
Twenty-fifth	4.00	2.86	1.14	80.47
Thirtieth	4.00	2.64	1.36	74.12
Thirty-fifth	4.00	2.39	1.61	66.57
Fortieth	4.00	2.08	1.92	57.61
Forty-fifth	4.00	1.72	2.28	46.97
Fiftieth	4.00	1.30	2.70	34.34
Fifty-fifth	4.00	0.79	3.21	19.33
Fifty-seventh	4.00	0.56	3.44	12.50
Fifty-ninth	4.00	0.31	3.60	5.30
Sixtieth	5.51	0.19	5.32	–

Source: Schedule 1 of the Agricultural Bank Ordinance, Chapter 132 of the Revised Edition of the Laws of Trinidad and Tobago 1925.

depressed state of the industry, and the financial encumbrances which were mentioned, that the rate of interest charged was too high.[53]

As Professor Shephard observed, "Low prices have afforded little opportunity for the collection of reserves and the profits realised by many mortgagors have been too small to pay interest on encumbrances." It is obvious, therefore, that if one accepted as the primary purpose of the bank that it was to provide for the redemption of mortgages and the restoration of the industry, the bank was not a success.[54]

Further assistance to the industry was given in 1935 when the government approved the adoption of a Cocoa Subsidy Scheme which provided

Table 14 Classification of Mortgaged Properties against which Loans Have Been Made by the Agricultural Bank to 31.12.1931

Class (Acres)	No. of Borrowers	Total of Individual Loans of						Total		
		£500 and Under			Over £500					
1–100		£	s	d	£	s	d	£	s	d
Up to 10	55	6,458	6	8				6,458	6	8
11–25	112	22,417	19	7	3,020	16	8	25,438	16	3
26–50	69	13,833	6	8	18,462	0	5½	32,295	7	1½
51–100	57	2,960	1	½	54,158	5	5	57,118	6	5½
Total	**293**	**45,669**	**13**	**11½**	**75,641**	**2**	**6½**	**121,310**	**16**	**6**
101–500 acres										
101–200	36	833	6	8	53,471	4	0	54,304	10	8
201–300	16	132	10	0	30,919	5	10	31,231	15	10
301–400	6	–	–	–	17,916	13	4	17,916	13	4
401–500	9	–	–	–	29,489	4	7	29,489	4	7
Total	**67**	**1,145**	**16**	**8**	**131,796**	**7**	**9**	**132,942**	**4**	**5**
Grand Total	**360**	**£46,815**	**10**	**7½**	**£207,437**	**10**	**3½**	**£244,253**	**0**	**11**

free grants of 1¢ per pound on cocoa production; the total amount of the subsidy sanctioned being $2.5 million spread over a period of four years.[55]

But the assistance given was not always free as in the case outlined earlier.

In 1932 the Cocoa Export Tax Ordinance imposed an export tax of 1½ d per 110 pounds on cocoa grown in and shipped from the colony during the year commencing 1 October 1932. The tax was to be increased to 2½ d per 110 pounds if the market price of cocoa rose to £2.1.8 per 110 pounds. The proceeds of the tax were to be used in dealing with the witchbroom disease.

Hence the industry was being forced to help itself.

Other Aspects of the Industry

Co-operatives and Marketing

These two institutions, co-operatives and proper marketing agencies, were largely absent in the cocoa industry of Trinidad and Tobago. It is proposed to treat them jointly because it is considered that one could have assisted the other in improving the industry.

In Trinidad and Tobago there were two types of owners of cocoa: the large estates and the more numerous peasant proprietors. The latter accounted for approximately 60 per cent of the total crop. The former were organized in the Cocoa Planters' Association.[56] The latter were unorganized. But the price received by the latter was often "$1.00 to $2.00 less per fanega" than that received by the large proprietor.

One explanation is to be seen in the better quality of the cocoa produced by the large estates. The chief cause of this higher quality was that the estates took great care with the fermentation process of preparing the beans for the market. By and large the peasants did not. Even if they wished to improve their methods the cost of proper individual fermentaries was beyond their means.

Co-operative fermentaries would have been the answer. The experience of peasant farmers in Tobago bears out this point. There were five co-operative fermentaries in that island and the quality of cocoa produced improved to such an extent that those producers received the same price as the larger estates.

The absence of a co-operative movement meant also that when in need of money for cultivation purposes or to maintain themselves until the crop

Table 15 Comparison between the Price of Trinidad and Tobago Cocoa at Store in Port of Spain and the Export Price of Cocoa, 1918–1931

Year	Price per Cwt	
	Store Price	Export Price
1918	86/1	90/-
1919	101/6	110/-
1920	42/5	112/-
1921	45/10	57/-
1922	40/5	70/-
1923	40/4	53/-
1924	55/2	63/4
1925	53/-	73/6
1926	64/8	68/2
1927	61/8	82/4
1928	49/-	69/2
1929	45/8	60/11
1930	32/3	57/2
1931	31/3	43/10

was sold, the small peasants usually became "indebted to the village dealers and were compelled to dispose of their produce through their creditors often on a very disadvantageous term instead of in the open market".[57]

Table 15 indicates the difference between the price of Trinidad and Tobago cocoa at store in Port of Spain and the price received in export markets. Even if allowance is made for the costs of marketing it is obvious that in certain years the middleman's profit must have been considerable.[58]

A proper co-operative organization should have been able to ensure a larger percentage of the market price for the producer. In this connection it must be remembered that the peasants contributed 60 per cent of total production.

The Claying of Cocoa

The claying of cocoa was a practice by which the cocoa beans were doctored to improve their appearance. Although when the trouble first occurred over this practice, it was because peasant proprietors were trying to make their cocoa appear of the same quality as plantation cocoa, claying originally applied not to the inferior type but to plantation cocoa. The practice originated in Venezuela which was famous for the high quality of its cocoa. A mixture of certain dyes was added to the cocoa to improve its appearance. In the process some weight (approximately 1–2 per cent of the total) was added. But those who clayed in Venezuela claimed that claying preserved the beans, improved the aroma and did not spoil the taste. The foreign buyers denied that any of these claims could be substantiated and maintained that the claying of cocoa did no more than deceive the purchaser as to quality and weight.

But the trouble over claying did not arise over Venezuela cocoa and the charges mentioned earlier were directed against Trinidad and Tobago cocoa of the "ordinary" or unfermented type which was doctored in this way to make it resemble the higher quality cocoa. There is reason to believe that claying of cocoa in Trinidad and Tobago was inspired by low prices when proprietors attempted to spend as little as possible on the proper treatment of the beans and yet earn the higher prices paid for the superior cocoa beans. The net result was the Trinidad and Tobago cocoa was discredited on the world markets. The Cocoa Manufacturers Association of America claimed that in 1922 "more than 60,000 bags out of a total of 118,000 bags examined were clayed to the extent of 5 to 20 per cent".[59] They also claimed that the recognized trade descriptions could not be applied to Trinidad and Tobago cocoa. It would appear, however, that this was something of an exaggeration and that the association was merely trying to get its own back.

It seems to have been the case that during 1919–20 an unusually large quantity of cocoa had been sold for future delivery and that in the meantime spot prices had risen substantially. It was during this time that claying became most prevalent. Since the spot price had gone up the buyer had gained on these forward transactions and so did not bother about the cocoa being clayed. The reverse situation obtained in 1921–22 when spot prices were considerably lower. It was to the advantage of buyers to reject delivery of sub-standard cocoa.

This they did in no uncertain terms. In an effort to restore the good name of Trinidad and Tobago cocoa, the government passed Ordinance No. 43 of 1922 which made claying illegal. Two inspectors were appointed under the ordinance. There were a few cases of prosecution, fines were imposed, some cocoa was confiscated and claying was stamped out by 1923. It is quite possible that producers' co-operatives enforcing high standards of production may have prevented the practice and maintained the good name of Trinidad and Tobago cocoa.

Summary and Conclusions

A study of the cocoa industry of Trinidad and Tobago in the inter-war period is largely a study of the decline of what was once the economic backbone of the islands. In twenty years its share of the value of total exports declined from $12.4 million to $1.2 million, from 51 per cent of exports to 3.3 per cent.

The causes of this decline were many. The "prime" cause was the fall of prices after 1920. This set in train a number of factors which combined to ruin the industry:

1. The insecure financial basis of the industry.
2. The incidence of diseases and pests, the eradication of which was made impossible in view of the low prices of cocoa.
3. Absentee owners.
4. The fact that expansion of the industry had been taken into unsuitable land.
5. The tendency of costs to rise.
6. Neglect of cultivation which was in fact the result of most of the preceding factors, and was itself largely responsible for the decline in yield per acre.

The decline was most marked after 1931.

In consequence of the decline the local "money market" was destroyed, confidence evaporated overnight, employment, commerce and government revenue suffered.

In the following chapter a comparison is made between the terms of the assistance given to cocoa and sugar. Briefly, therefore, it would appear that the treatment to cocoa was the more ungenerous and that it was unsuccessful. The lack of success did spring in part from the lack of generosity but it was not the only, nor the most important factor preventing success.

Government was not deliberately ungenerous. It appears ungenerous largely in retrospect. It must be remembered, however, that the shock of the depression of 1921 could have made clear thinking difficult. Also it must be remembered that the initial attempts to aid the industry were guided by the belief that the slump would be short, if sharp. Further the last remaining source of finance, the government, was in a very poor condition. Chapter 9, "Public Finance", shows that in the years 1921–23, the reserves actually became negative. In 1930 when sugar was aided, the overall condition was much better. Oil at least was making a contribution to revenue.

It is considered that the establishment of producers and marketing co-operatives would have assisted the smaller producer particularly. The industry also would have benefited from having 60 per cent of its output better organized and improved in quality.

The remainder of this book must be seen in the light of decline of this, the once most important industry and the only industry, the export revenues from which accrued almost wholly to domestic income earners.

4

The Sugar Industry

As was pointed out in the previous chapter, "The Cocoa Industry", the economy of Trinidad and Tobago up to the beginning of the twentieth century depended primarily on two principal industries – cocoa and sugar. These two industries shared in succession the distinction of being the most important economic activity of the colony. One saw also the French planter class selling out their sugar estates to British owners and investing in cocoa. At the beginning of the period of this study, therefore, the sugar industry of Trinidad was primarily in the hands of British owners. Trinidad and Tobago became one of those colonies in the West Indies, as were Jamaica, Barbados and so on during the eighteenth and nineteenth centuries, which were the main interest and source of wealth of the strongly organized West Indian sugar merchants and planters in the United Kingdom and having friends and representatives in Parliament.

The influence of these planters had declined with time and for the period of the study it was small compared with the eighteenth century when it was able to procure the revision of Acts of Parliament, for example, the Molasses Act of 1733, in its own interest.[1] They yet retain some influence, however, as can be seen from their efforts in the question of preferences on colonial sugar. From the point of view of West Indian sugar in general this has been fortunate; for the industry has not been without its problems. Throughout its post-emancipation history it has moved from crisis to crisis with brief periods of relative prosperity intervening. The industry has shown a remarkable resilience. It had at times been overtaken by other industries but it has time and again returned to become the most important agricultural industry of the islands. In the case of the other West Indian islands, for example, Barbados, sugar has remained the most important industry. In Trinidad and Tobago, although cocoa was superior in the period 1870–1920, it slumped badly in the late 1920s, and by 1930 yielded first place to sugar. In that same year, 1930, however, the sugar industry was in a state of crisis. What is therefore evident is that the agricultural economy was deteriorating or gravely threatened. For if cocoa had given way to sugar and sugar was itself declining, then the whole agricultural economy must have been declining somewhat rapidly.

It is not proposed here to go into the trend in production. Chapter 1, "Exports", has already indicated the main points – exports being closely lined with production. It is proposed, therefore, to deal with other aspects of the industry; for example, the concentration of the industry, the methods of production in the field and in the factory, the role of the peasant farmer and government assistance to the industry.

The Concentration of the Industry

The process of amalgamation of the estates in Trinidad had begun since in the nineteenth century. By the end of the nineteenth century, Tobago had virtually ceased producing and exporting sugar and its by-products.

> By 1897 practically all the sugar estates in Trinidad were in the hands of a few individuals and firms. Thirteen alone were in the hands of the Colonial Company and Burnley and company. Greig and Co., Messrs. Turnbull and Co. Sir Charles Tennant and the Lamont family were the other principal owners . . . The great Usine Ste Madeleine estate owned by the Colonial Company, and comprising an area of 4,000 acres formerly consisted of a number of small muscovado estates.[2]

During the period under study the process of amalgamation continued. At the beginning of the period there were fifteen estates engaged in the production of sugar. They ranged in size from the Usine Ste Madeleine which in 1919 produced 16,482 tons, that is, one-third of all the sugar in the colony, to Mon Desir which produced only 144 tons out of a colony total of approximately 48,000 tons. The main producers were Usine Ste Madeleine (16,500 tons); Waterloo (7,700); Brechin Castle (2,900); Bronte (2,900); Caroni (3,300); Tacarigua Factory (2,900); Woodfood Lodge (2,700); La Fortunée (2,500) (see table 16). By 1936 there were

Table 16 Cane Farming and Sugar Crop Returns 1919

Estates	Total Sugar Made	Tons of Sugar made from Estate Cane	Estate Canes (tons)	Canes Purchased (tons)	Amount Paid to Farmers BWI$	Number of Farmers		
						East Indian	West Indian	Total
Brechin Castle	2,910	2,270	25,410	7,650	33,000	349	220	569
Bronte	2,922	1,792	19,784	14,049	60,690	545	169	714
Caroni	3,360	1,515	18,951	23,061	88,383	1,603	925	2,528
Craignish	743	240	3,068	6,351	27,436	409	205	614
Esperanza	1,663	820	10,525	11,382	51,620	506	267	773
Forrest Park	1,851	1,525	15,533	6,790	29,325	430	122	552
Golden Grove	407	60	1,080	6,581	28,430	120	185	305
Hindustan	773	203	2,342	6,560	28,339	364	420	784
Mon Desir	144	–	–	1,077	4,303	10	15	25
Reform	669	191	3,447	6,870	26,651	500	400	900
Tacarigua Fact	2,940	1,381	18,195	21,033	100,911	911	977	1,888
La Fortunee	2,573	1,540	16,698	11,245	48,570	404	371	775
Usine Ste Mad	16,482	9,490	95,570	72,551	313,320	4,322	2,292	6,614
Waterloo	7,702	2,387	26,020	58,028	292,301	1,300	1,450	2,750
Woodford Lodge	2,711	1,440	18,837	17,096	73,850	597	368	965
Total	**47,850**	**24,656**	**275,451**	**270,324**	**1,210,155**	**12,370**	**8,568**	**20,938**

Source: Report of the Director of Agriculture 1919/20.
Note: Mostly estates producing 2,000 tons of sugar and over have been included.

eleven estates in operation and exports were about 143,000 tons (production about 155,000 tons). Again the most important factories were Usine Ste Madeleine (47,900), Caroni (21,860), Waterloo (19,200) and Woodford Lodge (18,900). These figures refer to the volume of sugar they were to be allowed to export under the ordinance regulating the production of sugar in 1936. They give, however, a fairly accurate picture of the relative importance of the various estates.

But 1937–38 there was further amalgamation with the advent of Tate and Lyle into the Trinidad sugar scene.

As was pointed out earlier, from the time that the French planters sold their estates to British planters the industry was predominantly directed from the United Kingdom. The Usine Ste Madeleine Sugar Company, for example, was managed by the London firm, Henckell Du Buisson and Co. The second largest estate was then (1938) Caroni Ltd, which was a West Indian subsidiary of Tate and Lyle. The company invested about £1 million in the venture which was made possible by the amalgamation of other smaller estates. A considerable sum, about half a million pounds, was spent in equipping and modernizing the factories.

Another aspect of the concentration concerns the Trinidad Sugar Estates Ltd, which was non-existent (at least in its later form) in 1919 but which, by 1936, was allotted an export quota of 10,400 tons out of a total allocation of 138,000 tons. Meanwhile such estates as Brechin Castle, Bronte, Esperanza, Golden Grove, Mon Desir and so on had disappeared as independent units, incorporated into one or the other of the larger estates.

Methods of Production

Both in the field and in the factory some measure of success was achieved in improving productivity. In the field the more primitive hand ploughing methods gradually gave way on the estates to mechanical ploughing. The Department of Agriculture and the Imperial College of Tropical Agriculture were instrumental in encouraging this more progressive approach. It was complained, however, that the peasants were reluctant to adopt the modern measures. As will be seen later, however, the peasants were on the whole small producers, cultivating on an average of less than 1 acre each and were nearly all part-time producers of cane. How these mechanical processes could have been attractive to them or been at all within their financial reach without a strong co-operative movement, is difficult to see. The estates, however, adopted some mechanical tilling. The figures for the import of agricultural machinery give some indication of the trend.[3]

In the government experiments in this field, the report from the St Augustine Station for 1922 observes that implemental tilling was substituted for hand labour wherever possible, "with a marked decrease in cost, with the further advantage that tillage can now be carried out at the right season". With implemental tillage was also introduced a greater use of artificial and natural fertilizers. Again the imports of fertilizers show a moderate increase over the period. This aspect of development as well as the experimenting with improved strains of cane was also assisted both by government and the Imperial College of Tropical Agriculture.

Factory extraction methods were improved over the period. New modern equipment was mainly responsible. See table 17 which shows the cane to sugar ratio falling from an average of 11.63 (1918–22) to 9.01 (1933–37). Of course both factory methods and quality of canes were responsible for this improvement. The weather is an important factor also but it is a fickle variable and would, on the whole, have influenced the earlier and later periods in the same way.

In spite of these improvements, however, the efficiency of the industry lagged perceptibly behind those of other sugar producing countries.

Table 17 Conversion Ratio: Tons Cane per Ton of Sugar

Year		Average (5 years)	Year		Average (5 years)
1918	11.47		1928	10.11	
1919	11.40		1929	9.19	
1920	11.36		1930	9.54	
1921	12.31		1931	9.58	
1922	11.60	11.63	1932	10.58	9.8
1923	10.56		1933	9.56	
1924	10.79		1934	8.84	
1925	10.38		1935	8.54	
1926	10.10		1936	8.86	
1927	11.87	10.74	1937	9.24	9.01

Source: Report on Cane Farming 1938, Trinidad and Tobago Council Paper 119/1938.

Mechanization

Although implemental tillage[4] was being gradually employed, for the whole of the period the use of bullocks and hand ploughing persisted. Norman Lamont claimed that West Indian backwardness in sugar production was directly due to two causes. First, the abundance of labourers (provided by indentures) working for a low wage; and secondly, the extreme rarity of skilled scientific direction. He pointed to Louisiana with its seasonal frosts, in which cane never fully ripens and where wages are high, and yet the very fact of this high rate of wages had compelled Louisiana planters to adopt every labour saving device conceivable, with the solitary exception at that time of the still uninvented cane reaper. "If some economic cataclysm could suddenly double the rate of wages in the West Indies or halve the working population it might be possible to save the sugar industry in spite of itself."[5]

Fertilizers

In spite of the increase in the imports of fertilizers, the agricultural industry was still lamentable ill-served in respect of this necessary factor in increasing productivity. Hereunder some comparison will be drawn between the use of fertilizers and resultant output changes both in Puerto Rico and Trinidad.

In 1932, S.M. Gilbert, the assistant director of agriculture in Trinidad, returned from a conference of sugar technologists in Puerto Rico and observed that "in Trinidad the advantages of soil work are not perhaps appreciated as fully as they might be and it is regretted that the Sugar Cane Investigation Committee cut down the work of this nature that was under way". Further, Trinidad was lagging far behind in the use of fertilizers.

In table 18 the figures for the imports of fertilizers into Trinidad are for all crops, not only for the sugar industry. Even if the total import figure were treated as imports for the sugar industry, Trinidad would still be seen to be lagging behind Puerto Rico in the ratio of fertilizers applied per unit of output.

> Thus in Puerto Rico there is an average of one ton of fertilizer used to every 7.7 tons of sugar produced. In Trinidad if all the fertilizers imported were used on sugar alone, it only works out at one ton of fertilizer per every 23.2 tons of sugar produced. An indication of the attitude of planters in regard to this phase of cane growing is that data for fertilizers used on sugar estates are not easily available.[6]

Table 18 Tons of Cane Produced per Ton of Fertilizer

Puerto Rico				Trinidad		Puerto Rico	Trinidad
Year	Fertilizer '000 Long tons	Year	Sugar Prod. '000 Long tons	Fertilizers Imports '000 Tons	Sugar Prod. '000 Tons	Tons of Cane per Ton of Fertilizer	
1921–23	38.6	1922–23	338.5	1.7	42	8.76	25.0
1922–23	50.7	1923–24	400.0	5.2	52	7.88	10.0
1923–24	67.6	1924–25	589.8	3.7	70	8.72	19.0
1924–25	60.7	1925–26	539.7	2.9	74	8.89	25.5
1925–26	71.0	1926–27	562.7	2.3	52	7.92	22.6
1926–27	83.0	1927–28	670.8	2.4	83	8.08	34.2
1927–28	81.7	1928–29	523.7	3.4	90	6.41	26.5
1928–29	83.9	1929–30	778.9	3.1	80	9.28	25.8
1929–30	90.4	1930–31	703.4	4.2	99	7.78	23.6
		1932	–	3.9	98	–	25.0
		1933	–	6.9	121	–	17.5
		1934	–	6.2	105	–	17.0
		1935	–	8.4	118	–	14.0
		1936	–	8.6	155	–	18.0
		1937	–	8.4	154	–	18.3
		1938	–	8.1	134	–	16.5
		1939	–	6.9	128	–	18.5

Source: "Notes on the Production of Sugar Cane" taken by M.S.M. Gilbert, BSc (London), assistant director of agriculture, Trinidad, at the fourth triennial Conference of the International Society of Sugar Cane Technologists, Puerto Rico, March 1932.
Note: The data for Trinidad have been extended to the end of the period under study, 1939.

The data for Trinidad have been extended to cover the period up to 1939. It will be seen that although there had been some improvement in the amount of fertilizer imported and used, the situation in 1939 was still worse than that of Puerto Rico in 1932.

Irrigation also was but little practised although it would appear that adequate irrigation together with the factors previously mentioned are necessary for increased productivity of cane per acre. Table 19 indicates the impact of irrigation and other factors on the growth of productivity per acre in Puerto Rico.

Compared with the high yields in Puerto Rico of 51.9 tons of cane per acre in the late 1920s and early 1930s, the yield in Trinidad was at its best in

Table 19 Cane per Acre in an Area under Irrigation in Any District Puerto Rico

Year	Total Cane per Acre (tons)	Remarks
1914	25.5	Prior to irrigation
1915	26.5	
1916	27.6	
1917	32.2	Irrigation system begins
1918	28.5	
1919	32.1	
1920	33.9	
1921	31.8	
1922	28.2	Long drought
1923	24.8	
1924	22.7	
1925	35.7	Change to new varieties
1926	35.5	
1927	43.1	
1928	51.9	
1929	36.5	Hurricane
1930	51.9	
1931	42.3	Drought

Trinidad Data

Period	Tons of Sugar Per Acre	Per Cent Increase over 1912–16
1912–16	2.98	–
1917–21	3.53	18.4
1922–26	3.49	17.1
1927–31	5.69	90.9

the period only *30 tons per acre*. The average yield was, even in 1939, about 22–24 tons per acre.[7] The factory process also, though as good as any within the empire,[8] was inferior to that in, say, Cuba and Puerto Rico. In the latter the large central factories were extracting 1 ton of sugar from 7 to 7½ tons of cane. In Trinidad this figure was not attained even in 1937–39.

Table 17 indicates that although there was some improvement over the period, the conversion ratio of 9 tons canes to 1 ton of sugar in 1937 was still too high: (a) by comparison, and (b) in terms of productivity.

In the smaller factories in Trinidad the ratio was even more unfavourable. The 1936 Legislative Council debate on the bill to allocate quotas to estates for the protected local market revealed that some of these small producers (estates) were still producing in the ratio of 13 tons of cane to 1 ton of sugar. It is therefore interesting to note that this lack of efficiency was used as an argument for giving them a relatively larger share of the domestic market.[9]

Restriction of Output

In an attempt to relieve the distress in the world sugar industry caused by low prices, the Chadbourne Plan was signed in 1931 by Cuba, Java, Germany, Czechoslovakia, Belgium, Poland, Hungary – the chief sugar producers. Later, Peru and Yugoslavia adhered to the plan.

The general aim of the plan was to restrict output by granting certain export quotas to each participating country. But the British Empire, French Empire and certain Asian countries were not participants. They increased production considerably and by 1935 when the plan broke down, only Cuba and Java had made any real sacrifice for its success.

In September 1937, the International Sugar Agreement was signed. It was larger in membership than the Chadbourne Plan and was to be operative for five years in the first instance. Although the former placed no restriction on Trinidad production, the new agreement restricted Trinidad's export quota to 138,000 tons per annum subject to such modification as might later become necessary. Total production in 1937–38 was 156,000 tons.

What was the effect of this agreement on the Trinidad sugar industry?

Firstly, consideration must be given to the overall export situation. Cocoa had been in steady decline. Sugar was attempting to absorb, but had only partly succeeded in absorbing, the unemployment in the economy. As will be shown in chapter 5 the search for an alternative had failed. While, therefore, from the point of view of world price and production trends there was need for restriction of sugar output, such restriction when applied in the particular case of the Trinidad economy was inimical to her interests.[10] If world conditions permitted, her best interests, given the decline in the rest of her agricultural economy, would have required an expansion of output through greater efficiency. However, as will be shortly explained even this course would have provided its problems.

As a direct result of the restriction on exports, came the Cane Farming Control Ordinance of 1937 designed to limit "the uncontrolled extension by cane-farmers of the acreage under sugar cane".[11] As was pointed out in chapter 1, "Exports", the economy had undergone a change during the inter-war period, a change which had shifted the nature of the imbalance of the export economy from a dependence solely on agriculture to a dependence on petroleum. Since petroleum was expanding rapidly, anything that retarded the agricultural sector tended to intensify that imbalance: thus narrowing the economic base.

Within the agricultural sector anything that tended to restrict the contribution to domestic participants intensified an imbalance that was concomitant with the first, that is, the tendency for the major industrial and agricultural units to become increasingly foreign owned and for the earnings of such foreign-owned enterprises to increase relative to those going to the domestic sector. This is not an argument against foreign capital. Development was impossible without it. This is an argument for some balance in that development.

The Cane Farming Control Ordinance, however necessary, given the international agreement, had the effect of assisting that process. Labourers and cane farmers were the only direct local recipients of a large part of the earnings of sugar. The incomes of the farmer were low. The earnings of the labourer were similarly low: restricting their output and thus that portion of total export incomes that accrued to local recipients tended to increase that imbalance.

But the problem has other ramifications and these are investigated and solutions are suggested in the section dealing with government assistance to the industry.

The Cane Farmer

This section is devoted to considering the contribution made by cane farmers to the industry, and the factors which affected their contribution, especially where those factors bear some relation to the export/import situation. Firstly, it is important to identify of whom one speaks when one refers to "cane farmers". The definition given in a booklet issued by the Sugar Manufacturers Association almost meets the case: "The term 'cane-farmer' means any cultivator who grows cane but does not own his own factory, whether small peasant cultivating one to two acres or the big farmer cultivating up to several hundred acres."[12]

The debate on the cane farming Control Ordinance 1937 introduced a new element, however: "It will be observed that for the purpose of this ordinance a cane farmer is not only a person who himself cultivates canes for sale to a manufacturer, but includes also those persons whom I may refer to as contractors and who sell to manufacturers canes which have been grown and sold to them by other persons."[13] When the question of the pricing of farmers' canes is discussed in a later section it will become obvious how undesirable it is that a third, middle man, element should have been encouraged and established in the industry.

The Birth of the Cane Farming Industry

This sector of the industry originated in the late nineteenth century. Here also the system of indenture had its role to play:

> The heavy expenses of repatriation of indentured labour led to the scheme whereby land was offered to East Indian labourers in lieu of return passage. Unfortunately, this scheme led to further shortage of labour in sugar estates. In consequence of this difficulty, in 1882, Sir Neville Lubbock persuaded a small number of East Indians to grow sugar cane for sale to the mills and in this way the Cane Farming Industry was born.[14]

Later West Indian (Afro-Trinidadian) farmers joined the industry.

The Contribution of Cane Farmers

In Trinidad the growing of canes is carried out by both the large sugar manufacturers and the cane farmers. The proportion of the total cane crop produced by these two sections has varied somewhat during the period. In the early part of the period under study, the cane farmers produced more than 50 per cent of the total (1921, 58 per cent). In 1934 their contribution was 40 per cent (see table 20).

Table 16, "Cane Farming and Sugar Crop Returns 1919", gives a clear picture of certain aspects of the structure of the industry and the part played in it by the cane farmer. The amount of cane bought from farmers is just about equal to that produced by from the estates of the manufacturer (270,324 versus 275,451). But their contribution to the individual

Table 20 Cane Farmers' Contribution to Sugar Industry, 1899–1939

	Canes Crushed '000 tons			Farmers' Canes as Percentage of Total	Total Sugar Produced '000 Tons	No. of Cane Farmers '000		
Year	Estates	Farmers	Total			EI	WI	Total
1899	426	107	533	20.0	59	2.8	3.9	6.7
1900	364	106	470	22.5	46	2.8	3.6	6.4
1901	334	170	504	33.7	61	3.8	4.7	8.6
1903	337	167	504	33.0	48	4.4	4.4	8.9
1905	244	145	389	37.2	38	5.4	5.5	10.9
1907	373	170	543	31.2	51	6.6	5.8	12.3
1909	451	155	606	25.5	53	6.1	5.3	11.4
1911	367	166	532	31.1	47	6.6	6.4	13.0
1913	347	137	484	28.3	42	6.9	5.5	12.5
1915	426	325	751	43.3	59	9.2	7.1	16.3
1917	379	385	764	50.4	70	12.1	9.0	21.0
1918	253	266	519	51.3	45	12.2	8.2	20.4
1919	275	270	546	49.5	48	12.4	8.6	21.0
1920	319	344	664	51.9	58	14.5	10.8	25.3
1921	287	389	676	57.6	55	15.0	11.4	26.4
1922	340	355	696	51.1	60	12.6	8.7	21.3
1923	253	186	440	42.4	42	9.7	6.8	16.5
1924	324	237	562	42.3	52	10.0	7.1	17.1
1925	395	328	723	45.3	70	11.5	8.0	19.5
1926	384	359	743	48.3	74	13.5	9.4	22.9
1927	330	287	617	46.5	52	11.9	7.5	19.4
1928	450	375	825	45.5	82	13.2	7.4	20.6
1929	426	400	826	48.4	90	11.5	6.5	18.0
1930	458	304	762	39.9	80	11.5	6.8	18.3
1931	559	385	944	40.8	99	11.9	6.1	18.0
1932	577	455	1,032	44.1	98	11.2	6.2	17.4
1933	666	488	1,154	42.3	121	11.7	6.2	17.9
1934	557	370	927	39.9	105	10.5	5.0	15.5
1935	603	402	1,006	40.0	118	12.1	5.9	18.0
1936	780	594	1,374	43.2	155	13.3	6.2	19.5
1937	813	630	1,443	43.6	154	13.8	6.9	20.7
1938	718	574	1,292	44.2	134	–	–	–
1939	758	389	1,147	33.9	128	–	–	–

Source: Appendix C of the Report of the Committee on Cane Farming 1938.
Notes: EI – East Indians; WI – West Indians (Africans).

estates shows considerable variations. In the case of the Usine Ste Madeleine, the largest factory, which produced just above one-third of the total sugar for that year, the farmers contributed 72,551 versus 95,570 tons of estates' canes. For Brechin Castle with a sugar output of about 6 per cent of the total for the colony, the respective contribution were farmers – 7,600 tons, estates – 25,400. Bronte with a similar sugar production had farmers' contribution of 14,000 tons versus estate production of 19,800 tons.

However, the picture is quite the opposite for most of the other estates. The second largest producer was Waterloo Estate (16.1 per cent of the Trinidad total). In this case, however, the cane farmers supplied more than twice as much cane as the estate, that is, 58,028 tons versus 26,020 tons by the latter. For many of the smaller factories the tendency is the same; the cane farmers are the chief source of canes. In the case of Golden Grove and Mon Desir the estate contribution is negligible. In the case of Woodford Lodge, with a production slightly less than that of Brechin Castle or Bronte, the contribution of farmers reflects the overall pattern, that is, almost equal contribution of estate and farmer. Table 20 gives an indication of how the contribution of farmer and estate or manufacturer varied from year to year throughout the period.

Size of Farming Units

Next to be considered are the sizes of the holdings of cane farmers and the contribution of the various categories of farmers to the total cane farming production. Table 21 shows the numbers of farmers supplying varying amounts of cane to the factory in the case of Woodford Lodge, a typical estate for the year 1953. Although this year falls outside the period under study, it gives a true indication of the smallness of the individual contribution of the majority of cane farmers. As pointed out earlier, Woodford Lodge was in a sense typical of the whole industry, that is, in so far as the contributions of farmers and manufacturers canes were concerned.

The picture presented by table 21 is similar to the situation of the interwar years as seen in the following extract from the report of the director of agriculture on the question of the appointment of a committee to consider the pricing of farmers' canes:

> The nature of the difficulties to be dealt with may be gauged by the fact that there were in Trinidad in 1927, 19,385 people returned as cane-farmers (i.e. who sold canes to factories) and although there were several producing from one to five or more thousand tons, the average production for the group was less than 15 tons of cane each.[15]

Table 21 Woodford Lodge Estate, 1953

Category of Canes Sold to Estates	Number of Farmers in Each Category
I – 5 tons and under	250
II – 6 tons to 20 tons	450
III – 21 tons to 50 tons	294
IV – 51 tons to 100 tons	158
V – 101 tons to 500 tons	40
VI – 501 tons to 1,000 tons	1
VII – 1,000 tons and over	7
	1,200 (850 East Indian) (350 West Indian, i.e., African)

On the basis of a productivity of 20 tons of cane per acre the average cane farming unit would therefore be a little less than 1 acre.

The Incomes of Cane Farmers

A later section will treat the methods employed in calculating the domestic price of farmers' canes. Here the history of cane prices provides a basis for discussing farmers' income (see table 22).

The price of canes was $3.46 per ton in 1927. This figure is the highest since 1924 ($4.52) (taking only the years of the study). Even on this basis of $3.46 per ton, the average cane farmer received about $51.75 (£10.15.7½) per annum from producing and selling canes to the factory.

This is not the whole of his income, however. When not working on his own land the cane farmer works in various capacities for the manufacturer or plants food crops in his plot. Woodford Lodge even in 1953 estimated that "approximately 40% of the estate crop was carted by farmers". There are also many cane farmers for whom cane farming is merely a sideline. It is important to distinguish between (a) the person who is a cane farmer first and foremost but who has other means of supplementing his earnings and (b) the person who uses cane farming merely as a means of supplementing his earnings.

The committee which investigated the cane farming industry in 1932 found that "very few cane farmers depend on the sale of cane for the major part of their income. It is usually a sideline; a method of creating security, with little effort, on which to base credit for food and other local purchase."[16]

Table 22 Price of Farmers' Canes (per ton) (1919–1939)

1919	**$4.74**
1920	8.40
1921	4.34
1922	2.57
1923	4.90
1924	4.52
1925	2.88
1926	2.88
1927	3.46
1928	2.97
1929	2.95
1930	2.95
1931	2.88
1932	2.92
1933	2.93
1934	2.64
1935	2.64
1936	2.64
1937	2.64
1938	2.64
1939	2.64

The majority of farmers also worked on estates for wages and planted their own plots.[17] Table 23 shows the number of cane farmers depending entirely on cane farming for a living as compared with those working only part time. Data were not available during the committee's survey, undertaken in 1933, for more than 13,000 cane farmers but from this sample which embraces about 70 per cent out of a total of 17,900 cane farmers it can be seen that only 12 per cent of those included depended solely on cane farming for a living.

In most works concerned with the economy of Trinidad a distinction has been drawn between the East Indian and the West Indian or African sections of the population. The committee that investigated cane farming in 1933 was no exception. On this question of full-time and part-time farming they drew attention to the fact that the West Indies provided in all cases, a much larger percentage of full-time farmers than the East Indian, and commented,

Table 23 Showing the Number of Cane Farmers Depending Entirely on Cane Farming for a Living as Compared with Those Working Only Part Time

Tonnage Class	East Indians					West Indians					All				
	Whole Time		Part Time		Total	Whole Time		Part Time		Total	Whole Time		Part Time		Total
	Farmers	Per Cent	Farmers	Per Cent		Farmers	Per Cent	Farmers	Per Cent		Farmers	Per Cent	Farmers	Per Cent	
10 and below	137	4	2,966	96	3,103	340	16	1,769	84	2,109	477	9	4,735	91	5,212
11–50	312	9	3,147	91	3,459	248	20	1,023	80	1,271	560	12	4,170	88	4,730
51–100	117	18	525	82	642	27	28	68	72	95	144	20	593	80	737
101–200	62	32	134	68	196	19	61	12	39	31	81	36	146	64	227
201–500	30	48	33	52	63	13	81	3	19	16	43	54	36	46	79
501–1000	5	29	12	71	17	1	50	1	50	2	6	32	13	68	19
Over 1000	3	33	6	67	9	9	82	2	18	11	12	60	8	40	20
Unclassified	88	7	1,151	93	1,239	105	13	719	87	824	193	9	1,870	91	2,063
Total	**754**	**9**	**7,974**	**91**	**8,728**	**762**	**17**	**3,597**	**83**	**4,359**	**1,516**	**12***	**11,571**	**88**	**13,087**

Note: Only 12 per cent of the 13,000 farmers examined in this sample depended solely on cane farming for a living.

"this may well be an indication of the greater industry of the East Indian". Since in the sugar industry these two racial groups are employed, it may be important to determine whether there is any ground for this conclusion.

The simplest kind of argument for the conclusion should be of the following nature. It must establish either that

a. The East Indian produces at least as much cane as the West Indian and then goes on to produce another commodity or follows some other economic enterprise, or
b. He produces less cane than the West Indian but then goes on to another commodity or enterprise, the returns from which are more than sufficient to compensate for the loss in output which resulted from his not working cane full time, or
c. He produces more cane than the West Indian (although he is not employed full time), and then continues to widen the gap in their productivities by pursuing other enterprises.

A study of table 24 which shows farmers classified according to the group and tonnage delivered seems to point to case (c) above being the most likely condition. For in the sample taken East Indians constituting 65 per cent of all farmers delivered 67 per cent of all canes to factories, that is, all canes grown by farmers while West Indians constituting 35 per cent of farmers delivered 33 per cent of canes. But there is another interesting point. In the under 50 tonnage class, the East Indians delivered an amount of cane more than proportionate to their numbers. In the middle groups, that is, 51–200 tons, there is no difference between the groups; in other words, the farmers of each group delivered an amount of cane proportionate to their numbers in the cane farming industry. In the slightly higher group, 201–500 tons, the West Indians are in the lead, however. The relative contributions are the same in the category 510–1,000 tons; but in the highest group the East Indians show, once more, a greater relative contribution.

Of course it may be unwise to attempt any firm conclusions about the relative productivities of the two groups merely on the evidence so far presented. It is not known for example what "part time" or "full time" means. If accurate figures of hours worked were available it would be possible to draw some conclusion. It is quite possible that, given in the words of the committee the "greater enterprise" of the East Indian, one would find that there was very little or no difference in hours involved between the part time of the East Indian and the full time of the West Indian.

Table 24 Farmers Classified According to Race and Tonnage Delivered

Tonnage Class	East Indians				West Indians				Total		Per Cent in Each Tonnage Class	
	No. of Farmers	Tonnage	Per Cent of Total		No. of Farmers	Tonnage	Per Cent of Total		Farmers	Tonnage	Farmers	Tonnage
			Farmers	Tonnage			Farmers	Tonnage				
10 and below	4,228	20,319	56	59	3,324	13,988	44	41	7,552	34,307	48.4	7.7
11–50	4,610	204,309	70	72	1,970	40,913	30	28	6,580	145,222	42.2	32.8
51–100	841	55,370	85	85	145	9,433	15	15	986	64,803	6.3	14.6
101–200	266	33,751	86	86	43	5,718	14	14	309	39,469	2.0	8.9
201–500	89	25,443	78	75	25	8,575	22	25	114	34,018	0.7	7.7
501– 1000	23	16,344	88	88	3	2,247	12	12	26	18,591	0.2	4.2
Over 1000	10	39,259	34	37	19	67,462	66	63	29	106,721	0.2	24.1
Total	**10,067**	**294,795**	**65**	**67**	**5,529**	**148,336**	**35**	**33**	**15,596**	**443,131**	**100**	**100**

The Pricing of Farmers' Canes

The problem of a just and reasonable price for farmers' canes has always troubled the sugar industry of Trinidad. The problem is so great for Trinidad because of the size of the contribution made by the cane farmer as a proportion of total cane production.

In British Guiana and East Africa, in the inter-war years at least, almost all the cane was grown on the estates connected with a particular factory and under the same ownership and control. In such a situation the size of the contribution of the cane farmer was such that it was possible to ignore him altogether if he became difficult. But in Trinidad the contribution was too great for the farmer to be ignored. Added to this was the tendency towards "increased size and centralization of factories" and "greater development of peasant farming as the most economical method of producing canes".[18] Where "economical" means "cheap" problems can arise.

This observation requires some elaboration. Its implications are treated in greater detail in a later section where the costs of producing estate and farmers' canes are compared. At this point, however, it is interesting to note the observation about cane farming being the "most economical method of producing canes".

The first justification for encouraging the cane farming industry was to secure a supply of skilled labour near to the estate. As factories became centralized, and this was happening even in the late nineteenth century, a further justification was introduced: ensuring a supply of canes sufficient to maintain large manufacturing units at full or near full capacity. But there was a third justification and one which from the point of view of the manufacturer gave the cane farming industry its greatest attractiveness. During periods of depression in sugar prices, the losses, instead of falling entirely on the manufacturer, were shared.

> Cane farming has been mentioned as a possible remedy for the depression, but I believe that at present prices it would but serve to diffuse the distress as planters cannot afford to pay a price for the canes which would be remunerative to the farmer. But in good times undoubtedly this industry would be a most useful adjunct, and serve greatly to direct the energies of the free coolies and Negroes and to develop the Colony by creating a small peasant land owning class.[19]

This was a singularly enlightened view even for 1897.

In the special case of Trinidad the farmers were at once a formidable and paradoxically a very weak force in the question of determining the price the manufacturers would pay for cane. Their strength sprang theoretically from the size of their contribution to the industry. Theoretically, they could almost halve the output of the factories if they wished to use any such weapon, and since in sugar factories efficiency falls rapidly at anything below optimum output, any such drastic withholding of canes implies losses for the manufacturer.

But the weakness of the cane farmers consisted in their lack of integration. The preceding sections have pointed to the fact that the average cane farmer cultivated just about 1 acre of land and delivered to the factory about 15 tons of cane. Over the period, there were on an average about 19,000 cane farmers. To organize such a large number of small farmers was a task which proved quite formidable. The difficulty is accentuated by the fact that cane farming was not their chief interest. As an example of the weakness of their position, note the following extract from the director of agriculture's report for 1924 on the question of the governors' efforts to appoint a committee to go into the question of the price of farmers' canes. "This effort as the previous one, failed, owing to the apparent impossibility of obtaining accredited representative cane farmers and the opinion of the manufacturers that a joint board would multiply difficulties instead of reducing them." Time and again this same attitude is encountered: the farmers are too many and too unorganized to make any contribution to any committee entrusted with the task of establishing the terms on which their produce should be bought or sold.

It must be pointed out also that the cane farmers were not as a body very concerned with the whole of the industry. They did not, for example, give much assistance to the campaigns for fighting diseases such as froghopper and at the same time, one observes their absence from committees set up to determine the price of canes. There is no doubt that they were partly to blame, but there is also the case that they were never considered as very important except as producers of canes for the factories. They were, therefore, not interested in any problems outside the narrow limits of their incomes from canes. They were, however, too disorganized to succeed even in this limited aim.

Methods of Determining the Price of Canes

During 1924–25, the sugar manufacturers agreed to pay for every 100 tons of canes purchased by the factory and delivered to the weighing stations the value of 4½ tons of grey crystal sugar based on the average free-on-board price thereof between the first day of January and the thirtieth day of June as quoted weekly by C. Czarnikow Ltd, subject to the following deductions, provided that there was a minimum payment of 12 shillings ($2.88) per ton:

1. The sum of $10.28 to cover the cost of transportation of the canes to their respective factories, of bags and of transport of sugar to the steamers.
2. Government taxes and impositions on such ton of sugar.
3. A fixed selling charge of 3 per cent of the average free-on-board price.

Secondly, 1926 saw the Report of the Committee on the Cane Farming Industry which recommended

1. "That the price be calculated on a sliding scale."
2. "That under the sliding scale the value of one ton of canes for each crop should be 5 per cent of the average f.o.b. price of Grey Crystal (96° polarization) sugar at Port of Spain from the first day of January to the thirtieth day of June subject to a deducted of $10.80 to cover the cost of handling canes from scale to factory, bags, haulage of sugar from factory to Port of Spain, lighterage and selling charges."

During 1927 and 1928 the sugar manufacturers agreed to standardize their prices for farmers on the basis of the committee's recommendations with the following modifications:

"The value of one ton of canes to be five per cent (5%) of the average f.o.b. price of Grey Crystal Sugar at Port of Spain from 1st January to 30th June of each year subject to the following deductions:

Transport to factory	)	
Cost of bags	)	$10.28
Transport of sugar to steamers	)	
Selling charges."	)	

Thirdly, in 1930 the Sugar Relief Ordinance was enacted. For the first time the pricing of farmers' canes was *removed from the sole discretion of the manufacturer*.[20] It provided for payment as hereunder:-

A minimum price of 12/- per ton subject to a reduction of 6d for every 10/- decrease in the free-on-board price of grey crystal sugar below

£10.10 per ton. If the price exceeded £16, a bonus was to be paid at the rate of *two-thirds of the sliding scale basis.*

The fourth formula was introduced on the recommendation of the committee appointed in 1938 to advise the government whether the scale of prices and the method of fixing such minimum price, to be paid by the sugar manufacturer to the cane farmer for cane under the Cane Farmers' Control Ordinance, were equitable.

Its report was published as Council Paper No. 119 of 1938 and in brief provided for the following solution. Price of canes was to be determined by the following formula:

$$\text{Price of canes} = \frac{A+B+C+D-(E+F+G)}{H}$$

where:

A = F.o.b. price for exported sugar

B = Premium on local sugar, for example, $\frac{(68 - A \: x \: 12{,}000)}{150{,}000}$

C = Value of molasses at $1.20 per ton sugar

D = Certificated preference, that is, $\frac{\text{value of certs}}{\text{tons of sugar}}$

E = Expenses of handling farmers' canes manufacturing and marketing expenses, say, $24.00

F = Depreciation, say, $1.92 per ton of sugar

G = Interest on sliding scale

$H = \frac{\text{canes crushed}}{\text{sugar produced}}$

This last formula was in many respects superior to the others. It includes all or nearly all the considerations which went into the other three and in addition breaks new ground. An analysis of this latter therefore serves to throw some light on all the others. It is also hoped to investigate not only the possible consequences of this formula for the industry but to show what were the factors which influenced the committee in arriving at its conclusions. As in the previous formulae the committee thought, and quite correctly, that the price of canes should be based on the price of sugar. But it went further and included the price of by-products, and the certificated preferences.

Locally Consumed Sugar

The cane farmers had argued that the previous formulae did not take into account the considerable premium accorded to sugar sold locally as against exported sugar. On 7 August 1930, government had fixed the price at which sugar was to be sold locally. Government was at the time taking various measures, for example, loans, to assist the sugar industry. In this case the price of sugar for local consumption was fixed at a rate higher than the free-on-board price in order that the industry should to a certain extent be subsidized by the local consumer. The measures to assist the industry were aimed at maintaining (a) the level of wages on the estates and (b) a minimum price for farmers' canes.[21] The quota (see table 30) for local consumption fixed by Ordinance No. 12 of 1937 was 12,000 tons. The committee found also that the average gross price for local sugar was about $68.00 per ton. It did appear, therefore, that previous formulae, at least those that followed after 1930, by failing to take into account the premium on locally consumed sugar[22] were in fact passing on the benefits of the subsidy only to the manufacturer and not in part to the farmer as was the intention of the government. However, later formulae were introduced – all improving the calculations.

By-products

The farmers argued that, in deciding what price they should receive, no account was taken of the value of the molasses which was produced from their canes. Since the whole or rather the main basis on which price of the canes was to be determined was concerned with the value of the products into which the canes should be converted, this seemed a reasonable request on the part of the cane farmers. The committee acceded to it. The committee, however, did not accept their contention that some consideration should be given to the value of the megasse (bagasse) or husk of the cane. This on the ground that that part of the megasse which was used as fuel made it possible to reduce the cost of the manufacturers, which costs were taken into consideration in determining the final price to be paid. Also it was argued that not much megasse was burnt and that what in fact happened was that the megasse formed unsightly heaps in the factory yard and had to be carted away at great cost to the factory.

It would appear, however, that while the cane farmers were pushing this line of argument almost to the point of absurdity in the case of megasse or bagasse, they omitted what may have turned out to be a much more fertile field – rum. Rum is produced from molasses. If they were going to be logical they could have argued that some consideration should be given to this by-product also. And their gains from this should have been considerable. But then the question would remain, how far would one be prepared to allow them to pursue their demands? Would every by-product, however far removed, qualify for consideration in determining the prices of canes?

Certification Preference

The reference here is to the certificate issued by the secretary of state in London to the effect that the sugar in question formed part of sugar that could be imported from the colony under a special preferential rate. The purpose of this special rate of preference was to *stabilize the sugar production of the colonies at the level prevailing in 1932*. Again, in this case as in the case of the subsidy through price discrimination against the local consumer, the purpose of the assistance to the industry was to help both the manufacturer and the cane grower. For example, the 1929 West India Sugar Commission, in discussing assistance to the industry, specifically stipulated preserving the interests of the cane growers. The farmers, therefore, were justified in asking that the benefits of such assistance be passed on to them, in part at least.

Expenses of Handling Farmers' Canes, Depreciation, Interest

For certain purposes these three items should be treated together. They represent some of the manufacturers' cost which the committee recommended should be deducted from the value of sugar before the net amount is divided by *H*, the conversion ratio of canes into sugar. And so one comes to see the fundamental argument in the formula. Ostensibly the aim is to apportion the profits from sugar through a sort of co-operative action. Note, for example, the following quotation from the committee's report: "Had there been one central factory our task would have been easy as a fair percentage on the net profits of the factory could have been fixed."[23]

It is proposed to discuss the two latter items before the one dealing with the cost of handling canes as it is hoped to treat first those items which concern the manufacturers alone, and then treat that item in which the cost of both parties can be compared. On the question of depreciation and interest the committee reported that it could not obtain much assistance or co-operation from the manufacturers. For they could not or did not provide figures showing the estimated value of factories and railway rolling stock and so on. Note the committee's view on this question:

> In view of the difficulty of arriving at the proper valuation we are constrained to refer to the estimate of $4.80 per ton for interest and depreciation based on the capital value at the rate of $48.00 per ton of sugar as set out in paragraph 50 of the 1929 Report of the West Indian Sugar Commission. From a reliable source we gather that that figure included interest at the rate of 7½ per cent and depreciation at the rate of 2½ per cent. We consider that depreciation at the rate of 2½ per cent is low as obsolescence should also be taken into account. For this reason we suggest a rate of 4 per cent equal to $1.92 per ton sugar.[24]

They found, however, that the allowance for interest payment should not, as in the case of depreciation, be on a fixed scale but on a sliding scale as the rate would change with movements of prices. Their conclusion, therefore, was

> We consider interest at the rate of 7½ per cent per annum reasonable but in view of the fact that share-holders would not be receiving dividends at a constant rate we are of the opinion that the sliding scale should provide for interest ranging from nil to a maximum rate of 12½ per cent to compensate the shareholders for the loss of or for very low, dividends when prices for sugar are low.[25]

The following is the sliding scale of interest recommended:

When total price of sugar is $50 per ton and under	Nil
When total price of sugar is $50 but not more than $55	5 per cent = $2.40 per ton
When total price of sugar is $55 but not more than $61	7½ per cent = $3.60 per ton
When total price of sugar is $61 but not more than $64	10 per cent = $4.80 per ton
When total price of sugar is $64 and over	12 per cent = $6.00 per ton

The Cost of Handling Farmers' Canes

Manufacturing and Market Expenses

The estimated expenditure of the manufacturer on these items is given by the 1938 committee as approximately \$24 (£5) per ton of sugar. Again one gets the impression that this figure is merely a very rough approximation based on figures supplied by the manufacturers.

The committee did not question the efficiency of any of the processes, that is, handling of canes or manufacturing. But this is crucial to the whole question. For since the amount that goes to the farmer is a quotient in the equation, the farmer may find that his share (i.e., the price) is reduced, not because of any shortcomings on his part but because some of the items of cost that are deducted from the export price of sugar are higher than they might have been in a situation of higher efficiency (in the factory).

The same argument holds for item *H*, the conversion or input/output ratio of canes to sugar, that is,

$$\frac{\text{canes crushed}}{\text{sugar produced}}$$

If the factory method is very efficient, this ratio is small and in the main formula the denominator is also small so that the figure for the price of canes is correspondingly larger.

But this question also was not *exhaustively investigated* by the committee. The figure of 9 tons of canes to 1 ton of sugar was accepted as the ratio in 1938. But even in 1932 the more efficient Cuban mills were obtaining a ton of sugar from 7 to 7½ tons of cane.

Once again some light is thrown upon the factory methods by the observations of Norman Lamont. He pointed to the absence or underemployment of chemists in West Indian sugar houses and a lack of co-ordination of processes. Most importantly, however, for the purposes of the problem under discussion was the absence of any attempt to determine not only the ratio but

> the actual number of pounds of sucrose contained in the cane, the juice, the syrup, the massecuite, the various grades of sugar, the filter press cakes, and the offal crop of molasses. In this way alone is it possible to compare the number of pounds of sugar coming into the factory in the form of cane with the numbers actually marketed and to ascertain readily at what point in the process of manufacture preventable losses occur.[26]

It is the case that since he wrote in 1902 the manufacturing methods had been improved but the relative backwardness of Trinidad extraction process still remained in the 1919–39 period.

The fairest, least exceptional method of price determination would have been one based on the sucrose content of the canes purchased. It would then have been in the interest of the manufacturer to have the most efficient factory processes to ensure the maximum extraction of the sucrose.

In Puerto Rico two methods of payment were used, both involving tests for sucrose and purity:

a. The sale price of 7 lbs of sugar (New York Exchange) per 100 lb of cane delivered , or
b. Sixty-five per cent of the sale price of sugar per 100 lb cane to the farmer (colono) and 35% to the factory.[27]

Although in Queensland, Cuba and Natal as in Puerto Rico, sucrose content was the guiding principle, "in Trinidad sucrose and purity are not taken into account in making payment for canes".

What is also of great interest in the Trinidad formula for determining the price of farmers' canes is the fact that all costs seem to be taken into account except the costs of production of the farmers themselves. Although in the text of the report there are references to the costs of production of the cane farmers, no mention is made in the formula of any method of ensuring that the price eventually paid to the cane farmer bears some relation to the cost to him of producing the canes. Against this must be noted the care taken to ensure that all the costs of the manufacturers are included. Even the dividends of the shareholders are calculated in advance and become a determinant in the equation instead of a resultant. The price of farmers' canes then becomes a residual, not a determinant of profits.

But the difficulties of assessing the costs of the farmers are great. In the first place the holdings are small and numerous. In the second place the farmers perform with the aid of their family nearly all the tasks on their plots. They use very little hired labour. In addition they work very exceptional hours, the value of which in terms of money must be difficult to assess. It has been possible, however, to arrive at some figures of their money costs which should be at least as acceptable as those put forward for some of the estates' expenses (table 25).

The figures were submitted by the cane farmers. The director of agriculture found the cost for plant canes reasonable but that for first and second ratoons high. It must be borne in mind, however, that in most cases the farmers' expenses are not cash but are the calculated value of their own

Table 25 Production and Transportation Expenses of the Small Cane Farmers, per Ton

Period	Yield per Acre (tons)	Cultivation	Reaping	Cartage	Rent	Total
First year	25	1.74	0.20	0.75	0.18	2.87
Second year	20	1.14	0.20	0.75	0.22	2.31
Third year	15	1.52	0.20	0.75	0.30	2.77
Total	**60**	**4.40**	**0.60**	**2.25**	**0.70**	**7.95**
Average	**20**	**1.47**	**0.20**	**0.75**	**0.23**	**2.65**

Source: Report of the 1938 Committee on Cane Farming, Trinidad C.P. 119/1938.

Table 26 Comparison between the Average Estimated Costs of Production and Returns per Acre on Estates versus Small Cane Farmers

	Estates		Farmers	
	Costs ($)	Yield (tons)	Costs ($)	Yield (tons)
	Per Acre		Per Acre	
Plants at	120	30	60–70	24
First ratoons	40	20	30–40	16
Second ratoons	35	15	?	13
Other ratoons	25	10–12	?	10

Source: Report of the 1938 Committee on Cane Farming, Trinidad.

labour and that of their families. It is therefore interesting to note that the 1938 committee found that an examination of the actual costs of the five principal sugar estates and the large cane farmers revealed that the average cultivation costs during 1935–37, including the estimated rental value of the land, exceeded the $2.65 submitted by the small cane farmers, and that this was possible in spite of the fact that the majority of manufacturers had a large portion of their land planted in Uba cane, the cultivation cost of which is cheaper. Cane farmers were more or less prohibited from cultivating Uba cane (table 26).

Table 27 shows the cost of production of estates' canes 1936–37 and compares it with expenses which the estates claimed were met in purchasing

Table 27 Cost of Estates' Canes Compared with Expenses Met by Estates in Purchasing Farmers' Canes

	Estates' Canes ($)		Farmers' Canes ($)	
	1936	1937	1938	1939
	Per Ton		Per Ton	
Transportation from scale to factory	0.27	0.26	0.34	0.34
Operating scales, derrick and equipment	0.16	0.18	0.22	0.22
Cost of administration, finance, etc.	0.14	0.15	0.13	0.14
Estimated rental value of land	0.16	0.16	–	–
Admin. of cane farmers dept	–	–	0.18	0.18
Cultivation costs (seedlings & Uba canes)	2.60	2.64	–	–
Purchase price of canes (seedlings)			2.65	2.64
Total	**3.33**	**3.39**	**3.52**	**3.52**

Source: Trinidad and Tobago Council Paper No. 119/1938.
Note: The statement summarizes the general average expenditure of the five sugar manufacturers.

farmers' canes. Table 26 is provided by the 1938 committee which also investigated the cane farming industry. In both tables it is seen that the cost of producing estates' canes was higher than the cost of producing farmers' canes.

This finding bears out the report in the Colonial Economic Survey[28] that peasant farming was less costly than estate production. But the implications seem to be, not only that the machinery employed by the estates was more inefficient than the hand ploughs of the farmers, but that the peasants were in fact working long and exceptional hours which were not properly valued in terms of money.

In this connection it will be useful to quote the observations of Norman Lamont,[29] himself a planter, on the relative methods of cultivation employed by the farmers and the manufacturers. He found that on the whole the methods of ploughing were inefficient in both sectors and went on to add: "It is conceivable that cane farming may succeed because it is cheap. It is probable that the methods of Trinidad Estates may succeed, because they are efficient. It is impossible that the average estates' cultivation should succeed, for it is neither cheap nor efficient."

But however cheap may have been cultivation by the cane farmer, it is obvious that the price he received for his canes made production unremunerative for him.

The price for farmers' canes for most of the period after 1923–24 has been $2.88 per ton. With the 1938 figures for expenses at $2.65 per ton there is a residue of only 0.23¢ per ton. But the estimate of $0.75 for cartage in table 25 is less than the figure found by the 1932 committee. They estimated the figure as nearer $1.00. Their comment therefore is interesting: "Carting charges are often over a dollar per ton and it is difficult to see, with canes at $2.98 per ton, how farmers can make much real profit in such cases."[30] For if the cartage costs are taken at $1.00 per ton instead of $0.75, the residual per ton becomes minus 2¢. The farmer is not even breaking even. Even if cartage costs are taken as $0.75, the residual seems still inadequate in the light of (a) the fact that his and his family's efforts were clearly undervalued in the first place, which is supported by (b) the fact that the money costs of cultivation on the estates were greater than his own.

If he delivered only 15 tons of canes per year as was indicated earlier, his profits were only $3.45 per annum. It was the narrowness of the margin of profit (even with undervalued labour effort) that resulted in the output of farmers' canes fluctuating so violently. At certain price levels it was not worth the effort and farmers concentrated on food crops or sought work elsewhere.

Further, if he had taken an advance from the estate on his crop, column 7 of table 28 indicates that the profit of 23¢ per ton would have been, in many cases, not enough to repay that advance. If in addition the cane farmer had to pay interest on his advance (see note to table 28), it is obvious that he could not but do so at a loss. It is therefore no wonder that he defaulted on his repayments.

Some other problems of the cane farmers will be mentioned briefly:

a. *Prohibited varieties.* Farmers were not allowed to grow Uba canes. The reasons given were that Uba canes had to be burnt before reaping. It was claimed therefore that with many farmers burning canes the danger of fires getting out of control was immense. But the farmers were not satisfied with the decision because the manufacturers grew Uba canes on the plantations and, what is more important, it was estimated that Uba were 10 per cent cheaper to cultivate than other varieties while their sugar yield was about 20 per cent less. In the first instance, therefore, the farmers' costs were relatively higher

Table 28 Showing Advances to Farmers by Estates According to Nature of Tenure and Setting Out the Amount Advanced per Ton of Cane Purchased (1932)

Estates	Estate Tenure		Outside Tenure		Total, $	Advanced per Ton of Cane Purchased
	Amount, $	Per Cent	Amount, $	Per Cent		
(1)	(2)	(3)	(4)	(5)	(6)	(7)
1	1,721.00	100	Nil	0	1,721.00	0.08
2	1,399.90	100	Nil	0	1,399.90	0.11
3	2,662.20	83	550.00	17	3,212.20	0.26
4	15,369.00	78	4,231.00	22	19,600.00	0.50
5	2,710.00	76	850.00	24	3,560.00	0.17
6	779.60	72	317.00	28	1,096.80	0.08
7	15,530.00	55	12,575.00	45	28,105.00	0.17
8	7,881.00	31	17,162.00	69	25,043.00	0.78
9	2,360.00	29	5,765.00	71	8,125.00	0.22
10	244.00	6	3,606.00	94	3,850.00	0.37
11	Nil	-		-		
12	No details available, therefore omitted					
					$95,712.90	

Source: Report of 1932 Committee on Cane Farming, Trinidad and Tobago Council Paper, no. 84/1933.

Notes: In addition, estates made advances of supplies such as food, fertilizers, implements and so on against the crop to be delivered. One estate advancing in all some $159,000 in 1932 does not differentiate between advances in cash and those in kind. It is not therefore included in the above table.

The total $95,712 is spread among some 5,000 farmers cultivating about 9,000 acres, that is, 28 per cent of the farmers are assisted in this way. Approximately 30 per cent of them receive cash advances by some means or other, while estates further assist by supplying fertilizers and so on as stated above.

Rates of interest. Several estates charge none. Others charge exactly what the banks charge them. In the case of credit societies, the money obtained from government carries interest at 6 per cent. Societies then lend at a rate, which by law must not exceed 12 per cent. Usually 10 per cent is charged, this being sufficient to pay working expenses and provide for a fund for building up reserves.

than they would have been had they grown Uba cane. In the second place, in calculating the yield of sugar from canes the factories aggregated the yields from both varieties, so that the farmer was further penalized as the formula has as its denominator the yield of sugar from all canes.

Table 29 Showing Amounts of Fresh, Poor Variety and Burnt Canes Delivered by 200 Canes Farmers in 1932

Canes delivered	Weight (tons)	Per Cent	Price ($)
Total	9,453	100.0	
Fresh, clean canes	8,781	92.9	2.88
Poor variety canes	592	6.2	2.16
Burnt canes	80	Less than 0.9	2.00

Notes: The amount lost to farmers through poor variety canes was $426.24.
The amount lost to farmers through burnt canes was $68.40.

There is a further point which was made by the 1932 committee. Some of the lands rented to the farmers by the estates supported such varieties as B.H. 10/12 with difficulty. Uba canes, on the other hand, would grow on the poorer soils. It is also difficult to find out how the estates valued the canes which they themselves had to burn before reaping, but as table 29 shows, burnt canes from the farmer were bought for $2.00 as opposed to $2.88 for the fresh ones.[31]

b. *Limitation of areas.* This is a system of zoning under which farmers in a given area were compelled to sell their canes to a certain factory. The system was inaugurated in the early 1920s. Just as the post–World War I boom led to the indebtedness of the peasant cocoa proprietor, in the same way that period saw the indebtedness of the cane farmer to the large sugar manufacturers. The high prices of the post-war boom led to considerable competition among sugar manufacturers for cane. So great was the competition that large advances were made to farmers with the object of encouraging them to grow more canes for sale to the particular factories from which they received loans.[32] After the collapse of prices in 1921 many farmers were unable to repay their advances. In many cases, however, there was direct evasion of responsibility – the farmers delivering canes to factories other than those from which they had received advances.[33] In this way they avoided having any deductions made from the value of their canes. It was to lessen this danger that some estates, in 1922 agreed to restrict the purchasing of canes and the provision of credit to defined areas.

One of the results of this was that nearly all farmers received the same agreed price for their canes. There is everything to be said for removing the uncertainty of price fluctuations if all parties are agreed on what the price of canes will be. In this situation, however, the stability in prices was the result of a unilateral agreement on the part of manufacturers. It is significant that in the southern part of the island, where the limitation of areas did not operate, the price paid for farmers' canes was nearly always above that paid in the northern and central areas where limitation of areas did operate.[34]

But the system had its advantages. It sometimes made for economies in cartage of cane, and it made it possible for factories to give financial assistance to their "own" peasant farmers without fear of their defaulting.

Government Assistance to the Sugar Industry

Sugar prices that had been declining fairly steadily for most of the early 1920s slumped even further in 1929 and 1930 under the impact of continued excessive production and the Great Depression. In the latter year the Government of Trinidad passed a bill designed to give assistance, in the form of a loan, to the sugar industry.

There were some very interesting aspects of the bill. In the first place, as the attorney general observed when he introduced the second reading of the bill: "This bill has (therefore) been framed at the instance of the sugar owners and has been drafted by their legal adviser in close consultation with Government and with the banks, who are also an interested party."

The following is the bill (article 9 was finally deleted):

> That this Council agrees to render financial assistance to the Sugar Industry as follows:
>
> a. That relief be given out of Surplus Funds to the extent of £2 per ton of sugar exported during the year 1930 for the purpose of carrying on the industry during 1931: this relief to be in the form of a loan on condition that the factory owners do agree to carry on next year and continue the obligation of a fixed minimum price of 12/- per ton in respect of farmers' canes during the 1931 crop and also agree not to make any reduction in the wages of labourers until June 1931. Provided, however, that in the event of the average selling price of 96° Grey Crystals falling below £10.10 per ton f.o.b. the minimum price paid to the farmers be reduced at the rate of 6d for every 10/- below that figure and provided further that in the even of the f.o.b. price exceeding

£15 per ton, the extra bonus payable to the farmers be reduced by one third.

b. That the loan be made a first charge on the properties subject to existing mortgages and yearly crop advances.
c. That the loan be repaid only after the f.o.b. price of sugar 96° test exceeds £14 per ton and at the rate of half the difference between £14 per ton and the figure realized. Repayment to be made on the total amount of sugar produced.
d. That no interest is to be charged on the loan unless and until the f.o.b. price of sugar is £15 per ton, when it will be payable at the rate of five per cent per annum on the unpaid portion of the loan during any year where £15 per ton and over is the average price.
e. That the f.o.b. price be determined by the figures furnished by Messrs. Czarnikow & Co. and be the average over the period 1st Jan. to 30th June in each year.
f. That the period for the repayment of the loan be limited to 15 years after which the principal sum and interest then outstanding shall be due and payable, and
g. That the factory owners be required to enter into deeds embodying the above conditions.

Rider: That the Council records its opinion that the question of making further advances in the year 1931 in respect of the 1932 crop should be sympathetically considered by Government when the time comes and that if the economic situation warrants it, similar relief be given.

Section (g) relating to the deed was deleted, the attorney general arguing that the process would require too much time, that the need for the loan was urgent, that searching for titles was a slow and expensive business, especially in view of the need for complying with stamp duty regulations and so on. He proposed therefore that these requirements be waived for the purposes of this bill. Another member of the Legislative Council ably summed up the bill in the following terms:

> a model of generosity, a model of relaxation of every condition, financial and otherwise.
> There is no searching of title in this bill – take the property for what it is worth.
> There is no registration – pass the application to the Registrar.

> There is no lawyer to make a fee.
> No interest to be paid until certain very remote contingencies happen.
> And it is doubtful if they will be called upon to pay the principal.

Later he remarked: "But as I said before, we have relaxed every canon of finance, and it is simply because we are trying to keep the industry alive that we consent to these unusual terms."[35]

The provisions of this bill and the attitudes of the government and some members of the Legislative Council have been set out at some length to underline the case of assistance to the sugar industry as compared with that to the cocoa industry. In the case of cocoa, the only laxity was in the question of exact valuation of the property of those applying for loans. On the question of mortgages, as L.A.P. O'Reilly pointed out

> The vice of agricultural relief was that the Government without the permission of mortgagees gave agricultural relief which passed as a first mortgage. That a mortgagee with a perfectly fixed right of property, with a fixed asset passing to him by virtue of his mortgage, should find himself ousted by a subsequent advance and without his permission! That was the vice!

In the case of sugar, not only were first mortgages respected, but provisions were being made for even subsequent crop advances to have priority over repayment of the government loan. This was a very sensible practical step.[36] The provisions for repayment were also widely different, most likely partly because of the difference in credit worthiness of the parties concerned.

In the case of cocoa there was a strict formula[37] for repayment of loans irrespective of the price of cocoa. In the case of sugar, the original intention was to make repayment conditional on the price of sugar. Finally, however, it was agreed to set a time limit; but it is evident from the debate on the bill that nearly everyone was prepared to regard the loan as a gift if the industry did not find better times.

Again, this was a most progressive approach which was stimulated largely by the following considerations. It was argued that they would soon have to go to the secretary of state for the colonies to ask for preferences. They could not expect to win the sympathy of the United Kingdom for this proposal if they did not show themselves willing to make a contribution, within their means, to the stability of the industry upon which so many persons (more than 100,000) depended for a livelihood.

On the question of interest rates also the provisions for the sugar industry were more generous than for cocoa. In the case of cocoa there was no "holiday period". In the case of sugar, the holiday lasted as long as the price of sugar remained below £15 per ton. But at no time during the period under study did the price of sugar rise to that level. Further, the rate of interest was lower for the sugar industry than it was for the cocoa industry, that is, 5 per cent versus 7 per cent.

There were other suggestions for aiding the industry. It was suggested that instead of giving the loan to the manufacturers, a subsidy should be given to the cane farmers. This proposal sprang from the contention that the manufacturers did not deserve any such assistance on such generous terms; and that the cane farmers were receiving for their canes an amount which was inadequate to cover the cost of production. Not only was this turned down but the government also refused the request of a private member that the same loan facilities as were extended to the manufacturers should be extended "to *bona fide* cane farmers, who are seized of and possessed large areas under sugarcane cultivation and who are not under financial obligations to such manufacturers". No reason was given for the refusal to extend the legislation to include cane farmers (in the case of cocoa, all classes of planters qualified for loans) but the reason seems to be that the government considered that by making the manufacturers agree to maintain a minimum price for canes they were ensuring that the benefits of the loan were passed on to the cane farmers (see section (a) of the bill).

If this is the case it would appear that the formula for determining the price of farmers' canes needs even closer study, and that further study should also be given to the question of costs of production of the cane farmers and the relative efficiencies of the various manufacturers. If it can be shown that this confidence in the manufacturers to pass on some of the benefits of the government assistance to the cane farmers was misplaced, then the case for direct assistance to the cane farmers becomes even stronger.

Assistance to the industry took another form also. A system of price discrimination was introduced under which the price at which sugar was sold locally was considerably above the free-on-board price of exported sugar. Of course this could not have been done without the prohibition of imports or the imposition of high tariffs. The latter course was adopted. In the event, the local price of sugar wholesale was about $68 (BWI) per ton according to the 1938 committee on the pricing of farmers' canes, while the free-on-board price never rose above, say, $50 per ton in the 1930s.

Immediately another problem arose. In what proportion were the companies to benefit from this subsidy? Local consumption was estimated at about 12,000 tons per annum. In 1936 a Sugar Quotas Ordinance was passed to fix the quota that each factory should have. According to the bill the four largest factories were to be allotted a proportion of local market equal to 5–8 per cent of their production, while the three smallest estates would get about 33 per cent of their production, intermediate sized estates getting amounts in proportion to their production (table 30).

Here, of course, is a case of the division of the market to make it safe for the least efficient to survive. For the smaller factories were in fact inefficient even by Trinidad standards. Note, for example, the argument used by one member of the council to ensure a larger quota for the small manufacturers:

> if the larger factories with more up to date machinery take only 10 tons of farmers' canes to manufacture one tone of sugar, whereas these smaller factories take 12 or 13 tons of the same canes to manufacture a similar quantity of sugar, in fixing a quota the position becomes very difficult and delicate. I will ask you, Sir, when fixing a

Table 30 Local Market Sugar Quotas (Tons)

Manufacturers	Exports (1)	Local Sale (2)	Column (2) as Percentage of Columns (1) Plus (2)
Usine Ste Madeleine	47,940	2,920	5.7
Waterloo Estates Ltd	19,230	1,475	7.2
Woodford Lodge Estates Ltd	18,930	1,460	7.2
Caroni Sugar Estates (Trinidad) Ltd	21,860	1,600	7.0
Gordon Grant & Co Ltd			
Trinidad Sugar Estates	12,880	1,155	8.0
Reform Estates (1928) Ltd	10,390	1,030	9.0
Alfred Laurie Esq. (Hindustan Estate)	3,880	700	15.2
Eric Murray Esq. (Craignish Estate)	860	550	39.0
J.B. Fernandes Esq. (Forres Park Estate)	810	545	40.0
	1,220	565	31.6
Total	**138,000**	**12,000**	8.0

Source: 1936 Sugar Quota Ordinance.

> quota, to consider carefully the man who is taking 13 tons of canes to make one ton of sugar as deserving of a higher percentage of the local market at enhanced prices.[38]

In this way inefficiency was to be subsidized.

What were the alternatives? The first was to allow the more inefficient factories to go out of business altogether. This would have meant hardship for those cane farmers who were tied by the limitation of areas scheme to the particular factories involved. Alternatively the smaller factories could have been incorporated into the larger ones, leading to a greater concentration of the industry. Actually the Sugar Commission had recommended such concentration.

> Centralization has been profitably developed in the South of the Island where, the Usine Ste Madeleine manufactured 32,000 tons of sugar in 1929 at a cost of £11.6.8 per ton f.o.b. which is considerably below the average cost. Before making large investments in machinery to bring the other factories up to modern standards careful study should be made of the possibilities of enlarging the better equipped factories and thereby centralizing the industry in a similar manner in the Northern part of the Island.

The need, therefore, was for greater efficiency. It should be observed, however, that though the speaker quoted in the debate was pampering inefficiency, he was motivated by another argument that cannot be entirely dismissed. He was trying to protect the Trinidad producer, inefficient though he was, from extinction.

The argument for efficiency required the improvement or demise of the small local-owned factories. Improvement was difficult, in view of lack of capital. Amalgamation of such factories into larger ones meant an intensification of the dependence on externally owned industries. That was the dilemma. For the free trader, the situation would have presented no problems. To those who thought that while inefficiency should be discouraged, the problem of having all the major assets of the country externally owned and operated, with the consequent export of profits while the share accruing to domestic income earners was merely low prices for farmers' canes, wages and government taxes: the solution was not so easy.

It must not be forgotten that the assistance to cocoa, the domestic income earner par excellence, was meager and ungenerous compared with the assistance to sugar and that partly in consequence of this the cocoa industry had died;[39] that the cane farming section of the industry, which apart from wages, was the only real alternative income earner and local recipient of export incomes, was also experiencing difficulties.

But if the efficiency argument requires the disappearance, as independent units, of the small factories and their amalgamation into larger central factories, that same argument pushed to its logical conclusion should require also the extinction of the whole Trinidad sugar industry in favour of more efficient Puerto Rican or Hawaiian production.

In the interest, therefore, both of efficiency and the maintenance of that proper balance between domestically owned and foreign-owned assets, what seems to have been required was a government-assisted co-operative movement among cane farmers, producing canes for a central factory.

But to increase efficiency in this section of the industry and in that run by the large expatriate companies, greater mechanization and a more intensive use of fertilizers and irrigation would have been necessary. The former would have resulted in a reduction of the labour force. It would then have been necessary to reorganize the whole economic structure to provide employment for those made redundant by the mechanization of the industry.[40]

5 Other Agricultural Products: The Search for an Alternative

This chapter analyses the factors which influenced production and exports in the "lesser" agricultural industries.

These minor industries – bananas, coconuts, coffee, grapefruit and limes – have an importance for the analysis of the development of the economy much greater than their small contribution to exports and employment would at first suggest. They are further indications of the instability of the prices of agricultural products. Their history shows the riskiness, the unpredictability of market conditions for agricultural products in the inter-war period.

In the context of the Trinidad and Tobago economy of the period they demonstrate the extent to which, given the decline of the chief agricultural industries (cocoa and sugar), the agricultural community was driven by the movement of prices to shift from crop to crop as world market conditions favoured now the one, then the other industry, but finally leaving them all (with but few exceptions) unsatisfactorily developed and unrewarded.

Cocoa had declined gradually until 1931 and fell catastrophically thereafter. Sugar, the total export value of which was barely maintained in spite of increases in total production, was increasingly concentrated into the hands of a few manufacturers, largely expatriate. The prices of farmers' canes were low. Into what avenues, therefore, should local enterprise and capital – such as it was – be directed? In so far as agriculturalists were concerned, what were the alternatives?

The year 1931 saw the report of a committee[1] appointed to consider measures to be taken to develop new agricultural export industries. This committee recommended the cultivation of bananas. That industry flourished for a while until, as will be shown later, it was overtaken by disease and price. All the other minor agricultural industries except grapefruit suffered in one way or another.

The resultant difficult position of agriculturalists is illustrated in the following observation of the director of agriculture:

> The question of alternative crops calls for immediate consideration on the part of owners of estates in those sections where pod infection has reached alarming proportions.
>
> The first consideration is a crop that is suited to the conditions of soil and rainfall – on this point the advice of the Department of Agriculture can be obtained.
>
> The second consideration is a far more difficult one. It is the question of the market prospects, and the proprietor must himself accept the responsibility of a choice that cannot but be a gamble on future world prices. Critical examination of such statistics as are available regarding existing world production and contemplated plantings are far from encouraging no matter what crop is selected, and the only justification for planting at all is the past experience of all countries that in spite of the ups and downs of agricultural enterprise some measure of prosperity from time to time rewards the planter.[2]

The following pages treat the factors involved in each of the minor agricultural industries, and illustrates how each of them fared in the "gamble on future world prices".

Coffee

Table 31 gives the quantity and value figures for the exports of coffee from Trinidad and Tobago for the period of the inter-war years. Up to 1923 the quantity and value of coffee exported were negligible. In 1924, however, coffee had made a jump, exports being 518,100 pounds valued at nearly £15, 900. Coffee then occupied fourth place (after cocoa, sugar, coconuts) among the agricultural exports of the colony. The upward trend continued into the next year, 1925, when exports were nearly 600,000 pounds valued at £28,000. The 1926 crop was somewhat less than that for 1925, due mainly to the dry season of the previous year. This was no deterrent, however, for coffee had come to be regarded as a crop of some importance and extensive plantings were being prosecuted in many parts of the islands. In spite of this,

Table 31 Coffee Exports, 1921–39

Year	'000 lb	£'000 (£1 = $4.80)
1921	1.0	0.024
1922	0.3	0.017
1923	1.7	0.06
1924	518.1	15.9
1925	597.7	28.2
1926	497.7	20.4
1927	163.9	7.2
1928	264.9	10.9
1929	818.0	32.3
1930	492.0	12.5
1931	857.9	16.3
1932	908.5	20.8
1933	339.2	7.4
1934	525.1	10.6
1935	1,187.9	18.3
1936	1,213.2	17.7
1937	1,752.9	28.1
1938	687.7	8.4
1939	736.4	8.7

however, it should be noted that the exports for 1926–27 to 1928 were all low. Drought was not the only cause.

As was the case with cocoa and sugar and then coconuts, the coffee crop suffered from poor methods of cultivation. In 1926 the director of agriculture reported that lack of attention to pruning was almost universal, with the result that although the area planted in new trees was expanding, these new plantings were scarcely more than enough to compensate for the falling off in yield of the older trees unless these poor methods were remedied.

One of the chief faulty methods of cultivation was the practice of interplanting the cocoa trees with coffee. It was stated earlier that efforts were made to find a substitute crop for cocoa. When the price of coffee was rising in the early 1920s, there was a considerable expansion of the area under coffee. But coffee was not treated as a crop in its own right. Planters tried to hold on to their cocoa estates and grow coffee at the same time. The prevailing idea seems to have been that coffee is a crop which can be grown in any old place. From the fact that they sought to maintain some vestige of cocoa estates together with coffee which they thought would grow anywhere, it does not seem unfair to conclude that planters thought that it was possible to grow an acre of cocoa and an acre of coffee on the same acre of land.

It should be observed, however, that the area in Trinidad and Tobago which is suitable for coffee is restricted by the very size of the islands and by the fact of other crops, for example, sugar, which were long established in certain areas. Weather conditions also had something to do with the small crops of 1926–28. However, in 1929 the director of agriculture could remark that it was still a rare sight to see a coffee plantation. The crop was still a "filler" in cocoa estates. Robusta was a favourite variety: "There are practically no coffee plantations in the Colony. The two popular types are 'Robusta' and 'Arabica' and they are used for filling in blank spaces in cocoa plantations."[3]

But condemnation of this practice should be guided by the difficulty of persuading planters to decide to destroy a cocoa estate and replant with another crop the market conditions of which perhaps were as insecure as that of the one to be destroyed. If the cocoa estates had been destroyed by fire, substitution would have been easier (though of course the difficulty of choosing a substitute would have remained). But where the cocoa was gradually declining and where prices rose from time to time to tickle the imagination of the planter and remind him of the golden age, such substitution was difficult to achieve.

This explains the hesitancy of the farmer and the attempt to have a stake in a number of crops on the same acre so that at least one of them would experience relatively favourable prices.

An attempt was made to secure the local market for local producers. In 1928, "in order to avoid the risk of disease of plants", a proclamation of 1 January "prohibited the importation of coffee into the Colony so long as the local supply was sufficient to fulfill domestic requirements".

This measure and the improvement in weather conditions seem to have stimulated production which increased in 1929, 1931 and 1932. Production then slumped but rose again after 1935, with 1937 as the peak year. The drop in 1938 could be explained in terms of two factors, a drop in the price of coffee and an increase in cocoa prices.[4] The result was that greater efforts were once more directed immediately to cocoa, the export values of which had increased thus:

	1934	1935	1936	1937	1938
Cocoa ($M)	1.7	2.5	2.3	3.1	2.4

Cocoa was still, in the mind of the agricultural sector, the prized crop. Coffee was only a filler, a substitute to be discarded as soon as conditions allowed.

Limes

The production of limes had long been a valuable though minor industry in Trinidad and Tobago. The products of this industry have been exported largely as concentrated lime juice, green limes, raw juice, pulp and distilled lime oil. But the demand for these different products varied from time to time with consequent periods of prosperity and depression. As the Economics Committee remarked, "the cultivation of limes is a speculative and risky enterprise, unsuited for specialization and more suitable as a subsidiary or even a catch crop".[5]

As with most of the subsidiary crops so far considered, the problems have been disease and cultural methods to which have been added the difficulty of finding and keeping markets in face of foreign competition.

Table 32 Exports of Lime Oil

Year	Quantities	Product Type	Value
1926	431 gal.		£5,312
1927	104 gal.		1,454
1928	495 gal.		5,894
1929	797 gal.		9,516
1930	1,647 gal.		19,457
1931	2,413 gal.		32,071
1932	929 gal.		12,840
1933	1,889 gal.		22,575
1934	2,882 gal.		25,055
1935	1,949 gal.		15,497
1936	22,016 lb	(Distilled)	17,702
	779 lb	(Hand pressed)[a]	1,403
1937	46,429 lb	(Distilled)	46,075
	1,222 lb	(Hand pressed)[a]	2,023
1938	33,403 lb	(Distilled)	22,904
	938 lb	(Hand pressed)[a]	1,688
1939	48,500 lb		25,700

[a]Hand pressed oil sold at double price of distilled oil.

Table 33 Exports of Lime Juice

Year	Concentrated Juice		Raw Juice	
	Exports (gal.)	Value (£)	Exports (gal.)	Value (£)
1926	7,886	1,926	Nil	Nil
1927	4,488	1,154	Nil	Nil
1928	5,653	1,487	Nil	Nil
1929	55,455	11,562	Nil	Nil
1930	21,762	3,759	47,554	4,096
1931	4,012	458	22,931	2,007
1932	8,583	427	46,629	4,250
1933	11,709	622	17,375	1,203
1934	9,110	535	3,479	294
1935	4,422	393	11,807	806
1936	3,521	321	66,881	4,758
1937	5,780	491	25,082	1,609
1938	2,640	253	74,752	4,667

As can be seen from tables 32 and 33 showing exports of lime products, the preparation of concentrated juice was the chief concern of the manufacturers in the early period. The process of manufacture involved the boiling down and concentration of the juice from the limes for making citrate of lime by the neutralization of the juice with calcium. With the development of a biological process for the manufacture of citric acid from molasses the demand for concentrated lime juice fell considerably. By 1931 the low price obtained on the London market both for the raw and the concentrated juice led to a considerable reduction in exports. The United States was the alternative market but here again the industry came up against the US tariffs of 1930 which had the effect of virtually closing the market.

Previous to 1936 attempts were being made to develop a trade in green limes in the United States. The exports were: 1935, 565 barrels; 1936, 1,391 barrels. In this field, however, the competition came from the Persian lime, which was considered by consumers as preferable in size and appearance to the West Indian lime.

Distilled lime oil, however, was the most important product of the industry. The chief market for this commodity was in the United States where it was used as a flavouring in confectionary and in the perfuming of toilet waters. Competition came from Mexico, but it would appear that the Trinidad and Tobago product was better than the Mexican and received a premium over the latter. The price of lime oil which was fairly steady for most of the later 1920s and early 1930s fell sharply after 1934.

In 1931, one could see once more the old familiar pattern of cultivation stimulated and diverted by price changes. Prices were good and the director of agriculture remarked, "the market price of lime oil has continued to be an inducement to extend the cultivation of this crop". The acreage devoted to this crop increased considerably, and exports of lime oil approached 3,000 gallons in 1934. The 1926 figure was only 431 gallons. Price fell sharply towards the end of 1934, however, to about 15/- per pound and growers and manufacturers were once more in trouble.

In face of these difficulties, West Indian lime producers came together in 1935 to form the West Indian Oil Sales Company, a co-operative marketing organization to ensure efficient marketing and to advise producers. At first only Trinidad and Tobago and St Lucia participated. Later all the other lime producing islands joined the organization with the exception of Dominica. In spite of the early numerical weakness of the organization it did succeed in steadying prices, most likely because of its policy of limiting production to forecasted demand.

Government Assistance during the Early Expansion of the Industry

In October 1930, the government approved an interest-free loan to the Tobago Lime Growers' Co-operative Association for the erection of a lime factory. Repayment of the loan was to commence after the third year of the completion of the factory, and was to be on a sliding scale based on the net value of a barrel of limes. The rest of the money for the factory, £1,000, was put up by the association.

In the inter-war period, the industry seemed to have weathered the storm fairly well, but if one should push the investigation into the 1940s, it is seen that "drying-out" disease reduced production in the fields to such an extent that the eight distilleries in the colony were all operating below capacity.

Grapefruit

As is indicated in table 34, the cultivation of grapefruit for export did not become important until after 1926. Here again is to be seen another example

Table 34 Grapefruit Exports

Year	Exports (Boxes)	Value (£) (£1 = $4.80)
1926	54	50
1927	1,649	1,427
1928	23	45
1929	807	606
1930	2,184	910
1931	4,377	1,874
1932	10,973	8,978
1933	3,433	2,586
1934	23,518	18,634
1935	51,119 (+7,724 loose fruit)	42,473
1936	42,958	41,357
1937	45,210 (+27,186 loose fruit)	39,078
1938	79,660	66,300

of the search for substitute crops to take the place of staples that have suffered either by world market conditions, disease or both. In this case grapefruit were planted in response to the difficulties occasioned by low prices of and witchbroom attacks on cocoa. Old cocoa plantations which had become unprofitable were turned over to this new crop.

But this planting of grapefruit was influenced not only by the difficulties of cocoa but also of limes. Limes were the citrus fruit attempted before grapefruit. With the reduction in the demand of concentrated juice owing to the increasing use of the fermentation process for the manufacture of citric acid from sugars, the demand for lime and its by-products tended to decrease – another example of the way in which scientific development and the production of synthetics endanger raw material production.

Trinidad and Tobago grapefruit production enjoyed an early acceptance on the English and Canadian markets where it received preferential treatment. The industry was built up rather quickly as the export figures indicated. The demand for this commodity was good as the quality of the fruit was soon recognized. The Trinidad and Tobago fruit received a premium over other types of grapefruit. To maintain the high standard of the fruit, the Co-operative Citrus Growers' Association, which was set up in 1932, encouraged improved cultivation and handling methods in the industry. Efforts were made in 1936 to cultivate the seedless variety of grapefruit which the market was then demanding. In this aspect of the development of the industry the Imperial College of Tropical Agriculture, as in most aspects of agricultural research in the islands, played an important role. The industry was developed around the Marsh seedless variety.

The industry was concentrated in the northern and central portion of Trinidad. The decision about this location was largely influenced by the following factors:

1. In the north and centre of the island there were larger areas of suitable soil than in the south.
2. The proximity of these areas to Port of Spain where the central co-operative packing shed was located. Also as Port of Spain was the export point, transport costs from farm to port were kept at a low level.

Although the packing shed was established in 1932, the cannery came four years later in 1936. That year production was 5,000 cases of juice and hearts. The juice was well received on the Canadian and the hearts on the English market. The canning process was necessary to prevent the wastage of bruised and over-sized fruit that was not suitable for export as whole-fruit. It also played a very useful role during the war when shipping space was difficult to obtain. All fruit was canned and later shipped when space became available. Without this process there would have been considerable wastage.

The industry grew rapidly both in respect of the actual fruit produced and the canning capacity of the factory. The plant was enlarged and in 1937 handled 26,000 field crates of fruit, producing 600,000 cans of grapefruit hearts and juice compared with 7,000 crates in 1935–36. In 1935 the export value of grapefruit had almost equaled that of coconuts which were third in importance among agricultural crops (grapefruit £42,500 versus coconuts £50,400).

As with some of the other crops government assistance was instrumental in the development of the industry. In 1929 the government made a loan of $24,000 available to the Citrus Growers' Association to build a fruit packing shed. When the co-operative was formed in 1932 legislation was enacted designating it the sole exporter of grapefruit in order that it might effectively control the quality and reputation of the fruit. In 1939 when the association wished to increase the capacity of its plant it received a government loan of $100,000 repayable on an amortization basis, by equal annual installments.[6]

Of the minor industries undertaken, the grapefruit industry may perhaps be regarded as the only one that succeeded. Its output expanded during and after World War II. In 1937 the area under grapefruit was 2,800 acres; by 1941 it was 3,430 acres.

The chief factors influencing the success of the industry were the high quality of the fruit; the quality of the entrepreneurship and the fact that "Trinidad enjoys the advantage of being able to market a large percentage of its crop at a period when the main crops of Florida and Palestine are becoming exhausted and when those of South Africa, Brazil and other places in the Southern Hemisphere are not yet available".[7]

Bananas

The vacuum created by the decline of the cocoa industry had to be filled by another crop which was predominantly peasant-produced. The increase in the production of the sugar industry could, by and large, compensate only in terms of the trade figures. In terms of the earnings of the majority of the population it was inadequate since the income from sugar was not widely distributed among the population. The search for such a peasant crop therefore went on, from coconuts and coffee to citrus and then to bananas in 1934.

Since 1914 bananas had not been produced for export.[8] In 1934, however, a number of experimental shipments were made through Elders and Fyffes. A profit of approximately £700 was made from the seven trial shipments. On this evidence the director of agriculture concluded that "the venture proved that Trinidad Gros Michel bananas were acceptable to the trade and could be marketed at a profit". Consequently, a Banana Board was set up and in May 1934 entered into a contract with the Canadian Banana Company. Under this agreement the company would purchase at a fixed price all the marketable Gros Michel bananas offered for export for a period of five years. With the sanction of the Legislative Council the company was given the monopoly for the purchase of Gros Michel offered for export during the period.

In this setting, therefore, the production of bananas was encouraged. The Department of Agriculture hoped that the fullest possible advantage would be taken of the "unique opportunity that now offers of growing a crop that involves little capital expenditure (where use is made of established cocoa lands), that brings in quick returns, and for which a market is guaranteed, at a fixed price for five years".[9] The department warned, however, of the dangers to be encountered especially Panama disease – which was already scattered throughout the colony, and the lack of experience in handling and cultivating the crop. Production for export had ceased since 1914.

In another section mention has been made of the tendency to over-produce any crop for which there appeared to be fairly good market conditions. In the case of bananas also there is evidence that the enthusiasm which was engendered by the profits of the trial runs led to this same difficulty. Banana cultivation spread into areas which were not suitable for the crop. Bananas need fertile soil and rainfall of about 80 inches. As the area planted expanded, poor quality soil became a menace. By 1935, for example, the mycologist reported that certain small blocks of pure stands had practically ceased to produce to any appreciable extent and this after only one or two crops. The reason for this was soil poverty or Panama disease or both. And he went on "Experience up to the present points to the fact that the commercial growing of bananas can only be regarded as a catch crop. The wise planter who clears land to grow bananas will promptly interplant a permanent crop to ensure the best results in the long run."[10]

Note especially the quick return to reality after the initial over-optimism:

> When the banana project for exporting Gros Michel was started there was a general feeling that abundant suitable land was available for the crop. But experience has shown that only very limited areas can be classed as good soils for this crop . . .
> Much disappointment has already resulted from more or less indiscriminate planting. In some instances only a meager crop has been reaped from the first plantings; in the other cases a marked decrease has resulted in the first ratoons. And in all of these instances, soil poverty has been a main factor for the failure.[11]

Production and Prices

Table 35 indicates the development of banana exports 1934–39. Note the swift expansion in 1936 and 1937 and the decline thereafter. It is very likely that the rise in cocoa prices could also have been influential in reducing interest in bananas. Also wartime conditions prevented further exports with the result that it is impossible to see how the exports side of the industry would have developed.

Before 1937 the price paid by the company was about 2/- (48¢) per count bunch. "In May (1937) as a result of representations made by the

Table 35 Banana Exports, 1934–1939

Year	Exports (No. of Stems)	Value (£)
1934	33,701	*
1935	66,369	£6,205
1936	159,085	14,797
1937	157,740	16,027
1938	80,506	9,174
1939	–	–

Source: Compiled from director of agriculture reports.
*In that year there were seven trial shipments through Elders and Fyffes and the profit realized was £700 (£1set = $4.80).

Fruit and Vegetable Conference, the contract price was raised by the Canadian Fruit Company to 54 cents per count bunch at the wharf."[12] Although formerly there was one flat rate applying to all "count bunches", that is, bunches of eight hands and more, the new agreement fixed the price to the growers as follows:

Bunches of nine hands and more	50¢–54¢
Bunches of eight hands and more	37½¢–40½¢

This system of pricing was an improvement on the other. It would appear, however, that the system of pricing by the "count bunch" is unfair to the producer of large bunches. The fruit is retailed by the pound and there is no way of relating the number of hands to the weight of the bunch. To relate price to the producer with subsequent retail price it would have been better to price the bunches according to weight, making some allowance for the weight of the stems.

Summary and Conclusion

Bananas failed as an alternative for the following reasons:

a. *Harvesting and handling.* As pointed out earlier, bananas had not been exported from Trinidad during the period 1914–34, with the result that, as the director of agriculture remarked, "We are still far from being banana minded." At the start of the new industry, therefore, the rejects caused by bad handling both on the field and on the trucks to the wharf amounted, in 1935, to about 25 per cent of exports. Also the Trinidad fruit was not as highly thought of as that from the other islands: "Rejections at the wharf are deplorably high and yet the fruit that is selected is reported upon less favorably than that from some of the northern islands."[13]

Lorries had insecure sides; loading and unloading without supervision was done by the roadside; attendants sat on top of the fruit in the trucks. Over time these faults were largely remedied; but the more serious drawbacks were difficult to eradicate.

b. *Disease.* Panama disease was the first to hit the industry, and the director of agriculture warned that "with the menace well in mind planters are wise not to cut down large blocks of other crops on the gamble that they will escape from this disease".[14] By 1936, Sigatoka leaf spot also made its appearance, especially in areas where rainfall was below 80 inches, which is considered the minimum for Gros Michel. In addition there were many pests of the banana to be eradicated.
c. *Cultural conditions.* These were, however, the prime cause of the failure. No soil surveys were made to determine which areas were most suitable for bananas. Cultivation was therefore undertaken at random with disastrous results. In the section on coffee, mention is made of the tendency to inter-plant that crop with cocoa. The same thing happened in the case of bananas. When in 1934 the production of bananas for export seemed profitable this method of production was one which commended itself to the Department of Agriculture. By 1935, however, the department was commenting that banana development was not satisfactory under shade and that inter-planting with cocoa was unsatisfactory especially for first ratoons.

It should be noted that adverse price fluctuations played no part in the decline of bananas. Unsuitability of soil and poor cultural methods were the chief difficulties. Also the war which seems to have stopped the banana trade in 1914 was also responsible for its decline after 1939.

Coconuts

The produce of the coconut industry (for most of the period the third most important agricultural industry) was exported in the following forms: whole nuts, copra, edible oil and coconut oil. The proportions of exports of

Table 36 Exports of Coconuts and Products

Year	Coconuts		Copra		Edible Oil		Coconut Oil	
	Millions	Value £'000	Millions lb	Value £'000	'000 Gal.	Value £	'000 Gal.	Value £'000
1919	33.9	322.4	1.8	34.8	0.1	0.3	–	–
1920	21.97	373.3	2.1	42.3	2.3	1.4	–	–
1921	20.5	108.7	4.2	62.0	7.7	1.6	–	–
1922	18.6	77.2	9.4	94.5	48.9	7.2	–	–
1923	12.2	47.2	13.2	147.5	8.9	1.4	–	–
1924	9.9	50.8	11.2	164.3	41.8	7.6	–	–
1925	8.6	45.8	9.9	131.2	76.3	15.8	–	–
1926	5.0	25.1	13.9	166.3	82.8	15.4	–	–
1927	6.5	32.3	12.5	146.9	58.1	11.1	–	–
1928	6.8	34.8	21.3	227.5	65.3	11.9	–	–
1929	13.6	66.3	23.9	209.7	–	–	34.7	5.4
1930	5.9	25.8	21.9	176.0	12.3	1.9	41.1	5.9
1931	4.5	12.5	19.5	101.1	20.7	2.9	20.7	1.8
1932	3.8	12.8	15.4	91.4	10.2	1.3	26.5	2.5
1933	7.9	21.4	19.4	82.9	6.5	0.7	45.6	3.6
1934	9.8	29.1	17.9	57.4	11.2	1.0	31.1	2.2
1935	5.4	14.4	8.8	34.7	5.3	0.7	14.9	1.3
1936	4.5	14.5	9.4	51.8	0.9	0.1	9.4	1.3
1937	5.0	20.7	17.3	113.1	3.6	0.4	19.9	2.3
1938	2.0	6.8	9.4	40.5	90.3	7.5	20.9	1.8
1939	0.6	1.6	12.5	39.5	319.0	29.6	17.2	1.6

Source: Director of Agriculture Reports.

coconut products represented by the various categories shown earlier varied over the period under study (see table 36). For an estimate of the trend of exports, however, see table 37. On the basis of three nuts to 1 pound of copra,[15] the whole of the exports are broken down and shown in table 37 in terms of nuts. Of course this method of calculation has its limitations. When, for example, the nuts are above average size, calculating from copra to nuts exaggerates the number of nuts. This is very likely what happened in the year 1928 for, owing to the favourable rainfall, the proportion of large nuts was higher than usual and consequently it would have taken less than three to give 1 pound of copra.

Table 37 Coconuts

Year	Exports in Terms of Nuts (Millions)	Prices per 1,000 Nuts	Copra per 100 lb	Value of Exports (£'000)
1919				357.6
1920	39.0			416.57
1921	33.0			172.08
1922	47.0			179.0
1923	52.1			253.76
1924	45.35			222.76
1925	41.96			192.83
1926	50.34	126/-	23/-	206.77
1927	46.57	117/-	22/-	109.29
1928	73.79	111/-	20/-	274.24
1929	87.11	93/-	17/-	281.5
1930	73.41	80/-	14/-	209.6
1931	63.8		8/9	118.4
1932	51.3		10/2½	108.1
1933	68.01		9/5½	108.7
1934	65.04		5/10	89.9
1935	32.34		8/6½	51.09
1936	33.30		11/5½	67.8
1937	57.75		11/11½	136.5
1938	31.55		6/4½	56.5

Source: Director of Agriculture Reports.

Despite allowing for this limitation, however, it can be seen that for the whole period 1919 to 1929–30, the trend of exports in terms of nuts has been upwards. After this a downward trend set in and in 1936 exports were the same as in 1921. The year 1929 saw the peak of exports, that is, 87.1 million nuts (see table 37).

Throughout the period export figures have been influenced by factors which are not always readily identifiable. It would appear, for example, that while the prices of most other products rose rapidly to their highest point in 1920, that of coconuts and copra fell heavily and this fact is given by the director of agriculture as one of the reasons for a comparatively low export figure. The other factors were the drought in 1919 and increased local consumption which took the place of imports of oils and fats, the prices of which had risen.[16]

The coconut industry was also troubled by disease. In 1919 it was red ring. By 1921 it was both red ring and bud-rot. The former, it was found, caused heavy losses on palms just on reaching the bearing age. In spite of this, however, the years 1922 and 1923 saw considerable increases in the crop. This increase was largely the result of the coming into bearing of new areas.

The year 1926 saw a continuance of the increase in importance of coconuts. Coconuts were at that time (1926) fetching 126/- per 1,000 nuts and both cocoa and sugarcane areas were turned over to coconut growing. In addition new lands made accessible by road extension were also brought under coconut cultivation.

In 1927 there was a slight temporary drop in exports due mainly to the drought of the previous year. In 1927 and for the next seven years the exports were more or less buoyant. The 1929 figure was 87.1 million, that is, more than double the number of nuts exported in 1920. A comparatively high level of exports was maintained until 1934 (65 million nuts) but thereafter the level of exports in terms of nuts dropped considerably. This drop in exports can be explained in terms of two factors: the hurricane[17] of June 1933 which damaged extensive areas, in Southern Trinidad and the greater use domestically of the copra crop for the manufacture of edible oil and coconut oil and lard substitutes. As indicated elsewhere[18] this expansion of the local industry was made possible by the imposition of tariffs on the imports of edible oil and lard substitutes, tariffs which had to be twice increased because the initial increase did not act as a deterrent to the importation of the foreign products.

It would appear that the history of the coconut industry is in many respects similar to that of the cocoa industry. The trend in production can be gauged by the prices ruling on the world market. Around 1926 there was a marked extension of coconut plantations owing to the comparatively high prices of coconut products and what was then regarded as the low prices of cocoa and sugar. Considerable areas were cleared of both crops and coconuts substituted. But here again one comes upon one of the fundamental drawbacks of Trinidad and Tobago as an agricultural country. Much of the land into which this new expansion of coconut production was pushed was unsuitable for coconuts and many of the palms succumbed to wilt disease when they should have come to maturity. The evidence for stating that wilt disease is caused by certain soil conditions is not really foolproof. What was established, however, was that as the coconut plantations were expanded away from the coastal areas, which are very suitable for coconuts, the output per tree fell considerably. There was almost a correlation between produce per tree and distance from the coastal areas.

The lesson, therefore, seems to be that as in the case of cocoa, expansion of certain agricultural industries soon came up against a frontier, a fertility frontier or suitability frontier, for lack of a better expression; that the urge to press beyond that frontier came largely from high world prices and the belief that those prosperous conditions would last. So followed the expansion into uneconomic land; an expansion which was only possible in conditions of unusual price increases. As soon as prices slumped the new extensions became liabilities rather than assets and were neglected.

There are other points for consideration. The West India Royal Commission Report of 1939 (Lord Moyne) observed that "the peace-time outlook for coconut producers, though far less desperate than that for cocoa, was on the whole decidedly unfavourable". In addition the market for whole nuts for confectionery was necessarily limited. The greater demand for coconuts was in terms of the fats and oils that they produced. But in this field they did not have a monopoly, but had to meet the competition of the other oil seeds. Therefore, in conditions where the supply of oil seeds is not restricted by war or other causes, or the demand for oils and fats is not increased considerably, the price of coconut products is not likely to rise to a high and long sustained level.

If one accepts such a situation, therefore, and adds the fact that the industry is one that involves, as in the case of cocoa, a long period of capital input in trees that do not yield a return for several years, and further the investment of fresh capital is not likely as long as market prospects are unattractive, then one sees the basic insecurity of this type of industry.

General Conclusions on Minor Agricultural Industries

High prices for any one crop relative to another produce the urge to maximize revenue from that favoured crop. There was therefore a switch, sometimes only a half-hearted switch, to the favoured crop. The margin of cultivation was soon reached and often passed, sometimes at great cost which was only warrantable in terms of high prices. Since the crops were often those involving investments of large sums and the returns were possible only after five or six years, the dangers of world prices changing meanwhile were very great. Even if demand and price conditions did not change before a crop was reaped, the amount invested sometimes demanded a number of good crops in favourable price conditions if the principal was to be redeemed and some profit made. Since these favourable conditions could not be ensured the possibility of disaster was great, and the resources necessary for continuing production and culture of the crops and estates were not forthcoming with the result that the fall in prices had a snowball effect on the domestic industry.

All developed countries have their agricultural sectors. They supply the local market and they export in the face of external competition. Is the answer then that countries like Trinidad and Tobago with its own petroleum industry should industrialize efficiently and profitably? Thereafter, assistance can be given to the agricultural sector and, this above all, the local population must learn to consume local products.

6

The Petroleum Industry

The Early History

Although active seepages of oil were reported in the forest of south Trinidad in the mid-nineteenth century, what can be called the earliest commercial attempt at producing petroleum came not from borings but the attempt in 1857 to manufacture liquid asphalt petroleum or pitch-oil by distilling crude lake asphalt. This experiment was short-lived.

Actual drilling was first attempted on the Aripero Estate by Walter Darwent in 1865 with a well of 150–160 feet, the limit of the drilling equipment available, and the well had to be abandoned. Shortly afterwards, about 1867, a well was sunk to a depth of 160 feet and oil was struck. Further attempts to find oil were made by a London company but here again the inadequacy of the equipment and the unproductiveness of the wells made search difficult and unrewarding.

There is no record of any other prospecting efforts until 1902 when more wells were sunk, again in the Aripero Estate in the south-west[1] and in the Guayaguayare area in the south-east of the island.

The earliest (nineteenth-century) system of sinking oil wells in the United States, and also in Trinidad and Tobago was the inefficient "percussion" method. Later, adopting the more efficient "rotary" method employed in the brine and salt industry, "oil men" drilled safer, better and deeper wells.

For all practical purposes the twentieth century, not the mid-nineteenth century, saw the birth of the local industry. It was in 1902, at Guayaguayare, that up-to-date drilling equipment was first used. Both at 750 and 1,000 feet oil was struck, the flow being about 40–50 barrels a day. Further strikes were made in 1903 and 1904. But in 1904 the company was forced by its financial difficulties to suspend operations.

Operations were resumed in 1906 for about one year. Four additional wells were sunk. But the oil from these wells was used only for fuel purposes on the fields or sold locally. But interest in oil had been aroused and another company commenced operations at about the same time, though in another district, Guapo, in the south-west of the island. By the end of 1910 they had sunk four wells.

The New Trinidad Lake Asphalt Co. Ltd, the concessionaires of the Pitch Lake, also took a hand in drilling operations and between 1908 and 1910 sank eight wells near the lake. They were the first to sink a really deep and successful well and were also the first to export a cargo of crude oil in bulk. The year was 1911 and the cargo 3,800 tons of crude petroleum.

One could divide the history of the oil industry so far into three periods: (1) the nineteenth-century explorations when wildcatting and the use of primitive drilling equipment were the rule; (2) the early twentieth century, 1900–1909, when equipment had somewhat improved. But even in this latter period the difficulties were immense; (a) roads in the oil bearing part of the island (i.e., the south) were non-existent through the forests and swamps. The difficulty was especially increased as equipment was heavy and cumbersome and would be bogged down on inferior roads; (b) the island was as yet unexplored for oil; (c) as later exploration showed, the geological structure was so irregular that many dry wells could be sunk around a gusher; (d) it was difficult to obtain labour in the areas in which prospecting took place. (3) 1910–11 onwards (see tables 38a and 38b) was a period of considerable expansion and it saw the real birth of the oil industry as a commercial proposition.

Ownership of Oil Rights

Before 17 January 1902 petroleum rights were not reserved by the Crown where the surface rights were alienated. The order of development in this question of oil rights was as follows:[2]

The grants issued since 1869 contained the following reservations:

> "The rights to reserve for works of public utility and convenience 1/20th part of the land granted except only land on which buildings

Table 38a The Growth of the Petroleum Industry 1908–1918

Year	Persons Employed	Feet Drilled	Crude Oil Produced (Million Imp. Gallons) (a)
1908			0.001
1909			1.66
1910			3.68
1911–12	1,208	40,418	10.0
1912–13	801	42,552	17.6
1913–14	1,209	41,933	22.5
1914–15	1,276	57,969	36.7
1915 (9 mths)	1,291	40,053	23.5
1916	1,511	58,390	32.5
1917	1,857	52,037	56.1
1918	2,311	54,238	72.9

Source: Handbook of Trinidad and Tobago, 1924, 54.
(a) 35 imp. gallons = 1 barrel.
See also table 38a on the following page.

Table 38b Principal Producing Fields of Trinidad

Field	Discovery	Producing Horizon	Gravity API	Production Av bpd First Half of 1976
Barrackpore	1911	Miocene	29.9–41.2	1,689
Brighton (incl. o.s)	1908	Miocene	32.8	1,805
Coora–Quarry	1936	Miocene	20.4–24.1	2,850
Forest Reserve	1913	Miocene	23.0	10,599
Fyzabad	1918–20	Miocene	20.8–32.7	3,859
Galeota (o/s)	1972	Miocene	31.6	1,374
Guayaguayare	1903	Miocene	33.7	4,374
Palo Seco/Erin	1915–26	Miocene	21.2	6,110
Point Fortin Central and West	1907–16	Miocene	20.4–45.1	1,567
Point Fortin East	1929	Miocene	34.4	1,342
Oropouche	1944	Miocene	10.8–38.6	1,067
Poui (o/s)	1974	Miocene	–	32,294
Samaan (o/s)	1973	Miocene	36.8	60,667
Soldado (o/s)	1955	Miocene	24.8	47,695
Teak (o/s)	1972	Miocene	29.3	35,660

Source: British Petroleum Company Limited, *Our Industry Petroleum*, 1977.
Note: Items marked o/s (off-shore) fall outside of the period of the study.

have been erected, or which may be in use as gardens or otherwise for the more convenient occupation of such buildings."

1869–89: All precious metals and coal were reserved to the Crown.

1889–1902 (January): All precious metals or coal together with asphalt in certain areas were reserved.

1902–10 (January): All precious metals or coal, oil and other minerals (except asphalt were reserved.

1910: All precious metals, coal, oil and other previous minerals were reserved.

For the purposes of the study, therefore, there were three kinds of land tenure:

i. Privately owned land in which the oil right was secured to the owner.
ii. Crown land on which the oil was the property of the Crown.
iii. Alienated land where the oil was the property of Crown although the surface rights were in private ownership.

This three-tier structure of land ownership soon produced its difficulties. Total production of oil for the years 1908 and 1909 at 37 barrels and 47,295 barrels, respectively, was from private land. Production from Crown lands began only in 1910 and soon overtook production from private lands. But in 1927 the situation was reversed again. The increased output from rich privately owned oil-bearing land in the Fyzabad area, and worked by Apex (Trinidad) Oil Fields Ltd,[3] turned the scales (table 39).

Put in another form the problem was that from Crown leases of 170,624 acres production was 339,351 tons, that is, 1.98 tons per acre; from private leases of 34,379 acres production was 416,088 tons, that is, 12.10 tons per acre. This meant that because of the earlier failure to reserve all oil rights to the Crown, private owners were receiving larger royalty payments than the government. The latter figures were dominated by an output of 259,351 tons from 1,136 acres of private land near Fyzabad.[4]

The remedies suggested included expropriation of oil rights. The remedy may have been effective but

i. It would have been contrary to the government's aim of encouraging private capital. Private capital may have resented this action.

Table 39 Oil Production from Private Lands, 1926–1929

Year	Oil from Private Land '000 bbls	Total (2)	(1) As Percentage of (2)
1926	2,030	4,971	40%
1927	3,044	5,381	56.6%
1928	3,561	7,685	46%
1929	4,101	8,716	47%

ii. It may have been hasty. In fact within a few years other rich areas were struck on Crown lands and the total of Crown oil once more outstripped privately owned oil.

Further, there was this important consideration. If one considered only the per acre yield of oil one might obtain a somewhat distorted picture. One of the chief reasons why per acre output on Crown lands was so small was the fact that the large acreage of Crown land was composed of many areas which were unproductive and could be deleted for the purpose of working out yield per acre. By 1927, for example, Trinidad Central Oilfields, which held no private land, had a lease covering 64,434 acres of Crown lands. Its production, however, was obtained mainly from two of its fifteen parcels of land.

However, three of the companies which held only private lands had a total output of 100,053 tons on 16,827 acres, that is, 5.9 tons per acre, which was distinctly above the per acre average for Crown lands.

To solve this problem of a large amount of royalties going to private rather than to government lands, Sir Thomas H. Holland[5] made the following proposal:

> A relatively small production tax on the oil obtained from lands which were alienated before 1902. The proposed tax would have to take into account the fact that companies in operation would have secured their rights either by
>
> a. paying a royalty to the landowners at a fairly high rate of 3/6 to 4/6 per ton or
> b. by outright purchase of the freehold, or
> c. by payment of a special rent.

Thus, the proposed tax would fall, in the case of (a) on the landowner, (b) on the company, and (c) on the landowner. So far for incidence of the tax. The amount of the tax was to be 2½ per cent of the value of oil. In each case the tax would be paid by the company and deducted from payments to the owner. In the case of (c) he proposed that the owner be charged one quarter of the rent which is normally 10 per cent of the value of oil so that this also works out at 2½ per cent of the value of oil.

Neither of these courses was adopted. The following extract from the debates of the legislature suggests the course adopted by government. The government did not deny it.

> The Government of the Colony every year receives the property of Indians who have married in this way (i.e. by Hindu laws) and who die intestate. The destination of that property is left to the gentle mercies of the Government . . . If your Excellency will permit me to use an Americanism, the Government in passing on such property to those morally entitled, not only takes a rake-off out of the estate but for some reason which I have never been able to appreciate takes the oil rights of these people away from them.[6]

In short a modified and secretive form of expropriation was practised. The failure of the Indians to reject their customary marriage practices became a means of off-setting the pre-1902 failure to reserve oil rights to the Crown. But the problem remained largely unsolved. In 1939, for example, both the amounts of currently produced oil and the cumulative total of all oil produced since 1908 showed a large contribution coming from private oil lands:[7]

1939 Productions (Million Barrels)

Year	From Crown Lands (1)	From Alienated Lands (2)	From Private Lands (3)	Grand Total (4)	Col. (3) as Per Cent of Col. (4)
1939	9.7	4.2	5.8	19.7	29%
Cumulative Production 1908–1939 (Million Barrels)					
1908–39	81.9	28.9	71.7	182.6	39%

While, therefore, the proportion of possible royalty payment going to government was increasing, the proportion and amount going to private individuals were still very considerable.

Prospecting and Exploration Licences

One of the most interesting points about the granting of leases for the development of the Trinidad oil industry was that such leases were granted, not in Trinidad but in the United Kingdom by an inter-departmental committee. The Trinidad government was therefore completely out of touch with many of the developments and agreements. This gulf between the government and the arrangements for exploiting the richest resources of the island comes out time and time again. But the government expressed complete satisfaction with the arrangement that leases be made in the United Kingdom.[8]

From this first important aspect of mining lease policy sprang many of the others:

An All-British Policy

As in the case of Iranian oil,[9] the aim was to produce oil fuel for the admiralty when ships were converted from coal into oil burners.

Crown land leases were therefore restricted to British companies. But this all-British policy was not carried to its logical conclusion and imposed on all lands, Crown and private. Foreign, mainly American, companies were able to rent private land. One result has been that there were certain pockets of Crown lands between private lands which could only be worked economically by the companies that secured the enveloping private lands.

There was another effect of the all-British policy. It seems to have "reduced the speculative element which necessarily accompanies the development of a promising oil field". There was some speculation, but "on the whole there has been (more completely than is generally usual with the development of a mining industry in an agricultural country) comparatively little disturbance of local values, and there has been marked co-operation among the companies themselves in pooling their information for the purposes of establishing a system of control over drilling operations".[10]

In this both American and British companies co-operated. In the 1919 report of Trinidad Leaseholds Ltd (TLL), the chairman reported that on the recommendation of the geologists, 1,500 acres of freehold land, oil rights over 1,450 acres and surface rights over 390 acres were purchased "before the increase in prices due to the present speculative activity in oil lands had taken effect".

This means that after ten years of exports by the oil industry, after production had reached 2 million barrels, it was still possible to purchase land and oil rights before the speculative fever had affected prices. The absence of such speculation was due not only to the all-British policy, as stated earlier, but to the fact that with negotiations for leases carried out 4,000 miles away the effect of the development of the industry on local interest, and so on land prices, was negligible. The industry though located in Trinidad, had its main spring and its *raison d'etre* abroad. Its great possibilities did not seem to enter fully into the consciousness either of the people or the government.

Leasehold Conditions

There was no set of published rules or statement of guiding policy governing the grant of concessions for oil. Conditions varied from lease to lease. There did appear to be, however, an upper limit of 100,000 acres on the extent of leases. Within this upper limit, leases of all sizes were granted. In this connection see table 40. It will be noticed that the largest lease area, 64,434 acres, went to Trinidad Central Oilfields Ltd. This particular lease is very important in that it, more than any other, shows up the inadequacy of the system which, in a geologically untested area, allowed large areas to be leased to companies which could relinquish unwanted though untested parts of their leasehold.

The lease of such a large area, much of which turned out to be unproductive, meant that the dead rent per unit of production was inordinately high. For example, the dead rent for the Trinidad Central Oilfields Ltd lease of 64,343 acres was fixed at £10,000 a year. The company found, however, that it had over-estimated its ability to exploit this considerable area. Its total output in 1927 from land exploited was only 6.769 tons of crude oil, that is, it was paying a minimum royalty or dead rent of approximately 29/6($7.08) per ton. Its total production up to 1927 (five years) was 59,980 tons and its total royalty charges £50,000 ($240,000).

Consequently, the company wished to exercise its right under the lease and relinquish a part of its holdings. This, however, led to the following considerations:

1. The patches which it wished to reject received, inferentially, a bad name, and this perhaps without justification since much of it had not been explored at all. Such land would therefore be difficult to lease to other less daring companies.
2. The relinquishing of such land frustrated the policy of creating spheres of influences.[11] This policy seeks to ensure for each company in operation a compact area of land which would mean among other

Table 40 Oil Lands Leases, 1914–1926

	(1)	Area Acres (2)	Date of Commence-ment (3)	Minimum Annual Royalty (4)	Minimum Royalty per Acre (5)
1.	TLL	63,894	1.1.14	£10,000	(A) 3.1
2.	Trinidad Central Oilfield Ltd	64,434	1.1.23	10,000	3.1
3.	United British Oilfields Ltd	5,986	1.7.15	(1) 2,000	(B) 6.7
			1.7.20	(2) 3,000	10.0
4.	Br. controlled Oilfields	5,367	9.9.25	2,000	7.5
5.	TLL	4,255	6.4.26	2,000	9.4
6.	Trinidad Pet. Dev. Co.	19,620	28.6.27	7,000	7.0
7.	T'dad Central Oilfield Ltd	6,996	9.4.29	3,300	9.4
8.	Pet. Dev. Co.	1,999	1.7.15	2,000	(C) 20.0
9.	C.C. Strollmeyer	500	23.11.25	500	20.0
10.	U.B. Oilfields	1,000	2.3.24	1,000	20.0
11.	Pet. Dev. Co.	1,865	19.2.25	2,250	24.1
12.	TLL	2,694	9.8.33	3,000	22.2
13.	Kern T'dad Oilfields	436	19.2.25	1,200	(D) 55.0
14.	Apex (T'dad) Oilfields	93	1.7.22	1,000	(E) 215.0
15.	" " "	52	1.7.26	440	169.0

Source: Compiled from data obtained from the Holland Report and mining leases published as Council Papers.

things certain internal economies, and better planning. When areas become isolated in this way the system breaks down.

In the case outlined earlier, the company wished to lease seven selected patches amounting to 6,770 acres (out of 64,434 acres) not concentrated around one centre and in no way conforming to the policy of "spheres of influences".

Period of Lease

While from the point of view of the company concerned the period of lease should be long enough to allow the lessee to be justified in the investment of his capital, it is also obvious that from the point of view of the state, limitation of the period of lease is essential to allow the state to adjust the rates and conditions of lease. Especially is this case with a commodity like oil, the price and market conditions of which can change rapidly.

The granting of leases for the period of fifty years (e.g., the TLL lease granted in January 1914, with an option of renewal for a further thirty years at rents and royalties not exceeding 150 per cent of the original rates) was unsound policy, at least from the point of view of the economic well-being of the colony. These conditions meant that whatever the upward movements in the price of oil for the first fifty years, the rents and royalty rates could not be changed and that in the event of a renewal, even if prices rose by 200 or 300 per cent, royalty rates could not be altered in step with such price changes to the benefit of the revenue. But there was a further condition to these leases: a "specific declaration made in 1913 to lease holders that no export duty would be levied so as to increase the agreed rate of royalty".[12]

In the event, the colony government considered itself bound hand and foot in its dealings with the companies.

Minimum Annual Royalty or Dead Rent

The dead rent was a minimum annual charge made in respect of each acre of land leased to the company. It was intended as a spur to the companies to expand production. Whenever the amount of royalty payable on oil produced exceeded the amount of the minimum annual royalty then the latter was waived and ordinary royalty alone was paid.

Tables 41, 42, 43 and 44 give some idea of the variations in dead rent charged and also of the periods over which the various leased areas produced enough to cover their dead rents. The chief purpose of the dead rent was to discourage or prevent the locking up of large stores of oil for the long period of a lease.

But, as stated earlier, dead rent was charged per acre of the leased area. Column 5 of table 40 shows to what extent the charges per acre varied. It is necessary, therefore, to determine, whenever possible, the factors which influenced this variety of charges per acre.

There would appear to have been two factors at work. The first concerns the regressive nature of the rents, that is, the charging of smaller rates per acre for large holdings. This policy is shown in table 40 as operating in respect of varying areas of land leased to various companies. In table 45, however, the policy is brought out most plainly in the agreement made in 1918 with S. Pearson and Son. Note how the fixed rents diminished with acreage.

Table 41 TLL Oil Mining Lease – Council Paper 1/1914

Year	Production in Tons '000	Production Free of Royalty	Royalty £'000
1914	8.5	0.4	0.8
1915	15.3	1.4	1.4
1916	30.5	2.1	2.8
1917	98.9	9.7	8.9
1918	133.2	14.2	8.9
1919	152.3	17.7	10.1
1920	155.7	23.5	10.0
1921	148.6	24.2	10.0
1922	116.2	19.6	10.0
1923	155.3	18.5	10.3
1924	232.8	18.7	16.3
1925	246.3	11.5	17.6
1926	203.2	8.1	14.6
1927	156.1	9.6	11.0
Total	**1,863.1**	**176.1**	**132.8**

Note: The dead rent was £10,000. Because of the concession of oil free for use on the works the company did not pay substantially more than the minimum until after 1923.

Table 42 Trinidad Central Oil Field Ltd Lease 1923

Year	Production in Tons '000	Free Royalty '000 Tons	Royalty £'000
1923	17.7	2.2	10.0
1924	11.7	1.3	10.0
1925	10.3	1.4	10.0
1926	13.6	2.3	10.0
1927	6.8	2.5	9.0
Total	**60.0**	**9.7**	**49.0**

Source: Holland Report.

Note: This lease earned nothing approaching its dead rent. In fact it has paid as royalty about £1 per ton on the oil available for sale, that is, after deducting the royalty-free oil used in drilling and other operations.

Table 43 Apex (Trinidad) Oil Fields Limited

Year	Production '000 Tons	Royalty Free '000 Tons	Royalty £'000
1/7/22–31/12/22	0.8	0.07	0.5
1923	15.4	0.7	1.3
1924	11.5	0.9	1.1
1925	26.8	1.6	2.5
1926	25.8	0.7	2.5
1927	17.6	0.3	1.7
Total	**98.0**	**4.2**	**9.6**

Note: Drawback payable in respect of half year ending 31 December 1922.

Table 44 Apex (Trinidad) Oil Fields Limited

Year	Production '000 Tons	Royalty Free '000 Tons	Royalty £'000
1/7/26–31/12/26	Nil	Nil	0.2
1927	4.6	0.2	0.8
Total	**4.6**	**0.2**	**1.0**

Note: Both areas approached the minimum royalty by output within eighteen months.

The preceding agreements and those labelled (A) in table 40 focus attention upon the ruling policy at the time when the early concessions were granted. Perhaps it was thought that every concession was necessary to attract the large investor. In the leases labelled (A) the royalty on 65,000 acres was £10,000, that is, about 31 shillings per acre.

Each of the leases in category (B), table 40, is less than one-tenth the size of those in (A) and the dead rent is larger: 6.7–10 shillings per acre. In category (C) the leased areas are yet smaller and rate per acre goes up correspondingly.

There was at least another important factor operating in respect of the dead rents charged on the lease labelled (D) and especially those labelled (E). Before discussing those, however, it is necessary to make certain comments on the policy of charging regressive rates of dead rent in the hope of attracting the large investors.

Table 45 Showing the Regressive Nature of the Fixed Rental Policy

Maximum Area of Lease	Fixed Rental (£)	Rate per Acre (shillings)
250 acre or less	500	40
Up to 500 acres	800	32
Up to 1.000 acres	1,000	20
Up to 2.00 acres	1,500	15
Up to 3.000 acres	2,000	13/4
Up to 5.000 acres	2,500	10
Up to 7.000 acres	3,310	9/5
Up to 10.000 acres	4,000	8/-
Up to 14.000 acres	5,500	7/10
Up to 20.000 acres	7,000	7
Up to 30.000 acres	9,000	6
Up to 100.000 acres	10,000	1

Note: From an agreement made in 1918 with S. Pearson and Son. Note how the fixed certain rents diminish per acre with increased acreage leased.

Firstly, it really was not necessary to grant any such concessions. The company reports indicate that investors were optimistic about the prospects of oil in Trinidad. They tried to outbid each other; to tie up as large an area as possible lest their competitors secured some area that proved in time to be particularly prolific.

Secondly, as Sir Thomas Holland observed, this scheme of regressive charges resulted from "confusing the fundamental objects of a prospecting licence and a mining lease".[13] In the case of prospecting licences large areas are granted over unproved ground but the period of alienation is short. For mining, however, the heavier burdens involved should not be undertaken except on ground already proved or on ground adjacent to proved ground. The need was rather "to impose conditions which ensure systematic prospecting in advance by qualified technologists".

It was his opinion that "there would have been fewer company failures and consequently less money wasted[14] if a more conservative policy had been adopted in the early days of Trinidad oil".[15]

To return to the categories (D) and (E) in table 40: the lease in category (D) paid dead rent at 55 shillings per acre. Those in category (E) paid 215 and 169 shillings per acre, respectively. It can be argued that here also the policy of regressive rents is evident. That may have been the case but it would appear that that policy was the least important factor operating in these categories of leases.

The principle operating in these latter cases was much more sensible. Although the rent is expressed per unit of area it was influenced by the well-known high productivity of the subterranean areas involved.

The areas involved closely adjoined the fields in the Fyzabad area where Apex (Trinidad Oilfields) Limited, operating on private lands, had made successful borings and earned large profits. This Fyzabad area was particularly prolific. Its contributions to total output were as follows:

1929	47.0%
1931	56.5%
1933	67.8%
1935	55.13%
1936	56.7%
1937	53.47%
1938	45.5%

The imposition of a high dead rent in this area was therefore justified.

The leases listed in table 40 were granted up to 1933. The year 1934 marked the dividing line between the old and the new policy of charging dead rents. Sir Thomas had recommended, *inter alia:*

a. a small dead rent for the first five years;
b. a rent not to exceed £1 per acre as it then became a handicap rather than a spur to greater activity.

The Land (Oil Mining) Regulations 1934 adopted some of these recommendations. The following table shows the new dead rent charges as listed in Schedule II of the regulations.

During the first year of lease 4s per acre
During the second year of lease 5s per acre
During the third year of lease 7s per acre
During the fourth year of lease 9s per acre
During the fifth year of lease 12s per acre
During the sixth year of lease 15s per acre

Some of the subsequent leases followed this pattern closely. It is obvious, however, that this pattern of dead rent was inadequate for prolific areas such as Fyzabad discussed earlier. Modifications were therefore made according to the known productivity of the adjoining areas.

Royalty Rates

"Compared with the terms granted in most countries there is no doubt about the leniency of the royalty rates hitherto demanded by the Government of Trinidad."[16] In the early leases the royalty rates were 2s to 3s per ton. The standard rate in Burma and Assam was approximately 4s per ton.[17]

The royalty rates and conditions of the early leases changed with each lease and also with the volume of output. It is therefore necessary to discuss royalty rates in terms of

a. variations of the rates over time;
b. variations as between companies;
c. variations with volume of production.

With regard to (a) there seems to have been a desire, even in the case of the earliest leases, to make the royalty rate approximately 10 per cent of the value of crude oil. It would appear, however, that the fear of fluctuating revenues (especially adverse fluctuations with falls in price) led to the royalty rate being fixed not as a percentage of the market value but as the money equivalent of what 10 per cent of the price was at some given date. In the first decade of the century when the price of crude oil was about £1 per ton the royalty rate was fixed at 2s per ton, that is, 10 per cent.

In 1924, effect was given to an Executive Council decision of April 1923 making 3s per ton the new royalty rate. Here again the assumption was that 3s would represent 10 per cent of price or declared value. Price fluctuations were taken into account and it was agreed that this 3s per ton valuation should be subject to change but only within certain limits. Either party could at the end of the first three years or for subsequent triennial periods ask for an adjustment of the rate by arbitration within the limits 2–5s per ton – 20–50s per ton being considered the range within which prices would be expected to move. The royalty on natural gas sold was also increased from ld to 2d per 1,000 cubic feet.

Regressive Royalty Rates (with Regard to b and c Aforementioned)

The companies which were earliest in the exploitation of Trinidad oil received exceedingly lenient treatment. In their anxiety to exploit the mineral resources of the island, the inter-departmental committee gave every inducement to the early companies. One wonders whether this question of granting favourable terms to the pioneer was first taken too far especially in an industry like oil where, although the losses can be great, the chances of making huge profits are considerable.

Consider the case of the lease to TLL granted in January 1910, over 63,894 acres of land. Here it was stipulated that, in the event of a renewal for 30 years, the royalties were not to exceed 150 per cent of original rates.

Further, under the agreement 10 per cent of the oil produced could be taken in kind by the government as royalty or in cash at the rates of 2s per ton of crude oil, while the annual output remained below 100,000 tons. For higher outputs there was a sliding scale reduction of royalty until, at 133,333 tons and over, royalty became 1/6 per ton.

This condition seems to have been directed at encouraging output. The idea was to reward large-scale production. The decision to grant this facility seems from the point of view of the welfare of the island to have been misguided.

If an oil company can increase its output to 133,333 tons, it is obviously in a position to make profits and needs no further encouragement in the form of reduced royalties.

Sir Thomas Holland suggested that this provision for reduction of up to 6d in the rate of royalty on production over 100,000 may have been a by-product of the Colonial Office negotiation with United British West Indian Petroleum Syndicate in 1913 and represented a premium on work on a large scale.

It would appear that since increases in production up to the point where the royalty rates were reduced could very well have resulted not from any greater effort or money cost in drilling and so on, but largely from the productive nature of the wells sunk, a higher royalty rate would have been in order and may not have been resented by the successful company. Even if it is difficult to defend a higher rate of royalty on the larger output, the charging of a lower rate on the higher output seems quite unjustifiable from the point of view of the colony's economy.

Products Free of Royalty

In addition to the leniency of the royalty rates, there were further concessions in the form of royalty-free crude oil, bituminous minerals and natural gas used on the premises.

It does seem reasonable not to charge royalty on that amount of fuel used by the company in the actual process of exploring, drilling and refining. In the case of Trinidad, however, the concession applied to fuel consumed on the works, in domestic consumption in houses and offices of

Table 46 Royalty-Free Crude Petroleum as Percentage of Production (by Companies)

Company	'000 (Tons) Production	Royalty-Free Crude	Per Cent of Prod. That Is Royalty Free	Royalty Paid £'000
UBOT 1915–27	451.3	27.7	6.1	44.6
UBOT 1914–27	13.2	4.9	36.8	3.8
TLL 1914–27	1,853.1	176.1	9.5	132.8
TLL. 1923–27	74.4	5.4	7.3	10.3
Trinidad Central Oil 1923–27	60.0	9.7	16.2	49.0
Petroleum Development Company Ltd 1915–27	467.1	41.7	8.9	45.1
Petroleum Development Company Ltd	8.6	0.9	10.6	6.4

Source: Holland Report.

agents and workmen, and also to motor spirit used in the cars of employees of the company.

It is difficult to check the amount consumed in isolated fields. Also where private lands are worked together with Crown lands it is difficult to apportion the amount so used as between private and Crown land. Table 46 shows that for the seven cases listed, the amount of total production up to 1927 that was royalty free varied from 36.8 to 6.1 per cent of total production. The average was 9.1 per cent. Normally, however, the percentage allowed royalty free dropped relative to output, see table 46.

Sir Thomas Holland estimated that the products allowed in 1927 free from excise duty to five of the principal companies would have paid as revenue if sold to the public for some £13,000–£14,000 ($62,400–$67,200).[18]

Other Conditions

Under all the leases the lessee was required not only to pay a certain minimum royalty as a spur to operating, but was also further required to operate a certain number of rigs for drilling; drill a certain minimum number of feet or produce a certain minimum output of crude oil.

In the case of the TLL lease of 1924, for example, the obligation was to drill with at least 3 rigs until a yearly output of 150,000 tons was obtained. (Note that it was at slightly below this output that the royalty rate reduction was operative.)

Table 47 Showing Minimum Footage and Output Obligations

Extent of Area Acres	Minimum Footage to Be Drilled	Minimum output of Crude per Acre Tons
Not exceeding 1,000	2,500	4,000
Over 1,000 but not over 2,000	4,000	8,000
Over 2,000 but not over 3,000	6,000	12,000
Over 3,000 but not over 5,000	6,000	20,000
Over 5,000 but not over 7,000	6,000	25,000
Over 7,000 but not over 10,000	7,500	30,000
Over 10,000 but not over 14,000	7,500	45,000
Over 14,000 but not over 20,000	7,500	50,000
Over 20,000 but not over 30,000	7,500	75,000
Over 30,000	2,500 per 10,000 acres	2½ tons per acre

The Petroleum Development Company, 1915, however, having a smaller lease, 2,000 acres, and a dead rent £2,000, was obligated to use three rigs continuously for twelve months or until an aggregate of 20,000 tons of crude oil was obtained. This minimum annual output remained obligatory until replaced by a supplementary lease granted in 1926.

As in the case of royalties, changes were made in 1924 in the obligation concerning footage to be drilled or output to be produced (see table 47).

As pointed out earlier, this obligation to drill or produce a certain amount was independent of and in addition to payments of prescribed dead rent. In the case of TLL, in addition to these two sticks the carrot of reduced royalty rates was added. For most of the others the goads were the only inducement: there was a definite and arbitrarily fixed task for every year without even the possibility of a good year compensating for a bad one.

The minimum footage obligation could be useful where a company is slacking. But the minimum royalty payment should be enough to spur it to action except in the case of a company that as an extreme example and for no apparent reason preferred to pay the dead rent, rather than incur the cost of drilling.

The obligation has no determinable relationship to exploitation. It becomes meaningless if the amount specified is too small and may merely be a waste of money if it is too large.

The annual output obligation introduces a risk of unknown value. At the time when these obligations were imposed, very little was known of the geology of the island. It was not known, except vaguely, which areas were profitable and at what depths.

The companies could not be certain of producing oil from any well. In addition, it may be uneconomical in some years to produce oil to the full quantity prescribed in the lease and in others profitable to push production to excess.

The possibilities open to leases were therefore as follows:

i. "burying pipe", a name frivolously applied by the companies to useless drilling to make up their footage obligation;
ii. drilling a number of shallow useless wells which are cheaper than one deep well which may have been profitable;
iii. turning out oil at temporarily unremunerative prices.

The Growth of the Industry

Production

Table 48 indicates clearly that in spite of the difficulties which faced the industry in its embryonic period in the nineteenth century when lack of finance capital and absence of modern deep drilling equipment restricted development, growth in the twentieth century has been, to say the least, spectacular.

The very great rate of growth of production from 37 barrels in 1908 to 927,000 barrels in 1916 can be explained simply in terms of the general tendency of industries or economies to register rapid rates of growth in their infancy when initial production is low and a doubling of the rate of output does not in fact mean a particularly high total output. The rate of growth is high, the volume of production low.

After 1916, however, the industry was more or less established; the periods of spectacular oil strikes became more commonplace and a rapid rate of growth of production reflected also a large volume of production. The industry had passed beyond the take-off stage.

Between 1917 and 1920, production increased from 1,602,302 to 2,083,110 barrels, an increase of about 400,000 barrels in four years, which is not a particularly rapid rate of growth.

One of the main factors making for this relatively slow rate of expansion of output was the shortage of drilling equipment due to World War I. The year 1920, however, saw an easing of the flow of machinery to Trinidad.[19] With the availability of machinery, drilling operation was intensified. But

Table 48 Annual Production of Petroleum

Year	Production in Barrels ('000)
1919	1,841.0
1920	2,083.1
1921	2,354.1
1922	2,444.6
1923	3,050.7
1924	4,058.0
1925	4,386.5
1926	4,971.4
1927	5,380.8
1928	7,684.5
1929	8,715.7
1930	9,418.9
1931	9,743.5
1932	10,126.1
1933	9,561.3
1934	10,894.3
1935	11,671.2
1936	13,237.0
1937	15,502.9
1938	17,737.2
1939	19,741.6

Source: Trinidad and Tobago Administration Report of the Inspector of Mines (1939–41).

in spite of the increase in the supply of drilling equipment the output of crude oil did not increase very rapidly and this was partly the effect of price and market conditions.

Although 1920 production was 2,083,110 barrels versus 1,841,036 for 1919, exports of crude oil and its products dropped from 40 million impertial gallons, that is, 1.14 million barrels (1919) to 36 million imperial gallons, that is, 1.03 million barrels (1925); and at the close of 1920 there were large stocks of oil awaiting export.

Another indication of the trend could be seen in the bunkering trade: 150 vessels took 9,707,047 gallons of oil for fuel in 1919. The 1920 figure was 13,519,148 gallons for 218 ships. This figure distorts the true situation, however, for the increase in the bunkering trade was confined to the early part of the year. Bunkering trade fell drastically in the second half of the year and continued to fall in 1921 when 176 ships took 6,750,569 gallons of fuel oil. Even in 1923 bunkering accounted for only 7,467,376 gallons for 167 ships.[20]

The prosperity and optimism of the immediate post-war years had suffered a check, with a resultant difficulty of finding markets for oil products, a reduction in the number of ships plying the high seas and demanding bunker fuel and consequently a fall in prices. The influences are reflected in the slowing down of the rate of growth of production and drilling in the oil industry in Trinidad in the period 1920–22.

The average values of petroleum exports had fallen thus: crude oil from 4.37 pence per gallon in 1920 to 1.77 pence in 1922.

Fuel oil 3.03 (1920) to 2.46 (1922)
Kerosene 10.20 (1920); 10.82 (1921) to 7.46 (1922)
Gasoline 15.62 (1921); 6.13 (1922); 8.07 (1923)
Lubrication oil 21.06 (1922) to 7.60 (1923)

The period 1923–27, however, shows a quickening of the pace of production. But even in 1923 the companies were complaining of the unfavourable effect of the financial conditions and development was chiefly confined to the already established companies and in already proven fields and no great amount of prospecting work was undertaken in new areas.

In the proven fields, however, a large and active drilling programme was undertaken and as can be seen in the table 48, the 1923 output was 606,000 barrels more than that of 1922. And this rapid rate of increase in output continued to 1925 when output was 4.38 million barrels. Meanwhile the 1924 output was 1,007,000 barrels more than that of 1923; 1925 production 329,895 barrels more than 1924.

Between 1925 and 1927 the growth of output continued apace. The 1926 production was 585,000 barrels more than output for 1925. In 1926 there was a considerable increase in the drilling programme in proven fields and considerable prospecting work in new fields with promising results.[21]

The year 1927 saw a continued increase in activity. An activity, however, which, great though it was, was hindered by two factors:

a. TLL which was developing as the chief refiner of petroleum not only from its own fields but from the fields of other operators, found that its pipeline and refining capacity were inadequate to deal with its own production from the fields at Fyzabad and Barrackpore and at the same time cope with the increased production of other companies whose output it purchased. While efforts were being made to expand refining, storage and pipeline capacity, TLL curtailed its own production for a considerable part of the year.

b. The low prices ruling for petroleum products in the world markets for the greater part of 1926. In spite of these handicaps, output for 1927 was 400,000 barrels more than that for 1926.

The quickening of pace which characterized the period 1923–27 was further accelerated in 1928 and 1929. Production in 1928 was 2.3 million barrels over that of 1927 (43 per cent increase) and in 1929 it was 1.1 million barrels over 1928. This acceleration of output was achieved in spite of the low world price of petroleum products in 1928. It was due partly to the removal of the bottleneck which was observed to restrict output in 1926–27, that is, refining, storage and piping capacity. TLL having completed both its programme of expansion in its Pointe-a-Pierre refinery, and also its pipeline programme, was able to cope with a larger throughput and therefore ceased the restriction of production mentioned earlier.

The year 1929 was in many respects a remarkable year for the Trinidad petroleum industry. Not only did the industry, for the first time, exceed the production of petroleum in British India, thereby becoming the premier producer in the British Empire, but for the first time the value of petroleum exports amounted to more than 50 per cent of total domestic exports.[22]

After 1929 and until 1933–34, the rate of growth of output slackened again so that the production curve is for the most part a gently rising plateau except for the year 1933 when production actually fell below that of the previous year by nearly 550,000 barrels.

This is the period of the Great Depression and the slackening of growth of output is largely attributed to it. Not only has the price of petroleum fallen with other prices. In addition there has been considerable over-production in the United States and other countries (e.g., Russia).[23] This over-production caused prices to fall even further.

Owing to the continued fall in prices of petroleum products most of the companies drastically curtailed their operations.

It is interesting to note that once an oil industry has established certain producing areas, demand and price conditions do not reverse production trends except where active measures are taken to cap wells. This is especially the case where the major part of production is through flowing wells. The oil will flow in spite of prices. This situation can be further ensured by mining lease obligations which stipulate minimum production and boring conditions. Of course with drastic price reduction these obligations can be shown to bear heavily on producers.

But the situation was not altogether bleak. In certain cases companies which had entered into sales contracts for their products based on prices ruling in the United States of America benefited from the rate of exchange since the departure of Great Britain from the gold standard.

1934 to 1939

For the whole of this latter part of the period under study, production of crude oil was expanding consistently at a rate of about 2 million barrels per annum.[24] For the years 1934–39, the percentage production increase for each year over the previous year until 1939 was as follows:

1922	5%
1934	13.9%
1935	7.13%
1936	13.2%
1937	17.12%
1938	14.4%
1939	11.3%

Between 1935 and 1939 the industry experienced a truly rapid rate of growth. The footage drilled in those five years exceeded the total of the period 1867–1934.[25] The crude oil produced exceeded the output from 1908 to 1931 and the quantity exported exceeded the total for 1909–32. Up to 1935, a total of 213,992 acres of Crown lands had been leased. During the period 1935–39, the number of mining and exploration leases granted increased from 34 to 90. Between 1935 and 1939 the average number of daily paid employees of the companies increased from 5,454 to 10,273 and the total number employed, including those employed through contractors, increased from 7,331 to 13,074.

There was also a considerable increase in the number of wells started. As against an annual average of 98 wells during the period 1930–34, the average for 1935–39 was 224.

This increase in activity and output would have been influenced by active market conditions, but as will be shown later, the upsurge in output was assisted to a considerable degree by the technological innovations which were introduced.

1939: War Year

The production of crude oil in 1939 was not as great an increase in production over that of 1938 as was the case with 1938 production over that of 1937, that is, 11.3 per cent versus 17.12 per cent increase, respectively. The year 1939, however, deserved special mention if only for the reason that it is the first year of World War II and that certain important developments and policy measures were being contemplated and given effect in respect of the oil industry.

Although increases in production in many of the immediately preceding years were due primarily to more intensive exploitation of already proven fields, the increase in 1939 was due partly to the "exceptionally satisfactory results which had been obtained from new wells drilled, the initial yields of which have been higher than usual".[26]

If the boundary of the study be pushed somewhat, the period 1939–40 saw the peak of production in Trinidad. Thereafter production fell in 1941 and until 1952–53 remained almost constant at about 19–20 million barrels. The period 1939–40 therefore saw the last big oil strikes or rather exploitation of oil strikes before the middle of the century. In many respects, therefore, the period 1919–39 covers the era of rapid development into maturity, of the Trinidad oil industry. It is the period of spectacular growth. It is invidious to predict future trends especially in view of recent attempts at marine exploration. From this position in time, however, the period under study covers a most interesting era for oil in Trinidad and for the economy as a whole.

The war had its effects directly and indirectly on oil production. Immediately upon the outbreak of war, efforts were made to increase output and this is reflected in the figures for monthly production for 1939, where the months of October and December show an increase over the preceding months.[27] "This rapid increase in production was made possible by opening up certain reserve wells which had been wholly or partially closed in."[28]

The demand of the war also resulted in the restriction of production to already proven areas to maintain the already achieved output without making greater demands on scarce resources for mining and exploring. This policy had its effects in slowing down and actually stopping the rate of growth of output for some time after the war.[29] There were no new proven areas to replace those which were no longer prime producers.

Trinidad Development versus Others

The growth of the Trinidad oil industry has been measured in terms of production of crude oil from year to year. In this section it is proposed to consider its growth in relation to that of some other oil industries.

The Report of the Mines Department for 1928 and the local mining interests at the time put great emphasis on the fact that in that year "for the first time on record Trinidad has produced more oil than any other part of the British Empire".[30] One would get the impression that Trinidad had outstripped India in the rate of growth of production. What is important to realize, however, is that Trinidad did not surpass an Indian production that was itself expanding. The comparison is somewhat similar to that between young athletes outstripping an old man past his prime, one albeit who may have lived too fast too early.

India had raced quickly to her peak. After 1926 with production at 8.5 million barrels production stagnated and the production levelled off until 1929.

In 1916 Trinidad on the other hand was producing only 0.9 million barrels. Trinidad's rate of growth was therefore large but it should not really be compared with the rate of growth in India over the same period.

If we took 1928 as a base year for both industries then Trinidad's output for 1926 would be only 12.1 and India's 102.3. India was past her peak.[31]

Refining

Trinidad was developing into an important centre for the refining of crude petroleum. Although the fact of an almost stagnated domestic production causes a greater emphasis to be placed on refining today, it should not be thought that this aspect of the industry is of recent origin and importance.

The factors which influenced the growth of Trinidad as a refining centre have their origins from the very inception of its oil industry. When, therefore, an attempt is made to analyse the refining section of the oil industry it is necessary to take the analysis back into the period immediately preceding the prescribed period of the study. This section therefore treats

1. the origin of the refining sector of the industry;
2. the growth of refining capacity;
3. the growth of actual refinery throughput;
4. the relation between (2) and (3) and between both and production.

With regard to (1), one of the most important motives that operated with Randolph Rust, the earliest pioneer of Trinidad oil, was the creation of an exclusively British source of oil for the British Navy; and this is long before the policy of converting naval vessels from coal to oil burners was introduced.[32]

This objective seems to have been shared by the British government, for later, with the object of providing a supply of oil fuel according to admiralty standards specification, it stipulated in the earlier leases in Trinidad that the lessees provide a refinery for at least 50 per cent of the crude output within two years after attaining certain levels of production which were arbitrarily fixed for each lease.

Here, therefore, we have the first factor influencing the birth and growth of the refining industry. It is quite probable that the oil operators would of their own accord have turned to refining. Sir Thomas Holland[33] found in 1927 that companies were making a loss on field operations and made profits, where these were made, only on refinery operations. It would seem, therefore, that if they became aware of the profitability of refining they would have entered the field also.[34]

What is in question, however, is whether such developments would have been as fast as was eventually the case. It seems most reasonable to conclude that the mining lease obligations led to the start of refining and that the profitability of the refining process, once realized, led to an acceleration of growth of refining capacity, an acceleration of growth which if viewed in isolation may give the impression that the earliest obligations to refine were unnecessary as a stimulus to this aspect of the development of the industry. However, without the obligation, companies may have refined in their home countries.

The Growth of Refining Capacity

It has not been possible to obtain accurate data on the refining capacity of the industry before 1934. Nor will it be particularly useful to use capacity throughput relations in the post-1934 period and by working backwards arrive at a rough figure of capacity. Growths in capacity and throughput were not uniform in time nor in respect of each other. The first part of this analysis would be, therefore, largely descriptive with some calculation and approximation included wherever they can be justified.

If, as a start, the figures given for oil refined in the colony in table 49 are taken, one can be sure of a minimum figure for capacity. Capacity could not have been less than throughput.

Table 49 Comparative Statement of Oil Refined in the Colony

Year	(1), Barrels	Column (1) as Percentage of Production (2), %
Before 1920	4,051,373	–
1920	1,395,487	66.97
1921	1,806,016	76.72
1922	1,820,018	74.43
1923	2,360,279	77.37
1924	3,433,902	84.62
1925	3,790,343	86.41
1926	3,786,876	76.18
1927	4,796,233	89.14
1928	6,725,383	87.51
1929	7,642,726	87.68
1930	7,989,679	84.82
1931	6,899,144	70.80
1932	7,635,296	75.39
1933	9,129,810	95.49
1934	10,846,584	99.55
1935	11,148,285	95.51
1936	13,028,161	98.42
1937	15,111,046	97.47
1938	17,596,932	99.21
1939	19,414,920	98.34
Total	**160,408,493**	

In 1920, therefore, capacity must have been at least 1.4 million barrels; 1921, 1.81 million barrels; 1922, 1.82 million barrels. After 1922 the amount of oil refined increased by the fact that in 1922 TLL completed its refinery at Pointe-a-Pierre and made considerable additions to its storage capacity there. We have also some further information. The Mines Department reports that "more than half the oil produced in the Colony is now refined at Pte-a-Pierre". Production for 1922 was 2.44 million barrels. TLL's refining throughput was therefore at least 1.22 million barrels, which must be the minimum of that firm's refinery capacity. There were no reports of further additions to TLL or any other refineries until 1926 when considerable additions were made. It would appear, therefore, that capacity between 1922 and 1926 must have been about 3.79 million barrels.

In 1926 TLL made considerable additions to its refinery at Pointe-a-Pierre by the addition of a Dubbs cracking plant for the treatment of fuel oil. By 1927 this company found its pipeline and refining capacity inadequate to handle production from its own wells and the production of those small non-refining companies that sold their crude to TLL. By 1928 TLL had further increased its refining capacity at Pointe-a-Pierre and had removed this bottleneck to increased crude oil production. The bottleneck is evident in the 1925 and 1926 throughput figures: 3.79 million and 3.786 million barrels, respectively.[35]

It would appear, therefore, that since the bottleneck in TLL refining coincides with the stagnation of total throughput, and TLL was even in 1922 refining at least 70–75 per cent[36] of total throughput, then the figure of 3.8 million barrels taken as refinery capacity for 1926 seems reasonable.

There may have been excess capacity elsewhere but there is no evidence of it and this seems unlikely. When in 1931 UBOT Point Fortin wished to increase refining capacity they had not the money for it.

In 1928 refinery throughput was 6.7 million barrels, nearly 2 million barrels more than 1927. It would appear that the increase in refinery capacity resulting from the 1927 programme was of this order of magnitude, that is, 2 million barrels.

After 1928 the picture becomes somewhat more difficult as for each of the years 1929 to 1933 inclusive, one or other of the operators beside TLL installed refineries. Except in one case, that is, UBOT in 1932, no figure is given for the capacity of the new refinery. For this period, therefore, it becomes more difficult to take refinery throughput as the possible level of capacity. Of course it can still be used as a minimum figure. The developments after 1929 were as follows:

1929 (1) West India Oil Co. set up a new refinery near La Brea to handle the production of Trinidad Oil Fields Operating Co. Ltd.

(2) TLL made large additions to its refinery and storage department at Pointe-a-Pierre.

1930 (1) Apex (Trinidad) Oilfields Ltd installed a plant for the recovery of casing head petroleum spirit from natural gas.

(2) The West India Oil Co. completed a pier and refinery at Point d'Or

1931 (1) TPD completed the installation of a plant for recovering light products from natural gas.

(2) UBOT attempted to raise fresh capital for a new refinery and loading facilities at Point Fortin.

1932 (1) UBOT raised the capital and were well on the way to completing a refinery with capacity of 1,000 tons of crude per 24 hours.
(2) KTO also started construction of a refinery of the same capacity.

1933 (1) UBOT and KTO schemes were completed.
(2) TLL commenced replacing the old Dubbs Cracking Plant installed in 1926 at Pointe-a-Pierre. See figure 5 of the new Dubbs Cracker.

What emerges? It is known definitely that the UBOT and KTO schemes of 1932–33 would together have increased capacity (each with a throughput of 1,000 tons per day, i.e., about 5.1 million barrels per year) in 1933 over 1932.

The increase in throughput 1928–1933 is 36.2 per cent. The figure of 9.1 million barrels for 1933 can therefore be regarded as a minimum figure of capacity. Obviously this minimum figure of 9.1 million barrels is an understatement of the true throughput capacity.

For it can be arrived at by adding the two UBOT and KTO developments of 1932–33 to the 1928 approximation of 3.8 million barrels per year. This excludes the additions made by West India Oil Co. and TLL in 1929, and

Figure 5: Historic 69 Tons Forged Reaction Chamber built in 1932 in Great Britain by Thos Firth and John Brown for terminal cracking of gas oil at Pointe-a-Pierre Refinery. Forged from a single steel ingot of 170 tons, it was at that time the largest single piece hollow forging ever made. In Dubbs Terminal Cracking Service from 1933.

the Apex and TPD schemes of 1930–31. This point seems to be further reinforced by the fact that in 1934, without there having been any evidence of further additions to the refining equipment, the figure of 14 million barrels is given as the refinery capacity of six main refineries.[37]

Before 1934 refinery capacity lagged slightly behind crude oil production. In 1921–22 and again in 1926–37 the inadequacy of refinery capacity led to bottlenecks which were quickly overcome and in some measure anticipated the subsequent rapid advances in crude production.

Up to 1934, therefore, whatever excess capacity there was in the petroleum refinery sector (i.e., excess in terms of production) was purely temporary. Wherever it existed it was a healthy sign of the anticipation of the growth of output.

After 1934 and perhaps for some time previous to this, however, refinery capacity was outstripping production and refinery throughput at a very fast rate. See table 50 which shows that refinery capacity was greater than crude production by 28.6 per cent in 1934; 39.1 per cent in 1935; 32.2 per cent in 1936; 12.9 per cent in 1937; 33.03 per cent in 1938; 21.07 per cent in 1939.

But production was also growing apace; 1940 was the peak year for production at 22.29 million until 1953 at 22.34 million barrels. During World War II the need to produce as much as possible with as little machinery and drilling as possible led to a curtailment of production to 20.5 million barrels in 1941. By 1941, however, refinery capacity, stimulated by the need for aviation and other fuels for war, had jumped to 32.0 million barrels, that is, 156.1 per cent of production, and refinery throughput was 20.81 million barrels.

The wartime conditions may have accelerated the pace but the period 1932–39 had set the pattern which in the 1920s appeared to be only tentative. Trinidad was to experience a change of emphasis in its petroleum industry, a change which had been predicted by Sir Thomas Holland. After referring to Trinidad's advantageous geographical position in the shipping and air routes of the Western Hemisphere, the large production of Latin America and the unstable political conditions there, the fact that Trinidad's domestic production could not last forever and that her land space did not give much hope of new finds, the difficulties of marine drilling and the expensiveness of the latter *vis-à-vis* land field operations, he stressed the opportunities of Trinidad as a refining base.

What are the merits and demerits of this change? This is not a purely theoretical point, for the sale of TLL to an American company, Texaco, elicited criticism based on this same question that the Americans were

Table 50 Comparison between Production, Refinery Capacity and Refinery Throughput

Year	Production (Million Barrels)	Refinery Capacity (Million Barrels)	Refinery Capacity as Per Cent of Production	Refinery Throughput (Million Barrels)
1934	10.9	14.0	128.4	10.8
1935	11.7	16.2	138.5	11.1
1936	13.2	17.5	132.5	13.0
1937	15.5	17.5	112.9	15.1
1938	17.7	25.6	144.6	17.6
1939	19.7	23.9	121.3	19.4
1940	22.2	28.5	128.3	22.1
1941	20.5	32.0	156.1	20.8
Index of Production, Refinery Capacity and Refinery Throughput: 1938 = 100				
1934	61.58	54.7		61.4
1935	66.0	63.3		63.1
1936	74.6	68.4		73.9
1937	87.6	68.4		85.8
1938	100.0	100.0		100.0
1939	111.3	93.4		110.2
1940	125.4	111.3		125.6
1941	115.8	125.0		118.2

interested in Trinidad only as a refining centre and so safeguards were necessary for continuation of production.[38]

Clearly refinery capacity was outstripping production at such a rate as to be justified by one or two possibilities or both.

a. The growth in domestic production of crude oil was expected to continue and increase at a faster rate.
b. It was intended to increase the emphasis on refining and depend on imported crude oil to fill the breach.

With regard to (a), (1) by 1939 a considerable part of the land areas of the southern part of the island had been explored by the then modern methods. But deeper formations were not yet explored. (2) Marine drilling as a possibility was likely to be expensive and likely to take some time to develop. (3) The old wells could not be expected to last forever. Some were already approaching twenty years old, some were past this figure and were experiencing senility and decline.

Point (b), therefore, became the likeliest prospect and in the 1930s crude oil was imported,[39] at first in relatively small, but in time, increasing quantities to meet the needs of an expanding refinery capacity.

The period after 1932 is most important in studying the refinery aspect of the industry and since the picture can be clarified somewhat by overstepping the bounds of the period of study it is proposed to do so.

One of the main objections to such a switch of emphasis has been that it may lead to a reduction of the rate of increase of royalties. Of course if production is neglected and minimum royalties and dead rents are not drastically upgraded, government revenue from this source can suffer. But the problem of ensuring maximum exploitation of crude petroleum should not prove insuperable.

It would appear, however, that if, as has been generally agreed, petroleum is a wasting asset and the life of the fields and reservoirs cannot be extended indefinitely, then stimulating the refining sector is at once an advantage in that it will fill, partially perhaps, a vacuum that would be left if production fell off drastically.

The refining process will not employ as many as the exploration and drilling processes. Further, not many roads will be built opening up the forests. But if the life of the fields had come to an end without the starting of a refinery process these losses would have been the same and their impact would have been greater.

The question of revenue is, however, of a different nature. If the reservoirs would have died then the anti-refiners have no case anyway. But even if crude production were allowed to stagnate at the expense of refining, the case for increasing refining capacity has, on the revenue level of the argument, at least one good point.

Since the larger profits of the industry are made in refining and not production[40] then if the imported crude is cheaper than domestic crude the profits they can make will be larger and what is most important for revenue purposes, the income tax contributions of the company will be larger.

Further, royalty rates, though variable, are fixed for a period and by a condition of the lease they are not varied easily. Further, in the pre-war context companies were assured that "no export tax would be possible which would merely increase in another way the rate of royalty settled by the lease".[41]

Of course it can be argued that the loss in local payments through wages and so on may be greater than the gain in income tax. But if senility of the fields had already set in or was approaching, this objection falls to the ground; and in that event the case for refining is incontestable.

The argument in favour of increasing refinery capacity is further strengthened by the case of India. As has already been indicated, India's production stagnated and even declined. Her production which in the 1920s and early 1930s averaged about 8 million barrels, fell in 1938 to 2.6 million barrels. It would appear that her refinery capacity was neglected at the time when her wells were flowing. Her 1938 refinery capacity was so low that in the *Petroleum Industry Bulletin Statistics* it is included among "others" which totalled 3.5 million tons. Trinidad's refinery capacity was then 3.9 million tons. Thereafter, however, India's refinery capacity increased and by 1955 was 3.8 million tons to Trinidad's 6 million.[42]

Compare also the Trinidad and Venezuela rates of growth of refinery capacity. The first Venezuelan refineries were built in the early twentieth century. Important operations started in 1925 in San Lorenzo with a refinery capacity of 10,000 barrels. In 1925 Trinidad's refinery capacity was at least 3.8 million barrels. It would be remembered that one of the arguments advanced by Sir Thomas Holland in favour of establishing Trinidad as a refinery centre was the fact that Latin America being unstable politically, companies interested in establishing a refinery would seek alternative, politically more stable centres in which to invest the large sums involved in refinery establishment. This opinion seems to have been amply borne out in part at least. In Venezuela "in the period 1931–1938 no new installations were built, since the existing capacity sufficed for the local demand of the period".[43] After 1938 capacity increased rapidly through expansion of old refineries and new construction.

It would appear that, as in Trinidad, government pressure aided the establishing and expansion of the refining industry. From 1945 onwards, in Venezuela and "largely as a result of their 1943 contractual obligations negotiated by the government, various petroleum companies intensified the construction of refineries so that by the end of 1950 the daily refinery capacity had been expanded to 375.000 barrels and by the end of 1952 to 484,000 barrels daily".[44]

It would be interesting to find out why it was required that refineries be set up in Trinidad instead of in the United Kingdom. This is contrary to what is recognized as the colonial form of investment. The answer may perhaps be seen in naval strategy. Actually Britain herself was late in developing her refinery capacity. In 1938 her capacity was only 1.9 million metric tons versus 3.9 million for Trinidad, and 2.7 for Venezuela; meanwhile Germany's was 2,400 metric tons and France's 7,600 metric tons.

Technological Advances

The section dealing with the growth of refinery capacity has already given some indication of the speed and readiness with which capital was invested in new machinery and methods of refining.

In addition to those advanced there were others in the field of exploration, drilling and pumping.

Exploration

Before 1931 the element of uncertainty involved in choosing the site for a well was very great. Wildcatting was the rule. In 1931 geophysical surveys were undertaken for the first time, mainly in the southern mining district. The 1936 Mines Department Report records the examination of extensive areas by geophysical (mainly gravimetric) methods.

By 1937 the use of seismic surveys had superseded the gravimetric method. This method, though more expensive than either of the two already mentioned, was probably the most positive method of determining the earth's substrata (especially where, as in Trinidad, the rock formations are sharply contrasted).

Drilling and Extraction

Mention has already been made of the poor drilling equipment which introduced the Trinidad oil industry. Maximum depth of the first drilling equipment was 160 feet. The drilling equipment improved steadily with time. But even in 1929 the importation of better drilling equipment and better control fittings could be referred to as features of operating technique most deserving of note.[45]

It was not only in the actual drilling of wells that techniques improved. One of the most and pressing problems was in the considerable volume of gas at very high pressure (up to 5,000 pounds per square inch) with which much of the petroleum in Trinidad was associated. The efficient control and conservation of this natural gas contributed a problem which was rendered more difficult by the complicated geological conditions of Trinidad.

The early history of oil in Trinidad has constant references to gushers and blowouts which were not only dangerous to human life but greatly reduced the flowing life of the well.[46] If the pressure in the well could be maintained, it acted as a natural syphon forcing the oil to the surface. If the pressure fell quickly, as happened in blowouts, pumping had to be resorted to very early in the life of the well.

The year 1929 saw (a) the use of Barytes-laden mud fluid for overcoming high gas pressures and (b) an increase in the amount of coring carried out in high pressure wells.

The 1931 report records the more general use of tubing in new wells brought in, which had a beneficial effect on the flowing life of the well. It helped to control the rate of escape of the high pressure gas in the reservoir.

In 1932 one company commenced experiments with replacing gas both in high pressure and low pressure zones with the hope that such repressuring and resealing would lead in time to a further natural repressuring of the well. It was thereby hoped to restore the well after a few years as a flowing well.

By 1936 the large companies tended to produce flowing wells through smaller chokes than formerly with the effect, in general, of reducing gas/oil ratios.

In the case of older wells various methods were used for lifting the oil to the surface. Table 51 shows the number of wells operated by the various methods. Note the number of wells that were freely flowing as a percentage of the total and accounting in 1939 for 67.5 per cent of total production, the number depending on pumping and especially the increase in 1935 of those operating the plunger lift. But even in 1939 this "very efficient method of lifting oil" was not widely applied.[47]

Pipelines, Storage and Piers

With the increases in refining capacity, the new techniques for drilling wells and bringing the oil to the surface, there was a corresponding growth of storage capacity, pipeline mileage and deepwater loading piers. Table 52 shows the growth in the storage capacity and pipeline mileage for the period 1934–39.

Both in 1923 and 1927, however, there is evidence of some activity in pipeline laying. In 1923, TPD constructed a pipeline linking up the field at Palmiste to a new tank at Claxton Bay, a deepwater pier. The General

Table 51 Methods of Recovering Oil, 1930–1939

Type of Wall	1930	1931	1932	1933	1934	1935	1936	1937	1938	1939	1939 Prod. in '000 Barrels
Flowing	170	185	215	231	222	235	273	357	405	478	13,311
Pumping	544	504	469	443	465	466	469	491	507	572	4,026
Plunger lift	–	–	–	–	–	8	38	68	108	138	1,553
Air or gas lift	19	13	15	29	70	105	107	100	75	69	734
Baling or swabbing	38	60	81	124	140	146	140	139	157	91	20
Displacement pump	–	–	6	9	9	14	15	15	8	9	37
Casing head gasoline returned to crude	–	–	–	–	–	–	–	–	–	–	61
Total							**1,041**	**1,170**	**1,260**	**1,357**	**19,741.6**

Source: Compiled from reports of the Mines Department.
Note: In 1939, flowing wells were 35.2 per cent of all wells but accounted for 67.5 per cent of output.

Table 52 Storage Capacity and Pipeline Mileage, 1934–1939

	1934	1935	1936	1937	1938	1939
Storage capacity (million barrels)[a]	3.9	4.09	4.03	4.5	4.8	5.1
Pipelines (miles)[b]	130	159	200	225	285	290

[a]The data for tank storage capacity are exclusive of the flowing tanks connected to the wells and the crude oil settling tanks.
[b]The data for pipelines refer only to main trunk lines. In addition there were many miles of subsidiary linking pipe.

Petroleum Company Ltd also laid pipelines from the rich Fyzabad fields to Los Bajos to link up with the pipeline of the United British West Indies Petroleum Syndicate Ltd and from there to Point Fortin where the petroleum was sold to the United British Refineries Ltd.

In 1927, at the time of the refinery and pipeline bottlenecks referred to earlier, TLL replaced its 6-inch pipeline from Fyzabad to Pointe-a-Pierre by a 10-inch pipeline and by 1929 had established a network of pipelines stretching across the width of the southern half of the island.

Piers

Even in 1923 there were four outlets for petroleum products:

Claxton Bay – Trinidad Central Oilfields Ltd
Pointe-a-Pierre – TLL
Brighton – Trinidad Lake Petroleum Company Ltd
Point Fortin – United British Refineries Ltd

Over the period under study these facilities were improved and a new one added. For example, in 1927 Trinidad Lake Asphalt carried out a considerable extension of its pier at Brighton. The same year Trinidad Oilfields Operating Company installed a new tank near La Brea and erected a pier at La Brea Point on which the shipping line was laid. This increased the shipping depots to five, all of which were capable of handling ocean-going vessels. In addition there were loading facilities at Port of Spain, the capital. In 1932, UBOT commenced construction of a pier, 8,500 feet long, capable of accommodating vessels with a draught of 30 feet. This addition to loading facilities went hand-in-hand with the increase in the company's refinery capacity (1,000 tons per day) referred to earlier.

The Direct Money Contributions of the Oil Industry to Government Revenue and the Domestic Economy

The analysis that follows seeks to establish two things:

1. It seeks to set out that part of government revenue that is derived directly from the oil industry. Where there are indirect contributions mention will be made of them but in view of the many possible degrees of indirectness it had been decided to restrict the analysis mainly to those revenue items that are readily identifiable.
2. It seeks to establish the money value of the contribution made by the oil industry to domestic incomes. The analysis does not cover the whole of the twenty-one year period of the study. It covers only the years 1927–39 inclusive. It is the only long period for which it has been possible to construct a consistent series from the data available. It has the advantage of covering in a continuous sequence
   a. one of the early boom periods of the industry;
   b. the Depression years and
   c. the post-Depression recovery, in that order.

Contributions to Revenue

The data have been set out in two series. Series I includes all the items which the Petroleum Association of Trinidad[48] considers as contributing either directly or indirectly to government revenue.

Series II is obtained by deleting from series I anything that is not a direct contribution of the oil operators to revenue.

The important item here is excise duty on petroleum products. It has been decided to exclude this item, as it is not a part of the cost to the petroleum industry. It is borne by the consumer; the petroleum industry being merely the agent for collecting the duty.

There is another reason why series I has been presented, however. There is a limited sense in which part of the earnings of the excise are a contribution by the companies to revenue: the Petroleum (Amendment) Ordinance No. 34/1930 provided for an increase in excise duties on petroleum spirit from 6d to 8d per gallon. The colonial secretary, speaking on the bill, referred to the fact that the oil companies, of their own accord, wished to reduce the price of petrol by 2d. When they informed the government of their intention, government promptly annexed the 2d by way of excise. Any improvement in sales which the companies hoped to effect by the reduction was therefore nullified and the government benefited by 2d per gallon on petrol. In this limited sense, therefore, they contributed a part of their share of the price of petrol to the government revenue. Of course it is quite possible that, as the unofficial members of council demanded, the excise duty on gasoline may, by a system of price controls, have been increased without the additional duty falling on the consumer.

In the final analysis, however, excise duty on petroleum products, as excise duty on rum (the contribution of which to revenue was larger than that of petroleum), was a charge on the consuming public[49] and should not be placed in the same category as, say, royalty payments, company tax and so on.

In the case of series I the contribution of the oil industry to revenue varies from 15.13 per cent in 1927 to 26 per cent in 1939.

Of course in this case as well as in series II there are certain indirect or second round additions to revenue, for example, taxes on salaries and wages paid. In series II the contributions vary from 12.16 per cent in 1927 to 19.4 per cent in 1939. Series II is the more accurate approximation of the industry's contribution to revenue.

Series II clearly shows the extent to which the policy of fixed rates in monetary terms of royalty and so on has influenced government revenue. In spite of variations in the price of petroleum products throughout the period the amount going to the government is more or less constant at about $1 million (BWI) until 1935. Except for the year 1930, royalty contributions increased with output. This was so even in the Depression years when the government was getting a larger proportion of the smaller export proceeds of the industry. Revenue from company tax, however, slumped from 1931 to 1933 as profits declined.

The chief factors in the post-1935 increase in the revenue contributions of the industry are company tax and royalties. The twofold increase in the former was due to the larger profits earned from greater output and increased prices. The increases in the latter are due to increases in production. It should be observed, however, that in view of the very substantial quantities of oil produced from private oil rights, government royalty receipts could not reflect the full increase in total output. Note, for example, the growth in item 16 in table 53, the greater part of which would have been private royalty payments.

In considering this question of the share of royalty payments accruing to private individuals it will be useful to bear in mind that little of it seemed to have gone into productive undertakings. It is interesting to note that in many cases some of those who received such payments were

Table 53 The Oil Industry's Contributions to Government Revenue ('000)

		1927	1928	1929	1930	1931	1932	1933	1934	1935	1936	1937	1938	1939
1.	Customs and excise	268.80	221.20	388.50	593.80	706.00	749.80	642.00	777.80	866.20	1,065.40	1,450.60	1,609.80	1,599.70
2.	Licences and other internal revenue not otherwise classified	285.10	323.40	379.80	52.10	61.20	54.70	57.80	52.10	68.50	80.40	78.70	85.40	71.40
3.	Taxes on incomes	378.80	435.60	284.90	384.50	260.80	318.20	252.50	365.20	249.10	592.00	532.90	879.70	794.20
4.	Royalities, land sales and so on	271.30	315.40	425.70	389.30	429.20	428.60	491.70	460.80	527.40	674.40	796.90	947.40	1,091.60
5.	Others	134.20	116.40	101.70	87.90	63.30	50.00	53.00	48.30	43.40	68.20	143.20	192.10	82.90
6.	Total contributions to revenue (series I)	1,338.20	1,412.00	1,580.60	1,507.60	1,523.50	1,601.30	1,497.00	1,704.20	1,754.60	2,480.40	3,002.30	3,714.40	3,739.80
7.	Series I less excise duty on petroleum products	203.10	278.40	339.70	363.80	478.10	457.90	518.40	542.50	641.10	704.00	805.40	890.60	963.80
8.	= Total contributions to revenue (series II)	1,075.10	1,133.60	1,240.90	1,143.80	1,045.40	1,143.40	978.60	161.70	1,113.50	1,776.40	2,196.90	2,823.80	2,776.00
9.	Series I as per cent of gross government (%)	15.13	15.32	16.35	16.17	17.96	18.28	17.11	19.41	18.84	18.70	22.90	26.00	26.00
10.	Series II as per cent of gross government (%)	12.16	12.13	12.84	12.27	12.33	13.05	11.19	13.23	11.95	13.40	16.80	19.70	19.40

(*Table 53 continues*)

Table 53 The Oil Industry's Contributions to Domestic Incomes ('000) (*continued*)

		1927	1928	1929	1930	1931	1932	1933	1934	1935	1936	1937	1938	1939
11.	Salaries	3,036.50	1,021.70	1,028.60	1,453.00	1,103.40	990.60	1,089.50	1,230.00	1,276.40	1,477.70	1,847.90	2,421.80	2,731.70
12.	Wages		2,056.70	2,245.50	2,421.00	1,540.10	1,504.20	1,731.60	1,729.10	1,915.90	2,270.40	3,127.20	3,935.60	4,103.90
13.	Contractors payments mostly wages	700.50	444.90	679.90	613.50	284.30	396.70	470.80	443.60	491.40	816.20	1,232.60	1,626.60	1,416.00
14.	Total salaries, wages, contractors payments	3,736.00	3,523.30	3,954.00	4,487.50	2,927.80	2,891.50	3,291.90	3,402.70	3,683.70	4,564.40	6,207.60	7,984.00	8,251.60
15.	Local purchases of materials	1,828.10	1,487.10	1,593.10	1,652.30	812.6	1,055.10	1,202.70	1,246.00	1,071.20	1,771.10	2,574.10	3,030.40	2,809.00
16.	Other local expenditure private royalties, rents retainer fees	965.20	815.10	902.20	795.10	791.90	1,139.10	831.10	827.30	941.80	1,416.30	1,984.80	2,963.10	2,906.20
17.	Total contributions to incomes (series I)	6,529.30	5,834.50	6,449.30	6935.40	4,532.30	5,085.80	5,325.90	5,476.00	5,696.70	7,751.70	10,766.50	13,977.60	13,966.80
18.	Series I less local pur chases of materials = series II	4,701.20	4,347.40	4,856.20	5,283.10	3,719.70	4,030.70	4,123.20	4,230.00	4,625.50	5,980.60	8,192.40	10,947.20	11,157.80
19.	Series II + one half local purchases of materials = series III	5,615.20	5,090.90	5,652.70	6,109.20	4,126.00	4,558.20	4,724.50	4,853.00	5,161.10	6,866.10	9,479.40	12,462.40	12,562.30
20.	Contributions to revenue (series II)	1,075.10	1,133.60	1,240.90	1,143.80	1,045.40	1,143.40	978.6	1,161.70	1,113.50	1,776.40	2,196.90	2,823.80	2,776.00
21.	Total contributions to revenue and incomes	6,690.30	6,224.50	6,893.60	7,253.00	5,171.40	5,701.60	5,703.10	6,014.70	6,274.60	8,642.50	11,676.30	15,286.20	15,338.30

also those persons responsible for the chain of cinemas which exist in Trinidad.[50]

Series I, however, shows total contribution to revenue increasing even until 1933 $1.6 million and the main cause was the contribution of the excise duty which was increased at the end of 1930 from 12¢ per gallon to 16¢ per gallon. Incidentally there seems to have been no lasting adverse effects on sales consequent on this increase. Actually domestic consumption of petroleum products (spirit and oil) for 1930–38 were as follows:

Year	Petroleum Spirit '000 Gallons	Petroleum Oil '000 Gallons
1930	2,329.6	702.3
1931	2,509.7	718.8
1932	2,413.2	716.1
1933	2,715.8	729.9
1934	2,870.0	694.0
1935	3,064.0	746.8
1936	3,449.2	779.5
1937	3,966.2	845.0
1938	4,603.4	966.7

In the final analysis the effect of including excise duties changes the picture to the extent that whereas, with excise duties excluded, the contribution to revenue (1927–35) is static, with duties included one gets the picture of a growing contribution to revenue. Note the growth of petroleum excise duties from $203,100 in 1927 steadily to $963,800 in 1939, a more than 470 per cent increase in thirteen years.

Column (2) of table 54 indicates that between 8.3 and 11.9 per cent of the value of exports went to the government in the form of revenue of one kind or another. The post-1935 period shows a distinct improvement in the share going to the government.

The Contribution to the Economy as a Whole

Here the same period is covered as for the analysis of the contribution to government revenue alone.

As in the case of contribution to revenue it has been found useful to set out the data for the contribution of the industry to the local economy in

Table 54 Contributions of Oil Industry to Revenue and Incomes

Year	Wages Bill as Percentage of Pet. Exports (Value) (1)	Contribution to Revenue II as Percentage of Pet. Exports (2)	Total Contribution to Revenue and Incomes as Percentage of Pet. Exports (3)
1927	33.4	9.6	59.9
1928	29.4	9.5	52.0
1929	27.0	8.5	47.1
1930	33.5	8.5	54.1
1931	31.3	11.2	55.3
1932	25.3	10.0	49.8
1933	30.4	9.0	52.7
1934	24.2	8.3	42.8
1935	27.7	8.4	47.1
1936	28.7	11.2	54.3
1937	32.9	11.6	61.8
1938	33.7	11.9	64.6
1939	30.9	10.4	57.5

more than one series. The Petroleum Association of Trinidad includes the item "local purchases" in its statement of the contribution of the industry to local incomes. It does appear, however, that not all of it should be included. The difficulty is to decide what part of it to include.

It is doubtful that all of the, say, $1.8 million represented by local purchases in 1927 was spent on domestically produced commodities. They were purchased locally as opposed to mining and refinery equipment purchased directly by the company from Great Britain and the United States, but they were most likely commodities imported by local merchants and then resold to the oil companies.

Firstly, the $1.8 million (1927) representing locally produced goods purchased by a single industry is large by any standards. Compare this with the value of exports of sugar ($3.8 million) which supported more than 100,000 of the population; coconut products ($0.9 million); asphalt ($2.2 million); cocoa, as yet still buoyant ($8.0 million).

Secondly, the economy was, apart from oil and asphalt, agricultural. The needs of the oil industry are mostly for capital or semi-capital goods, spare parts, bricks, cement, gravel, sand and so on.

Thirdly, note the statements made in the Legislative Council by representatives of the oil industry on the dependence of the mercantile class on the oil industry. The merchants imported goods for sale. Their sales of domestically produced goods were small.

In the debate on preferences for empire oil, for example, Lt Col. Hickling[51] observed that

> the largest class of imports appertaining to any one of the industry imported into the Colony from any one country is that of mining machinery from the UK The figure of 1932 was £152,000 and the total direct imports from the UK in that year by the Oil Industry were worth £214,250. There were also indirect imports of approximately half that amount.

The last sentence provides a clue. The indirect imports are those imported by local merchants and resold to the industry. In 1932 Lt. Col. Hickling estimated them at about £100,000 ($500,000) from the United Kingdom alone. Table 53b shows that the figure given for "local purchases" in that year was about £200,000 ($1 million). Without putting too fine a point to it, therefore, it would appear that a figure equivalent to one half the stated "local purchases" would be a closer approximation than either that which includes the whole of that item or that which excludes it entirely.

Fourthly, the item "local purchases", large as it is, does not cover all local expenditure on goods and services. Apart from wages and so on, there is another item "other local expenditure" which covers private royalties, legal fees and so on.

But it is impossible to determine exactly the part of this item that was due to local products. It has therefore been decided to present the data in three series:

Series I contains all items as given in Petroleum Association statements.
Series II contains all items in series I, less the total or "local purchases".
Series III is a compromise. It is series II plus 50 per cent of "local purchases" as in series I.

For the purpose of this study, series III appears to be the most accurate.

Salaries and Wages

The first point to be emphasized is the way in which employment follows the same pattern as in any other industry. There is nothing counter-cyclical about it. After rising steadily until 1927 employment drops by more than 2,000 in 1928 and then levels off until 1930 when under the impact of the Depression there is a steep, swift fall. In 1930, employment in the industry was 8,172. Within a year, in 1931, it had fallen to 5,027. Thereafter the revival was slow and was not completed until after 1935 when it climbed steeply. The numbers employed nearly doubled between 1935 and 1939.

There was a corresponding trend in the wages bill. The total of salaries, wages and contractors' payments (mostly wages) dropped from $4.5 million in 1930 to $2.9 million in 1931 and $2.89 million in 1932. Not even in 1935 was the 1930 level regained. But the post-1935 period saw the wages bill increase from $3.7 million (1935) to $8.25 million in 1939. The percentage increases in the wages bill were

1935 – 8.3 per cent
1936 – 23 per cent
1937 – 36 per cent
1938 – 28.8 per cent
1939 – 4 per cent

As indicated earlier this increase in employment and the wages bill resulted from increased activity to meet increased world demand for petroleum products.[52] The strikes for better wages and riots of 1937 against oil and sugar also contributed.

The absence of complete data prevents an analysis of the relationship between wages and the total current costs of the industry. Column (1) in table 54, however, shows the relationship between the wages bill and the declared value of petroleum exports. There was, in addition to the value of exports, certain revenues from the domestic sales of petroleum products. These have not been included as their total value is not known. The industry estimates that 4–10 per cent of production is consumed locally. In that case the value of total output is increased correspondingly and the ratio of wages to total values of finished products falls. Taking the declared export values alone, however, it is seen that labour earned its highest share of the export values of the industry in 1938 (33.7 per cent) and 1930 (33.5 per cent), with 1927 (33.4 per cent) not far behind.

The figures for the total money contributions to the economy (item 21of table 53) are arrived at by summing the contributions to revenue series II and the contributions to incomes series III.

Here also the most interesting aspect of the period is the rapid rise after 1935. Column (3) of table 54 indicates the portion of the export values of petroleum products that accrued to domestic income earners and to government revenue. As with wages and revenue, 1938 was the best year, the contribution being 64.6 per cent of oil exports.

The Companies

The number of firms operating for oil in Trinidad varies considerably throughout the period.[53] In 1919 there were thirteen. By 1920 there were twenty; 1923, seventeen; 1928, fourteen; 1929, fifteen; 1934, fifteen; 1938, nineteen. These variations can be explained in terms of new entrants, amalgamations, absorptions, liquidations, associations, formation of subsidiaries and outright buying up of one company by another.[54] Thus:

1. *The Trinidad Central Oilfields Ltd,* for example, registered in February 1917 was an amalgamation of (a) a company of the same name registered in January 1911; (b) the Ortoire Syndicate Ltd; (c) oil concessions of Mayaro (Trinidad) Ltd and Cruse Syndicate Ltd.
2. *Trinidad Consolidated Oilfields Ltd,* the whole of the initial capital issue (£400,000 in £1 shares) of which was applied for privately, was formed "to acquire all or any of the shares of Oropouche Oilfields Ltd and Moruga Oilfields Ltd both incorporated in Trinidad".[55] In February 1936 it acquired the leasehold property, 1,886 acres, of M.L. Bramson, with plant, machinery and so on for £168,000 payable in cash and £133,500 in 267,000 fully paid shares of 10/- each.

   In 1939 its capital was increased to £600,000 including five and a half per cent debentures to the value of £75,000 which were created in October 1938 and were held by British Burmah Petroleum Co. Ltd. These were redeemable by a cumulative sinking fund over fifteen years.
3. UBOT, registered in 1913, acquired the properties of Trinidad Oilfields Ltd. In 1919 it acquired by purchase the whole of the share capital of United British West Indian Petroleum Syndicate Ltd, one of the earliest operators in the field and the company with which the earliest and most favourable (to the company) lease arrangements were made.[56] The transactions involved £450,000 in fully paid £1 shares and cancellation of £125,000 indebtedness of the syndicate.

   At the end of 1933 it acquired from the Petroleum Development Co. Ltd on a royalty basis, Crown leases adjoining the company's own Parry Lands fields comprising 2,000 acres of proven and semi-proven land and a number of producing wells. It also purchased as part of the arrangement a freehold estate of 245 acres in the Point Fortin district containing potentially oil bearing lands near which its refinery was situated. By 1939 it owned over 1,000 acres of freehold land and oil-rights over a total of 40,000 acres.

4. *Apex (Trinidad) Oilfields Ltd,* was registered in 1919 to acquire from Anglo-French Exploration Co. Ltd, the British Borneo Petroleum Syndicate Ltd and others, certain oil rights in the Fyzabad district.[57]
5. *Premier (Trinidad) Oilfields Ltd,* registered in Edinburgh in April 1934 as the Caribbean Oil Co. Ltd (a private company), was converted into a public company in October 1936. In July 1937 it acquired a lease granted by government over the Stollmeyer Concession of 500 acres in the Palo Seco district.
6. *Lipana (Trinidad) Oilfields* was registered in June 1930 with a share capital of £500,000 in £1 shares; but TLL and its association owned £225,000 of the shares.
7. *Trinidad Northern Areas Limited* was registered in January 1936 with capital of £150.00 comprised of 50,000 £1 shares in each of the categories "A", "B", and "C". All the shares were issued and ranked equally and were held equally by TLL, UBOT and D'Arcy Exploration Co. Ltd. The accounts were issued to shareholders only.
8. *Trinidad Oilfields Operating Co. Ltd,* registered in August 1926 is a subsidiary of Standard Oil Co. New Jersey.
9. *Petroleum Options,* registered in May 1925 is a reconstruction of Petroleum Options Ltd.
10. *Antilles Petroleum Co. (Trinidad) Ltd,* incorporated in 1935 is a subsidiary of the Canadian firm of McCall Frontenac Oil Co. Ltd. Its capital in 1939 was £200,000 in £1 shares fully paid up.

The giant of the industry was Trinidad Leasehold Ltd (TLL) with a share capital at the end of the period, 1939, of £1,700,000 in £1 shares. The original share capital in 1913 was £550,000 which was increased in December 1917 to £850,000. In 1918, 112,000 fully paid shares were issued to acquire the undertaking of Trinidad Oil and Transport Co. Ltd. Further, 132,500 shares were taken up at par under an option granted to the lenders of an advance of £200,000 the debt being reduced by this amount. The lenders further agreed to accept 37,500 shares at 36s each in discharge of the balances of £67,500.

In May 1919, the capital was further increased to £1,500,000, and 349,750 shares were offered to shareholders at 45 shillings each on the basis of one for two.

In January 1928, 262, 312 shares were offered to shareholders at 55s each (one for four). In October 1936 the capital was increased to £1,700,000 by the creation of 200,000 shares of £1 each. Also 327,890 shares were offered to shareholders at £3.15s each (one for four). It had interests in North Venezuela Petroleum Co. Ltd, Tocuyo Oilfields of Venezuela Ltd, Lipana Trinidad Oilfields Ltd, Trinidad Northern Areas Ltd, and Lipana Trinidad Oilfields. Thus, therefore, the growth of the capital of the largest petroleum company in Trinidad. It was the largest producer of oil; owned the most extensive pipeline network, stretching across the entire width of the Island; purchased the crude oil production of most of the minor and some major oil operators and was the largest refiner of crude oil not only in Trinidad but also in the British Empire.

In 1938, the year of its silver jubilee, its efforts were described as "twenty five years of tremendous industrial development started with the drilling of a single well on the beach at Forest Reserve and going on to the erection of the largest oil refinery in the British Empire".[58] Even in 1939–40 its refinery input capacity was in excess of 1 million barrels a month.

The other four of the five main operators were UBOT (capital in 1939 £1,850,000); Apex (£550,000); Trinidad Central Oilfields (£1,350,000) and TPD (£1 million).

The figures for profits for 1938–39 are as follows:

	£'000 (£1 = $4.80 BWI)
TLL	£580.5 after depreciation
Apex	£256.0 after writing off £151.5 amortization of wells
TPD	£181.1 after writing off £153.8 wells plants and so on
UBOT	£83.3 after writing off £172.6 depreciation
Trinidad Central Oilfields	£28.3

Tables 55 and 56 give further data on the financial position of the "Big Five" and the less fortunate companies for the years 1938–39.

In so far as the amount going to profits is concerned, TLL is in the lead. But the most profitable enterprise for the shareholder was Apex. Note that while TLL's maximum dividend rate was 30 per cent in 1928–29 and her minimum was 5 per cent in 1930–31 and also that for two years

Table 55 Dividends Declared by the Five Most Successful Companies

Year	Trinidad Central Oilfields (%)	Trinidad Leaseholds (%)	Trinidad Petroleum Develop	United British		Apex
				Pref + Participating	Ordinary	
1919	10					
1919–20	10	12½				
1920–21	Nil	Nil				
1921–22	-	-				10
1922–23	-	10				25
1923–24	-	17½				25
1924–25	-	25				25
1925–26	-	27½			7½	50
1926–27	-	27½			7½	80
1927–28	-	27½			-	35
1928–29	-	30	20		-	52½
1929–30	-	7½	-		-	25
1930–31	-	5	-		-	20
1931–32	-	12½	20		-	25
1932–33	-	15	-		-	35
1933–34	-	12½	-	9 3/7	3	35
1934–35	Nil	17½	35	11 4/7	7½	27½
1935–36	6	25	20	12 1/6	8¾	35
1936–37	6	30	7	12 1/6	8¾	45
1937–38	7	27½	12		-	40
1938–39		15	15			30
1939		7½				12½
1940						12½

Note: Pref. dividend (8 per cent) payable March and September paid to 1939–40.

1920–21 and 1921–22 no dividends were paid, Apex was moving on an altogether higher plane. Her minimum figure was 10 per cent for nine months in 1922. Her highest dividend was 80 per cent in 1926–27. Thereafter she averaged about 30–55 per cent. In no year did she fail to declare dividends.

In the depression years 1930–33 when even TLL's dividends fell to 5 per cent in 1930–31 Apex's figure was 20 per cent. It should be borne in mind,

Table 56 Financial Situation of Oil Companies, December 1938

Companies	Profits	Credited Balance	Total	To Dividends	To General Reserve	To Taxation Reserve
			£'000 (£1 = $4.80 BWI)			
Trinidad Central Oilfields	28.3	3.7	32.0	20.2	7.5	
Trinidad Consolidated Oilfields Ltd	-22.2	16.8	5.4			
TLL	580.5	145.9	726.4	245.9		310.0
Trinidad Petroleum Development Co.	181.1	59.2	240.3	150.0		25.0
UBOT	83.3	13.1	96.4	24.4	50.0	
Apex (Trinidad) Oilfields Ltd	256.0	128.4	384.4	165.0		80.5
Petroleum Options	-7.0	-20.9	-27.9			
Premier (Trinidad) Oilfields Ltd	-11.0	-9.8	-20.8			
Lipana Trinidad Oilfields	5.2	-90.5	-85.3			
Antilles Petroleum Co.	-114.0	-311.6	-425.6			

Note: In addition, Apex put £8,300 to directors' further remuneration and £239,400 to cash.

however, that in every case the capital base of TLL was larger than that of Apex.

Trinidad Central Oilfields declared 10 per cent in 1919 and 1920. Thereafter she paid no dividends until 1936 when 6 per cent was declared.

TPD declared 20 per cent free of tax in 1928–29. Thereafter no dividends were declared until 1931–32 (20 per cent less tax); in 1934–35 dividend was 35 per cent less tax; in 1936–37 it was 7 per cent less tax and in 1939 it was 15 per cent.

UBOT whose capital was composed partly of preference shares participating in dividends and ordinary shares paid the preference rate of

8 per cent for the entire period and in addition paid an additional 1 3/7 per cent in 1934; 3 4/7 per cent in 1935; 4 1/6 per cent in 1936; 4 1/6 per cent in 1937.

Ordinary shareholders received nothing except for 1926 and 1927 when dividend was 7½ (less tax) and again for 1934–37 inclusive when dividends were 3, 7½, 8¾ per cent, respectively.

J. Fred Rippy, in his article "Trinidad and Ceylon: Two Profitable British Crown Colonies",[59] gives at once an interesting though at times distorted picture of the profits earned in the Trinidad oil industry. He states, for example, that Trinidad Central Oilfields Ltd paid an annual average dividend of 6.1 per cent during the 32 years beginning 1919.

Table 55 of this chapter indicates, however, that his findings could only have been arrived at by averaging dividends over long periods. What is most interesting for any study and in particular for the study of the interwar period is that for fifteen years – 1921–1935 inclusive – no dividends at all were declared. The post-1935 upturn did restore the company's profits but during the long depression period no dividends were paid. The finding that this company was for long periods in great difficulty is further supported by the account given on pages 139–40 of this chapter which shows that things went so badly with the company that it had to reduce drastically the area under lease.

Sir Thomas Holland in his report came to the conclusion that companies were making losses in their field operations and made profits only on their refinery operations. He was only partly right. In the case of TLL, the large-scale refiner (producer of crude), high dividends were indeed regularly declared. The lesser refiners were not so fortunate. But in the case of Apex the success cannot be explained in terms of refining at all. She did none. Her success was due entirely to her good fortune in having obtained the Fyzabad area for her drilling. It is the most prolific (per acre) oil-bearing area in Trinidad.

But even the success of TLL was greatly influenced by that of Apex. The TLL 1926–27[60] report, for example, records that profits were maintained though prices were falling and that this was possible because the company's refinery input rose from 444,989 tons in the previous year to 475,882 tons, that is, 7 per cent. "Of this total 229,303 ton were purchased against 171,454 tons a year ago", and "it paid to refine a greater amount of purchased oil than oil produced on the company's properties".

The bulk of the oil purchased came from Apex with whom the contract was in 1927 renewed for a further ten years. "The basis of the contract is a minimum price plus a percentage of the refining profits so that in a period of falling prices for refined oil products TLL is protected."

"The company is in a strong position by reason of its field reserves; its purchases of oil contract with Apex and its sales contract with the British Admiralty for fuel oil. On a small scale it is a complete and well organized unit in the oil industry."[61] One might go further and say that it was demonstrating certain definite monopolistic tendencies.[62]

In assessing the profitability of the industry, however, it is necessary to look not only at the "Big Five" but at the other companies which have perhaps just broken even or more likely have made consistent losses and continued operating in the hope of tapping rich fields. They also make a contribution to the island's economy. They have to pay royalties or dead rent whether or not they made a profit. They contribute to wages, salaries, and road construction. Their wage rates have to be the same as or similar to those of the successful operators.

Table 56 gives an idea of their position in 1938–39. Note the current deficits of £22,200 for Trinidad Consolidated Oilfields making her net credit position only £5,400, and the current debit of £7,000 of Petroleum Options swelling her overall debit position to minus £27,900. Lipana Trinidad Oilfields made a profit of £5,200 which only served to reduce her debit balance position to £85,300.

The Antilles Petroleum Co.'s, current deficit of $547,200 (£114,000) made her overall position minus $2,043,000 (£425,600).

There are other companies whose financial position cannot be given as they were subsidiaries of other companies and did not publish separate account or others which supplied statements of accounts only to shareholders. It is clear, however, that Rippy's[63] observation in a footnote to his article that his statistics "take no account of capital losses, which were rare", needs some modification.

In 1945, for example, Commander H.V. Lavington[64] who represented the oil interests in the Trinidad and Tobago Legislature reported that since the commencement of the industry there were thirty-nine companies in operation. Of these twenty were liquidated; of the nineteen remaining twelve were still operating. Of the thirty-nine only six had ever paid dividends. Further, the total cash capital invested in the thirty-nine companies was approximately £15 million ($72 million) and over twenty years the total dividends paid were less than half the capital.

Of course, in view of his interest in the industry and the subject of the debate[65] any consideration of Lavington's account of developments should make allowance for a possible lack of objectivity on his part. Some of the thirty-nine companies were subsidiaries whose accounts were never published. If and how these were manipulated will perhaps never be known. The fact is, however, that considerable losses were made. That considerable profits were also made is also beyond question.

7

Population

The previous chapters have analysed the developments in the various export industries and in imports. It is necessary to turn now to the question of the population and its growth to see how it compares with the trends in the productive spheres of economic activity.

The Long-Term View

Table 57 gives a picture of the growth of population before and including the period under study. It covers the period 1891–1946. It has been thought necessary to go beyond 1939 because the 1946 census was the first after the 1931 census and provides the only really accurate data about population growth for the latter part of the study. It will be noted, however, that estimates for 1939 are also included. These, while perhaps less accurate than the census figures and while giving end of year figures as opposed to the April figures of the census years, will give some indication of what the situation was at the end of the period under study.

Immediately, the rapid rate of growth in the population from 1891 to 1946 is evident. In each of the first three inter-censal periods listed the population increased annually by an average of 54,000 persons. This was the period of rapid increase in the immigrant population, both free and indentured. The increase in the population continued after 1911 but at a reduced rate; the figure for 1911–21 being 32,400 as opposed to 59,700 for the preceding inter-censal period. This reduction is in part accounted for by the

Table 57 Population Increase, 1891–1946

Year	Census Date	Census Population	Increase since Previous Census		
			Persons	Total Increases (%)	Equivalent Annual Rate (%)
1	2	3	4	5	6
1891	5 April	218,381	47,202	27.57	2.46
1901	21 April	273,899	55,518	25.42	2.28
1911	2 April	333,552	59,653	21.78	2.00
1921	24 April	365,913	32,361	9.70	0.92
1931	28 April	412,783	46,870	12.81	1.21
1939	End of year estimate	473.5	60.7	14.70	
1946	9 April	557,970	145,187	35.17	2.04

Source: Census Reports of Trinidad and Tobago.

slowing down and eventual cessation of indenture in 1917. Thereafter the growth of population accelerates once more, and increases thus:

1921–31 being 46,900 (estimated)
1931–39 being 60,700
1939–46 being 145,200

This latter phase in the growth of the population which will be analysed in greater detail in a subsequent section is most interesting. It took place in spite of the cessation of indenture. It is in fact due to natural increases assisted by immigration from the other islands, seeking work in the building of American wartime bases and so on. It presents the picture of a population rapidly increasing and poses the question and problem of finding the economic resources for sustaining that population.

Column (5) of table 57 sets out the total increase percentage over the period; column (6), however, is more eloquent. It shows that the annual rate of growth of the population having fallen gradually from the high point of 1891 (2.46 per cent) to about 1.00 in 1921–31 shot upwards again and between 1931 and 1946 regained the 2.04 per cent level.

A new country experiencing rapid development of its natural resources through immigrant labour can record high rates of population growth without undue concern, for example, America in the period of pushing back the frontier to the West. A population of 218,000, therefore, increasing at 2.46 per cent need not be a cause for alarm. But a population of 558,000 possessing the same extent of land,[1] and increasing at 2.04 per cent may be another matter. Especially is this the case when the rate of growth is influenced so much more by natural growth than by migration. Of course there was considerable immigration during the period 1941–44, during the building of the American bases. The fact of the acceleration of natural increase remains, however, as will be seen in a later section.

As an indication of the problems posed through the data in column (6), table 57, the following examples are given of the time required for a population to double itself at different rates of population growth:

At 0.25 per cent a year	278 years
At 0.5 per cent a year	139 years
At 1.0 per cent a year	70 years
At 1.5 per cent a year	47 years
At 2.0 per cent a year	35 years

Even if it is assumed, therefore, that the rate of growth will settle at around 2.0 per cent or slightly less then the population of Trinidad and Tobago judged by 1946 figures will double itself in about thirty-five years. Whether the economic resources necessary to sustain such a population could be generated in that same period of thirty-five years is difficult to say. It is clear, however, that considerable change in the economic structure will be necessary.

Table 58 compares the rates of population growth in Trinidad and Tobago with that of other West Indian islands. In every island the rate of growth since 1921 has been high. The highest, however, are Jamaica, Trinidad and Tobago, British Guiana, and British Honduras. The last two are vast territories and can support, theoretically at least, many millions of people. Trinidad and Tobago is not seriously threatened, at least not as seriously as Jamaica where the problem of population pressure has assumed great proportions.

Table 59 sets out the growth of population for the period under study 1919–39 in greater detail. The sudden drop after 1920 is due mainly to the repatriation of East Indians who had then completed the period of their indenture. This decline was assisted by the fact that there were no replacements as Indian immigration had ceased in 1917. Also the depression of the 1920s had just set in and its effects were being felt in Trinidad and Tobago, through high prices of imports and a reduction in wages. Many people from

Table 58 Annual Intercensal Rates of Growth (%) for West Indian Populations

Intercensal Interval	Jamaica	[a]Trinidad and Tobago	British Guiana	Windward Islands	Leeward Islands	Barbados	British Honduras
1844–51	–	1.84	2.50[b]	–	–	1.53	–
1851–61	0.92	1.87	1.66	0.82	–	1.17	–
1861–71	1.38	2.41	2.71	–	–	0.59	-0.36
1871–81	1.38	3.06	2.37	1.37	0.16	0.59	1.06
1881–91	0.97	2.46	1.03	1.25	0.65	0.62	1.38
1891–1911	1.32	2.14	0.33	0.88	-0.39	-0.29	1.26
1911–21	0.32	0.92	-0.02	0.79	-0.91	-0.95	1.13
1921–31	–	1.21	0.48	0.42	–	–	1.26
1931–46	1.67[c]	2.03	1.15	0.94	0.98	0.84	0.96

Source: Roberts *The Population of Jamaica:*

[a]Note that the Trinidad and Tobago rate of population growth (after 1921 especially) is greater than that of any other territory.

[b]1841–51

[c]1921–43

the other West Indian islands returned home preferring to face the rigours of the Depression in their own island.

After this setback, population rose steadily; the 1920 figure being reached again in 1926–27. During this period, however, there were smaller leakages through continued repatriation of formerly indentured Indians.

The Factors Involved in the Rapid Growth of Population: Age Distribution

Table 60 indicates that the population was essentially a young one. Persons of 44 years of age and below, in each of the census periods, account for at least 83 per cent of the total population. Also there has not been any great variation in the percentage size of this age group, that is, 0–44 years. Compare this with the American population in which in 1890 those below 44 years accounted for just about the same proportion, that is, 82 per cent of the population, as in Trinidad and Tobago. By 1945, this age group accounted for only about 73 per cent of the US population as opposed to 82.9 per cent in Trinidad and Tobago. Similarly in America the below twenties fell from about 46 per cent of the population to about 33 per cent.

Table 59 Population Increase, 1919–1939

	Population ('000)
1919	384.2
1920	388.9
1921	367.4
1922	371.8
1923	376.4
1924	380.0
1925	383.4
1926	386.3
1927	391.7
1928	397.1
1929	403.3
1930	413.1
1931	414.6
1932	419.6
1933	425.6
1934	432.1
1935	440.0
1936	448.3
1937	456.0
1938	464.9
1939	473.5

In the case of Trinidad and Tobago the age group below 14 years was fairly constant for most of the period and by 1946 instead of falling as was the case in America it actually increased to 36.8 per cent of total population. The age group 0–14 had increased relatively to that of the group 15–44. If anything, this meant that that proportion of the population which in the next generation would be producing the children was increasing. Without going into the question of the net reproduction rate for the moment the very youthfulness of the population seems to indicate, *ceteris paribus*, a further increase in the rate of growth of the population, or at least maintaining that rate.

The proportion of children below 15 years is indicative of a population increasing rapidly through natural reproduction. There has been a steady but very gradual fall in the population represented by those aged 15–44.

Table 60 Trinidad and Tobago Population by Age 1891–1946

Population Aged	1891	1901	1911	1921	1931	1946
0–14	71,395 (32.70%)	90,868 (33.18%)	112,902 (33.85%)	124,937 (34.15%)	140,046 (33.93%)	205,015 (36.81%)
15–44	112,670 (51.61%)	141,099 (51.52%)	169,576 (50.85%)	180,802 (49.41%)	200,750 (48.63%)	256,830 (46.11%)
45+	34,264 (15.69%)	41,922 (15.30%)	51,074 (15.31%)	60,166 (16.44%)	71,987 (17.44%)	95,124 (17.08%)
Not stated	52	10	–	8	–	1,001
Total	**218,381**	**273,899**	**333,552**	**365,913**	**412,783**	**557,970**

Source: Census reports.

This age group is essentially the one responsible for production and for the reproduction of the population. Its size therefore indicates that whatever the problems involved in this rate of population growth, it will not be that of how a shrinking labour force must support an increasing population of aged citizens which is the problem with a stagnant population.

But the proportion of population above forty-five was increasing also during the period 1891–1946. This does not necessarily contradict the last statement about caring for the aged. In fact far from this being a cause for apprehension it is to be regarded as a very good sign.[2] It indicates that more people are surviving above the age of 45 or 60. It indicates a greater life expectancy. It indicates, in part, a change from the situation described in a statement attributed to Dr Seagar[3] "that the working man in Trinidad over the age of 40 is already past his best years, his arteries are beginning to harden and his life shortened because of lack of nutrition".

Table 61 indicates that during 1921–31 this increase in the population of above forty-four was biased in favour of the female population. In 1921, males exceeded females in the age groups 30–70 only. This was due largely to the system of indenture in which most of the immigrants were male. It would appear that up to the end of the 1930s at any rate the male population was still subject, perhaps to a lesser extent, but subject all the same to the ill effects of vitamin deficiency; that the female population enjoyed a longer life span than the male.[4]

In chapter 8, "Labour", the conditions experienced by the working man will be more fully elaborated. For the present, however, it would suffice to say that long hours of work in the fields (agricultural or petroleum)

Table 61 Ages and Sexes

Age	Males '000		Female '000	
	1921	1931	1921	1931
15–20	16.4	19.0	18.1	21.6
20–25	17.3	20.2	18.9	22.2
25–30	15.3	17.1	16.3	18.4
30–35	14.3	15.3	13.7	15.3
35–40	14.0	13.2	12.4	13.5
40–45	13.6	11.5	10.5	11.8
45–50	10.4	9.2	7.8	9.6
50–55	7.9	5.6	6.3	7.8
55–60	4.5	5.1	3.6	4.6
60–65	4.5	2.8	3.7	4.7
65–70	2.2	1.8	2.0	2.7
70–75	1.6	1.0	1.6	2.0
75–80	0.8	0.7	0.9	1.1
80–85	0.6	0.2	0.7	0.9
85–90	0.2	0.1	0.2	0.3
90–95	0.1	0.1	0.2	0.2
95 and above	0.1	–	0.2	0.1
Total	**123.8**	**136.2**	**117.1**	**136.5**
	Net increase 12,400 10.0 per cent increase		Net increase 19,400 16.6 per cent increase	

coupled with a deficiency both in the quantity and the nutritive value of the diet of the population, and assisted by such factors as low real wages, brought about a shortening of the life expectancy of the male labouring population. The female escaped somewhat because she was to a less extent exposed to the hardships of work in the fields under an enervating tropical sun and sustained by a poor diet. While wages of female workers were poorer, the following factors seemed to have operated to their benefit relative to the male.

1. They were mostly domestic servants. The hours were long but the work not as arduous as the fields.

2. As domestics they could obtain a better, more regular, more consistent balanced diet than their male or female counterpart in the fields.

The clerks, stenos or typists have a life less strenuous than that of the males. But women seem to be naturally endowed with longer life.

Birth and Death Rates

It has already been indicated that after 1917 the upward movement in population was due largely to natural increase.

This has been due to

1. a birth rate which increased from 30.10 per thousand in 1919 to 34.7 in 1923 and declined and fluctuated thereafter but which nonetheless never fell below 29.5 (1928). It averaged about 32.00 per thousand of the population (table 62).
2. the drastic reduction in death rates from 24.46 per thousand in 1919 to 15.8 in 1938. The crude rate of natural increase therefore rose from 6.64 per thousand in 1919 to 17.01 in 1938.

Causes of Reduction of Death Rates

Infant mortality rate fell from 154.75 (1919) per thousand births to 98.42 in 1936–38. As table 62 (column 5) indicates there were the inevitable fluctuations but the downward trend was maintained.

The reduction in infant mortality rates was brought about chiefly as a result of measures initiated in 1918 which included the setting up of mothers and infants clinics at the Colonial Hospital, Port of Spain.[5]

Previous to this, "The Early Notification of Births Ordinance 1916" was proclaimed to be in force in Port of Spain. It provided for the notification to the district medical officer, Port of Spain, of all births within 36 hours. It soon spread its branches to neighbouring centres of population.

By 1921 mother and infant care clinics had been set up in many districts, far from Port of Spain, and by 1927 the government had set up special clinics for free treatment of children and was providing instruction in hygiene.

Table 62 Birth and Death Rates per 1,000 of Population

Year (1)	Birth Rate (2)	Death Rate (3)	Crude Natural Increase Rate (4)	Infant Mortality Rate (5)
1919	30.10	24.46	6.64	154.75
1920	29.85	23.76	6.09	174.93
1921	31.1	24.0	7.1	139.75
1922	31.8	22.3	9.5	138.68
1923	34.7	20.8	13.9	129.78
1924	33.6	20.0	13.6	124.07
1925	33.1	20.5	12.6	134.47
1926	31.9	21.9	10.0	142.8
1927	30.4	18.7	11.7	120.6
1928	29.5	19.8	9.7	–
1929	31.7	19.4	12.3	127.91
1930	31.2	18.9	12.29	127.02
1931	29.9	19.97	9.93	144.10
1932	28.97	17.08	11.89	108.90
1933	31.08	19.57	11.51	131.30
1934	29.72	18.6	11.12	127.40
1935	32.92	17.47	15.45	99.42
1936	32.93	16.28	16.65	96.82
1937	31.46	17.4	14.06	120.48
1938	32.83	15.85	17.01	98.42
1939	–	–	–	–

The overall death rate fell also as indicated in table 62. Here also the chief causes were improved medical facilities and health and sanitation measures. Note that deaths caused by malaria (table 63) fell from 214.63 per 100,000 (1921–25) to 102.88 per 100,000 (1936–40). This decline was achieved principally through the schemes undertaken by government to drain the many swamps which formed the breeding grounds for mosquitoes.

Ankylostomiasis (hookworm) accounted for 75.19 deaths per 100,000 of population in 1921–25 but only 26.19 in 1936–40. In this case the chief factor in the decline was the operation of the Rockefeller International

Table 63 Principal Causes of Death in Trinidad and Tobago

Causes of Death	1921–25	1926–30	1931–35	1936–40
	(Rates per 100,000 of population)			
Enteric fever	53.06	27.48	31.31	24.93
Influenza	27.56	15.00	10.02	5.86
Malaria	214.63	182.86	148.06	102.88
Dysentery	60.87	61.67	33.67	16.30
Pulmonary tuberculosis*	121.53	112.12	91.61	92.24
Syphilis	44.30	53.91	37.26	34.01
Cancer*	36.17	37.49	34.69	46.68
Cerebral haemorrhage*	45.65	47.74	50.40	46.28
Infantile convulsions	31.57	19.64	8.21	8.49
Cardiac and valvular disease*	105.85	120.88	114.67	112.44
Bronchitis (all forms)	144.25	131.41	103.97	72.21
Broncho-pneumonia*	35.49	32.42	29.90	40.80
Lobar pneumonia	85.64	41.39	44.36	46.44
Pneumonia (n.i.d)*	2.16	6.20	11.93	11.84
Diarrhoea and enteritis	157.15	128.51	100.32	84.43
Ankylostomiasis	75.19	56.93	39.44	26.19
Nephritis	139.60	125.81	99.67	93.48
Diseases of the puerperal state	14.57	27.66	23.86	22.22
Diseases of early infancy	231.13	215.72	216.86	201.90
Old age	144.88	153.92	188.11	166.46

Note: Items thus marked * indicate where there has been either very little improvement or a worsening of the situation over time.

Board of Health Hookworm treatment scheme. This operation which was carried out with great intensity from 1914 was stopped by the Rockefeller International Board in 1925 but was maintained thereafter by local staff under the central board of health.

These twin factors (a fall in the infant mortality rate and in the overall death rate) were both brought about by government health measures. Here, therefore, is the important and often discussed problem: that government by taking measures to improve the health of the population provides at high cost those very amenities which lead to a rapid growth of the population. This in turn creates and accentuates other problems of employment and standard of living which may be beyond the financial power of the government. But the problem is even more complex for it is arguable that (and in the case of Trinidad and Tobago the enervating effects of hook-worm disease are well known) these social amenities must be undertaken to improve the health and efficiency of the population.

In the case of Trinidad and Tobago the problem of choosing between social overheads and productive enterprise seems to have been resolved largely in favour of the former.[6] In the 1920s especially the emphasis seemed to have been on health improvement measures.

The results, for the purposes of this chapter, therefore, have been a marked increase in population, its rate of growth and the general health of the population.

Migration

The early development of Trinidad and Tobago was associated with migration of one kind or another. There were the Spanish settlers of the seventeenth and eighteenth centuries, the French planters from the neighbouring islands who fled the terror of the French Revolution and later there were the indentured Indians and migrants from other West Indian islands. These last two categories are the ones most important for the purposes of this study of the inter-war years. Table 64 gives a comparison of the migration from the smaller West Indian islands.[7] Note the decline between the years 1921 and 1931 in the number of immigrants especially from Barbados. This decrease is indicative of the absolute and relative decline of Trinidad and Tobago as a source of employment: absolute in view of the fall in prices of agricultural exports; relative in terms of the prosperity of Aruba and Maracaibo which were developing greater oil refining industries than that of Trinidad, were offering better and more employment opportunities and so attracted the migrants. Grenada and St Vincent, however, continued the rate of migration to Trinidad and Tobago.

The inflow of indentured East Indians stopped in 1917 and was partly reversed thereafter. Why then should this migrant population deserve special mention in a study on the period 1919–39? This section of the population is important because of the rate at which it has been reproducing itself. It has been doing so much faster than the rest of the population and its rate of growth goes on unchecked. The problem, therefore, is that of a migrant population which after making its initial (migration) contribution to the size of the population, settles down to cause the natural rate to increase at a very fast rate.

Table 64 Immigration from Other West Indian Islands

Island	1921	1931
Barbados	16,744	13,823
St Vincent	10,113	10,425
Grenada	12,838	14,949
St Kitts/Nevis	1,486	1,003
Antigua	701	646
Other BWI	5,162	4,916
Others of East Indian parentage	633	629
Total	**47,667**	**46,391**

Table 65 Growth of East Indian Population, 1851–1946

Census Year	East Indian Population	Increase since Previous Census		Proportion of East Indians to Total Population*
		Number	Per Cent	
1	2	3	4	5
1851	3,993	–	–	4.81
1861	13,488	9,495	237.79	13.51
1871	27,425	13,937	103.33	21.65
1881	48,820	21,395	78.01	28.52
1891	70,218	21,398	43.83	32.15
1901	86,383	16,165	23.02	31.54
1911	110,911	24,528	28.39	33.25
1921	121,420	10,509	9.48	33.18
1931	138,667	17,247	14.20	33.59
1946	**195,747	57,080	41.16	35.09

Source: Census Reports.
*Inclusive of Tobago. (The population of Tobago is overwhelmingly African. In 1946 93.39 per cent of population were African or of African descent.)
**Excluding East Indian Creoles.

Table 65 shows the growth of the East Indian population from 1851 to 1946. Column 4 shows the percentage increase at each census over the preceding census and column 5 shows the East Indian population as a

Table 66 Birth, Death and Natural Increase Rates per 1,000 of Population 1921–1945

Period	Birth Rate		Death Rate		Natural Increase	
	East Indian	Other	East Indian	Others	East Indian	Others
(1)	(2)	(3)	(4)	(5)	(6)	(7)
1921–25	38.88	30.28	23.81	20.59	15.07	10.22
1926–30	38.07	27.48	21.50	18.96	16.57	8.54
1931–35	36.90	27.30	20.09	17.76	16.81	9.33
1936–40	40.64	28.38	17.27	15.67	23.37	12.60
1941–45	45.24	32.44	15.58	15.99	29.66	16.59

percentage of the total population. This column is particularly interesting for the post-1921 period, that is, after the positive (immigration) and negative (repatriation) effects of direct migration can be considered to have largely worn off.

The picture is further elaborated in table 66. It shows that the East Indian birth rate rose from 38.88 per thousand (1921–25) to 40.64 (1936–40) and shot up to 45.24 (1941–45). The death rate fell for the same period from 23.81 to 17.27 and then to 15.58. Other races experienced a much smaller change in both birth and death rates. Columns 6 and 7 show that the 1921–25 East Indian rate of natural increase was 15.07 per thousand versus 10.22 for others; that for 1936–40 the figures were 23.37 versus 12.60 and for 1941–45 29.66 versus 16.59.

As a measure of the respective rates of growth it has been estimated that if the 1941–45 average rate of growth is maintained, the East Indian population will overtake "others" in 1993 at 800,000 persons in each category. If the average 1931–45 is maintained, the East Indian population will overtake "others" in 2005 at 779,000 each.

Predictions about rates of growth of population can be very dangerous but it does appear that even if the rate of growth slackens somewhat the population will soon become very large relative to land space and, unless other economic activities are more available, relative to employment opportunities.

How does one explain this great natural increase of the East Indian? Death rates would have fallen rapidly with improved health. Initially they were physically less robust specimens than "others". Proper medical treatment would therefore have saved many lives. But the 1941–45 figures seem to indicate that their death rates had become as low as that of the other races. Why? One possible explanation is that while the East Indian was prepared to take full advantage of all free or cheap medical facilities the others were more inclined to regard such facilities as a form of charity and were less inclined to make full use of them.

Population Growth and the Social Services

The rate of population growth outlined earlier must place great strain on the social services that an underdeveloped country can supply. One may go further and argue that the high rate of population growth is partly responsible for the country being less developed. But the growth of the petroleum industry, its contribution to revenue and its input into electricity generation, the creation of other industries and higher quality employment contributed positively to the economic development. For the present, however, it will be interesting to see how at least one of the public services fared in the struggle to keep pace with population growth.

Hospital facilities, and so on, will not be used as precise data about them is not available. It can be taken for granted, however, that population pressure on these facilities must have been great. It is proposed to examine the impact of population on the facilities for education and housing.

Literacy

Table 67 shows a considerable increase in the proportion of literates.

Table 67 Literacy Including All Children Below 5 Years

Period	Able to Read and Write	Per Cent	Able to Read Alone	Per Cent	Unable to Read and Write	Per Cent
1946	342,799	–	7,861	–	205,359	–
1931	223,865	54.2	11,158	2.7	177,760	43.1
1921	172,617	47.1	12,600	3.7	180,696	49.4
1911	139,053	41.7	15,205	4.6	179,294	53.7

Primary Education

At a conference on "Financing the Economic Development of Underdeveloped Countries" organized by the United Nation Association, Professor W. Arthur Lewis made inter alia, the following statement:

> My view on education priorities, that is to say immediately rather than ultimate objectives, is that all countries should aim at having universal primary education. . . .
> Universal primary education should be an immediate objective. Everything on top of that should be related to productive purposes. You should have such a number of people going ahead as you will require for nurses, typists, technical people, people who have to go into technical schools, who are to become teachers, who are to become administrators, and so forth.[8]

Table 68 gives an indication of the problem of providing such universal primary education in Trinidad and Tobago where the population of school age was increasing at a considerable rate. Even if in any one year it were possible to accommodate all children of school age it must be remembered that every year saw the survival of from 10,000 to 13,000 new children aged 1 year.

The burden of providing schooling facilities, places and teachers for such a large annual addition to any school population must have been considerable.

In fact they were not all provided school space. As table 68 indicates, while the children of school age increased in number from 92,130 to 102,960 between 1921 and 1931 (increase of 20,630) the number in attendance at schools increased by only 7,400 (from 59,260 to 66,730).

Even in developed and prosperous countries with lower rates of growth of population the problem of providing school space has been great. In the case of Trinidad and Tobago, relatively poor and having a rate of natural increase of approximately 1.5–2 per cent per annum, the problem becomes almost impossible of solution: the problem, that is, of finding money for school building and teacher training on a scale sufficient to keep pace with this increase in population.

Another aspect of the problem for education authorities and one which springs from the rapid rate of population increase is that of malnutrition in childhood with its consequent ill effects on powers of concentration and absorption. Low wages and large families make proper nutrition impossible.

Table 68 Children of School Attending Age

Period	No. of Children of School-Attending Age (1)	Per Cent of Population (2)	No. of Children at School (3)	Per Cent of Children of School-Attending Age (4)	Number Not Attending (5)	Number Gainfully Employed (6)	Number at Govt. School (7)	Number at Assisted Schools (8)	Number at Private School (9)
1946									
1939									
1931	102,960	24.9	66,729	64.8	36,231	5,494	8,237	53,471	5,022
							(12.3%)	(80.1%)	(7.4%)
1921	92,128	25.2	59,260	64.3	33,875		8,469	46,621	4,170
1911			52,273		60,112		10,210	38,595	3,468
1901			42,006		52,227		10,972	26,120	4,914

In this connection it may be interesting to quote from a speech of the governor in the Legislative Council on 9 July 1937: "I was looking into the question of free breakfasts (lunches) in Port of Spain recently. There are some 15,000 school children, and I was told that a very large majority of them do not get a breakfast (i.e. lunch) in the course of the day; and they are not the children of agricultural labour."

Density of Population and Housing

In this section it is proposed to analyse the population in terms of

1. its density
2. its distribution as between urban and rural areas
3. its housing accommodation.

Table 69 shows the growth in the area of towns; changes in the areas of counties; the population changes in each area and the density of population.

In each case the figures are given for the census periods 1911–46 with an estimate for 1939 included wherever possible.

Density

Between 1911 and 1946 the population density had increased from 169 persons per square mile to 281.8 per square mile. This period includes the war years which are not strictly within the scope of this study. The 1939 approximation seems to be necessary, therefore, to clarify the picture. The increase were as follows:

	1911	1921	1931	1939	1946
Density	169	185	208	235	281

Some of the increase after 1938 can be accounted for through migration from other West Indian islands during the war. But the increase of 50 per square mile in 1921–1938 was almost all natural increase. It would appear that the hardships of two depression periods 1921 and 1930–34 had little, if any, adverse effects on the growth and density of the population.

These increases in density were not uniformly distributed. It is therefore necessary to consider the growth in area and population of towns and rural districts.

Table 69 Density of Population, 1911–1946

Areas (Urban)	1946	1939	1931	1921	1911
Port of Spain					
Area (square miles)	3.70		2.80	2.80	2.09
Population	92,793	89.6	70,334	61,580	59,796
Density	25,079		25,119	21,992	28,160
San Fernando					
Area (square miles)	2.50		1.05	1.05	1.05
Population	28,842	16.2	14,353	10,610	8,667
Density	11,537		13,669	10,104	8,320
Arima					
Area (square miles)	0.98		0.91	0.91	0.91
Population	8,069	5.7	5,089	4,210	4,020
Density	8,234		5,592	4,626	3,840
	Areas (Rural)				
St George					
Area (square miles)	354.68		355.06	314.30	
Population	138,362	86.4	85,904	67,535	–
Density	390.1		242.0	215.0	
Caroni					
Area (square miles)	213.99		213.99	253.39	
Population	61,739	57.7	51,193	53,961	–
Density	268.8		239.0	213.0	
Victoria					
Area (square miles)	313.49		313.53	313.43	
Population	87,441	77.8	60,086	67,079	–
Density	278.9		192.0	214.0	
St Patrick					
Area (square miles)	260.80		260.80	260.67	
Population	69,183	52.4	46,531	34,075	–
Density	265.3		178.0	130.0	
St Andrew					
Area (square miles)	282.74		282.74	286.40	
Population	23,285	26.3	23,337	23,576	–
Density	82.4		82.0	82.0	
Tobago					
Area (square miles)	116.24		116.24	111.4	
Population	27,208	28.5	25,358	23,390	–
Density	234.1		218.0	201.0	
Colony					
Area (square miles)	1,980.66		1,980.06	1,980.06	1,980.06
Population	557,970	464,900	412,800	365, 900	333,552
Density	281.8	235.0	208.0	185.0	169.0

Urban Population

The growth of towns and increases in the proportion of the population that is designated "urban" can give some indication of the extent to which

1. the economy is becoming less dependent on agricultural production;
2. it is becoming increasingly a money rather than a subsistence economy;
3. employment in secondary and tertiary industries is expanding;
4. the nucleus of a possible industrial labour force is being created;
5. dissatisfaction with the employment possibilities, and social amenities of rural life makes urban life more attractive;
6. the unemployment and underemployment of the rural areas is shifted to the urban centres.

All of these factors seem to have operated in the process of urbanization in Trinidad and Tobago. The total urban population increased from 72,500 in 1911 to 111,500 in 1939 and 129,800 in 1946. As a percentage of the total population the figures are 21.7 per cent (1911), 24 per cent (1939) and 23.3 per cent in 1946.

In the three census periods – 1911, 1921, 1931 – the proportion of the population that was urban remained at about 21 per cent. In 1938 it went up to 24 per cent. This increase is partly explained by shifts in the geographic boundaries. The population of Port of Spain increased by 19,300 in 1931–38. This was due largely to extension of the boundaries of the city. Both Port of Spain and Arima are in county St George and San Fernando is in county Victoria. Note how rapidly the populations of those counties have increased. If an attempt is made to estimate the urban labour force a large part of the population of the surrounding county should be added to the actually designated urban population, especially where, as has been the case, there is nothing but an arbitrary boundary marking the limits of the city. The urban and semi-urban population would then be much nearer 30 per cent than 24 per cent.

A.R. Prest[9] takes the view that in Trinidad the drift to the towns from agriculture was caused by the attraction of employment and wages on the American bases. This conclusion is in fact only partly correct. The drift to the towns had started in the 1930s. Also the number of persons and the proportion of the population engaged in agriculture were falling steadily.

While the shifts in population may have been accentuated and accelerated, they have been in fact only a continuation of a long established trend.

To some extent, therefore, hardships and lack of reward experienced in rural Trinidad contributed to this shift to the towns. It must be remembered

	1911	1921	1931	1939	1946
Numbers in agriculture ('000)	97.12	95.6	89.3		53.8
Per cent of population	29.12	26.12	21.69		9.6
Or as per cent of adult population	43.9	32.4	39.4		–

that the period was largely one of depressed prices for agricultural products. Note how the population of Port of Spain with its commercial and light industrial enterprises, service industries and social amenities and that of San Fernando near to the oil fields, expanded. In San Fernando the 1921 census contains the following observation:

> The town of San Fernando has shown an increase beyond all expectations but on investigation it has been found that there was and still is an itinerancy caused by the Oil Fields and Refineries immediately North and a little South of that town. Inadequate housing accommodation in the former making it imperative that employees should live in this the nearest centre.

Bearing out the connection drawn between the growth of centres of population and economic activity is the following remark from the same source. "The town of Arima has also shown a slight increase. This small but picturesque Borough at one time the centre of a flourishing cocoa industry and possessing many commercial attractions now stands depleted in population and crushed by a trade diversion from which it would seem there is to be no relief."[10]

Oil mining and refining and to a lesser extent sugar, made for an increase in urbanization to the south (see San Fernando's population growth). Table 70 shows that between 1931 and 1946 (15 years) the population was more than double.

The preceding extracts put into clear outline the shift in economic activities in Trinidad. The latter shows the decline of the cocoa industry, formerly the chief agricultural industry, and in fact the foremost industry. The former shows the growth of oil mining and consequently the shifts of population density from the agricultural to the oil mining areas.

Housing

To what extent did housing keep pace with the rapid rate of population growth?

Table 71 compares the number of rooms recorded in each of the census year 1921, 1931 and 1946. It shows that for 1921–31 there was a 22.14

Table 70 Increase in Urban Population (since Previous Census)

Year	Port of Spain		San Fernando		Arima		Urban Population as Percentage of Total Population
	Number '000	Increase (per cent)	Number '000	Increase (per cent)	Number '000	Increase (per cent)	
1901	20.3	60.12	1.0	14.79	–	–	–
1911	5.7	10.53	1.1	13.84	-0.06	-1.37	21.7
1921	1.8	3.00	1.9	22.42	0.2	4.73	20.9
1931	8.8	14.22	3.7	35.28	0.9	20.78	21.8
1939	19.3	27.4	1.9	13.2	0.6	11.7	24.0
1946*	22.5	31.93	14.5	100.95	3.0	58.68	23.3

Source: Census reports.
*The 1946 figures refer to increases in 1931–46.

per cent increase in the number of rooms and for 1931–46 an increase of 39.7 per cent. For the colony as a whole the number of rooms increased proportionately much faster than the population.

Table 71 Rooms Recorded at the Censuses of 1921, 1931, 1946

	1946	1931	1921	Increases	
				1931–46	1921–31
Port of Spain city	51,885	43,734	31,479	8,151	12,255
San Fernando	17,948	8,723	7,005	9,225	1,718
Arima	4,856	3,289	2,580	1,567	709
St George county	75,796	44,935	34,993*	30,861	9,942
Caroni	34,055	26,712	25,006**	7,343	1,706
Victoria	46,239	33,962	32,814	12,227	1,148
St Patrick	37,623	24,419	16,137	13,204	8,282
St David	2,585	2,881	2,117	-296	764
St Andrew	14,484	13,453	12,148	1,041	1,295
Nariva	6,318	5,112	3,832	1,206	1,280
Mayaro	3,082	2,847	2,591	253	256
Tobago	13,392	10,533	9,876	2,859	657
Colony total	308,263	220,600	180,578	87,673	40,012
per cent increase				39.7	22.14

*Including San Rafael.
**Excluding San Rafael.

Year	Population Increase (per cent)	Housing Increase (per cent)
1921–31	12.81	22.14
1931–46	35.17	39.7

These findings are further substantiated by table 72 which shows that the number of persons per room for the colony fell from 2.00 in 1921 to 1.84 in 1931 and 1.77 in 1946. In nearly every area the number per room had fallen from above 2 in 1921 (St David 3.15) to somewhat below 2 in 1946.

But even so in 1946 it was estimated that the number of additional rooms needed to reduce the density of occupation (without taking into considerations additions to population) in every case to 2 persons per room was estimated at 2,488 and to 1.5 persons, at 52,526. But the fact that the increase in the number of rooms seemed to more than keep pace with population

Table 72 Persons per Room 1921–1946

Towns	1946	1931	1921
Port of Spain	1.68	1.57	1.92
San Fernando	1.56	1.61	1.49
Arima	1.64	1.53	1.62
Other (County) Areas			
St George	1.75	1.82	2.05
Caroni	1.81	1.91	1.89
Victoria	1.88	2.03	2.04
St Patrick	1.83	1.90	2.11
St David	1.95	1.97	3.15
St Andrew	1.61	1.73	1.94
Nariva	1.87	2.11	2.21
Mayaro	1.36	1.41	1.48
Tobago	2.01	2.40	2.36
Colony total	1.77	1.84	2.00

Note: Density in Port of Spain at 1.68 is really an average between a high density in the south-eastern and south-western wards of the city where, especially in the south-eastern ward, slum clearance was urgently needed, and a lesser density in the wealthier northern and north-western ward where there was very much more room space per person.

is no cause for regarding the problems as solved. The data on the number of room say nothing either about room space (size of rooms) or quality of the accommodations; it gives no idea of new building, replacement of old dilapidated buildings or domestic conveniences.

Actually it is fair to say that in spite of the increase in the number of rooms, housing was far from satisfactory. Especially this was the case in Port of Spain. Note that in Port of Spain population and housing increased.

	1931–46	**1921–31**
Population growth	22,500	8,800
New housing rooms	8,151	12,255

This shows that 50 per cent less new building was done in 1931–46 than in 1921–31 while the population increase in 1931–46 was more than double that of 1921–31.

The West India Royal Commission Report (1939) points its finger on the two most important aspects of this problem: "Dwellings containing space that might be more or less sufficient for families of a moderate size become palpably overcrowded when they are inhabited by families containing eight, ten, twelve or more children. At the same time, there is a steady increase in the numbers of family units requiring to be housed."[11]

The Forster Commission report pointed specifically to a "village" adjacent to Port of Spain which was described as "an entangled conglomeration of unsightly ruinous huts and privy cess pits placed helter-skelter on a sloping, steep and slippery hillside – a danger to health, life and limb for the local residents and a menace to the surrounding city population". This was clearly a case for slum clearance but "it is in our view inevitable that power of slum clearance vested in a City Corporation composed in sufficient part of persons who are owners of or who have interests in unsanitary property, to create opposition to schemes for its abolition, will not be effectively carried out, and that in such circumstances slum clearance is doomed to failure and the public interest must suffer".[12] Population growth, therefore, must have a heavy burden on the resources of the colony. One is therefore forced to consider solutions for the problem.

Birth control measures were not encouraged. If they had been they may have made a contribution to relieving the pressure. But it is necessary not to expect too much from this approach to the problem. Such measures even where they are accepted take time to show any effect on population growth.

Too often one gets the impression that the solution to the problem of population pressure is considered mainly in terms of trimming and restraining population to suit a given socio-economic potential. That is to say, a certain per capita level of national income is aimed at or is considered desirable. Sometimes considerations of the distribution of such incomes are ignored. Where it is not ignored it is sometimes by-passed with the comment that it is not important; that as long as the average level is high enough, as long as it is at least theoretically possible for the population as a whole to be better off, the main problem has been solved.

To arrive at this level of per capita income one or both of two factors have to be influenced: incomes and population. Very often it seems to be the case that the former is thought to be more intractable than the latter. Greater emphasis is therefore placed on reducing or restraining population.

But in fact restraining or reducing (by emigration) the population is not as easy as one would at first think. Birth control methods are expensive, especially for low-income countries. One can therefore construct another "vicious circle" to show why progress is impossible. It is, above all, not easy to make them generally accepted and efficiently employed by illiterate and certain religious people. The incident is related of a woman in Trinidad who, upon being approached by another who wished to convert her to practising family planning, rejected the suggestion with the reply, "That is all right for you Madam but, I am a decent woman." [13]

Such attitudes were typical of large sections of the society. They were countered, on the part of a protagonist of birth control, by certain suggestions which are so brutally logical as to appear inhumane. It was suggested, for example, that if babies must be born indiscriminately let them also die indiscriminately. Destroy all welfare clinics and so on. [14]

It would appear that while one must face squarely the problems created by population increase and do everything possible to restrain the increase, one should give equal prominence to the question of maximum utilization of the resources of the country. Further, if it becomes possible, in spite of the obvious difficulties, to educate and improve the skills of the larger population, the sacrifice will be amply rewarded by increased production in the future.

One should be concerned not only with the numbers but with the quality of the population. If this training can be achieved in spite of its cost[15] (and both the process of educating and the resultant benefits will be cumulative), size of population may yet prove to be the greatest single asset possessed by the islands.[16]

In the case of Trinidad and Tobago, however, which is blessed with a petroleum industry with its increasing production of petroleum products and natural gas, the problem is capable of solution. Secondary schools have increased in number, student capacity and the quality of education. They are to be found not only in Port of Spain but in several centres throughout both islands. Further since we must, where appropriate, step somewhat beyond the period of our study, 1919–39, and the developments of that period have influenced the years following, one should note that tertiary education has come to the West Indies through the University of the West Indies (UWI) and the largest campus is in Trinidad and Tobago, established in 1960. The UWI in Trinidad is largely government assisted, financially.

8 Labour

Labour Supply

An understanding of the labour situation in Trinidad and Tobago in the interval between the two world wars requires, at least, a brief statement of historical developments in the field of labour before this time, especially from the immediate post-emancipation period, 1840–1920. The most important single influence was exerted by the indenture system.

Indenture

To maintain the labour force on the plantations after emancipation, when former slaves refused to continue in the service of their former masters, the planters in the West Indies sought successfully to secure indentured labour from Africa, China and India. For the purpose of this study the most important stream of indentured labour came from India.

Some indication of the inflow can be gained from the fact that for the period of indenture, 1846–1917, Trinidad received 143,000 indentured Indians (some of whom were of course repatriated), that is, 33.3 per cent of the total indentured immigrant inflow into the British West Indies.[1]

To emphasize the characteristics of the post-indenture period it is proposed to state briefly the advantages to the planter of the system of indenture: the indenture system made available to the planters an abundance of cheap, flexible, industrious and obedient labour.

Abundance and Cheapness of Labour

The 143,000 indentured labourers brought into Trinidad kept the labour market perpetually overstocked. In the face of this constant inflow of indentured labour, free labour was of necessity more amenable to discipline.[2]

Male persons party to such agreements received by the terms of their contract 25¢ (1/0½d) per day or performed tasks which earned them slightly higher wages. The labourer was entitled to five days work a week "out of crop" and six days "in crop".[3] He could not work voluntarily more than 15 hours a day nor be compelled to work more than 9 hours. He was entitled to payment of wages for all days on which he should be supplied with work, whether or not work was provided. Few immigrants actually demanded such employment or payment, preferring to work their own plots on such days.

Flexibility, Industry and Obedience

The immigrant was required to live on the estate to which he was indentured. He was always available and could be trained to perform any task the planter required without the payment of any additional financial inducement.

Chapter 4 on sugar showed that on the sugar estates the East Indians, both as cane farmer and labourer, were more numerous than the West Indians. They appeared also keener, more efficient workers. Note the larger amount of farmers' canes produced by the East Indians.[4] In addition they cultivated enough rice and ground provisions to make themselves almost self-sufficient in these commodities.

As further evidence of their industry and thrift was the observation of the protector of immigrants as to the number of repatriates and the amounts that they were each able to save out of their meagre wages and take back to India.

Post-indenture

The year 1917 saw the end of indentured immigration; but some immigrants' contracts did not expire until 1920. This latter year, therefore, saw the real end of indenture, saw in fact in the eyes of the planter, the cutting off of the flow of this abundant, cheap, flexible and industrious labour force. It is in this context of change from an overstocked and cheap agricultural labour force to one of labour shortage and higher wages that this study of the beginning of the period should be seen.

Indentured labour no longer stood between the efficient and the inefficient estate. Competition for labour which was unknown under indenture came into existence and in the immediate post-war boom was severe. For this cessation of indenture coincided with the boom of the immediate post–World War I period and free labour, realizing that its hands were strengthened by these twin factors, agitated for and obtained higher wages.[5] One further factor assisting the labourer was the fact of improved transportation facilities (omnibuses, trains and so on) which increased his mobility and allowed him to take advantage of differentials in wages between different areas and estates.[6] Also planters were attempting to expand their output to take advantage of the rise in prices for their exported products. This shortage of labour and the increased world prices situation led in 1920 to wage increases to 60¢ per day.

In addition to the system of indenture the following factors affected the supply in Trinidad in the period.

Other Immigration

Before 1921 there was considerable emigration from the other West Indian islands into Trinidad.[7] The slump of the early 1920s checked this flow considerably. Chapter 9, "Population", showed[8] that this flow was diverted largely to Aruba and Maracaibo where large oil industries were being developed and employment opportunities were more favourable.

Population Growth

But the chief factor influencing the size of the labour force after the second decade of the twentieth century was population growth.[9] While indentured immigration was stopped and reversed in 1917 and the post-war depressions of 1921–24 diverted would-be immigrants, the rate and size of population increase contributed a permanent and self-reproducing increase in the labour force that affected the economy, not for stated periods but for all time. While population increased and emigration possibilities were not favourable, the economy had to find some way of living with the problem.

Land Settlement

At various times since emancipation restrictions on the sale of land to peasants or on the occupation of land by them had the effect of ensuring labour supply for agricultural industries. In some cases the motive was clear; in others it was not, but the effect was the same.

Shephard maintains that "with the object of maintaining a labour force for the principal export crops Crown Lands were seldom alienated in small sizes prior to 1847. In that year the price was fixed at £2 per acre with the deliberate intent of making purchase by labourers impossible."[10]

The Montserrat "Experiment"[11] under which squatters were permitted to buy the land on which they squatted put an end to this barrier.

Sugar

In more recent times, however, the sugar estates adopted a similar method of ensuring a labour supply. When in the 1890s the sugar estates were suffering from capital shortage, they persuaded East Indians whose terms of indenture had expired to remain in the island. The inducement took the form of renting or leasing lands to the East Indians at cheap rates, for the planting of canes.[12] Thus was started the cane farming system which ensured to the sugar industry a supply of canes irrespective of world prices and without much cost to the manufacturers, and also ensured them a readily available labour supply.

In the 1930s, however, sugar estates tended to reduce the area allotted to cane farmers. This tendency was checked by the Cane Farming Control Ordinance. Had it gone unchecked, however, its net effect on the labour market would have been to convert a certain number of cane farmers either into full-time sugar workers or make some cane farmers part-time sugar workers or leave them unemployed.

This tendency to reduce or to prevent further expansion of cane farmers' output was coincidental with the upturn of sugar prices after the Depression. The proportion of farmers' canes showed a tendency to rise with rising prices and fall with falling prices.[13] This in fact meant that at the time when estates were more eager to harvest their crops the farmers who would normally be expected to help on the estate were busy with their own crops. Reducing the acreage available to cane farmers may not have had as its motive, as Shephard claims, the increasing of the labour force. The net effect, *ceteris paribus*, would, however, have been the same.

Oil

Before the discovery of oil in the south of the island, large tracts of Crown lands were sold to peasants who readily cultivated cocoa and other crops. The reservation of about two-thirds of the Crown lands of that area for oil prospecting hindered the expansion of the peasant proprietary. In 1924 some 98,000 acres were temporarily withheld from sale and a further 124,833 acres licensed on bond for oil prospecting. In this way a land shortage in cultivating cocoa or perhaps ground provisions was thrown upon an already over-crowded labour market.

Health

The high incidence of certain diseases had an effect, if not on the numbers of the labour force at least on its efficiency. The mortality rate did fall throughout the period from what was a very high level.[14] In this context, however, of an already large labour force the question of the health and stamina of the survivors is of the greater significance than the lower death rate. Although the number of deaths from malaria had fallen greatly by 1936, the disease was in fact still seriously affecting the producing powers of large numbers of the population. In 1936 also some 19,000 cases of malaria were reported to the health department. The number actually affected could have been larger as in the country districts many persons would have attended no doctor.

Hookworm also was reported to be one of the principal causes of disability, especially among the East Indian population. The Forster Commission reported that one of the factors in the Trinidad disturbances of 1937 was the rather drastic preliminary hookworm treatment insisted upon by some companies before labour was employed.

Education

The spread of education had an effect upon agricultural labour in the following ways:

1. Children went to school until they were somewhat older than was formerly the case;
2. Education made them more ambitious, and less likely to accept employment in the fields.

But the increase in population had to be absorbed in some way and so the ranks of clerical employment were swollen by the out-turn of the schools. This type of education, however, while making young persons alive to the disadvantages of agricultural employment in the context of Trinidad, sugar and so on gave them few skills which they could employ. Even shorthand and typing were, in the 1920s and 1930s, rare achievements for the majority.

The Demand for Labour

In the preceding section, factors influencing the supply of labour which were entirely or largely independent of demand considerations have been isolated and analysed. While indenture was the result of an increase in demand for labour the cessation of indenture was controlled by other forces.

Population growth, while it may be shown to have connections with standard of living and so on was in fact independent of the demand situation for labour. Note that the birth rates of the depression period did not fall at all, on the contrary they rose.

The land sales policies outlined would in the first case (1846) have been influenced by the demand for employment opportunities – the policies of the sugar planter perhaps less certainly. That which was connected with oil exploration was most likely not motivated by a desire to provide labour for plantations though it would have had the same effect.

Education affected the supply of labour only insofar as it changed the type of labour that became available – labour for agriculture being reduced while that for clerical jobs increased.

The health factor would have affected both numbers and quality of the labour force – the greatest impact (with the fall of the death rate) being on the stamina and initiative of the labour force.

The factors which have not yet been touched upon are closely connected with demand considerations and will be treated in this section.

The demand for labour in Trinidad and Tobago can be divided broadly into two kinds: agricultural and non-agricultural; and agricultural demand can be divided into cyclical and seasonal demand. Cyclical demand for labour is associated with world market conditions for the export crops. Seasonal demand is associated with the actual planting and reaping of the crops; that is, the times of planting and reaping when labour is needed and time of growing when little labour is needed – "crop season" and "out of crop season".

The first is a derived demand. It follows the demand and price trends on the world market with or without some time lag.

The period 1870–1921 saw the contraction of sugar and the expansion of cocoa. It was in this period that cocoa also was allowed to import indentured labour. The end of that period, however, saw the cessation of indenture and the post–World War I boom. At this point therefore, that is, 1917–20, the demand for labour increased precisely at the time when supply was contracting.

The period 1921–24 was one of post-war depression in which the prices of the chief export crops of sugar and cocoa fell considerably. Following the trend in the export industries the demand for labour fell also. But there was a difference. Cocoa, the expansion of which was based on rather insecure financial foundations, could employ few labourers. Sugar, better supported financially and influenced by the necessity for relatively more continuous labour supply, survived the impact of the Depression more easily than cocoa.

To meet the lower price level sugar estates reduced their unit cost of production by increasing output, improving their methods of cultivation and sugar refining. This process of rationalization involved an additional demand for labour which was not, however, proportional to the increase in output of sugar. Further this process of rationalization was accompanied by reduced labour wages.[15]

The net result of the depression of the 1920s on the demand for agricultural labour was to reduce that demand both in agriculture itself and in industries dependent on agriculture. Sugar, by expanding production, absorbed some but not all of the redundant labour resulting from world price conditions and disease in cocoa.

The period 1925–29 saw complaints of an acute shortage of labour from planters in nearly all districts.

World prices had turned up again, not very much but enough to lead to an increase in the demand for labour. But meanwhile other factors had come into operation. Firstly, the repatriation of indentured labour still continued though at a reduced rate.[16] Another factor and one not so far touched upon was the demand for labour by the oil industry. So far the analysis has been concerned largely with agricultural labour. As was seen in chapter 6, however, this period from 1925 saw the rapid increase in the growth of the oil industry. Before 1918 that industry employed less than 1,500 persons. By 1927 it was employing more than 5,000.

But it will be misleading to over-emphasize the direct effects of this competition for labour. At no time could the demand for labour by the oil companies really jeopardize sugar, and for the following reasons: firstly, the labour employed by oil was small relative to capital invested. In addition to a low labour/capital ratio, and labour/output ratio, the oil companies' demand for labour was small relative to the total labour force.

Secondly, the oil industry employed mostly West Indians (Africans) to do the heavy work of preparing sites, roads, drilling and so on. East Indians, less robust, found this type of work rather heavy and were actually more efficient at sugar cultivation. The extent of the sugar/oil competition for labour was therefore not very great. There was, in fact, an element of complementarity. Of course, in any given situation of labour shortage the higher wages and better conditions of employment in oil would have meant that sugar estates would have lost some of the West Indian labour which would otherwise have been available. Later, East Indians also joined the oil industry labour force.

In the actual situation competition for labour affected chiefly the mechanical, transport and factory sections of the sugar industry. Cocoa, which employed mostly West Indian labour and which was still suffering somewhat from world prices and more so from disease, lost some labour to oil. On the whole, however, cocoa was demanding less labour, economizing (sometimes unwisely) on its cultivation methods to reduce costs. The labour flowing to the oil industry could not therefore be said to have embarrassed cocoa in any way.

Although the demand for labour by oil did not greatly affect, directly, the supply of labour to agriculture; indirectly, however, it had its effects. The higher wages and better conditions of labour in the oil industry set a standard which neither sugar nor cocoa could emulate. Labour, however, found it attractive. It is not possible to state precisely to what extent this disparity of wage rates and so on affected the labour situation. It is to be expected, however, that the existence of this disparity made for dissatisfaction on the sugar estates especially. It strengthened the prior dissatisfaction of cane farmers and sugar labourers, was evident in every labour dispute and must have contributed to the drift from agriculture.[17] Other factors (in World War II) were to have the same affect of strengthening and acting upon an already growing dissatisfaction with sugar conditions: dissatisfaction with conditions in the industry and dissatisfaction with conditions in the industry relative to other industries.

During the Great Depression, 1930–34, the prices of sugar and cocoa fell. While the decline in cocoa prices continued, sugar prices had been more or less stabilized following the Imperial Preference Agreement.

In the case of cocoa, therefore, work was curtailed, wages reduced and the size of tasks was increased, so that production costs could be kept in

Year	Cocoa per Fangea (110 lb), $	Price (Cocoa) per Ton, $	Sugar – Grey Crystals per Ton (f.o.b.), $
1929	10.99	219.80	55.20
1930	9.34	186.80	49.20
1931	6.88	137.60	43.20
1932	6.94	138.80	46.60
1933	5.03	110.60	45.60
1934	6.00	120.00	40.00

line with export prices. But in the midst of these attempts to reduce costs, in spite of an increased total labour force (through population growth) there were reports of labour shortages on estates.

This shortage was largely offset in the following way. The lower prices ruling for cocoa resulted in smaller incomes to the small peasant proprietors. They were unable to cultivate as intensively as before, also they needed money. They therefore made their labour available, at least part-time, to the larger estates.[18]

Government Assistance to Agricultural Industries

Perhaps there would have been no "shortage" of agricultural labour if the government had not given relief both to sugar and cocoa through the Sugar Industry Relief Ordinance No. 157/1930 and the Cocoa Industry Relief Ordinance No. 36/1930 (amended by No. 22 of 1932).

The Great Depression had shown (if such a lesson was needed) the complete dependence of the agricultural community upon export crops, a dependence which rendered it particularly susceptible to fluctuations in prices on the world markets. The fall in export prices had completely altered the situation from one of labour shortage to one of shortage of employment even in agriculture.

The government relief measures steadied the situation somewhat but the drop in revenue to both industries and the general market situation had been too strongly adverse to be reversed by the government relief measures. In the case of sugar the relief was very substantial and the sugar industry did contribute to reducing the incidence of unemployment. In the case of cocoa the relief was not well-organized, not as substantial, and this, coupled with the prior unsound financial position of the estates and disease and senility, made it impossible for cocoa to employ large numbers or pay high wages.

1935–1939

Chapters 1 and 2 dealing with the export/import situation and subsequent chapters dealing with the chief industries have already indicated that the period 1935–39 was one of considerable expansion.

This increase of activity is reflected in an increased demand for labour in every sector.

In sugar the downward trend in the number of cane farmers which started in 1928 was checked and the numbers increased from the low point of 15,500 in 1934 to 20,700 in 1937. The general absence of employment figures[19] prevents one getting an accurate picture of the increase in sugar labourers. It would appear, however, from the reports of the director of agriculture for the period that there was some increase in the number of labourers employed.

In cocoa also there is similar difficulty about obtaining precise data. The upturn in prices and export values in 1937 would, however, have led to some increase in employment. The most spectacular increase in employment, as in exports, was, however, in the petroleum industry. The numbers employed by the companies and contractors increased, thus doubling in four years.

1935	1936	1937	1938	1939
7,331	9,740	12,363	14,952	13,074

This all-round increase in employment in the export industries would have had secondary effects on employment in the other sectors; effects which, in the absence of better data, are impossible to determine.

One important problem stands out in the 1935–39 situation, however. Why did the strikes and riots occur in 1937 (an apparently prosperous year) and start in that industry (petroleum) in which employment had been increased so rapidly, and in which wages and conditions of service had advanced beyond the standards set in every other industry?

This problem and that concerning the other labour disputes will be analysed in a subsequent section of this chapter.[20]

Seasonal Demand

So far the cyclical demand for labour influenced, as it is, by world market price and demand considerations, has been examined. This section treats the purely seasonal factors that affected the demand for labour.

Sugar

Except when the sugar industry is expanding or contracting the sugar estates, taken together, show very little variation in the aggregate demand from year to year for labour. This is largely because a more or less fixed pattern of cultivation is employed. Of the area reaped in any one year, about one-third is in plant canes, and the other two-thirds in ratoons of two or three years. Every year, therefore, about one-third of the area is planted. The year to year labour force is therefore, *ceteris paribus*, fairly constant. But within any one year the variations in the labour force are considerable. The year is conveniently divided into "crop season" and "out of crop season". The crop season may employ twice or three times as many persons as the out of crop season. Also work is available in crop for six days a week, but out of crop only three to four days a week.

The supply position is also rather fickle. Many workmen do not desire all-week work on estates. Some prefer to plant rice and other crops on some days. It is difficult to reconcile the point of view of labour and employer on this question. The employers' view is that labour is unreliable, often shiftless; this is partly true; labour does prefer to work part-time "on the estates". The last three words are the operative ones.

The main difficulty is to distinguish between the man who is involuntarily unemployed, who is genuinely desirous of extra employment but is unemployed on the estate because the estate is not offering enough employment, and the man who wishes to work only a few days, earn enough and then have a rest or work on his own plot.

The following point emerges clearly, however. Whatever may be the attitude of labour, the irregularity of employment offered on sugar estates reinforces low wage rates in discouraging regular attendance of labourers. To ensure his survival during the out of crop season, the labourer finds it prudent to maintain his own cultivation all the year round.

He will work more intensively on the estate during crop. But he will not sacrifice his own subsistence crops for work on estates. The Wages Advisory

Board in 1935 found that on one estate labourers were offered extra pay on the following basis:

a. ¼ day's pay extra for four days work per week;
b. ½ day's extra pay for five days;
c. One day's pay for six days per week.

In spite of this, only 50 per cent of workers worked four days or more. The average was three to five days per week.

In one respect irregular working helped the labour situation. It allowed for the spreading of employment among more men, but it handicapped the large estates.

This offer was not very attractive to the following categories of labour for the following reasons:

1. *The cane farmer*. Since the financial incentive given by the sugar estates was made possible by higher prices of sugar, higher prices would also have been ruling for canes. It would therefore have been more profitable for him to tend his own canes rather than work as a labourer on estate canes.
2. *The ordinary labourer* would have weighed the immediate gain through more regular employment against the deterioration through neglect of his subsistence crops.[21] If he were East Indian, which he most likely was, his crop would have been rice, his principal article of diet. For him, ensuring his supply of rice is vital, it ensures almost complete self-sufficiency. Wages must be high and employment very regular to make him forego his rice planting. It has been found that in 1928 10 out of 17 sugar estates and 10 out of 14 cocoa estates in the western counties experienced shortages of labour on account of rice planting.[22]

It is evident, therefore, that the irregular supply of labour is caused largely by the irregularity of employment offered. Estates do not complain about irregularity of employment during the "out of crop" season. There may be some element of laziness involved as the employers claim; there are, however, in the eyes of the labourer at least, good economic grounds for preferring to work part-time all the year round rather than full-time for half the year and then part-time for the other half.

There is evidence that part-time working is not an essential characteristic of the labour force of Trinidad. It is characteristic only of the agricultural labour force. In the oil industry, commerce, clerical employment, there is no complaint about irregular working.

Government Expenditure and its Effects on Demand for and Supply of Labour

The demand for labour by the Public Works Department (PWD) was partly seasonal and partly regular. It was seasonal in that in areas where road surfaces and banks were not very secure the rainy season caused landslides and so road repairs. These occurrences did not necessarily coincide with the peak demand on sugar and cocoa estates. Whenever they occurred, however, they won labour from the estates.[23] The PWD wage rates were higher.

Apart from this type of seasonality of employment there were

1. the regular demand for labour for ordinary and recurrent schemes;
2. demand for labour for extraordinary schemes. By and large expenditure on extraordinary works varied with the financial position of the colony, which in turn, linked the PWD demand for labour with the exports/imports situation. In times of government financial difficulties, expenditure and demand for labour were curtailed. The Moyne Commission, commenting on government schemes for relieving unemployment, found that they "all had the character of hastily devised experiments and nothing in the way of long range policy to deal with the problems of unemployment emerged during our investigation".[24]

But it seems that labour prefers seasonal government employment to seasonal employment on the estates. In an interesting and informative study of a rural Trinidad village, Melville and Frances S. Herskovits observed:

> For many reasons work for the P.W.D. is considered desirable by Toco people. Payment is in ready cash, made promptly at fixed intervals, and, more important still, is assured. Even more than this, the remuneration, at the period of this research, was at a higher rate than any estate owners were prepared to pay.
>
> The temporary and limited character of government employment was from their (labourers') point of view, the only element that relieved what otherwise would have been for them a critical labour situation.[25]

Wages and Conditions of Work

In agricultural labour which predominates in Trinidad, men are usually paid not by day but by the task.[26] In the oil industry hourly rates apply for most wage earners, with daily, weekly and monthly rates for other categories.

Agriculture

Tasks

There is no rule about the size of tasks. The Moyne Commission found that "the rates are not fixed by any general agreement or collective bargaining but are usually decided on the spot". More frequently they are arbitrarily decided by the overseers.[2]

Also, quite apart from the amount, that is, physical measurement of the task, there are considerations of the difficulty of the task varying with the season, hardness of the ground, nature of undergrowth and so on.

Table 73[28] gives an idea of size and rates of tasks and also the corresponding average daily earnings. A task was supposed to be approximately what could be done by an average man in one day (8 hours). At least this was the standard demanded by the outstanding labour leader of the day. Even this definition is obviously vague. It has been claimed, and supported by the table, that some men actually perform one, one and half or two tasks per day.

Cocoa Industry

Day's Work

The daily earnings for a day's work on cocoa in 1935 were no higher than in 1913. Earnings for men rose from 35¢ to 40¢ per day in 1913, to 50–60¢ in 1920, the height of the post-war boom, and fell again to 30–40¢ in 1935. The 1935 minimum is even lower than that for 1913. The Trinidad *Handbook* for 1924 gave the agricultural wage for that year as 40–50¢. It would seem, therefore, that wages fell gradually from 1920 under the impact of the generally depressed condition of export prices and incomes and did not recover until about 1937[29] when the daily earnings went up to 44–80¢. This gradual reduction in wages until 1924 at least is seen in the following quotation from the *Handbook*: "Since 1921 the rate of wages have through force of circumstances been gradually decreased though not to any great extent, and this has led to a desire at the present time, on the part of certain sections of the community to emigrate to the USA and other countries where the wages offered are more attractive."[30]

Of course a fall of wages from 50–40¢ minimum is much greater than the *Handbook* suggests. Also the desire to emigrate confirms the severity

Table 73 Agricultural Wages

	Pre-War 1913	1920	1924	1935	1938–39 ($)	End of 1937
Men	35–40	50–60	40–50	35–40	2.50–3.50/wk 44–80	
Women	30	30–40	25.35	25.30	1.65–2.25/wk 25–35	
Children	12–25	15–30		15.25		
Cacao Estates (Earnings per Day)						
Days work						
Men	35–40	50–60		30–40		
Women	30	30–35		25–30		
Children	15–25	15–30		15–25		
Tasks						
Cutlassing	35–40	50–75		30–40	Men 40–50 Women 25–35	40–50
Draining	50–65	70–90		50–60	4.50 wk	
Round ridging	30–45	40–60		30–40		
Pruning generally		50–60		40–60	2.50–4.00 wk	
Picking day work		60–90		40–60		
Oil					15,000	
Sugar and cocoa					+41,000 employees	

Notes: 1924: Handbook
1913, 1920, 1924: Wages Advisory Board, CP 88/36
Cacao: Stockmen and Watchmen and those with long service may earn 5–10¢ more. Pre-war tasks adhered to, perhaps more effort required. Total disbursement 50 per cent less than 1929.

of the post-war depression. Jamaica, Barbados and so on have been the great sources of emigration in the West Indies. Trinidad had so far been the recipient of immigration. That the trend in the case of Trinidad should have been reversed shows that the employment/wages situation was indeed serious.

This same trend of a falling wage rate and daily earnings is evident where tasks were concerned.

Sugar

In sugar the pre-war wages or earnings were low, they rose in 1920 and though they subsequently fell, they did not, by 1935, again reach the low pre-war level.[31] A comparison with cocoa shows that while the trend in wages paid in the cocoa industry reflects the trend in world cocoa prices and Trinidad incomes from cocoa, this was not always the case with sugar. The period 1870–1920 which saw the "golden age" of the ccocoa industry was a period of decline in the sugar industry. Note that in 1913 the wage for cutlassing on cocoa estates was 35–40¢ while in the same year cutlassing on sugar estates earned only 25¢. The following factors explain this difference in wage rates:

a. Firstly, and most important, was the prosperity of cocoa and the depression in sugar.
b. Secondly, the overstocking of the sugar labour force through indenture.[32]
c. Thirdly, the better relations between employer and labour in cocoa leading to a greater willingness to share the profits with labour. The Forster Commission found, for example, that during the Depression agricultural labour willingly accepted lower wages. After the Depression, cocoa alone voluntarily increased wages as a result of improved prices of cocoa.[33] Further the frequent riots and disputes affected oil and sugar but not coca. There was also a feeling of close affinity between employer and labour engaged in an industry that was largely peasant owned, and that was domestic in a way that neither sugar nor oil was.

The wages for 1920 show the same trend: the peak of cocoa's prosperity with cocoa wages still above those on sugar estates for the same tasks. But even these higher money wages were not commensurate with higher export prices and were not enough to offset the rise in import prices. The 1920 cost of living committee found that owing to the high prices ruling for sugar, cocoa and coconuts, the planters were in a position to pay better wages (tables 74 and 75).[34]

By 1935 sugar wages were in most cases above those in cocoa for the same kind of task. But in 1937 the rise in cocoa prices, temporary though it was, had again led to an increase in wages on cocoa estates, bringing cocoa wages above those in sugar, for example, cutlassing, sugar 35¢ a task; cocoa 40–50¢ a task (thus the voluntary wage increase). Although wages in the cocoa industry varied freely with the prices of cocoa on the world market, the wages on sugar estates did not. The Forster Commission pointed to the readiness with which labour accepted lower wages during periods of

Table 74 Sugar Estates

Male, Female, Juvenile	Pre-war 1913	1920	1935	1939 Average Daily Earnings	End of 1937	
Cutlassing	25	40–60	30	40–50	35	
Banking	30	40–60	40–50	45–60	45	
Draining	42	50–80	55–65	60–90		80–100
Cutting plants	25	35–40	35–40		35	35–50
Weeding plants	25	35	25–35	35–40	35	35–50
Cutting canes	35	50–90	45–60	50–75	35	80–100
Carting	42	55–70	55–65	80–90		40–50
Coconut Estates						
Day						
Men	30–40	45–60	35–45			
Women	25–30	35–40	25–30			
Children	15–25	15–30	15–25			
Tasks						
Cutlassing	40		25–35			
Weeding	25		25–30			
Picking per 1,000 nuts	60–70	1.20	60–80			
Collecting dropped nuts		60–90	40			
Extracting copra			45–60			
Husking	60–90	1.20	60–90			

Notes: Sugar – Expert workmen may make more per day, for example, the more skilled drainer as much as 75¢ and cane cutters who do three tasks up to 90¢.
Tasks same as pre-war.

rationalization and, in an oblique reference to sugar, to the fact that wages were not restored in all industries after the Depression. The governor had previously, in a politically injudicious, but nevertheless accurate analysis of the causes of the 1937 disturbances, mentioned the fact that the subsidy to sugar was not intended to allow them to pay dividends but wages.[35]

Mineral Industries

Data on the wages paid in the oil industry before 1924 are not considerable (table 76).

Table 75 Agricultural Labour Rates of Wages*

Sugar			
			Factory Workers
Skilled labour	$1.00 to $1.60 per day		8–8½ hours
Semi-skilled	70¢ to 95¢ per day		8–8½ hours
Unskilled	55¢ to 65¢ per day		8–8½ hours
Cultivation			
Operation	**Size of Tasks**	**Rate**	**Average Daily Earnings**
Cutlassing	30 rods	35¢	35–40¢
Forking	18–20 rods	45¢	45–65¢
Banking	28–32 rods	45¢	45–65¢
Lining	per acre	40–45¢	80¢–$1.00
Planting	1,200/1,400 plants	40–45¢	45–60¢
Cutting	1,000/1,200 plants	35¢	35–50¢
Draining	25/30/40¢ per chn	–	80¢–$1.00
Weeding	varies	35¢	35–40¢
Carting pen manure	8–9¢ per ton	–	70¢
Head pen manure	150 baskets	35¢	35¢
Cutting canes	varies	35¢	35–70¢
Carting canes	14¢ per ton	cartermen/loaders	80¢–$1.00
Small gang	day of 8 hours	20–30¢	40–50¢
Applying artificial manure	"	25¢	–
Stock keepers	"	75–90¢	–
Stockmen	"	50–55¢	–
Grooms	"	50–60¢	–
Tractor drivers	"	$1.60–1.90	–
Ploughmen	"	80¢	–
Watchmen	"	50–55¢	–
Loading derrick hands	"	55–60¢	–
Cocoa			
Cutlassing per 100 trees		40–50¢	
Pruning per 100 trees	Light	50–65¢	
	Heavy	80¢–$1.20	
Draining per 100 feet	Lateral	40–60¢	
	main	40¢–$1.00	
Picking and breaking		60¢–$2.40 per barrel depending on the quantity of ripe cocoa at the time of picking	

Note: Day rates average approximately 45¢ for an 8–8½-hour day for men and 30–35¢ for women. On coconut, citrus and other estates the rates paid follow generally those paid on cocoa estates.

Government estates:

Minimum rates for an 8th day:

Port of Spain 60¢ Country 45¢

In estimating the average daily earnings of any class of agricultural labourer it must be remembered that the greater part of the work performed on estates is task work. A task is completed in approximately 4 or 5 hours and labourers can, if they so desire, increase their daily earnings by undertaking an additional half or a second task.

In addition to actual cash payments, a number of estates provide a proportion of their regular labourers with free barrack accommodation, fuel and other pre-requisites.

*The table gives the wage rates in force on agricultural estates at the end of 1937. Labour on sugar estates was about 12½ per cent more than in 1938.

Table 76 Wages in the Oil Industry

	1924	A 1935	B 1935	1939		
				1939 (¢)	Average Weekly ($)	Normal Week (Hours)
Blacksmiths and strikers	18–24	18–24	12–17	9–26	5.13–14.34	45–56
Boilersmiths				9–26	7.00–14.55	"
Carpenters				9–26	3.90–12.17	"
Electricians	12–19	18–24	12–17	9–26	4.64–17.29	"
Fitters		18–24	12–17	9–26	4.32–14.82	"
Masons	13½–24	18–24	12–17	9–26	4.13–12.60	"
Motor mechanics		15–20	9.14	11–26	4.75–15.50	"
Rig-builders	7½–28½	15–20	12–17	9–26	5.56–11.86	"
Welders	9–22	15–24	10–14	9–26	3.40–15.12	"
Rigmen		18–24	12–17	9–27		"
Drilling		18–24	9–12	9–26	7.80–14.16	"
Prod.		12–15	9–12	9–26	6.03–14.52	"
Enginemen	9	15–20	10–15	9–26	5.53–1209	50–56
Firemen	9	10–18	10–14	12–26	6.93–12.67	52–56
Surveymen		15–20	9–15	11–26	4.05–9.00	45–56
Watchmen		10–15	7–10	9–19	6.48–13.44	48–84
Road gang		9–12	7–8	9–14	3.22–8.00	45–51
Sanitary men		9–12	7–8	9–14	4.17–8.20	45–56
Clerical staff				3.25–35.00	3.25–31.00	–
Shipping						
Shipwrights		18–24	12–17	14–26	6.97–10.72	45
Pile drivers		18–24	12–17	14–26	12.85–14.17	48
Round captains and engineers		12–24	10–18	12–26	6.80–9.90	48–56
Dock-hands		15–18	9–15	11–17	7.20–9.58	56
Canning operators				14–16	6.80	56–67
Bosuns				1.60+	14.10	48–56
Stewards				1.00	6.85	"
Firemen				1.27	10.80	"

It seems, however, that from 1924 to 1939 there was not a very great change in the wage rates. Wages, which were hourly, had increased but the increases were not great in themselves nor perhaps in relation to the profits earned in the industry.[36]

Taking those cases in which there is a consistent series we see that blacksmith's wages, for example, for the highest grades were the same in 1924 as in 1935. There was a new classification A and B as for all other categories but this only created a less skilled grade receiving a lower minimum and maximum. Actually the maximum of the lower grade is below the minimum of the higher. By 1939 the position of the lower grade seems to have deteriorated for the wages given (compressed into one classification) are 9–26¢ per hour compared with 12–24¢ for 1935. This may have been an attempt to bring in apprentices at the lower rate, however. At the highest grade the wage rate has been increased by 2¢ per hour, that is, about 8½ per cent.

The increases for enginemen, firemen, surveymen at the top of the grade seem to have been more substantial.

The hours of work given for 1939 vary from 45 to 56 per week according to occupation. The wage policy of the Petroleum Association of Trinidad was as follows:

1. The minimum rates for labour shall be as follows:
   Men above eighteen years – 5¢
   Women above eighteen years – 5¢
   Apprentices and boys below eighteen years – 4¢
2. No wages were to be below the minimum.
3. Overtime was to be paid at hourly rates to men after 10 hours in one day or in excess of 56 hours in any one week provided that no overtime rate should be paid for the extra hours worked, due to the changing of the shift. No overtime was to be paid to watchmen (as a matter of interest their hourly rates were, taking the whole period, 7¢ minimum to 19¢ an hour) Overtime was to be paid for all time worked from midnight to midnight on public holidays and so on.

The 10-hour day (56-hour week) seems therefore to have been the rule, that is, a 5½ day week.

The 45–56-hour week mentioned as normal for, say, blacksmiths is misleading in that it was only after 56 hours of work (not 45 hours) that overtime could be earned.

A comparison between the wages and earnings of labour in the sugar and petroleum industries reveals the following interesting fact. The Apex Company estimated that the average wage per man day for the 8 weeks ending 8 October 1935 was 91.5¢. The Wages Board[37] found also that in the case of sugar, "cane cutters who do three tasks" can earn up to 90¢ a day. If one accepts the director of agriculture's opinion that a task takes from 4½ to 5 hours, one finds that to earn anything like the normal wage in the petroleum industry, the skilled cane cutter (the ordinary unskilled labourer was worse off) had in 1935 to work three tasks, that is, 13½ to 15 hours.

This difference in wage rates is accounted for largely by the more prosperous position of the oil industry versus sugar. Another factor was the high proportion of total costs accounted for by labour in sugar as opposed to the oil industry in which both the labour/output ratio and the labour/cost ratio were very low. It has been estimated that in 1935 an increase in ordinary wages from 45¢ to 60¢ a day would have increased the cost of sugar production by 10 per cent and that of cocoa by 20 per cent.[38]

Both the Wages Board of 1935 and the Forster Commission of 1937 found that while the petroleum industry was willing and able to pay higher wages, agriculture was in no position to do so. But even in oil there were difficulties. The prosperity in the petroleum industry was restricted to five to six big firms. The other lesser companies were hardly winning enough oil to meet some of their current expenditure.[39] A general increase of wages would therefore have brought greater pressure upon them.

The asphalt industry was also in an unfortunate position, due largely to the Depression. During 1927–31 an average of 187,742 tons asphalt per annum was mined and removed from the lake. During the succeeding five years, 1932–36, the average dropped to 82,763 tons, that is, 44 per cent of the pre-depression average. In view of the fact that this drop in output occurred at a time when a new concessionaire was operating it was hardly likely that the industry was in a position to pay really high wages.[40]

Public Works

The pre-war (1913) wage to PWD labour was 50¢. By 1922 it was 65–70¢; the majority of labourers receiving 70¢. At the time of the Depression and until 1937 it was 56¢. The 1937 money wage was therefore only 6¢ a day above the 1913 wage (table 77).

Table 77 Average Wage to Skilled Workers in Port of Spain

		Pre-war 1913	1920	1924	1935
Cabinet maker	(Day)	1.00	1.80	1.50–1.60	1.60
Coppersmiths	(Hour)	16	23	17–20	22
Fitters	(Day)	1.50	1.87	12½–25	1.40
Moulders	(Day)	1.00	1.25	10–18	1.44
Pattern makers	(Day)	1.10	1.44–1.89	12–20	1.17–1.62
Shipwrights (carpenters)	(Day)	1.20	2.00	$2.00	1.81
Caulker	(Day)	1.50	2.25		2.20
Metal turner	(Day)	80–150	1.62–2.25	10–18¢	1.50
Wood turner	(Day)		Not Included		90
Tinsmiths	(Day)	81–1.17	1.17–1.62	90–1.00	1.45
Plumber	(Day)	85–90	1.10–1.20	$1.30	1.45
Chauffeur	(Week)	–	–	$6–8.40 (without b. and 1.)	3–5.50
Blacksmiths	(Day)	70–1.20	1.37–1.56	18–24	1.67
Painters	(Day)	80	1.20	1.30–1.45	1.30
Wheelwrights	(Day)	1.20	1.65	1.20–1.80	1.50
Masons	(Day)	1.00	1.20–1.44	1.20–1.50	1.55
Carpenters	(Day)	80	1.20–1.44	1.20–1.50	1.40
Compositors	(Week)	–	–	–	3–15
Printers	(Week)	–	–	5.28–11.44	3–12
Bookbinders	(Week)	–	–	–	3–12
Paper rulers	(Week)	–	–	–	7.50–10.50
Semi-skilled					
Chippers	(Day)	63	63–1.08	80–120	80
Stevedores	(Day)	1.20	2.50	1.95	1.62
Coal trimmers	(Day)	1.44	2.50	1.20	1.62
Firemen	(Day)	1.00	1.20	9–11	1.20
Stationary engine drivers		81	1.26	9	1.32
Tram conductors and motormen		93½	1.37½	12	1.20
Lightermen			Not Included		

The wage position in the export industries and in PWD can therefore be briefly summarized as follows:

1. The depressed condition of agriculture for nearly the whole of the period made it difficult, if not impossible, for agricultural industry to pay higher wages.

2. The oil industry, though affected by the Depression, was in a better position to pay higher wages. But the following factors operated to prevent payment of higher wages. (a) The uneven incidence of prosperity in the industry. (b) The tendency of the industry to be united in its wages policy so that wages were fixed to suit the least prosperous or efficient firms. (c) The unorganized state of labour in the industry pre-1937 and (d) The fact of a large available labour force from which to fill the places of dissentients. But even if the oil industry paid higher wages, the total effect of such wages on the total of wages would have been relatively small. Agriculture, not oil, was the large-scale employer of labour. High wages in agriculture would affect the standards of living of larger numbers.
3. The government attempted to maintain as large a number of men as possible in employment which paid a wage above the agricultural wage. As in the case of oil, however, the number thus employed was much too small to have a great effect on the depressed labour situation. Also government's ability to employ labour and pay good wages was adversely affected by the Depression.

Agriculture, therefore, was at the base of the trouble. The commission (1937)[41] found a vicious circle of depressed agriculture and an overstocked unskilled labour market, depressed wages and low labour efficiency due to malnutrition.

Domestics and Shop Assistants

The large number and proportion of the population engaged in domestic service,[42] personal services and employed as shop assistants are indicative of a society lacking in more productive employment opportunities.

In this overstocked labour market low wages are bound to be the rule. Major Orde-Browne found that "conditions in these occupations appear to stand decidedly in need of regulation and definition".[43]

Shop assistants suffered from long hours of work and low wages. Although the Shop Hours Ordinances[44] limited the hours during which shops were to remain open, the employers often made the assistants work after shop hours when considerable backdoor trading took place. On this question of long hours it is interesting to get the opinion of a member of the Legislative Council: "In many occupations of this colony people are worked almost beyond endurance and despite a very spirited effort on this side of the House we were unable to convince Government of the necessity for a change." So overstocked was the labour market, especially in the towns, that assistants were diffident about complaining through fear of possible discharge.

According to the Moyne Commission (1939)[45] the wages paid were from £1–£5 per month ($4.80–$24.00). Major Orde-Browne[46] found the average for males to be $29 and females $18–$19 per month. These low wages had decidedly adverse effects both economically and socially, for the working population. Girls were forced to supplement their wages by undesirable means so that petty theft and prostitution became prevalent.[47]

Domestics

Note how the number of domestics increased in the 1920s and 1930s. Taking the category of "female domestic servants not otherwise classified", one finds that their number increased from 8,000 in 1911 to 18,600 in 1921 and 16,700 in 1931. In 1946 it was 7,900.[48]

The hours of work for domestics, 6 AM to 9 PM, were even longer than for shop assistants. Very few accepted the condition that they live at the place of employment as this would have meant that they would be almost always on call. The Depression led to increased numbers competing for these jobs and even at these low rates of wages. The Moyne Commission found that in certain cases wages were as low as 1/6 per week in the rural areas.

In addition domestic servants enjoyed no security of tenure in their jobs and could have been discharged without payment in lieu of notice.

Both in the export sector and in the domestic sector, therefore, wages were low. The chief causes were, firstly, the decline in that part of the exports sector which employed most labour and secondly the continued increase in the size of the labour force. The labour market was therefore overstocked. In addition labour, as will be shown later, was unorganized. In these circumstances it was inevitable that wages were low.

Wages and the COL

An earlier section on money wages showed the manner in which wages were, partly at any rate, influenced by the impact of trading forces on the industries producing for export. In this section an attempt is made to compare the trend in real wages. How much could the wages of 1919 purchase compared with those of, say, 1939?

Incidentally this sort of analysis is likely to give a more realistic picture of the position of the population than that analysis which treats the overall terms of trade. The overall terms of trade analysis would necessarily include all these items, large absolutely and relative to the total trade, which are imported by the mining companies.

Comparing wages and prices of a given representative basket of commodities consumed by the population (nearly all personal income is spent) is therefore a better way of assessing changes in real wages and in standard of living.

Some of the data used have been obtained from the report of the Wages Advisory Board.[49] The board's analysis is very simple; it takes certain commodities which it considers essential, makes a rough estimate of per capita consumption and prices that basket for the periods pre-war, 1920 and 1935: meat 3½ pounds, potatoes and vegetables 7 pounds, bread and biscuits 8 pounds, sugar 1½ pounds, butter or lard 14 ounces. It considered this collection of products the minimum for a healthy man and priced it as follows:

	Pre-war	1920	1935
Port of Spain	(100) $1.18	(205) $2.42	(121) $1.43
Country districts	(100) $1.12	(196) $2.20	(132) $1.48
Tobago	(100) $1.42	(180) $2.55	(108) $1.53

Taking Port of Spain pre-war as 100, according to this calculation 1920 is 205 and 1935 is 121.

The board found that the relation between rates of wages and COL in Port of Spain was in 1935 rather better than before the war and very much better than in 1920, but the position of agricultural labour, while much better than in 1920, was on the whole less favourable than before World War I.

Lieutenant Colonel Hickling of the petroleum industry carried out an investigation in 1937 and found that the COL figure had in that year risen by 17 per cent over that of 1935.[50]

Certain points emerge clearly:

1. The absolute poverty of wages and consequently the small number of items on which such wages could be spent.
2. The inadequacy of the basket selected from the point of view of nutrition.
3. The extent to which the boom of 1920 had led to a greater proportional increase in the prices of consumption goods than in wages.

(The change in the ratio of exports/imports[51] may not have been so unfortunate or large.) Real income analysis, however, is better served by the wages/prices ratio analysis.

4. The fact that on the whole skilled, semi-skilled and unskilled labour in Port of Spain was relatively better off than country labour. Indeed, allowance must be made for the extras which the country labourer obtained, for example, housing, such as it was, a little food and so on. But the town dweller had certain amenities also. On the whole the balance seems to have been in favour of the urban worker. This must in part explain the drift from the country to the town which was taking place throughout the period.[52]
5. Rents: While the price of foodstuffs fluctuated somewhat and the 1935 prices for instance were considerably below those for 1920, the opposite was the case with rents.

The following table shows the upward trend in rents (cents per week):

	Pre-war (cents)	1920 (cents)	1935 (cents)
Port of Spain	48	60	70
Country	23	23	35

The correlation between the upward trend in rents, and the rate of population growth (especially the rate of growth of the urban population) and the failure of new room space to grow correspondingly make it reasonable to assume a causal relationship between these factors, that is, population and rents. It had been noted that housing rooms had been increasing perhaps step by step with population, but that more rooms were constructed in 1920–30 than in 1930–46, while population increased more rapidly in the latter period. It would appear that such was the demand for housing in the towns that even the Depression had but little effect on rents.

Minimum Wage

The shortage of agricultural labour in the midst of a rapidly growing population and total labour force, the general pronouncement against the level of agricultural wages and the conditions of work of most of the labouring population were indications that something had to be done to improve the position of labour. Local labour leaders and unofficial members of the Legislative Council attempted to make the government provide for a minimum wage. Time and again the secretary of state was moved to write as in the following dispatch: "I am inclined to the view that some simple provision empowering the government to intervene in any case which may come to its notice (such cases undoubtedly occur) of the exploitation of illiterate employees by the payment of unduly low wages would be fully justified."[53]

This dispatch was in 1932 in reply to previous Trinidad government insistence that a minimum wage was impossible since tasks, not hourly or daily work, were the rule.[54] In 1935, however, the government introduced into the Legislative Council a Minimum Wages Bill.[55] At first sight the ordinance appears to provide all the power required to meet the situation. The government could fix a minimum rate, would appoint a board to investigate any occupation; employers could be prosecuted for non-compliance with the government's ruling; magistrates could order reimbursements in cases of underpayment; employers could be required to keep records.

But no minimum wage was in fact specified[56] and the Minimum Wages Advisory Board, appointed in 1935 to make recommendations on agricultural labour, confessed itself unable to recommend a minimum wage.

Why was no minimum wage provided? Although the board found from the evidence put before it "that many labourers today are suffering severe hardships, especially those who in the past earned reasonably comfortable incomes on cocoa estates", they would not recommend a minimum wage and for the following reasons:

a. They argued that tasks, not daily or hourly work, were the rule and it was impossible, in view of the varying degrees of "labour effort" required under different conditions of soil, weather and so on to predefine size of tasks.
b. If the economic position of the agricultural industries was to govern the fixing of the minimum wage, it must be on a level to suit estates with only medium potentialities and labour may receive less than at present.
c. If the need of the labourer and not the position of the industry was to be the guiding principle then the large number of cocoa estates struggling to make two ends meet must be abandoned and the position further prejudiced against the labourer.

d. Finally, the minimum wage would inevitably lead to the building up of a labour roster of picked labourers and the discharge of the less efficient.

In short, therefore, a minimum wage would defeat its own end.

Each of the arguments advanced by the board contains some considerable merit. Each, however, exaggerated and distorted the picture somewhat.

As was pointed out in a Minority Report,[57] the difficulty about tasks versus day's work can be largely if not entirely overcome by making a task equal to the average performance per man-day.[58] The idea that a labourer could do two or three tasks a day could only be supported by labour being over-worked.

On the second and third points (b and c), the powerful argument of the depressed exports industries is employed. But the presentation of the argument in (b) is at least disingenuous. The argument there implies that the then existing wage was above the level at which it would have been fixed had consideration of the estates with only medium potentialities been the guiding principle. This is seen in the contention that "labour may receive less than at present".

The question, however, can also be discussed in terms of the factors which resulted in the level of these medium potentialities.

Inability to pay higher wages, where it was largely or overwhelmingly the result of world price considerations or disease in the industry, could reasonably be accepted as a ground for lower wages. As was shown earlier world market conditions did affect estates at certain periods and in those periods labour was willing to accept lower wages.[59]

But reduced potentialities were often governed by factors other than world prices: by indebtedness of owners, mismanagement, absentee ownership, over-spending of the profits of good years on luxuries. In such cases labour should clearly not be required to suffer.

Both in cocoa and sugar there was evidence of this second type of factor undermining the estates.

In chapter 4, "The Sugar Industry", this pampering of inefficiency was seen in the granting of quotas for sale of sugar in the local market, 12,000 tons, where prices higher than export prices to the tune of $68 (BWI) versus free-on-board price of $50 per ton ruled, as a subsidy to the industry. The least efficient producers were given larger quotas than the more efficient.

The question arises then: what would have happened if a higher minimum wage than the existing wage was in operation? Shephard[60] had estimated that an increase in wage from 45¢ to 60¢ would have increased the cost of cocoa production by 20 per cent and of sugar by 10 per cent. At the ruling prices some estates, the senile, mortgaged, diseased, badly run ones would have had to cease production or be sold to other agriculturists. Whether this situation would have been better or worse than the previous one it is impossible to determine. It is reasonable to assume, however, that the dislocation would have been considerable if the more prosperous estates had not bought up and operated the less successful ones.[61]

Regarding (d), an effective labour roster would have resulted only if (i) the labour supply was already too large. This was not the case. There was a shortage of agricultural labour for many years. The increased wages may have increased the supply of labour but it would hardly, by itself, have made labour redundant. (ii) More machinery would have been substituted for labour, only if labour costs consequent on the increased wages were high enough to make machinery competitive, that is, taking into account the relative marginal productivities of these two factors. But in certain processes in agriculture labour has, as yet, little to fear from machinery, for example, in the cutting of canes in certain areas, and more so, the picking and trimming of cocoa. However, after abolition when estates could have introduced machinery they insisted on asking for cheap indentured labour.

Another objection to the minimum wage and one related to (d) aforementioned was presented in another minority report. It contended that before a minimum wage could be considered, the government must undertake an extensive campaign for improvement of the health of the working classes, so that they could earn the minimum wage. If not, large numbers would be thrown out of employment.

The fact of the health of the working population has already been referred to in earlier sections. But this fact is being misused here. It is possible to argue with equal force that the lowered stamina and vitality of labour were the result of continued long hours of hard work for low wages.

The minority report adduced no evidence that the wages then being paid were equal to the marginal productivity of labour and that the then marginal productivity of labour was the maximum labour effort of which labour was then capable. The argument assumed that the wage was equal to the output of labour and that increased wages require a proportional increase in output. The minimum wage demand implied the opposite argument, that is, wages were less than labour's contribution to the value of the final product.

But how often in fact are wage rates determined on precise calculations of the marginal productivity of labour? It would therefore appear that the most important arguments against a statutory minimum wage are, firstly, that the minimum wage tends, in every case where it is upheld by statute only, to become a maximum wage. Secondly, wages and conditions of labour are largely determined by the relative strengths of employer and employee in the industrial struggle. Where trade unions are strong no statutory minimum wage is needed or desired by labour.[62] There can be no substitute, therefore, for a strong trade union and collective bargaining.

> Legislation can act as a palliative and prevent the graver abuses, but there are strict limitations to the power of Government and the public to protect workmen who are unable to protect themselves. Labour laws, indeed, find one of their most effective sanctions in the support of organized unions.
>
> It is in the power to combine that labour has the only safeguard against exploitation and the only lasting security against inhumane conditions.[63]

Finally, however, it may be useful to mention that in the particular industry under discussion, that is, agriculture, the organization of labour is difficult. Too many persons exist in a sort of never-never land between being employee and semi-independent peasant proprietors, some of whom may also employ labour. Whether trade unions could in fact be depended on to help the wages situation in agriculture was therefore difficult to assess. However, table 78 shows that a union was established on 24 November 1937 in the sugar industry, that is, after the strikes and disturbances.

Trade Unions

The Need for Trade Unions

In the earlier discussions on wages it was pointed out that both the size of tasks and the wages to be paid to labour were nearly always unilaterally decided by the employer. As the Forster Commission rightly observed, this state of affairs was due to the fact that no means of collective expression or bargaining were available to labour.

Once again the inter-war picture demands explanation through an earlier one, that is, the period of indenture 1846–1917. The indenture system not only provided a supply of labour, it also provided for certain legal safeguards, albeit hardly observed, for the immigrant. His wage was fixed;

Table 78 List of Workers Trade Unions in Trinidad and Tobago up to 1939

Title	Date of Registration	Description
Trinidad Working Men's Association	Never registered as trade union	All industries
The Amalgamated Builders' and Woodworkers' Union	30 March 1936	Building trade
Federated Workers' Trade Union	21 September 1937	All workers in all trades and industries
Oilfield Workers' Trade Union	15 September 1937	Oil industry
Seamen & Waterfront Workers' Trade Union	19 November 1937	Waterfront
Public Works & Public Services Trade Union	26 November 1937	All workers in all trades and industries
All Trinidad Sugar Estates & Factories Workers' Trade Union	24 November 1937	Sugar industry
All Trinidad Transport & General Workers' Trade Union	8 June 1938	All trades and industries
Railway Workers' Trade Union	25 July 1938	Male workers of the Trinidad government railways
Trinidad and Tobago Union of Shop Assistants & Clerks	30 August 1938	Retail distribution
Printers' Industrial Union	11 October 1938	Printing industry
Civil Service Association of Trinidad and Tobago	23 March 1939	All officers on the fixed government establishment

Note: Compiled mainly from P.W. Dalley: "Trade Union Organization and Industrial Relations in Trinidad", CO. No. 215, and other sources.

housing, such as it was, was provided, and the employer was under a legal obligation to government for the well-being of the immigrants.

The cessation of the system of indenture removed all these obligations on the part of the employer. Labour, all labour, became free to work or not to work and if possible to demand its own standard of wages. But, as was pointed out earlier, the general economic situation more often than not militated against high wages. But this was not the only factor. Another and as important, was the absence of trade unions. Cessation of indenture had created a vacuum and resulted in the shift from an established and understood, if somewhat unsatisfactory, relationship between labour and employer, to one in which there were no obligations on the part of employers and no powers on the part of labour to make any demands.

Labour was unorganized, mainly agricultural and scattered physically over the islands. In addition, labour was already financially poor. The Moyne Commission,[64] commenting on the absence of trade unions which must provide the countervailing power so necessary to keep the labour–capital relationship in balance, observed: "On the other hand employers in the West Indies have long been associated for purposes of trade and in some cases – for example among sugar manufacturers – their organization has attained a high state of efficiency."

There were therefore only informal arrangements for fixing wages, no collective bargaining and "wage rates have followed standards laid down by the employers alone".

Note also that in addition to the unsatisfactory condition of the removal of obligations under indenture, the absence of trade unions, the financial poverty of labour, the absence of any medium of expression of grievances on the part of labour, there was another factor to complete the vicious circle of poverty and low wages. The population was increasing at the rate of about 2 per cent per annum with the result that the labour market was becoming more overstocked and the bargaining power of labour correspondingly reduced.

In cocoa, the employer–labour relation was good, less impersonal. In oil, the relation was very impersonal but though wages and housing were better than in any other industry labour was as ill-equipped for bargaining as in agriculture.

In sugar the relationship was bad. Housing was unhealthy, wages low and the attitude of employers to labour most unenlightened. This fact is perhaps explainable in terms of the historical employer–employee relationship in the industry. The Forster Commission[65] refers to the callousness of sugar employers towards their labour both in matters of wages and housing. Another indication of their attitude to labour was mentioned in the chapter on sugar where the governor's proposal that all sections of the industry be represented on a committee to consider the price of farmers' canes was noted.[66] The sugar manufacturers objected on the grounds that the sugar workers and farmers were unorganized and could not find a representative and that their inclusion would only "multiply difficulties instead of reducing them". What sort of "agreement" could have been arrived at without the participation of the farmers is difficult to imagine.

The following extract from the Moyne Commission regarding wages and housing on estates is also applicable to the whole labour–management relationship and succinctly sets out the indenture and post-indenture conditions:

> On many estates the labourer is given free housing, but he has no security of tenure and may feel that, should he complain, he will be in danger of dismissal. He has gained in freedom but his employer is not under an obligation to give him good living conditions and what he receives today is not a right but an act of a benevolent autocracy.[67]

Further,

> to say that the West Indies labourer is placed at a disadvantage in bargaining with his employer who in all probability owns the range in which he lives and would evict him at short notice is to understate the case. Devoid of any effective protection by means of Trade Unionism, the labourer is helpless and, if he wishes to live, must accept the rate of pay offered to him. In the light of this it is not surprising to find that earnings have remained extremely low even in periods when planters were making good profits.[68]

Trade Union Legislation

How was the necessary countervailing power of labour to be brought to hear on the Trinidad and Tobago situation? The history of trade unionism in Great Britain showed that without the necessary legislation trade unions could not function.[69]

Again, as in the case of minimum wage legislation the secretary of state took the initiative in directing that legislation be enacted to make possible the setting up, growth and functioning of trade unions in Trinidad and Tobago. As with minimum wage, the colonial government saw no need for trade union legislation.[70] Before this there had been only one organization, the Trinidad Working Men's Association, which could approximate to a trade union.

The first piece of legislation on the subject to come before the Trinidad and Tobago Legislative Council was Trade Union Ordinance No. 20/1932.[71] This ordinance was in many respects limited and unsatisfactory. It was concerned only with the organization, registration and control of trade unions. While the ordinance sought to "prevent the exploitation of illiterate workmen and simple-minded people by unscrupulous organizers" by insisting on the rendering of accounts and so on, the role of trustees, the safeguarding of funds, liability to sue and be sued, political levy, it was considered undesirable to include the provisions regarding trade disputes, strikes, lockouts, picketing, and liability to action for torts.

The ordinance therefore sought to set up trade unions; to make them safe for working men and while ensuring the internal "correctness" of the trade union took no steps to give them any external power in industrial relation.

And the reason for these commissions was that "care has been taken not to include in the Bill any mater of a contentious nature".[72] Actually it was so uncontroversial as to appear innocuous.

The limitations of the ordinance were not solely the responsibility of the colonial government. They were set on the recommendation of the secretary of state for the colonies. Not even the provisions about picketing in the 1927 UK Trades Disputes and Trade Unions Act, unsatisfactory as they were and retrograde in relation to the acts of 1897 and 1906, were to be considered. See the extract from Lord Passfield's dispatch: "It is, however, necessary for me to observe that the provisions of the Trade Disputes and Trades Union Act of 1927 are (or may become in the near future) subjects of acute controversy in the country. I could not agree therefore to their adoption in the Dependencies."

Lord Passfield's intentions may have been laudable, that is, to prevent the inclusion of such unsatisfactory legislation in the Statute Books of the Dependencies. Whatever the justification for that course of action, however, the result was that it left a vacuum.[73] In effect, the 1932 ordinance brought trade unionism in Trinidad only up to the friendly society stage of development.

The attorney general insisted that there was nothing to prevent peaceful picketing. His statement was only partly correct, however. Whereas peaceful picketing in industrialized countries largely involves the placing of pickets on public roads and public land, picketing on sugar estates could involve the pickets in action for trespass and for the following reasons:

1. Where labour is partly resident on estates it could not be approached to be persuaded to strike without trespassing on estate lands.
2. Some of the roads leading to the fields are estate owned so that placing pickets there would also be trespassing.
3. The estates are so large that picketing the boundaries or entrances is impossible; to speak to workers pickets would have to trespass.

The 1932 ordinance was followed by the Trade Dispute (Arbitration) and Inquiry Ordinance of 1938. It provided for the replacement of the old Industrial Court (Ind. Court Ordinance 26 of 1920) with its permanent president and sanctions and an atmosphere of compulsion by a tribunal of arbitrators, and assessors. It sought to replace compulsion with conciliation.

The formal removal of the provisions for the Industrial Court was in fact no great loss. It had never functioned. The encouragement of conciliation was a laudable change. It must be observed, however, that conciliation is satisfactory only where the persons or organizations involved are fairly evenly matched or are not too selfish. In labour/management disputes where labour is weak, unorganized and cannot even resort to legalized peaceful picketing, while management is strong and organized, labour is at a decided disadvantage. But the very existence of a tribunal can be an incentive to labour to organize. This in fact happened as can be seen from the growth of trade unions shown in table 78.[74]

The Trade Dispute (Arbitration and Inquiry) Ordinance 1938 was amended on 4 November 1938. "To protect parties from incriminating themselves by allowing them to refuse to produce evidence on grounds of self incrimination." The amendment was reasonable but government had been so keen to give the impression that the original ordinance had "full powers to demand evidence" that the comment of the *Port of Spain Gazette* is justified:

> to give an arbitration tribunal or Board of Enquiry as the case may be, "full powers to require any person to furnish in writing or otherwise, such particulars in relation to such matters as the Tribunal, or Board may require", and then to give the right to any witness so ordered to refuse to answer questions or to produce relevant documents is highly farcical.

What was most unfortunate was the timing of the amendment. It came only about four months after the original ordinance and, more to the point, a few weeks before the first arbitration proceedings to be experienced in the colony (between the oil industry and the workers). Immediately the ever-present if latent suspicions of labour that government was taking sides was awakened and the *Port of Spain Gazette* remarked that the "proceedings would probably disclose at whose behest the draft bill has been issued and its real objects and reasons".

Of course the ordinance would in principle operate both for labour and management. In fact, however, at that time labour had nothing to hide, no books or documents, the presentation of which would weaken their case for better wages and conditions. Few commercial undertakings are prepared, however, to disclose their books to arbitrators who may decide in view of their position and profit that they could afford higher wages.

Legally, however, not even the Supreme Court could have required anyone to give evidence or produce documents that would incriminate him. The original ordinance therefore gave the tribunal greater powers than those possessed by the Supreme Court.

There was no other trade union legislation in the period, though towards the end of the period of study further legislation was contemplated on the question of peaceful picketing and non-liability of trade unions to action for torts.[75]

Workmen's Compensation

The other labour legislation during the period was the Workmen's Compensation Ordinance No. 8 of 1926 (amended in 1932). Workmen's compensation was, however, very limited in its application. It did not apply in the case of (1) agricultural labour unless employed with machinery; (2) domestic, clerical, shop assistants and drivers of motor vehicles. In short the largest section of the working population could not benefit from workmen's compensation.

Further the workman had to suffer too long a period of disability (ten days) before he could be eligible for compensation. The Forster Commission and Major Orde-Browne recommended a reduction of the period from ten to three days.

Labour Administration

The lack of organization on the part of labour is paralleled by an absence of government departments concerned with labour matters. Up to 1935, labour matters were handled by the labour exchange which was run conjointly with the immigration and warden's departments. Its function was merely to direct registered unemployed to employment vacancies when these occurred and were notified to the exchange.

This situation existed in spite of the secretary of state's circular dispatch of November 1935 regarding the creation of labour departments. As an indication of the official attitude towards trade unions, not only was no action taken to set up a labour department but no reply was sent to the dispatch until after the riots and disturbances of June–July 1937. Even then, only a temporary, part-time appointment of a secretary of labour was made.

In 1938 an industrial adviser was appointed. Consequently labour matters assumed a new importance in the colony. Major Orde-Browne reports that thereafter trade unions were better guided and grew in integrity and self-discipline.

Growth of Trade Unions

Before the 1932 ordinance which legalized trade unions, as indicated earlier, there was in Trinidad and Tobago but one organization, the Trinidad Working Men's Association, which could be described as a trade union. Acting upon the advice of the British Labour Party, the leader of this organization of about 18,000 members refused to register his organization as a trade union under the unsatisfactory Trade Union Ordinance of 1932.

Thereafter the first union to be registered was the Amalgamated Builders' and Woodworkers' Union in March 1936, for the building trade. As table 78 indicates the growth of labour unions after this was fast and confused. There was considerable overlapping and competition for membership, a situation which was not likely to strengthen the position of labour in its struggle against management.

But it must not be imagined that the 1932 ordinance was the chief factor promoting the growth of trade unions. It gave the necessary legal sanction but the factor chiefly responsible was the disturbances in Trinidad in 1937. Note, for example, the rapid increase in the members of trade unions registered in and after 1937.

List of Disturbances in Trinidad in the Inter-War Years, in Which the Causes Were Entirely or Mainly Economic

1919. A two week strike of stevedores, accompanied by the riots of 1–3 December. The 1918 annual report refers to the high prices of imported and locally grown goods and the little corresponding increase in wages (committee appointed, report in 1920).

1934. Disturbances on sugar estates: demands for reduction in the size of tasks (local commission appointed, report CP).

1935. (February) (1) Strike at Apex (oilfields) for higher wages and better conditions of work. (2) Hunger march to Port of Spain (the capital).

1937. General disturbances, affecting largely the oilfields and sugar estates (Forster Commission appointed, Cmd. 5641).

Strikes and Public Disturbances

The complex and difficult labour situation in Trinidad and Tobago in the period between the two wars was influenced by two sets of factors, external and internal.

The former concerned the vagaries of world demand and price conditions and this has already been analysed. Some of the internal factors, for example, increases in the population and labour force, legislation and so on, have also been analysed. In this section it is proposed to deal with that one aspect of the labour situation which, in the absence of trade unions, labour departments, statistics and so on, most eloquently portrays the impact of the labour/wages situation upon the working population.

The Moyne Commission reported:

> One of the outstanding phenomena in the history of the West Indies during the last few years is the occurrence of public disorders of such magnitude as to have led in all except three cases to the appointment of a Commission to investigate the causes and character of the outbreak, which are only the symptoms of which the principal causes are low earnings and irregular employment.[76]

For the particular case of Trinidad and Tobago the preceding list indicates the disturbances of the inter-war years and the chief causes of such disturbances.

It is interesting to note the pattern of the disturbances. They occurred in every sector save cocoa where the management–labour relationship was best, and where wages increased voluntarily with improvements in the trading situation. There was only one in the first decade of the period when, as seen in the section treating the distribution of export incomes,[77] cocoa was still relatively prosperous and made a considerable contribution to domestic incomes.

The three that took place in the 1930s occurred almost within a year of each other and were restricted more or less to the sugar and oil industries. As the two kinds of imbalance (mentioned in chapter 1, "Exports")[78] developed, the position of labour deteriorated. In the absence of means by which labour could express its discontent the economic pressure built up in the 1930s culminating in the very serious disturbance of 1937. Like the others its main causes were economic but it was more important than the others. It marked the end of one phase and the beginning of another – both in political development and in the position of labour.

The Forster Commission,[79] in its summary of the causes of the disturbances, understated the economic forces. It referred to "a more or less general sense of dissatisfaction"; a sense of dissatisfaction which reached its culminating point when, the cost of living having risen, the earnings of the working people were not adjusted with sufficient promptitude to offset its effects; it then mentions the threats of intimidation, the activities of "Buzz" Butler, and the hesitant policy of government.

While these factors all operated, it would appear that the purely economic factors were somewhat underplayed. Whatever importance may be attached to the other factors (and some of them were important), the basic underlying factor, as the Moyne Commission of 1939 reported, was economic distress.

In this connection it is proposed to list certain extracts from the speech made in the legislature after the disturbances by the then governor of the colony. However injudicious may have been the speech from the political point of view, it gives a vivid and true picture of some of the economic factors which caused the outbreak:

> When I arrived in Trinidad I was somewhat painfully impressed by the poverty here . . .
>
> We have been told that the younger generation are disinclined to work on the land. Is it to be wondered at that in these circumstances, the younger people leave the country and move into town. . . .
>
> In Trinidad the difference between unskilled and skilled workers is 150 per cent . . . (In the U.K. it is 33½%).
>
> I have a definite instance of pressure being brought to bear to prevent an industry paying higher wages because it must thereby embarrass estate owners . . .
>
> There was obviously lack of contact between the men at the top and the men at the bottom (of industry) . . .
>
> Agriculture has been depressed, the unskilled labour market has been overstocked, and wages have been pressed down. When a man has not got a living wage, he cannot possibly be efficient . . .
>
> In a recent dispatch to the Secretary of State I wrote: "Since the time of my arrival in the Colony it has been apparent to me that steps must be taken to establish a minimum wage for the purpose of preventing the exploitation of the poverty of the unemployed and the strike situation has given me the opportunity."[80]

9

Public Finance

The most important single feature of central government finance in Trinidad and Tobago during the inter-war years has been its dependence on fluctuations in the value of exports and imports. This dependence on trade which has been shown to exist in the case of every other section of the economy is illustrated in the case of public finance in figure 6. The upturns and depressions are identical except for slight time lags at certain periods.

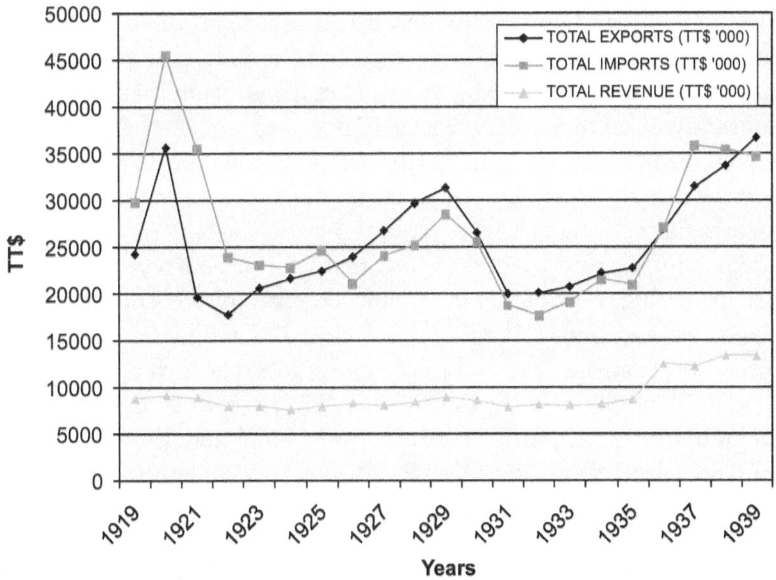

Figure 6: Total imports, exports and revenue in the period 1919–1939.

Both imports and revenue rose sharply, 1919–20, under the impact of the post-war boom in the export industries. But the subsequent downturn in exports preceded and was somewhat sharper than was the case with revenue. After 1922 when the revival in export values had taken place, the lag was once again evident. This time both revenue and expenditure continued downwards with imports for a year or so after the values of exports had turned up.

In the Depression years also, the stagnation in the export trade which was directly restraining imports was reflected both in revenue and expenditure during the period 1930–31 to 1934–35.[1] The Depression adversely affected export values not only in the agricultural industries but also in the mineral industries with the result that revenue both from customs duties and company taxes fell. The fall in the receipts from customs duties – which it will be seen later constituted the largest part of revenue – can be explained in terms of a fall in incomes which led to corresponding fall in the value of imports. And since the customs import duties were mostly *ad valorem*, the shift in the value of imports led directly to a corresponding shifts in revenue.

In the post-Depression period, especially after 1935, one would perhaps have expected that this dependence of revenue on trade might have been reduced.[2] Although this may have happened it did not do so to any significant extent. Customs duties still remained the chief source of revenue. The fault may, however, have been twofold: failure of the domestic income earners to retain and utilize internally a significant part of income that had been accruing in the past from exports and the failure of government to devise a system of taxation which would tax incomes internally rather than significantly when they were spent on imports.

Taxes on imports are paid by the whole population; but the burden falls more heavily on the low-wage earner than on the wealthy or the high income earners.

It must not be considered, therefore, that internal sources were not making an increasing contribution to revenue. For example, revenue from excise duties increased from $1.5 million in 1935 to $2.2 million in 1939. But the contribution from customs and excise duties together increased from $4.9 million to $7.3 million in the same period. Also, in spite of the fact that the value of petroleum exports doubled between 1935 and 1939, the revenue from land sales and royalties increased from $0.7 million to $1.1 million in the same period. The failure of revenues from royalties to increase *pari passu* with the increase in the value of petroleum exports was due to two factors: firstly, the fact of a large part of oil production having taken place on land the oil rights of which were privately owned; secondly, this trend could have been influenced by the system of regressive royalty rates which obtained for some of the larger companies. This point has already been discussed in chapter 6, "The Petroleum Industry". While revenue had to continue to be influenced by the changes in export values, it should have become less dependent on customs and excise duties. However, the colony was still largely underdeveloped and change could only come later.

The arguments set out earlier are not intended to suggest that, overnight, revenue should have ceased to be closely influenced by trade – this would have been impossible. What is aimed at in the foregoing statements is not self-sufficiency in respect of imports but, given the low labour/output ratio of the principal export industry (petroleum), in view also of the relative poverty of agricultural labour, it would appear that less should have been spent on imports of food (see appendix 2). Further, more revenue could perhaps have been earned directly from the oil industry. The leak through imports, which accounted largely for the size of the contribution of import duties, could have been reduced. The aim should have been obtaining increased revenue from a combination of the following:

a. payment of better wages and a better distribution of such incomes;
b a tax system devised to achieve an increase in the number of persons assessed for tax; and
c. further, a raising of the tax revenues both on personal incomes and company profits. In this context the tax department had to learn the nature and intricacies of the petroleum industry, locally and internationally, the better to assess oil company taxable incomes.

Revenue and Expenditure[3]

The policy in government finance for the period can be summed up in one word – "caution". The extreme cautiousness of the policy is seen clearly both in public debt policy (which is discussed later) and in current revenue and expenditure transactions. At two periods only, 1920–21 to 1921–22 and again in 1930–31 to 1932, did expenditure exceed revenue. The excess of expenditure over revenue in the first case was perhaps due largely to the difficulty of making prompt adjustments to expenditure.[4] Adjustments to revenue would have been almost impossible in the short run. But a likelier and a much more powerful factor seems to have been the buoyant confidence[5] in the continuation of the prosperity associated with the previous fifty years of the "golden age" of cocoa. This downturn was therefore seen as a temporary and transient phase, not requiring any immediate cuts in expenditure.

Compare now the first and second deficit periods and it is seen that while they are of equal duration the deficits in the first period (1921 and 1922) are almost of the same size, that is, $1 million, while that of 1931 is $2 million and that of 1932 is only $19,000. Quite apart from the severity of the Great Depression, the force of its initial impact and the promptness with which it was recognized, the quick check on expenditure in the 1930s must be seen in terms of the effects of the stringencies of the 1920s which had succeeded in destroying the earlier confidence, had imposed a restrictionist mentality and had made government psychologically more ready for immediate cuts in expenditure.

There are other differences also. The deficit of the 1920s resulted in the depletion of the surplus balances from $2.3 million in 1920 to minus $61,000 in 1922.[6] The deficits of the 1930s were different both in their size, and their impact on reserves. They also were met from surplus[7] funds, but although the former deficits had exhausted the balances the latter did not. Surplus balances had been built up to the point where they could stand the strain. Further the figures of $2.04 million and $19,000 for deficits in 1931 and 1932 are misleading. The 1931 figure includes (classified under "expenditure") a sum of $1.44 million which was put to reserves. The 1932 figure is also similarly distorted by $255,400 which was put to reserves and $100,200 to the special reserves.

Reserves and Surplus Balances

Successive annual reports and those of Royal Commissions refer to the strong financial position of Trinidad and Tobago, at least *vis-à-vis* the other West Indian islands. This financial strength was due in part to the presence of the mineral industries in Trinidad, but it was due in a large measure to the financial policy which had as one of its chief aspects the accumulation of reserves both in the form of surplus balances and general and specific reserves.

Apart from the four deficit years mentioned earlier the period was one of budget surpluses. In 1936 the budget surplus was $3.4 million when gross revenue was $13.3 million and in each case the surplus was put into the accumulated surplus balances. Further, a reserve fund of $1.3 million was started in 1931 and was increased to $2.2 million in 1935 after which it was liquidated. Note that the initiating and liquidation of reserves coincided with the beginning and the ending of periods of austerity. The accumulation

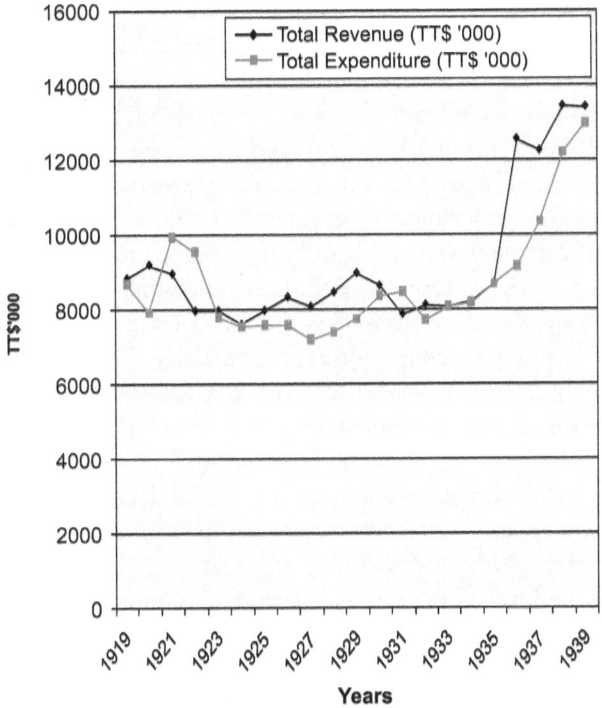

Figure 7: Total revenue and expenditure, 1919–1939.

of surplus balances continued apace, however, and rose from $2.7 million in 1935 to $6.1 million in 1936 and to $9.2 million in 1939 (figure 7).

This policy of cautious finance aimed at increased security rather than greater expenditure on public works that were plainly necessary is in a sense open to attack. But there are other considerations. Reserves are not merely idle resources. What is paradoxical about reserves is the fact that they are most useful when one does not have to use them. One who has ample reserves hardly ever needs to use them. It is precisely the economy that has no reserves, that can find no other way of financing its projects, that is most handicapped. For reserves impart to the holder and to the rest of the world a confidence in the particular economy which improves the credit-worthiness of the holder and facilitates the undertaking of large development projects.

From this point of view, therefore, the policy of accumulation of reserves, even at the expense, for some time, of certain development projects, can be justified. It is one of the views of this book that the achievements of the post–World War I period were largely influenced by the difficulties, the restraint and the accumulations of the inter-war period. Of course, the important question is to determine when the policy of caution and reserve accumulation had succeeded and more specifically at what point should the switch have been made from restraint to expansion. It is clear that a continuation of the drains of 1921–22 would have been disastrous.[8] It is clear also that this period showed the inadequacy of reserves that were as low as $2.5 million when expenditure averaged $8.9 million. It has been shown to what extent revenue fluctuated with both exports and imports. The steadiness of expenditure both for social services[9] and administration can also be seen. In the case, therefore, even of a mild recession in external markets and consequent unstable revenue sources, plus a fairly rigid expenditure trend in certain categories of expenditure, large reserves are absolutely necessary.

The Memorandum on the Sterling Assets of the Colonies[10] stated that some colonies kept reserves equal to 4–6 months of revenue. But the Trinidad and Tobago reserves of 1921 and 1922 were only slightly below the lower limit referred to and they proved quite inadequate. Sir Donald MacDougall[11] in developing the argument for adequate reserves quoted the findings of the United Nations Committee on Measures for International Economic Stability that "experience shows that a country's export proceeds can easily fall by 25% between one year and the next". Where, as in Trinidad and Tobago, the link between trade and revenue is so strong reserves should be adequate to meet at least a fall of the size referred to earlier. Especially is this the case in view of the relative inflexibility of certain expenditure items.

The question still remains, however, of determining the best possible time for a switch from the policy of restraint to that of expansion. The critical date in the case of Trinidad and Tobago appears to have been 1935–36 when prosperity had returned to the export economy. After the experience of the 1920s and the Great Depression[12] when both in 1921 and 1929–30 the downturns came at the precise moment when the economy seemed set for a period of prosperity, a wait of another year or so after 1935 would have been reasonable. It would appear, therefore, that the policy of expansion which was inherent in the ill-fated 1938 Five Year Development Programme could well have been undertaken in 1936–37. The 1938 plan failed because the war supervened and prevented the raising of loans. Without the war the plan could well have succeeded. But any judgment involving a choice of dates so closely linked can only be taken in the calm atmosphere of retrospect. In the given situation the decision is much more difficult and perhaps, a combination of cautious reserve building and gradual expansion may have been best.

Revenue

Table 79 shows the growth of revenue and the chief revenue sources for the period 1919–39. Throughout the period customs and excise continued to be the chief source of government revenue. In fact instead of falling as one would perhaps have expected the contribution to revenue from this source rose from 48.77 per cent of gross revenue in 1919 to 50.7 per cent in 1939.

The chief item under the heading "customs" was import duties which accounted in 1936 for 63 per cent and in 1939 for 65.2 per cent of customs and excise revenue. The importance of the item unmanufactured tobacco can be gathered from the fact that in, say, 1935 it accounted for approximately one quarter of the entire revenue from import duties. Port and harbour dues and export duties are next in order of importance under "customs". Export duties which were very important in the earlier part of the period fell off considerably about 1931–32 with the curtailing of operations on the pitch lake. Asphalt was the chief product on which export duties were levied. There were no export duties on petroleum. Export duties were levied on agricultural produce but the imposition of these duties was a fitful process. For example, taxes were levied in 1919–21 and then suspended; revived in 1924–26 and again suspended on account of the low export prices of agricultural products; then revived once more in 1935–36 until the end of the period to subsidize the cocoa industry. The rates of this produce tax varied from time to time but were in fact low and did not result in a large contribution to revenue. The highest contribution was $417,500 in 1938.

Excise

Revenue from the imposition of excise duties was second in importance only to the revenue from import duties, being just about one-half of the latter, thus:

	1935	1936	1938	1939
Import duties (million)	$3.09	$3.44	$4.66	$4.74
Excise duties (million)	$1.54	$1.69	$2.06	$2.20

Table 79 Growth and Sources of Revenue ($'000)

		Chief Components			Earnings of Land Sales		
Year	Gross Revenue	Customs and Excise (per cent)	Licences (per cent)	Taxes on Incomes	Government Department	Royalties	Railway (per cent)
1919	6,445.8	3,144.1 = 48.77	847.3 = 13.14	310.5 = 4.81%	436.9 = 6.7%	230.2 = 3.6%	1,039 = 16.1
1920	9,205.2	4,740.3	995.9	518.2	536.5	270.0	1,081.9
1921	8,966.1	4,048.1	936.2	1,027.0	810.2	222.1	1,070.4
1922	7,975.7	3,977.9	922.0	944.3	664.6	283.6	982.4
1923	7,841.0	4,139.3 = 52.8	1,155.6 = 14.7	327.8 = 4.2	768.0 = 9.8	291.2 = 3.7	893.1 = 11.4
1924	7,616.8	3,913.1	940.8	512.3	728.2	342.6	824.5
1925	7,981.8	4,092.5	939.4	577.3	768.8	456.6	796.6
1926	8,339.0	4,174.8	965.5	589.0	886.8	568.7	888.5
1927	8,841.1	4,684.1 = 53	1,016.6 = 11.5	775.4 = 8.77	815.2 = 9.2	520.1 = 5.8	748.0 = 8
1928	9,214.1	4,854.0	1.061.8	895.8	781.7	569.0	745.0
1929	9,663.1	5,255.9	1.052.5	865.0	755.7	684.0	684.4
1930	9,320.2	4,988.0	1.029.8	914.3	704.6	627.0	676.7
1931	8,478.5	4,414.1 = 52.1	1,161.1 = 13.7	673.4 = 7.9	648.0 = 7.6	589.7 = 6.9	601.0 = 7.1
1932	8,756.6	4,182.8	1,064.0	611.6	603.7	601.0	624.7
1933	8,744.4	4,566.7	937.4	645.9	178.6	557.7	646.4
1934	8,776.7	4,555.5	981.8	715.6	172.0	557.8	566.4
1935	9,312.2	4,938.3 = 53.0	1,263.7 = 13.6	671.4 = 7.2	199.1 = 6.8	661.1 = 7.1	619.5 = 6.6
1936	13,276.9	5,406.0	1,253.7	878.0	219.4	648.9	716.6
1937	13,103.6	6,821.0	1,331.3	1,140.0	285.3	749.3	850.8
1938	14,338.6	7,062.0	1,412.0	677.0	411.4	925.5	893.4
1939	14,331.4	7,269.0 = 50.7	1,341.3 = 9.4	1,405.0 = 9.1	407.2 = 2.9	1,081.2 = 7.5	910.1 = 6.4

The important duties under this heading were on rum and spirits[13] and on petroleum spirit and petroleum oil. In spite of the greater prominence often given to the role of petroleum in the economy it is interesting to note that rum and spirits, not petroleum products, were the chief contributors to revenue under this sub-head. The figures for the two items of the last five years of the period are as follows:

$'000	1935	1936	1937	1938	1939
Rum and spirits	826	900.3	999.4	1,072.7	1,130.3
Petroleum products	635	704.0	805.4	890.6	963.8

In 1939 rum and spirits accounted for 51 per cent and petroleum products for 43.8 per cent of excise revenue. Excise duties were also charged on matches, beer and copra products. The contribution from the latter was about $50,000 a year for the last five years of the period. But in no case was the rate of duty high on these secondary products. Also the quantities entering into Trinidad and Tobago were small so that revenue from these products was not considerable.

The rates of duty applicable for all these products varied slightly from time to time but the following rates operated for most of the period:

Rum and spirits	(per proof gallon)	$3.12
Petroleum spirits	(per gallon)	16¢
Petroleum oil	(per gallon)	12¢
Beer	(per gallon)	17¢
Deodorized edible oil		10¢
Lard substitutes	(per 100 lb)	42¢
Matches	(per gross box)	6¢
Laundry soap	(per 100 lb)	20¢

The rates of petroleum seem to have been very low. Actually until 1930 they were even lower, at 12¢ per gallon. Compare, for example, the rates ruling in India at about the same time.[14]

Motor spirit (per gallon) 10 annas plus a surcharge of 25 per cent
= 22½¢ plus 5 5/8¢? = 28 1/8¢?

Matches (per gross box) RI = 36¢

Taking petroleum spirits first it would be clear that the rate of tax in Trinidad and Tobago was considerably below that in India. The same applies in the case of matches. But the argument for an increase in the petroleum spirits rate of tax can be strengthened from another direction. A.R. Prest[15] in his work on the Fiscal Survey of the British Caribbean refers to the fact that the number of persons paying income tax in Trinidad and Tobago was smaller than the number of persons owning private cars. The consumption of petrol in the inter-war years indicated an upward trend. It is not being suggested that the excise duty should be a substitute for efficiency in the assessment and collection of income tax especially from the petroleum companies but that the excise duties could have been increased and that those who would have borne the increase would have been in a position to bear that increase. One does not know what the elasticity of demand at the ruling price was. It appears likely, however, that elasticity was less than one so that an increase in price consequent on a small increase in the tax would not have affected sales considerably as long as people remained prosperous enough to purchase cars.[16]

Licences and internal revenue not otherwise classified accounted for 13.14 per cent of revenue in 1919 and maintained that proportion more or less throughout the period. The chief items included here are licences for spirit retailers, motor vehicles and driver's licences and so on. Note how rum and spirits make a contribution to revenue in every conceivable way.

Taxes on incomes occupy third place, that is, after customs and excise and licences in the order of importance of revenue sources.[17] Since the growth of the contribution of direct taxes has long been looked upon as one of the ways of measuring the development of a fiscal system, it should be interesting to examine the factors involved in this rather slow development of income tax revenue.

It was only in 1918 that taxes on incomes, then regarded purely as a war tax, were imposed in Trinidad and Tobago. The yields of this tax varied with the export position of the chief products, cocoa and then petroleum. The yield from this tax was as follows:

1919	$310,000
1920	$518,200
1921	$1,027,000
1922	$944,300

In 1923 a new income tax bill was introduced which was to make income tax permanent.

In 1923 tax revenue fell to $327,800. Thereafter there was an upward trend as prosperity slowly returned to the export industries. For example, the relatively high yields from 1926–27 to 1929–30 correspond to increased profits in the oil industry which can be seen in the dividends declared as hereunder:

	1924–25 (per cent)	1925–26 (per cent)	1926–27 (per cent)	1927–28 (per cent)	1928–29 (per cent)	1929–30 (per cent)	1930–31 (per cent)
TLL	25	27½	27½	27½	30	7½	5
Apex	25	50	80	35	52½	25	20

The trends for the rest of the period correspond also to trends in the revival in trade after the Great Depression, that is, after 1935. In spite, however, of the increase in yield of the tax after 1935 the percentage contribution to gross revenue remained disappointingly small. It was 11.45 per cent in 1921 and after averaging 8½–9 per cent for most of the period jumped to 12½ per cent in 1938. Even this increase left revenue from this source insignificant compared with that from customs and excise.

Why did income tax revenue play so insignificant a part in total revenue?

a. The insignificance of income tax is in part relative, that is, to customs and excise. Since the proportion of the national income (if that could be known accurately) accounted for by trade is very large and the goods involved pass through a few ports, then customs duties recommend themselves as the cheapest, most effective means of collecting revenue. The propensity to import out of any given income is high and in addition about 35–40 per cent of all items imported pay duty of 10 per cent preferential and 20 per cent non-preferential. Other items such as motor vehicles pay 15 per cent and 30 per cent. In addition there was a surtax of 10 per cent up to 1934, thereafter increased to 15 per cent. Also certain items paid high specific duties. The duty on unmanufactured tobacco varied from 78¢ to $1.30 per pound according to moisture content. As a result of this wide, safe net placed[18] precisely where most incomes pass, in one form or another, the revenues from this source were very large. As will be seen later the income tax net was nowhere so safe or widespread so that by comparison the revenues from the former are considerably larger than those from the latter.
b. But the revenues were small in an absolute sense also and this fact is accounted for by the following factors:
   i. The low rates (average and marginal) of income tax. From 1918 to 1923 the minimum taxable income was £500 and the minimum

tax rate was 4½d (9¢) in the £ in 1918; 3½d in 1919; 3d in 1920–21 and 6d in 1922–23. The governor explained in 1919 that "the position is that with the present machinery the Government cannot deal with incomes below £500".[19] In 1924 the minimum chargeable income was lowered to £250. There were eleven instead of six income scales. Also the marginal rate in the post-1924 scale was higher than in the earlier ones. The increase in the number of intervals coupled with higher marginal rates meant that for any increase in personal incomes government received an increasingly greater share.

ii. In 1934, to meet the increased expenditure necessary to satisfy the popular demand for increased social services, there was imposed an all-round increase of 25 per cent on the standard 1934 income tax rate. In 1935 there was a further levy of 10 per cent on the basic tax payable under the tax ordinance. The purpose of this levy was to assist the subsidization of the cocoa industry.

A few comments are necessary on this outline of the development of the income tax.

a. The first is that there was an obvious searching for a "proper" level of minimum taxable income and rate of tax. It must be remembered that income tax was something new and all sorts of experiments and mistakes were possible.
b. The levies of 1934 and 1935 can be criticized on the following grounds:
    i. Whatever may have been the justification for higher rates of income tax (and it will be shown that there were good grounds for such an increase), it does appear that any popular demand for increased and improved social services should have been met by a wider casting of the tax net or rather by a more efficient system of assessment and collection even if it were thought necessary at the same time to increase the tax rates. In 1935 only 2,500 persons (including companies), that is, less than 1 per cent of the population were assessed for tax.
    ii. The imposition of piecemeal and *ad hoc* levies to meet particular increases in expenditure seems to have been a most unsatisfactory method of operating an income tax. These levies caused resentment among those upon whom the increases were likely to fall,[20]

> especially as it was the general belief that others with taxable incomes were escaping an inefficient tax net. The knowledge that others were escaping tax led also to attempts at evasion and false declarations by those who actually paid. Further, these levies did not give the necessary impression of permanence to the taxation of incomes which is necessary if this more equitable, progressive and potentially lucrative source of revenue was to play its part in economic development.

A large once and for all increase would have been better. Also it could have been justified, at least by a comparison of the Trinidad and Tobago rates of tax with those of the other West Indian islands. Even with the two levies imposed in 1934 and 1935 the rates of tax were lower in 1935 in Trinidad and Tobago than in any other West Indian island.

	Tax on $4.800	Tax on $14.400
Grenada	252	1.872
St Vincent	210	
St Lucia	248	1.868
British Guiana	252	1.458
Trinidad and Tobago	186 (+10% levy) = 204	1.290 (+10% levy) = 1.419

If it is accepted that the social amenities already available in Trinidad and Tobago were superior to those in the other islands it would appear that a tax level equal at least to the lowest of the other colonies could have been justified.

The small number of persons assessed for tax could have been due to one or all of the following factors: the smallness of incomes, the inequality of incomes and evasions. In 1927, 1928 and 1929 there were respectively 1,953, 2,174 and 2,620 persons assessed for tax. In 1935, the number had dropped to 2,530; 1936, 2,614; 1937, it was 3,061 and 1939, 3,220. In this latter year the proportion of taxpayers to total population was less than 1 per cent (0.677 per cent).

In 1935 of the 2,095 shops on which the treasury proposed to levy a trade licence only about 1 per cent or 20–25 shop owners had ever paid income tax. One of the chief difficulties involved in assessing these petty traders was the fact that most of them were Chinese and made up their accounts in that language. The income tax assessor found it necessary, therefore, either to accept the original declaration or to get a translation from another Chinese. It was not possible to check the reliability either of the original declaration or of the subsequent interpretation. It was only in 1938 that the difficulty was met by a new ordinance[21] which provided that all books and ledgers be kept in English.

Income Distribution

Table 80 shows the chief sources of income assessed for tax. Here again the importance of trade is shown in the size of items "Profits or gains from trade, business or profession". The size of the items "public salaries" points to the ease with which that class of income earner can be taxed.

Table 80 also indicates, even if the deficiencies of the tax system are taken into account, how unequally incomes were distributed. Even in 1938 (the best year) there were only four categories with over $1 million and of these, one of them alone (i.e., profits and so on) accounted for more than 62 per cent of total income assessed for tax.

Company Tax

The rate of company tax operating for most of the period was 12½ per cent for ordinary companies and 2½ per cent for life insurance companies. This rate of 2/6 in the pound corresponds to the rate on personal incomes in the bracket £8,001–£10,000 in 1919 or £3,000–£4,000 in 1924–25.

In spite of this low rate of company tax, however, the yield from this source was in 1929, 81 per cent of total revenue from income taxes.

By 1951 income tax had become the chief source of revenue and in 1953 company tax represented 85 per cent of total tax collected. By then, however, the company tax rate had been increased to 40 per cent. By far the greatest contribution was from the oil industry. This is shown in table 81.

The following factors appear to have affected the yields of company taxes in the inter-war period:

a. The fact that the company form of organization though growing had not yet developed on a really large scale;
b. The generous depreciation allowances allowed to companies.[22] Although in oil mining generous depreciation allowances are necessary there did not appear to be any clearly worked out policy for depreciation allowances;

Table 80 Sources of Incomes Assessed for Tax $'000

	1926	1927	1928	1929	1933	1934	1935	1937	1938	1939
Profits from trade, business, or profession	6,117.1	7,750.6	9,037.9	7,831.2	6,815.2	7,425.4	7,304.4	10,352.6	15,091.1	13,920.3
Profits from estates and lands	582.2	737.4	1,002.4	1,622.8	289.7	671.9	442.0	901.5	1,518.6	396.2
Interests and dividends within the colony	1,967.5	943.6	1,160.1	979.2	813.7	685.3	613.8	700.7	749.4	1,927.0
Rent of property	409.4	423.8	450.7	451.6	485.0	486.5	480.9	502.1	569.2	787.6
Incomes, interest and other from abroad	67.2	68.1	92.1	137.7	159.1	96.8	112.7	102.2	131.7	151.2
Salaries and so on from public treasury	924.9	883.2	888.9	897.6	990.3	982.3	978.4	1,067.3	1,104.0	966.2
Salaries and so on from private concerns	2,446.5	2,544.4	2,923.6	3,141.6	3,093.4	3,172.8	3,371.8	3,918.8	4,741.3	5,161.8
Pensions, annuities received in colony	–	–	–		–	–	–	–	–	254.5
Total gross income	12,514.8	13,351.1	15,555.7	15,061.7	12,646.4	13,521.0	13,304.0	17,545.2	23,905.5	23,564.8
Total net chargeable income	9,631.2	11,586.2	13,292.9	12,637.4	9,898.7	10,535.3	7,971.2	11,701.7	16,634.4	14,638.4

Table 81 Contribution of Oil Industry to Tax Revenue

Year	Total Direct Tax Revenue $'000 (1)	Total Revenue Oil Industry (2)	(2) as Per Cent of (1)
1927	775.4	378.8	48.8
1928	895.8	435.6	48.6
1929	865.0	284.9	32.9
1930	914.3	384.5	42.0
1931	673.4	260.8	38.7
1932	611.6	318.2	52.0
1933	645.9	252.5	39.1
1934	715.6	365.2	51.0
1935	671.4	249.1	37.1
1936	878.0	592.0	67.4
1937	1,140.0	532.9	46.7
1938	1,677.0	879.7	52.5
1939	1,405.0	794.2	56.5

c. Double taxation which is in turn linked with and largely determines the level of company taxation. The largest and most important companies operating in Trinidad and Tobago were registered in the United Kingdom and were therefore liable also to UK income tax. Under the Double Taxation Agreement relief of tax in Trinidad and Tobago was given "on that part of (his) income at a rate equal to the amount by which the rate of the tax appropriate to (his) case exceeds half of the appropriate rate of the UK tax. If, however, the rte of tax appropriate to his case under the ordinance exceeds the appropriate rate of UK tax he shall be entitled to relief at a rate equal to half the appropriate rate of UK tax." [23]

The net effect of the Double Taxation Policy, therefore, was to tie the Trinidad and Tobago rate of company tax to the UK rate and at one half of the latter. For the imposition in Trinidad and Tobago of any rate lower than one-half of the UK rate meant that Trinidad and Tobago was giving to the UK Treasury the amount by which the Trinidad and Tobago rate was less than one half of the UK rate. Nor could Trinidad and Tobago derive any benefit from UK companies by raising its rate of tax above the level of one half of the UK rate up to the level of the UK tax. Such benefit could only be achieved by the most likely course of raising the Trinidad and Tobago rate above the UK rate. See the following hypothetical example:

Trinidad Tax Rate (pence in the £)	UK Rate (pence in the £)	Trinidad Tax Receipts (pence in the £)
6	12	6
8	12	6
12	12	6
16	12	10

But any increase in the domestic rate of tax above the UK rate to overcome (partially) the effects of the Double Taxation Policy would have meant that, unless discriminatory taxation were employed, the local companies would have had to pay a very high rate of tax. Correspondingly also the UK companies' total tax payments would be even greater.

Perhaps a graduated company tax would have solved both this problem and the problem of increasing revenue at the same rate as incomes. It has been argued against this, however, that a graduated company tax scale is likely to lead to the formation of subsidiary companies. But against this latter argument must be advanced the fact that in Trinidad and Tobago the formation of subsidiary companies was already taking place. See, for example, the number of subsidiaries formed by Trinidad Leasehold Ltd.[24] In any event the increase of company taxes to 40 per cent and the consequent increase in revenue seems to give further support to the argument that the original 12½ per cent was much too small.

Whatever may have been the disadvantages of the Double Taxation Policy, in revenue terms, to the country in which the capital was employed, the fact of the local tax rate being tied to the tax rate of the metropolitan country had the following ill effect. The automatic linking of the local to the UK rate removed any necessity on the part of the dependent country for serious thought on the important questions of company taxes, level of profits or depreciation allowances. In fact, in spite of the hypothetical case outlined earlier, it is quite likely that the rate of company tax actually charged was much higher than it would have been had the tax rate not been automatically tied to the UK rate.

Land sales and royalties are the next important contributor to revenue during the period. Their contribution to revenue increased from 2.3 per cent in 1919 to 8.1 per cent in 1939. For a fuller development of this question, see chapter 6 on petroleum where the low royalty rates and the regressiveness of those rates are dealt with.[25]

Interest

The growth of this item from $33,800 in 1919 to $332,100 in 1939 is indicative of both the healthy reserves that were being built up and the reinvestment of unspent balances from loan funds.

It is this sort of gain through investment of colonial funds in British securities which has been used as an argument[26] both for the 100 per cent Sterling Backing arrangement and the obligation to invest in British securities rather than, even partially, in the securities of the investing colony. Against this increase in revenue from interest, however, must be placed the possible loss from depreciation in the values of these securities over time.

Table 82 shows both the appreciation and depreciation by year and in the value of securities for the period 1928–1939.

Table 82 Value of Securities, 1928–1939

Year	Market Value 31 December ($M)	Amount by which Securities Had Appreciated $'000	or Depreciated during the Year $'000
1928	7.2		211.7
1929	7.5		431.0
1930	8.1		224.6
1931	7.7		902.9
1932	10.0	1,447.2	
1933	11.2	230.9	
1934	12.1	246.2	
1935	6.3		52.7
1936	7.3	18.0	
1937	10.4		193.7
1938	10.7		360.8
1939	11.6		178.8

Note: On balance, a loan of $792,700 over twelve years.

Expenditure

The following list shows a functional classification of expenditure over the period.[27] Any such classification is bound to be arbitrary and it is therefore necessary to indicate the items included in each category and to point out that such classification has been employed consistently throughout the period.

Public debt:	All interest charges and sinking fund charges for the servicing and redemption of the public debt.
Administrative services:	Normal administrative departments plus legislative council, governor, pensions and gratuities and also law and order.
Social services:	Health, education, orphanages and other social services.
Economic services:	Public Works Department recurrent and extraordinary, agriculture and forest departments subsidies to industries, total railway expenditure has also been included in gross expenditure. Railway revenue is also included under gross revenue.
Other:	Military, subventions and other items.

The amount of gross revenue devoted to different categories is shown in table 83, and the percentage of gross expenditure devoted to different categories is shown in table 84.

Table 83 Distribution of Gross Revenue, 1919–1939

	1919	(1921)	1924	1929	(1931)	1934	1939
			'000 BWI				
Public debt charges	505.0		898.5	742.6		750.9	992.4
Administration	1,340.8		2,029.2	2,106.5		2,269.4	2,761.9
Social services	1,144.7		1,444.8	1,616.4		1,878.8	2,945.0
Economic services	2,463.5		2,975.0	3,791.5		3,330.3	5,851.0
Others	831.2		201.8	173.7		527.3	1,360.5
Total	**6,285.2**		**7,549.3**	**8,430.7**		**8,756.7**	**13,910.8**

Table 84 Percentage Allocation of Gross Expenditure, 1919–1939

	1919 (%)	(1921)	1924 (%)	1929 (%)	(1931)	1934 (%)	1939 (%)
			'000 BWI				
Public debt charges	8.03		11.9	8.8		8.6	7.1
Administration	21.3		26.9	25.0		25.9	19.9
Social services	18.1		19.1	19.2		21.4	21.1
Economic services	39.1		39.4	45.0		38.0	42.0
Other	13.2		2.7	2.0		6.1	9.9
Total	100.0		100.0	100.0		100.0	100.0

Administrative

Throughout the period there was a steady increase in all the items under this heading irrespective of the trends in exports or revenue. The increase between 1919 and 1924 is largely explained by the development of the departments which were, before this, very rudimentary. Customs and Excise Department, for example, almost doubled ($52,300 to $92,100) and Treasury and Income Tax expanded from $55,600 to $233,000. Also contributing to this general increase was the item pensions and gratuities which rose from $241,900 to $417,700. In spite of the fact that the amount going to administrative services more than doubled between 1919 and 1939 ($1.3–$2.7 million), the proportion which expenditure on this item bore to total expenditure rose only from 21.1 per cent in 1919 to remain at about 26 per cent for the whole of the intermediate period, and actually fell to 19.9 per cent in 1939 with the rapid increase in expenditure which took place in this later period.[28]

Social Services

Here again the growth of expenditure was, with but one small exception, steadily upwards, rising from $1.1 million in 1919 to $2.95 million in 1939. The two main components were health and education. Health claimed $642,600 in 1919, $757,400 in 1929 and $1.1 million in 1939; the same as for all social services in 1919. Education claimed $339,800 in 1919, $679,200 in 1929 and $1.05 million in 1939. Although education was neglected in the earlier part of the period, it came by the end of the period to have similar priority treatment as health. As an indication of the order of priority observed at this time it should be pointed out that until 1926 the amount spent on "constabulary" exceeded that spent on education and was nearly as much as the amount spent on health services.

The increase in expenditure on education after 1934–35 was largely the result of the report of the Education Committee which recommended a speeding up of the building and equipping of schools and a general rethinking of the whole education system. On the whole, social services took 18 per cent of total expenditure in 1919 and 21 per cent in 1939.

Economic Services

In contrast with the steady trends and the lack of fluctuations in the other services one sees the violent fluctuations in the amounts spent on the economic services. It is most interesting to note that these fluctuations correspond, point to point, with the fluctuations in exports and revenue.

Consider the size of this expenditure and its relation to gross expenditure. In 1919 it was $2.5 million out of a gross expenditure of $5.3 million (47.2 per cent); in 1929 it was $3.8 million out of $8.4 million (45.2 per cent); in 1939, $5.85 million out of $14.3 million (40.9 per cent). In the lean years, 1924 and 1934, the figures were $2.98 million out of $7.5 million (39.7 per cent) and $3.3 million out of $8.8 million (37.5 per cent), respectively.

A comparison between expenditure on economic services and on social services brings out some interesting points:

a. It is easier to vary (upwards or downwards) expenditure on economic services than on social services.
b. It is therefore necessary to examine social service commitments closely both for their immediate and their recurrent costs. Once schools and hospitals and so on have been provided, there will be constant popular demand for maintaining them in a high state of efficiency and even for their improvement and expansion. Social services expenditure is therefore likely to increase regardless of the trend in exports and revenue.

The expenditure on economic services may be haphazard and unplanned. Any threatened drop in revenue can be reflected with a minimum of time-lag in the postponement or reduction of public works without incurring the same popular resistance as is the case with social services once undertaken. The trend in expenditure on economic services can therefore be said largely to reflect, in an unplanned economy, the general prosperity, or lack of it, of the country. The currents of world trade affect first the values of exports and so imports and revenue and, in the field of expenditure, the economic services which, as has been shown in the case of Trinidad and Tobago, are the first and main victims of the adjustments.[29]

The other major items here are concerned with military and defence measures. This other accounts for the fact that the figures for 1919 (end of World War I) and 1939 (beginning of World War II) are so much larger than those for other years.

The Public Debt and Capital Expenditure

Table 85 shows the growth of the public debt from $8.4 million in 1919 to $19.4 million in 1939. This increase, however, corresponds to an increase in gross revenue from $6.4 million to $13.4 million over the same period. Also the surplus balances which were shown to have been deliberately increased, grew from about $1 million to approximately $9.2 million. So that even at its highest point the total public debt was only twice the size of the surplus balances and about $6 million more than the gross revenue for that year. This takes no account of the sinking funds that were being accumulated for the redemption of the debt. On 31 December 1939 the market value of sinking fund investments was $1.07 million.

An examination of table 85 reveals some prominent and interesting shifts in the size of the debt. The immediate post-war increase in the public debt from $8.4 million in 1919 to a peak of 16.5 million in 1922, encouraged most likely by the post-war prosperity, is accounted for thus:

1. A loan of $4.8 million in 1920 partly for the improvement of railways and roads.
2. The second steep rise in 1921–22 is accounted for by the $960,000 loan for the reclamation of the Caroni Swamp.

It is interesting to note the similarity in the current (a) fiscal and (b) debt policies. The disillusioning effect of the depression of the early 1920s which imparted caution to the former and led to a policy of reserve accumulation had the effect in the latter of stopping completely the raising of loans.

Table 85 Public Debt

Years	Amount of Public Debt ($)
1919	8,393.246
1920	13,189.005
1921	13,180.328
1922	16,475.639
1923	16,443.060
1924	16,352.415
1925	16,322.418
1926	16,041.871
1927	15,752.904
1928	15,444.594
1929	15,135.467
1930	14,824.952
1931	14,512.886
1932	14,555.524
1933	19,205.918
1934	20,366.366
1935	16,689.168
1936	20,274.816
1937	20,013.312
1938	19,730.304
1939	19,442.016

For a period of ten years, between 1922 and 1932, no new loans were issued and the size of the debt was being gradually reduced through annual redemptions until 1933 when the amount of the debt shoots up again.

This increase in 1933 of $7.2 million was composed of the following loan issues:

i. $4 million for the Central Water Scheme
ii. $1.2 million for the Agricultural Bank
iii. $2 million, a conversion loan for the repayment of a debt to the Imperial Treasury, incurred during World War I.

Item (iii) calls for special comment. Up to this time the debt to the Imperial Treasury was being repaid by annual installments. The interest rate on the debt was mainly 5 per cent, though there were small amounts of

4½ percent. It was intended therefore to take advantage of the relatively low rates of borrowing then prevailing on the London market (it was expected to be no more than 4 per cent and perhaps less) and by this manoeuvre to convert the treasury loan of 5 per cent into one of 4 per cent at most with a resultant saving to the Trinidad and Tobago treasury.

The further upward movement in the size of the debt in 1934 is the result of a new loan of $1,440,000 less repayments of $279,600 (mostly on locally issued debentures).

The steep drop in 1935 came in spite of new loans totalling $4.1 million. For in that year the 3 per cent stocks ($2.88 million) and the 4 per cent stocks ($4.67 million) were redeemed. The amount by which the sinking fund for the 3 per cent stock fell short of the amount to be repaid was made up by transferring £65,000 ($312,000) from the supplementary non-statutory sinking fund. The deficit in the case of the 4 per cent stock was made up by a "private" loan of $1.44 million at 2.9 per cent which was issued in London, and repayable in September 1944. In addition, further loans to a total of $8.0 million were authorized for the following:

The new harbour scheme
Country water supplies
Hospital buildings
School buildings
Housing commission
Electricity scheme

The final position, therefore, was the reduction of the public debt by approximately $3.7 million to $16.7 million. In 1936 the completion of the subscription to the 3 per cent loan issue of $8 million brought the public debt almost back to its 1934 level at $20.3 million. Thereafter until the end of the period no new loans were issued. Repayments on the debenture issues continued at an annual rate of about $250,000 causing the gradual reduction which is shown in table 85.

Debt Charges

The charges on account of public debt almost doubled between 1919 and 1939 from $505,000 to $992,400. The corresponding per capita figures were approximately $1.00 in 1919 and a little over $2.00 in 1939; in spite of the fact that the size of the debt doubled over the period it is obvious that the burden was very light. The charges were 8 per cent of expenditure in 1919 and 7.1 per cent in 1939.

In the absence of national income figures, this debt burden is measured in terms both of gross revenue and the value of exports:

Year	Public Debt Charges as Per Cent of Gross Revenue	Public Debt Charges as Per Cent of Exports
1919	7.8	2.8
1923	12.99	4.9
1927	6.67	2.2
1931	5.67	2.9
1935	7.63	3.1
1939	7.39	2.8

Also compared with other West Indian colonies the percentage of debt expenditure to total expenditure (exclusive of expenditure on railways) was very small towards the end of the 1930s.[30]

Barbados	5.3%
British Guiana	21.1%
British Honduras	20.0%
Jamaica	11.1%
Grenada	10.2%
St Lucia	12.4%
Trinidad and Tobago	9.5%

Trinidad and Tobago's debt burden as a percentage of expenditure was therefore smaller than that of all the other colonies with the exception of Barbados. In monetary terms both the Jamaica and British Guiana debts in 1938 at $20.6 million and $21.1 million, respectively, were larger than Trinidad and Tobago's debt of $19.7 million.

In the case of Trinidad and Tobago though, not all of the amounts stated for some years represent genuine public debt. Of the $19.7 million of public debt in 1938, for example, $9.3 million were raised on behalf of other "public bodies", for example, the Port of Spain City Council. When further deductions are made for the sinking funds it can be seen that the actual debt in any one year is somewhat less than it at first appears.

The Structure of the Public Debt

Apart from small and temporary advances with local banks the public debt of Trinidad and Tobago was held in two forms only: debentures and inscribed stock. The former was a local issue; the latter was issued in London through the Crown agents. The former was repayable by annuities. The period of redemption was usually thirty years commencing after the tenth year. The latter was also long term, twenty years or more and often undated.

An analysis of the composition of the debt over the period gives another insight into public debt policy.[31] Between 1890 and 1912 all loans issued were with inscribed stock at 3 or 4 per cent. Between 1915 and 1920 all loans were in the form of debentures at 4–6 per cent. From 1931 onwards there was a reversion to London flotations. The exceptions being the Agricultural Bank and Central Water Supply Scheme: 4 per cent debentures to a total of $2.3 million authorized by Ordinance 41/1931 (table 87).

If one compares the situation in 1930 with that in 1936 for example, the position is as follows:

	1930 (per cent)	1936 (per cent)
Debentures (as per cent of debt)	41.00	24.1
Inscribed stock (as per cent of debt)	59.00	75.9

There is an obvious shift away from locally issued to London-issued loans. But before further discussion of the reasons for this shift it is necessary to observe that this distinction between locally and foreign issued loans does not necessarily correspond to a classification of internal and external debt. London issues are most likely entirely external debt in the usual sense. The position with locally issued loans, however, is more ambiguous. This is so because a large part, if not the largest part of local issues would have been taken up by the local branches of foreign owned banks. Why then the distinction? Even though the local contributions to a loan issue (i.e., the domestic saving in a local loan issue) is small, the very fact of raising the loan locally sets up over time a tradition of dealing in government loans. It creates a rudimentary money market which can grow in time leading to the gradual mobilization of local savings and capital for domestic economic development. A policy of switching all loan issues to the London market is therefore detrimental to this development (table 87). But the shift has been explained in terms of other factors.

Cost

As can be seen from the tables 86 and 87 for 1930 and 1936,[32] the average rates of interest on the two forms of loan issues were as follows:

	Debentures (per cent)	Inscribed Stock (per cent)
1930	5.3	3.5
1936	5.0	3.1

It has been estimated that even considering the fact that the local issue involves no expenses as opposed to the cost of London issues, the disparity in interest rates was enough to make the London issue more attractive from the point of view of the local treasury.[33]

Depletion of Local Circulation

In 1930 this argument was advanced in favour of foreign issues: "it is not considered advisable to withdrawn from circulation in the Colony so large a sum as is required, particularly as at any moment we may have to raise locally the Agricultural Bank loan". It can be argued in opposition to this point, however, that

a. in as far as local issues are largely subscribed by foreign owned banks the argument about depleting local circulation losses much of its importance. As long as the difference between the local and the London

Table 86 Showing Public Debt as at December 1930

4 per cent inscribed stock	Ord. 18/1890	£322,593
4 per cent inscribed stock	Ord. 10/1892	£100,000
3 per cent inscribed stock	Ord. 20/1894	£400,000
3 per cent inscribed stock	Ord. 34/1895	£100,000
3 per cent inscribed stock	Ord. 13/1896	£100,000 (repaid 1935)
4 per cent inscribed stock	Ord. 26/1912	£550,000
4 per cent debenture	Ord. 2/1915	£49,140
6 per cent debenture	Ord. 15/1918	£80,020
6 per cent debenture	Ord. 15/1920	£950,000

Table 87 Statement of Loans Outstanding and of the Sinking Funds for their Redemption (1936)

$'000		Amount Raised	Out-standing at 30/9/1936	Sinking Fund 30/6/1936	Annual Drawing	Annual Pay-ment to Sinking Fund
Local Loans (Debentures)						
4% Cap. 220		337.2	134.5		16.9 June	
6% Cap. 221		480.0	218.2	7.1	22.6 Sept	
6% Cap. 220		4,800.0	3,120.0		240.0 Aug	
4% Ord. 41/1931:-						
Agriculture Bank	1,200.0)					
Central Water	)	2,348.2	2,348.2	61.8		23.5
Supply Scheme	1,148.2)					
Loans Raised in UK						
Inscribed Stock						
3½ Ord. 41 of 1931						
C.W.S.S.	2,867.5)					
	)	4,968.0	4,968.0	24.8		49.7
Ord. 38/1932 Debt to Imp	)					
Gov.	2,100.5)					
2.9% Conversion Loan		1,440.0	1,440.0	132.7	Repayable Sept	132.1
3% Ord. 3 of 1934						
& 3. 9 and 21 of 1935						
Habour Scheme	4,756.0)					
Country Water Supplies	489.0)					
Hospital Buildings	489.0)			2.0		14.7
School Buildings	244.5)					
Housing Commission	244.5)					
Electricity Undertaking	1,793.0)	8,016.0	8,016.0			1,793.0
		22,389.4	20,244.9	228.4		

rates of interest is such as to leave a profit after meeting the cost of transfer, funds would have flowed from the parent bank in London to Trinidad. There was this difference in interest rates.

b. There had never in the past been any difficulty in raising local issues so that even if a large part of such issues was locally financed government had never really tested the limits of the local market both as to interest rates and to size of the issue.

But there is a further consideration. The issuing of large domestic loans could have had this further disadvantage. Continuation of the practice of maintaining large sums of unexpended loan funds plus the necessity for investing those funds in London would have meant that, as the London rate was lower than that in Trinidad and Tobago, such reinvestment would have been threatened with losses from four directions:

a. The difference between higher domestic and the London borrowing rates.
b. The difference between the local borrowing rate and the London investing rate.
c. The possibility of losses through the depreciation of securities (which may have occurred, however, whatever the source of the loan).
d. The higher cost of the London flotation.

Public Debt Policy

This section treats the public debt policy both in regard to the size of the debt and the question of whether loan funds or current revenue should be employed in financing development projects.

For the purpose of this analysis the period can conveniently be divided into three phases: 1919–34, 1934–38 and 1938–39.

i. The keynote of the first period especially was caution; the same caution which was characteristic of the then current financial transactions. It has already been seen how relatively light was the burden of the debt, the infrequency with which loans were raised and the smallness of the early loans. Note that no new loans at all were raised between 1923 and 1931; that even the loans of 1931 and 1935 did not greatly increase the size of the public debt because the redemptions which were effected at the time just about compensated for the new borrowing. To understand the reason for this caution it is essential to recall that the position in the early 1920s was so adverse that sinking fund payments on the Imperial Treasury loan had to be suspended in 1923–24. Fortunately the surplus balances filled the gap.

The coincidence of the loans of 1921–22 and 1931 with the depressions may convey the impression that a counter-cyclical fiscal policy based on loan funds was initiated to lessen unemployment and so on. In fact the issuing of these loans at these times was largely fortuitous. Further it would be wrong to conclude that such large-scale counter-cyclical policy did operate with or without a conscious policy. In each period the projects for which the loans were issued were either postponed, abandoned or curtailed; precisely at the time when they would have done most to combat unemployment. In place of these large-scale projects, provisions were made from current revenue for initiation of small projects in certain areas. In 1931, for example, £20,000 was allocated to the Department of Public Works for road construction work "for the relief of unemployment".[34] In mid-1935 relief works were also initiated in certain areas to ease unemployment.[35]

The effects of postponement and curtailing of vital projects plus new loan issues can be seen in the growth of unexpended loan balances, as follows:

Year	Unexpended Loan Balances ($M)	Unexpended Loan Balances as Per Cent of Debt
1933	3.5	18.2
1934	3.7	18.1
1935	5.1 (plus specific funds of $3.69 million)	30.3
1936	6.7 (plus specific funds of $3.72 million)	33.0

Apart from caution, the chief characteristic which emerges of debt policy is the lack of a concise policy or plan. Loans were raised for individual projects without any consideration about balanced development. They were easily postponed or curtailed, also without any consideration of the overall effect on employment.

ii. *1934–35 to 1937–38*. This period differed from the earlier one in one fundamental respect only. For the first time something like an overall plan emerged. A large loan of $8 million was issued and also the projects were somewhat different from the usual roads and bridges type of development. It provided for:

a. The Deep Water Harbour Scheme ($4.8 million) which was to make Trinidad the focal point of Eastern Caribbean shipping and a vital stage in the shipping lanes linking North America and Europe to South America.

b. An electricity scheme ($1.8 million).
c. Country water supplies ($489,000).
d. Hospital buildings ($489,000).
e. School buildings ($244,500).
f. Housing scheme ($244,500).

For the first time, therefore, there was to be undertaken simultaneously a variety of projects calculated to increase and improve the overhead social and economic capital of the colony and provide the basic elements for further economic development. Further the inclusion of housing and slum clearance as a concern of government was a milestone in the history of government policy – a direct reversal of attitude

iii. *1938–39.* The idea of long-term planning came in 1938, as can be seen in the speech in which the acting governor introduced his new proposals: "What is immediately required in Trinidad and Tobago is a comprehensive development programme to be carried out over the course of the next five years. It is quite clear to me that matters have reached a stage where any attempts to meet requirements solely by annual expenditure will result merely in a perpetuation of the present state of affairs."

To make up the leeway in the spheres of housing, social services, schools and hospitals, therefore, it was proposed that in addition to allocating $3.1

1 Housing for the working classes	$4.8 million
2 Aerodrome	$1.3 million
3 Country water supplies	$0.6 million
4 Electricity schemes	$0.9 million
5 Slipway	$0.3 million
6 Hospital buildings ($2.5 million less loan funds available $0.2 million)	$2.3 million
7 Schools and other educational buildings	$0.3 million
8 Roads	$3.1 million
9 Other	$0.4 million
Total	**$14.0 million**

million from surplus balances to expenditure on certain capital works, a new loan, for similar purposes, of $10.9 million should be issued. From this loan fund appropriations should be made as and when required. The scheme was ambitious by past standards. Hereunder are some of the major items:

Not only was the policy new in terms of the nature and extent of the projects that were to be undertaken, a new approach was evident also in the official plans for raising and servicing the new debt. It was surprising how little conscious thinking was devoted by government before this time to gearing development projects to the presence of the oil industry. Before 1938, apart from unofficial statements in the press to the effect that the islands were not benefiting as much as they should from the presence of the oil industry, the only concrete approach to the problem came from the unofficial members of the legislature. In the early 1930s they proposed the earmarking of oil revenues for certain development projects. Although this was an improvement on government thinking on the subject of utilizing the revenues from a wasting asset, it did not go far enough. For the implementation of such a proposal would have meant in fact the continuation of piecemeal planning and execution of projects based solely on annual revenue flows from oil companies.

Earlier still in 1919 another unofficial member,[36] speaking on this same topic, had said, "I feel that in suddenly tapping resources that were unknown to the Colony before, and unsuspected a few years ago, and throwing the revenue from these sources into the general expenditure of the Colony we are to some extent prejudicing the advancement of the Colony with respect to permanent works in the future." He continued, "I think some such policy should be adopted of setting aside the money annually to pay interest and sinking fund on a large loan to carry out development works in the Colony."

The new government policy of 1938 set out to do precisely that. It is at once apparent that unofficial economic thinking was in this respect at least twenty years in advance of official policy. Another question arises, however. When the 1919 proposal was made the economy was on an upward plane. The shocks of 1921 and the Great Depression had not yet been felt or foreseen. Although the point about prejudicing the advancement of permanent works remains incontestable, it should be borne in mind that in 1921–1922, for instance, all revenue from whatever sources plus surplus balances were inadequate to sustain expenditure.

In the event this 1938 policy of long-term planning on the relative stability of oil revenues was immediately hard hit by World War II. The loan could not be raised and in 1939 a more modified plan, but one which still showed the influence of the new thinking of 1938, was introduced. It was to be financed in its modified form by surplus funds.[37]

Revenue and Debt Financing of Development Projects

A.R. Prest[38] has referred to the difficulties involved in dealing with published data on Trinidad and Tobago finances. It is almost impossible to determine capital items from current items. It would appear, however, from the size of and the increase in the category economic services (particularly extraordinary works) that a considerable portion of such expenditure was revenue financed. This point is further supported by the speech in 1919 of the unofficial member referred to earlier. The following extract from a speech in 1938 by the acting governor points to the same conclusion: "the amount of work waiting to be done and urgently needed is far more than could possibly be met yearly from revenue or even by the expenditure of the three million four hundred thousand dollars estimated to be available from surplus balances".[39]

Apart from these references to revenue financed public works (roads and so on), however, there were other projects which are difficult to put into one or the other category.

Tables 86 and 87 showing the number and size of loans raised indicate that the following projects were at least almost entirely debt financed.

Railway and roads extension	1920
Caroni reclamation scheme	1922
Deep water wharf scheme	1935
Housing and so on	1935

Perhaps to be included also were the planned 1938 projects. What can be called the major basic undertaking to provide essential social and economic overheads were therefore largely debt financed.

But the classification is not complete. Certain debt financed schemes had to be completed from budget funds. In this category are, for example, the 1936 estimate of $312,000 to complete the Central Water Scheme, and new appropriations for the completion of the Harbour Scheme and consequential work connected with the reclamation of land linked to the deepening the harbour.

Yet another category of public works is illustrated by the Central Water Supply Scheme mentioned earlier. Although authority was sought for raising the loan to finance the project in the first instance, it was proposed "to do the whole or as much as possible of the work with Surplus funds" and then according to the financial position of the colony to take a loan for such portion of the expenditure as the treasurer thought fit. It was intended to reimburse the surplus funds as far as possible.

The final category concerns the 1939 revision of the 1938 plan for a five-year development programme. Here, $3 million of a disposable surplus of $3.6 million were to be employed to finance the scaled down programme. The difference between this and the aforementioned category is that surplus balances were not to be restored by a later loan as in the earlier case. Specific revenue increasing measures were taken to help finance the project, for example,

1. *Income tax*. An emergency levy equivalent to the then rate of income tax provided that the levy and the tax combined did not exceed a maximum of 7/6 in the £ (which is to be the increased rate of tax "at home", that is, UK).
2. *Companies tax*. To be revised to one half the standard rate of income tax "at home".
3. A surtax of 50 per cent was to be added to estate and succession duties.
4. A cess of 2¢ per barrel was to be charged on all crude oil produced in Trinidad.

Summary and Conclusion

In the context of the economic development of Trinidad and Tobago, therefore, the inter-war years were a period of transition from an economy dependent for its exports mainly on agriculture to one dependent mainly on petroleum; a transition from a situation in which the chief industries yielding export incomes were domestically owned to one in which they were foreign owned.

This shift was not brought about in a race in which both agriculture and petroleum were expanding, the latter at a faster rate. Such a state of affairs would have been very favourable. It was brought about by the almost complete decline of the chief agricultural industries (cocoa and sugar) and the expansion of petroleum production. Total export values in 1939 were not much higher than in 1920.

The period experienced two depressions: that of the 1920s was short and sharp and that of the 1930s was more prolonged. Or perhaps one can say that the period experienced three upturns. For on the whole the economic climate was one of depression and the plateaux of prosperity appear as mere interludes in a long period of depression. There was a levelling off and a slight downturn in export values after 1937 and one wonders whether the cycles of upturn and recession would have continued, had it not been for the advent of World War II and the construction of American bases.

The decline of cocoa was the result of the interaction of external and internal factors. The initial setback came from the fall in world cocoa prices. This was in turn occasioned by the expansion of West African production and the decline of living standards in certain importing countries. But the internal weaknesses of indebtedness, over-expansion and disease were as much to blame for the subsequent decline of the industry.

Sugar was able to maintain a more or less stable position. Prices fell until 1932 when they were rescued by imperial preference. There was a remarkable thing about sugar; whereas in cocoa, prices and output reinforced each other in a downward trend, the opposite happened in sugar. As prices fell output was increased, sometimes more than correspondingly with the net result that total incomes from sugar exports were maintained at a stable level. The industry was, however, inefficient both in the field and in the factory, when compared with, say, Puerto Rico, or Cuba. Too little attention was paid to implemental tillage, irrigation and fertilizers.

Compared with the high yields in Puerto Rico of 51.9 tons of cane per acre in the late 1920s and early 1930s, the yield in Trinidad was at its best in the period only 30 tons per acre. The average yield was, even in 1939 about 22 to 24 tons per acre. The factory process also, though as good as any within the empire, was inferior to that in, say, Cuba and Puerto Rico. In the latter the large central factories were extracting 1 ton of sugar from 7 to 7½ tons of cane. In Trinidad that figure was not attained even in 1937–39 (8.89), some small producers were achieving only 13 tons of cane to 1 ton of sugar.

One of the basic difficulties about the industry, however, was the pricing of farmers' canes. As farmers produced more than 40 per cent of all canes grown, any discontent in their ranks could not therefore be lightly ignored. But they were largely unorganized, part-time cane farmers and could not really influence prices in the industry as much as their contribution warranted. It was quite a long time before they could have a voice in the fixing of prices for their canes. Even then, the formula devised for determining price took no account of farmers'costs of production, nor of the sucrose content of their canes. In fact it made the price of canes the residual in an equation in which dividends and efficiency of the factory process were determinants.

In the 1930s efforts were made to limit the area under farmers' canes. One of the results of this was that it tended to strengthen the trend towards concentrating relatively more and more of the sugar resources of the island into the hands of persons not resident in Trinidad and Tobago. The process of amalgamation of estates which had progressed considerably even in the nineteenth century was carried even further in the inter-war years. By the end of the period, production was mainly in the hands of about five large firms which were mainly expatriate.

The minor agricultural industries confirmed the picture of fluctuating export prices. The coconut industry was particularly vulnerable in view of the number of other agricultural products from which oils and fats were produced for the world market.

The important point demonstrated by the analysis of these industries is the fact that in searching for an alternative to cocoa, Trinidad in the inter-war years was confronted with no really worthwhile alternatives. Trinidad shifted from crop to crop as world prices and market conditions favoured now one and then the other. Except in the case of citrus fruit the success achieved was limited. As with cocoa, the external factors of price and markets were reinforced by unsuitable soil conditions, inefficient cultivation and disease. Coconuts also suffered from a severe hurricane in 1933. On the whole, therefore, agriculture had ceased to hold out much hope of prosperity and Trinidad and Tobago was fortunate to have had the petroleum industry upon which to rely.

In the petroleum industry itself the 1930s was the period of rapid development of production; the surveying of the geological structure of Trinidad; the building up and extension of refinery capacity, so that, if and when domestic production fell, the industry could be maintained by imported crude oil. The period saw, therefore, the development of what was to become in the 1950s the chief source of government revenue: the fuel for electricity generation and the developing of a bunkering trade.

It was a period also of rapid population growth in which, curiously enough, the indentured population played a twofold part. Having made its initial contribution to population increase, this section of the population seems to have over-played its part by having a net reproduction rate greatly in excess of that of the rest of the population. The 1920s and 1930s gave to pre–World War II Trinidad and Tobago a population growing at the rate of 2 per cent per annum and heavily weighted in terms of the younger age group. This in itself meant that, *ceteris paribus*, the post-war period could expect population growth to continue apace. This population, if trained, can make great contributions to economic development. But as in the inter-war period, or even more so in the post-war period, the cost of education and other social services will prove formidable.

The inter-war years bore the full brunt of the transition from indentureship to free labour. From 1845 to 1917 the indenture system provided agriculture with a large and sustained flow of relatively well-disciplined, industrious and cheap labour. The full effects of the cessation of indentures were not felt until 1921–22, however, when the last contracts had run their course. Indentureship no longer stood between the efficient and the inefficient estates. Competition for labour which was unknown during indenture came into existence, and in the immediate post–World War I boom was very severe. The period saw also the passing of labour legislation, the development of trade unions and labour departments in the public administration.

In the field of public finance the period saw the search for a proper system of income tax. The suddenness and sharpness of the depression of the 1920s denuded reserves in 1921–23 when they became negative. Thereafter the building up of reserves seems to have become an article of faith and took precedence over important development works. But this build-up of reserves was important for stability. It is clear that together with American spending on the construction of bases and the growth of the petroleum industry, it was largely responsible for the sound, even prosperous, conditions of post-war Trinidad and Tobago.

Some of the important social overheads were then provided. The inter-war years gave to Trinidad and Tobago the Deep Water Harbour and Piarco airport which are very essential for her position in the main shipping and air routes linking South America with North America and with Europe. Also initiated were the Central Water Scheme, Electricity Scheme, and housing for the working classes.

In conclusion it is proposed to refer to and to develop a point which in the midst of the varied strands of the study may be selected as the most important single characteristic of the period. Reference here is to the tendency of the economy in the inter-war period to become more and more orientated towards the overwhelming foreign ownership of productive resources both in mining and agriculture. The lesson seems to be that as more capital-intensive economic activities were engaged in (mining and refining) or became necessary to maintain and improve efficiency (sugar), the economy had to look to foreign sources to finance such developments. The main difficulty was absence of (internally generated) capital for certain undertakings.

This trend of becoming increasingly dependent on external sources of capital was strengthened by government debt policy. In the mid-1930s it broke with the 1920s by issuing the greater part of its loans in London rather than in Trinidad and Tobago. There were some good economic reasons for the switch. But it would appear that longer term policies should have been considered. The creation and encouragement of a local stock exchange should not have been completely jeopardized by considerations of small differences in the relative rates of interest and cost of flotation. If the economy is to develop along sound lines, it is necessary to encourage the accumulation and employment of a domestic economic surplus. Domestic income earners must make a contribution to economic development and there must be some institution through which the savings which they are encouraged to make are properly channelled into development projects. The benefits, interest and capital growth from the investment of such savings would have been enough encouragement.

It has been mentioned that the later phase of imbalance in the economy was better than the earlier phase if only because the bulk of export incomes were concentrated into fewer hands, and the profits could therefore be more easily taxed. Some modification to this general point is necessary. From the point of view of welfare considerations the earlier phase may have been better. For the moment, however, it is proposed to deal with the question of the use to which the increased revenues accruing to government as a result of this imbalance were put. A policy of "sowing the oil" (to borrow an expression from Venezuelan context) though advocated in 1919 by an unofficial member of the legislature was not officially recognized until 1938, but the 1938 longer term plan had to be modified with the advent of World War II. The absence of long-term government planning based on stable revenues was one of the most important shortcomings of the inter-war year, once more we must look into the future. The first issue of Treasury Bills was not made until 1962 with an annual upper limit of $50 million per annum.

Although in the 1970s government required the foreign owned banks and large corporations to make a percentage of their shares available for purchase by the general public, it was only in 1981 that the Trinidad and Tobago Stock Exchange was established.

Appendix 1

The Terms of Trade

An account of the economic development of Trinidad and Tobago which is dependent on trade would be incomplete if it did not give some indication of the terms of trade, which were obtained during the period under study.

It is not proposed to do an elaborate analysis of terms of trade. P.T. Bauer[1] circumvented some of the problems of this sort of analysis by making his treatment very simple. He compared the prices of the chief income-earning export (cocoa) with the prices of one of the main imports (cotton goods).

The approach of Professor and Mrs Hicks[2] was more elaborate. They considered the whole of Jamaica's exports and imports. In the case of Jamaica, however, it was possible to obtain indices of import and export values.

The Trinidad and Tobago situation was different from the two (West Africa and Jamaica) mentioned earlier. In the first place it has not been possible to obtain any indices of export or import values for the period. Also the single commodity selected by Bauer comprised about 25 per cent of imports, and in the exports sector the single commodity chosen was petroleum – the most important earner of export incomes. A comparison between these two commodities was therefore very significant.

Compared with this, the largest single item imported in Trinidad and Tobago was machinery for the oil and other industries. Also the largest export item was eventually petroleum products. Quite apart from the difficulty of obtaining significant average values for so heterogeneous an item as "machinery imports", terms of trade analysis based on this industry would not say anything at all about the position of consumers.

A midway course between the Jamaican and the West African methods has been adopted. In the export sector the prices (free on board) of cocoa have been chosen. In addition the prices received at store in Trinidad and Tobago by cocoa producers (as opposed to exporters aforementioned) have also been considered. This latter is of special significance since middlemen seem to have made considerable profits. It also contributes more to an understanding of the final position of small producers who were responsible for 60 per cent of cocoa production. Further, consideration is given to the cane farmer – the price he received for his canes being taken for comparison with import prices next to be discussed.

On the imports side, one commodity has not been taken but a basket of five: cotton goods, boots and shoes and the three food items - flour, rice and milk – combined in the proportions in which they were imported.[3]

It is hoped to indicate, therefore,

a. The income terms of trade of
   i. Cocoa exporters
b. The net barter terms of trade of
   ii. Cocoa exporters
   iii. Cocoa producers (i.e., prices at store)
   iv. Cane farmers (price of canes).

In terms of the basket of commodities listed earlier, table A1.1 sets out the position.

The income terms of trade were favourable for cocoa exporters for all of the period except 1921, 1934 and 1939. The adverse movement of the terms of trade in the 1921 depression was quite spectacular and reinforces the findings of the earlier section that the abrupt and steep fall from prosperity undermined confidence. But for the rest of the 1920s, especially 1928 and 1929 the terms of trade were in their favour.

The net barter terms of trade of this same group (cocoa exporters) showed similar characteristics with these two important exceptions.

i. When the barter terms of trade were favourable in 1932, the income terms of trade deteriorated considerably and were unfavourable.
ii. In 1936 and 1937 when the barter terms of trade improved almost to the 1929 level the income terms of trade were barely favourable. In both cases the trouble was with production. By the late 1930s the cumulative effect of neglect, disease, expansion into poor soils, underpopulation of estates and so on, listed in the chapter on cocoa, had

Table A1.1 Terms of Trade, 1919–1939

Import Price Indices

	1919	1920	1921	1922	1923	1924	1925	1926	1927	1928	1929	1930	1931	1932	1933	1934	1935	1936	1937	1938	1939
Flour (35)*	235	262	596	149	130	138	173	155	142	137	130	127	89	88	79	82	85	90	119	100	80
Rice (20)*	310	355	207	207	140	160	176	184	154	150	147	128	97	96	83	81	87	90	94	100	92
Milk (13)*	231	77	238	238	193	206	197	170	187	166	167	165	167	144	102	98	94	82	82	100	111
Boots and shoes (22)*	215	222	194	194	174	166	148	151	146	149	138	137	137	103	105	103	91	96	95	100	97
Cotton piece goods (10)*	156	264	119	123	170	132	119	123	118	116	135	106	106	82	80	87	89	93	105	100	102
Combined import rice Index	237	248	358	179	154	157	166	159	149	144	140	132	107	100	89	89	88	91	103	100	92

*Weights in brackets.

Export Products Price Indices

	1919	1920	1921	1922	1923	1924	1925	1926	1927	1928	1929	1930	1931	1932	1933	1934	1935	1936	1937	1938	1939
Cocoa																					
Average value	364	443	153	203	164	178	218	218	275	243	200	182	121	118	93	111	102	146	209	100	119
Total value	525	654	276	238	261	236	255	257	339	335	293	230	167	117	113	71	107	99	130	100	51
Price at store	280	330	138	149	131	131	180	173	211	200	159	149	105	105	72	79	83	97	147	100	90
Cane																					
Farmers price	180	318	164	97	197	182	109	109	131	112	109	109	109	109	109	100	100	100	100	100	100

*The total value index is in respect of cocoa exports only.

Terms of Trade

	1919	1920	1921	1922	1923	1924	1925	1926	1927	1928	1929	1930	1931	1932	1933	1934	1935	1936	1937	1938	1939
Cocoa Exporters																					
Income T of T	221	264	77	133	169	150	154	162	227	233	209	174	156	117	127	80	122	109	126	100	55
Barter T of T	154	179	43	113	106	113	131	137	184	169	143	138	113	118	104	125	116	160	203	100	129
Cocoa Producers																					
Barter T of T	118	133	39	83	85	83	108	109	142	139	114	113	98	105	81	89	94	107	143	100	98
Cane Farmers																					
Barter T of T	76	128	46	54	128	116	66	69	88	78	78	82	102	109	122	112	114	110	97	100	109

> made themselves felt and the economy could not take advantage of the rise in export prices.

One must compare the barter terms of trade of producers with the barter terms of trade of exporters. Although the terms of trade of the latter had recovered by 1922, the terms of trade of the former (producers) did not become favourable until 1925. Even then it was considerably below that for exporters.[4] Also, whereas the barter terms of trade of the exporters were favourable for the rest of the period, that of the producers fell again around 1931–32 and were not favourable again until 1935–36. In 1936–37 they seemed to have benefited but little from the increase in the export price of cocoa.

The cane farmers' position is very interesting. It would best be compared with that of cocoa producers. The two numbers seem to reflect, after 1923, the competition between the domestic agricultural industries. Although the terms were favourable to the cane farmers in 1923 and 1924, they were unfavourable to the cocoa producers. Both values then cross in 1924–25 and throughout the 1920s when cocoa producers were experiencing favourable barter terms of trade, cane farmers were experiencing very adverse terms of trade.

Further grounds are therefore obtained for finding that cane farmers were justifiably dissatisfied especially in the 1920s. The terms of trade improved in the 1930s but the gains were never considerable. It is significant also that improvements in their barter terms of trade occurred at the same time as the granting of preferences to sugar in 1932.

Appendix 2

Domestic Food Production

One of the problems that has faced those concerned with the economic development of Trinidad and Tobago has been that of domestic food production. The first indication of the gravity of the problem is seen in the large bill which the colony has had to meet year after year for the imports of food. What is most disturbing is the fact that the food bill remained large in times of depression as in times of prosperity. In 1920, for example, the food bill was $11.6 million. In 1930, the landed cost of food and drink imported amounted to $7.7 million or roughly three-fourths of the value of the agricultural exports of the same period. That year the important items were as follows:

Rice	$1,055,500
Vegetables and ground provisions	$349,400
Beans and peas etc.	$173,300
Beef cattle	$379,200
Pork, bacon, poultry, and so on	$558,200
Milk (condensed)	$565,400
Butter and butter substitutes	$297,100

An examination of the data for the entire period shows that the 1930 situation is typical. But the fact of a persistently large bill for food imports is not alone cause for concern; it is of concern when the following points are considered jointly with the preceding data:

a. a large and rapidly increasing population;
b. fairly large-scale unemployment and underemployment;

c. depression in the agricultural industries producing for export, and
d. a generally low income per head of the population.

That the problem is drawn into proper perspective.

Since high imports of food (both in the aggregate and per capita) are not new to Trinidad and Tobago and the other West Indian islands, it should be useful to see how this pattern was built up and with what sort of economies these import patterns were associated in the past.

From the earliest development of the West Indies the pattern has been a specialization based on the production of export crops, for example, sugar, and the importation of food. In chapter 2, "Imports", it was shown that in the eighteenth century, so infinite was the profit on sugar that land and slave labour could not be spared for the "lesser activity" of food production. Also it was shown that the director of agriculture, while upholding this same pattern of development for the fifty-year period up to 1920, thought that in the inter-war period this pattern was outmoded. He thought that while the specialization and trade argument was sound up to 1920 it was considerably weakened thereafter because, while "it was sound business during the earlier period to neglect food crops in favour of an export crop, the return from which allowed an ample margin for the purchase abroad of relatively less valuable articles i.e. food", the position had altered "for cocoa is worth half what it used to be".

Before analysing the problems of food production in Trinidad and Tobago, it should be useful to consider to what extent the director of agriculture was justified in his conclusion that price changes had weakened the specialization and trade argument which seemed to hold for the earlier period pre-1870–1920.

In appendix 1 treating the terms of trade, it is seen that although the export price of cocoa fell considerably during the period 1919–39 the price of imported food items fell too. In terms of the export prices and the total values of cocoa both the net barter and the income terms of trade seemed to have favoured cocoa. But in terms of the prices received by the cocoa producer at store in Trinidad, the period 1924–25 to 1930–31 was the only long period during which the net barter terms of trade were favourable. This wide difference between the export price and the price paid to the producer has already been referred to in the chapter on cocoa. This section is concerned with showing that in so far as cocoa producers were concerned the justification for the earlier division of labour had largely disappeared – in the 1930s especially.

The cane farmer was not much better off. In fact for most of the 1920s the barter terms of trade moved decidedly against him and in the 1930s, though they were favourable, the margin was not large even with the preferences granted to sugar in 1932.

From the point of view of the barter terms of trade of these two groups, therefore, a greater production of domestic foods would have been desirable.[1]

In addition to the preceding specialization and trade argument, the director of agriculture advanced four other factors which affected local food production negatively, that is, (1) soil, (2) praedial larceny, (3) markets and (4) shortage of land suitable for rice.

The first has some merit. The soil composition is very complex, and, as has been pointed out in the chapters on the other agricultural industries, it places definite limit to expansion. The heavy clays of the central plains of Trinidad were not suitable for ground provision though ideal for sugarcane. But although it places difficulties in the way of increased production, such difficulties are not an insurmountable barrier. The fourth links up with the first, that is, soil. The third (markets) is very important, especially because of the great emphasis which has in the past been placed upon the supply side of the problem. One of the aims of this section is to show that while note must be taken of the supply difficulties, the demand side of the problem presents the greater difficulties.

An outline of the build-up of the emphasis on the supply side of the problem is discussed first. Even as far back as October 1917 when the Ground Provision Depot was established under the supervision of the Ground Provision Committee, the emphasis was on the supply side of the problem. Peasants, and even larger agriculturists, were exhorted to produce more ground provisions. The figures of receipts of the depot which was operating on an advance account were for the year 1918–20 (inclusive) as follows: $8,917.50; $26,898.20; $41,525.27 – almost a fivefold increase in three years. From the point of view of the encouraging of local food production, therefore, the establishment of the depot was a success.

But this fivefold increase in the purchases of the depot did not solve the problem; for in 1921 the director of agriculture reported "an annually recurring glut of sweet potatoes, grown largely as a catch crop with sugar cane". Efforts were made to find an outside market but without success. He further reported that storage experiments, on a larger scale than had hitherto been seriously undertaken, had met with some success.

In spite of these annually recurring gluts, however, what attitudes prevail and where is the emphasis placed in 1930? "There is far too great a tendency to neglect the growth of food crops for local consumption."[2] And once again he used as his argument the size of the import bill for food. He advised more attention to the growth of food crops and rearing of livestock for domestic consumption but in the following year the market was glutted: "In 1931, for example, the maize crop was larger than usual and growers experienced the greatest difficulty in effecting its sale, even at the very lowest prices."[3]

But the glut in the Trinidad domestic market did not occur only from production in that island. Tobago was for many years known as the "bread basket" of Trinidad. The rich Tobago soil and, except in hard dry seasons, the regular natural irrigation by rain water resulted in the production of ground provisions of all kinds always of a good quality and abundance. The coastal steamer, the SS *Trinidad* which was capable of carrying livestock (a few cattle, sheep, goats and pigs) and cocoa from the many estates and the ground provisions of all kinds (plantains, yams, pigeon peas, sweet potatoes and so on) did a round-the-island trip around Tobago every other week. It stopped at all the main ports at which a significant cargo could be loaded and transported to Port of Spain, Trinidad.

Before the joining of the two islands in 1898, Tobago shipped its cocoa, sugar, cotton and so on direct to England and America. After their unity all produce (cocoa and ground provisions) was transported to Trinidad where together both islands' cocoa production was exported to all relevant markets. Unfortunately no reliable data are now available about Tobago's contribution to Trinidad and Tobago's cocoa exports, nor of the amount of ground provisions sent to Trinidad.

However, Tobago producers of sweet potatoes tried always to have their supply of that commodity arrive at the market in Port of Spain before that of St Vincent. The latter island with its light volcanic soil produced an excellent product.

The sailings of the SS *Trinidad* continued during peace and World War II without attack from enemy submarines. Only one submarine surfaced near to the vessel during the war. No one knew its nationality but no attempt was made to stop or damage the vessel.

But the emphasis on production as opposed to consumption and so effective markets was not changed. Pressure was brought to bear upon the peasants to produce more ground provisions in spite of the annually recurring glut. One of the conditions imposed upon small proprietors who received assistance under the Cocoa Subsidy Scheme was that attention was to be given, where land was available, to the growth of food crops for family use.

Here again pressure was being put on the wrong persons. Those who contributed most to the import bill were not the small peasant proprietors. The proceedings of the Wages Committee of 1920 brought out quite clearly the importance to peasants of food gardens as a supplementary means of income or as a method of curtailing expenditure.

Once again, therefore, the emphasis was misplaced. The peasants were already producing for their own consumption and some for the market. The only further urging they needed was an expanding market at reasonable prices.

The Demand Side of the Picture

It becomes evident, therefore, that in spite of soil deficiencies, praedial larceny and so on, peasants were prepared to produce domestic food crops and even to sell them at very low prices. It is necessary, therefore to examine the demand side of the problem for a solution.

Consumption Pattern

As was pointed out earlier, the economic specialization which was inherited from the past emphasized production of export crops and imports of food. This specialization engendered a consumption pattern which has persisted through time, one of the major factors in the problem. When, therefore, the director of agriculture points to the size of the items: fish, meat, poultry, vegetables, and so on, an explanation comes readily from the following extract from Eric Williams's *Capitalism and Slavery*:

> In 1770 the continental colonies sent to the West Indies nearly one-third of their exports of dried fish and almost all their pickled fish; seven-eights of their oats, seven-tenths of their corn, almost all their onions, five-sixths of their pine, oak, cedar boards, over half of their staves, nearly all their hoops, all their horses, sheep, hogs and poultry, almost all their soap and candles.[4]

Examine the imports of Trinidad and Tobago, and the similarity and continuity are evident. Many of the items that were important in the import list of the West Indies in 1770 were imported in Trinidad and Tobago in the 1920s and 1930s.

One of the main problems, therefore, has been an inherited and perpetuated consumption pattern; a pattern which was perhaps suited to the economic fortunes of the islands in the seventeenth to nineteenth centuries but which is out of place in the depressed state of agriculture in the 1920s and 1930s.

And although evidence of this consumption pattern is to be found among the peasants (salt fish, salt beef and so on), the towns are the real centres of it. It is the wealthier classes and the wage earners in the towns who are mostly responsible for the large imports of food. Note, for example, the following extract from the director of agriculture's report, 1936: "While it is true that the basis of the diet of the working classes is imported flour and rice in the aggregate a very large amount of ground provisions are grown and consumed annually by the smaller peasant proprietors."

From the foregoing it will be seen that there were problems both on the supply side and the demand side. It should be emphasized, however, that the problems on the demand side were more important, that those of the supply side would have yielded to treatment, if only the demand difficulty were removed or lessened.

First, it is necessary to get the problems into their right perspective and within the right limits. There can be no question of self-sufficiency resulting from increased domestic food production. Since there cannot be complete substitution of local for imported foods all along the line, it is necessary to determine

a. the extent to which local foods are readily substitutable for imported foods;
b. the relative prices of home produced and imported foods which are substitutable;
c. methods of so influencing the established consumption patterns and standards as to facilitate the substitution of local for imported foods.

Regarding (a), conditions of climate and so on rule out the growing of wheat which is one of the chief imports. Wheat flour is nutritious and an almost permanent fixture in the diet. It would be difficult to replace it by local production. The rearing of cattle on a large scale on grasslands on relatively small islands is also impractical.

Poultry and meats can be produced locally and are almost perfect substitutes. Almost perfect because, though the articles may in fact be similar or identical, there is in every country a section of people who will not believe their own country can produce anything as good as the imported items. They will wish to continue importing some foods. There is the social boost which they experience when they think of themselves as different. About

(b) it is not known precisely what the prices of the identical domestically produced food items were. It would appear, however, that local producers could not clear the market even at very low prices. And this, apart from the fact of given long-standing consumption patterns, must have been affected by the low prices of imported foodstuffs. On the other hand, it can be argued that the local foods would have been fresher and more nutritious and their production would have given employment to many who were then unemployed or underemployed.

Altering the consumption pattern would have been a difficult task. It was perhaps this difficulty over influencing consumption patterns that led to the easier though less fruitful course of stressing the supply side of the problem.

An examination of the domestic food production during World War II gives support to the argument that the pre-war problem was largely on the demand and not the supply side.

The Report of the Economies Committee 1949 explains the success of the wartime "Grow More Food Campaign" in terms of the estimated increase of 10,000 acres in rice lands; 13,000 acres from cocoa lands for corn; 15,000 acres from sugar estates for ground provisions; plus a further 14,000 acres from large estates for ground provisions. It estimates 1944 production to have increased over 1938 production as follows; rice two and half times, corn six times, pigeon peas thrice, root crops twice.

	1938 = 100
1944: Rice	250
Corn	600
Peas (pigeon)	300
Root crops	200

Once more, interested mainly in the supply side of the problem, the committee gives the following factors responsible for the increase (a) release of labourers from the decaying cocoa industry; (b) the natural increase in population; (c) immigration; (d) the draining of workers from the staple agricultural industries; and (e) the spare time activities of thousands in their backyard gardens.

The report then went on to mention the special provisions which guaranteed "both a market and minimum prices for certain commodities".

It is the contention of this book that while the supply factors aforementioned were contributory, they were far from sufficient to ensure the increase in domestic production; that the increase in production was made possible by the increase in demand and that the increase in demand was caused by the following factors:

The submarine warfare which in the early years of the war closed off foreign sources and gave local producers a virtual monopoly. Certain local foods which were previously eaten largely by those of the lowest income groups were in great demand by all classes.

The amount of American spending[5] led to increased and well-distributed incomes which formed the basis for this increased demand. Note that when imports became easier and before the complete curtailment of American spending both imports and domestic production increased side by side.

Increased demand brought about by the increase in numbers of immigrants and the large number of troops. Many traders made their fortunes supplying domestic foods to the American armed forces and nationals working on the construction of the bases who could not be released to leave the bases for lunch.

As a result of this stimulated demand for domestic foods farmers found it profitable to grow more food. Some left the sugar estates not to work on the American bases but to cultivate food crops: "Both garden and rice crops give the farmer a bigger and quicker return (than cane-farming) for his outlay and are cheaper crops to cultivate."[6]

Finally one is forced to the conclusion that, in spite of all the apparent concern over the size of the bill for imports of food the government never really intended to take active steps to remedy the situation. Since import prices were low in the early 1930s this attitude may have been justified. Since unemployment and underemployment were growing, however, it may, on balance, have been better to take active steps to discourage certain food imports while encouraging their production at home.

After all, active steps were taken to exclude cheap Japanese-made shoes and other items not in the interest of the Trinidad and Tobago consumer but in the interest of other empire manufacturers. When the bill for the high tariff on shoes was introduced into the Legislative Council in 1932, one member was moved to ask whether Canada was demanding such preferences from a barefooted country.[7]

No attempt is being made to decide what course of action should have been taken. What is of concern here is that whatever objective was decided upon, the policies should have been geared to its attainment. There was no point in lamenting the growth of food imports while at the same time closing an eye to the true cause of the difficulty. Further, there seems to have been a marked absence of co-ordination in the policies of the government departments. It becomes at least confusing when at the same time as the director of agriculture was exhorting peasants to produce more foodstuffs and thereby glutting the market, the government through its controller of customs was in 1935 lowering the duty on potatoes (in return for Canada's preference on crude oil),[8] onions and other vegetables, and was in the same breath saying that it would be a good thing to develop a local supply of these items.

Appendix 3

Commercial Policy

Perhaps the title of this appendix is somewhat over-ambitious. In the first place, although the island government did have some say in the formulation of certain aspects of its commercial policy, such policies were largely influenced, in fact, by the secretary of state for the colonies. The colonies, for example, were not directly represented at the Ottawa Conference.

This section does not propose to deal, except very briefly, with the general question of imperial preference. F.V. Meyer and Sir Donald MacDougall,[1] and others have already analysed some of the important points.

This section does not propose to say much about revenue tariffs too. Customs and excise duty accounted for slightly more than 50 per cent of gross government revenue for the whole of the period. The import duty on unmanufactured tobacco was most important, contributing in 1935–36 at least one quarter of the value of revenues from import duties. In 1935 increased duties were imposed on milk, flour, vegetables, boots and beer to provide revenue for assistance to the cocoa industry.[2]

What it is proposed to analyse in greater detail is the question of protective tariffs for local industries. Even here, however, only the main principles and the industry to which they were chiefly applied will be discussed.

Protective Tariffs for Local Industries

In April 1931 the Trinidad and Tobago legislature approved the principle of protective tariffs for local industries in all cases where:

i. the consumer is protected against increase of price;

ii. the local producer of raw materials shares in the profits of the unmanufactured articles;
iii. the quality of the local product is not inferior to that of the imported articles, and
iv. the Revenue of the Colony suffers no loss.[3]

At once one is tempted to ask whether these four principles were examined for mutual compatibility before they were enunciated.[4] Also even when taken singly, does their application present any problems?

Take principle (ii) for example. The enforcement of standards of quality is nearly always a difficult matter, especially where the fall in quality is not considerable. What happens if a new process is developed abroad so that the quality of the foreign article changes or is improved? Does the local product then lose its protection? Any lapse from the quality standard was threatened with complete removal of protection. But if the lapse applies to a particular firm, then general relaxation of tariffs would have hit all manufacturers in the same way. In the case of protection for coconuts it would have affected coconut growers also.

The other three principles could perhaps be enforced singly. Whether or not they were mutually incompatible will be discussed later. It is necessary, however, to make two comments at this point.

Firstly, the resolution said nothing about the length of time during which protection would be provided. It did not even state whether the protection was mainly for infant industries. If it is assumed that infant industries are implied, it states nothing about limitation of their state of infancy.

Secondly, it was quite definitely not going to be a protection designed mainly to provide employment:

> The kind of industry which it is not proposed to help is where local material forms an insignificant portion of the total value of the finished product. Such an industry might be profitable. One can conceive that most of the materials would have to be imported, but that in the finished product 70, 80, or even 90 per cent of the total value might be attributable to local labour, so that material is the least part of the expense.
>
> But the industry which this resolution seeks to help is where the value of the local materials used and the value of the labour each forms a substantial portion of the value of the finished product.

With the second paragraph of this elucidation of the original resolution one cannot take issue; but the earlier section which refuses protection even in the exaggerated case where "70, 80, or 90 per cent of the total value is attributed to local labour" but where the material is imported, might be open to serious objections.

Even reluctant protectionists will allow protection where it promotes employment. In the peculiar circumstances of Trinidad and Tobago in the 1930s, the need for promoting employment was overwhelming. The rapid rate of population growth; the decline in the agricultural industries; the decline in the actual numbers and in the proportions of the population of those employed in agriculture; the growth of the towns; the growth of unemployment and underemployment, all indicate that protection would have been justified if it did no more than provide employment.

In a country where raw materials were scarce and where labour was the surplus factor, the employment and skilling of the population would be ground enough for protection. The type of industry that was needed was precisely that which encouraged the development and utilization of domestic skills.

How did the principles stand up to practical applications? The one important case in which they were employed in the 1930s was for protecting the copra products industry. This case brought out the inconsistencies of the principles; demonstrated that though they appeared to be broadly conceived this was not the case; that their applicability was limited and that the slightest change of circumstances from those envisaged when the principles were conceived would make them of no effect.

In 1930 tariffs were imposed on imported copra products from all sources[5] (empire and foreign) with the aim of preserving the local market for a new copra product manufacturing industry that was being set up. The protection was sought because an English company, Lever Brothers, was employing a system of price discrimination on a regional basis. That is to say, prices varied from island to island and country to country according to local conditions in each.

It was therefore decided to encourage and protect the local market from such practices.[6]

The four principles which were enunciated in 1931 were already embodied in the bill for the protection of the copra industry.

Having argued that this new industry needed "protection against unfair foreign competition", the treasurer proceeded to protect the general revenue. Since he expected that the increase in duties would be a considerable deterrent to importers of foreign produce and that as a consequence there would be a drop in revenue, he required the protected companies to pay excise duties on the locally produced commodities. In addition he assured the council that even if this did not suffice there was another channel. The company would have to import ingredients for hardening their compounds. On these they would have to pay duty which should make up any deficits that might occur.

To protect the consumer he proposed that the wholesale price ex-refinery be fixed at a level not above the lowest prices prevailing between January 1925 and April 1930. In addition the companies would guarantee to pay $3.00 minimum for every 100 pounds of copra used by them in manufacturing the articles. Government was to fix weekly the selling price of copra. The companies would pay the producers of copra from whom they purchased, at that price, but they would undertake to deposit into the treasury or with the collector of customs the difference between the fixed prices and the $3.00 guaranteed. The amount held in deposit would subsequently be distributed among all producers of copra regardless of whether they had sold to the companies or not, in proportion to their sales to local produce dealers. Producers of copra were required to submit sales slips to the collector of customs and in the case of exports, their shipping bills, so that it could be ascertained how much copra they had disposed of.

This bill was designed to ensure that there be no loss of revenue and no hardship to consumers; a new field of employment and a prosperous industry. The agreement was for two years in the first instance after which the government had the right to revise all its conditions.

The minimum price of $3.00 per 100 pounds meant that the price of copra would be raised from an unguaranteed 2½¢ (BWI) per pound to 3¢ guaranteed.

In fact the plan broke down. The level of tariffs first imposed proved inadequate and had to be increased by 50 per cent as a check to the section of the population who would not believe that their country could produce anything good. It was estimated that 25 per cent of the people continued to prefer the imported commodity. "Thereby feeding those very people by whose efforts the copra market has been reduced to its present level."[7] The new duties did reduce considerably the value and quantity of imported oils and fats.

But the persistence of imports was only a minor difficulty. In 1933 the empire rate of duty had to be reduced. The part played by the Ottawa agreement in this matter was insignificant. What was important was the weak economic and bargaining power of the local copra products industry and the economy as a whole.

The local industry, in spite of its being protected, had the capacity to handle only 25 per cent of local copra production (which was enough for local consumption plus a small surplus for export to the rest of the West Indies). The colony was dependent as to the other 75 per cent of copra production on British manufacturers of copra products. The latter demanded and had to be granted a share of the soap market. The main condition imposed by the British company was that "the same differentiation shall be maintained between imported soap as regards customs import duty and local soap as regards excise duty, as always used to exist before the local soap factory was built". That is to say a differentiation of one shilling per case of 100 pounds under the British Preferential Tariff plus surtax.

The wishes of the British company had to be met because "we are more or less in their hands . . . The local company realizes that they are not in a position to resist this offer."

What were the drawbacks of the four principles? Why was it possible to undermine protection in this way?

1. Although before the granting of protection care was taken to ascertain that the capacity of local industry would be sufficient for the whole of the local market no thought was given to the throughput of the factory in relation to total production of raw materials. The lesson that was being learnt was that it is well-nigh impossible to impose protection against a competitor who is himself in the monopolistic position where he purchases 75 per cent of the raw material in question produced by the economy. Further, the market for the raw materials was a buyers' market.[8]
2. The check from the foreign company demonstrated also the difficulty of establishing a system of protection so that everyone would be perfectly satisfied and in which no sector suffered any loss. Normally protection involves some sort of loss: either in terms of quality or price, consumers' surplus and if the market is to be preserved for the local industry, some loss of revenue from import duty or excise. Such loss may, however, be temporary and compensated by gains in another sector or at a later date.

In the case under discussion the demands of the foreign company could only be met by a loss being incurred by one of the domestic sectors named in the "four principles". Principle (iii) was the one thrown overboard and revenue bore the loss and the following explanation was given: "I think it will be agreed that, especially at a time like this, since soap is one of the prime necessities of life, we cannot impose any excise duty and shall therefore revert to the former customs duties, i.e. an import duty of one shilling per case plus surtax."

In other words, this was the British Preferential Tariff. The general rate was to remain unchanged.

It was anticipated that the loss of excise duty would be £500, but it was anticipated that this would be passed on to the consumer.

It should be interesting to compare the measures taken in Trinidad and Tobago with those taken in Jamaica about this same time to protect their copra industry. Although Trinidad and Tobago relied upon high tariffs, Jamaica employed total prohibition of imports. Whereas Trinidad and Tobago imposed four conditions for protection, conditions which were designed to protect revenue and the consumer, in respect both of quality of the product and price, and the producer of the copra, Jamaica did not impose statutory regulations for controlling the prices of copra, nor did it impose conditions of quality of the product, nor did it safeguard revenue. In the event, the only loss to Trinidad and Tobago was to the public which had to pay a higher price for its copra products than would have been the case if imports were free. For meanwhile the price of copra and copra products on the world market had fallen. In the case of Jamaica, in addition to the aforementioned loss to the consumer, that is, the loss of what could be described as consumers' surplus there were the following losses. Government suffered a substantial loss of revenue since there was outright prohibition and no imposition of excise duties; the coconut growers failed to secure any benefits for there was no minimum price fixed for coconuts and copra. Statutory conditions as to the price of copra were not imposed with the result that competition forced the price down to the level better than that obtainable in export markets.

> The chief beneficiaries of the scheme have been a number of competing edible oil factories each operating on a small scale far too small for efficiency, but succeeding nonetheless in making profits. Measures for the rationalization of edible oil production and for the regulation of the price of copra appear to be essential in Jamaica if the main objectives of the exclusion of imports are to be secured.

However, since Trinidad and Tobago, Jamaica and other developing island colonies (later nations), have to trade (export and import), or they die, is it really feasible or wise for them to attempt to achieve a total exclusion of imports of any small international important commodity to achieve whatever objective?

Especially is this relevant when (a) the largest portion of their government revenue comes from trade taxes, that is, import and excise duties and (b) the infant industry that needs protection is so small and inefficient that it utilizes only a small percentage of the basic domestic commodity required for their operation and the balance must be exported to foreign countries and industries.

Appendix 4

Statistical Data

Since this book considers the export/import trends and economic development of Trinidad and Tobago, note the relevant statistical data for the period (tables A4.1 through A4.10):

1. Principal export products (1,000)
2. Quantities of principal exports
3. Percentage contributions to export
4. Imports of flour
5. Imports of rice
6. Imports of milk
7. Imports of fish
8. Imports of textiles
9. Imports of boots and shoes
10. Imports of cement

Table A4.1 Principal Export Products ($'000)

Year	Cocoa	Sugar Products	Petroleum Products	Asphalt Products	Coconuts Products	Others	Total
1919	12,446	4,999	4,050	647	1,717	451	24,310
1920	15,485	13,139	3,116	1,274	2,002	674	35,690
1921	6,538	7,293	3,483	1,130	828	376	19,648
1922	5,641	5,561	3,656	1,631	859	444	17,792
1923	6,173	5,383	5,919	1,813	942	403	20,633
1924	5,597	6,129	6,563	1,852	1,069	491	21,701
1925	6,034	5,412	7,490	1,729	925	860	22,450
1926	6,096	4,937	8,976	2,170	993	862	24,034
1927	8,026	3,768	11,167	2,230	913	719	26,823
1928	7,925	5,906	11,968	1,933	1,316	638	29,686
1929	6,941	5,192	14,647	2,074	1,351	1,185	31,390
1930	5,453	3,848	13,395	1,504	1,006	1,381	26,587
1931	3,965	4,486	9,358	1,136	568	506	20,019
1932	2,779	4,263	11,437	632	519	508	20,138
1933	2,669	5,569	10,820	724	522	452	20,756
1934	1,679	4,569	14,056	797	431	706	22,239
1935	2,531	4,693	13,322	1,093	245	891	22,775
1936	2,343	6,426	15,911	960	325	971	26,935
1937	3,087	6,426	18,896	1,195	655	1,272	31,531
1938	2,369	5,157	23,657	1,131	271	1,157	33,742
1939	1,213	6,200	26,672	1,200	n.a.	n.a.	36,732

Table A4.2 Quantities of Principal Exports

Year	Cocoa (million lb)	Sugar '000 tons	Copra (million lb)	Dried Asphalt '000 tons	Petroleum, Fuel Oil (million gallons)	Gasolene, Motor Spirit (million gallons)	Kerosene (million gallons)
1919	60.7	37.8	13.2	54.7	30.4	2.4	2.1
1920	62.7	48.0	9.5	7.6	27.3	2.4	1.9
1921	75.2	46.1	11.0	67.9	33.8	2.8	2.0
1922	50.6	51.9	15.6	100.0	39.5	5.5	2.2
1923	67.7	35.5	17.2	126.4	61.7	10.5	1.3
1924	56.4	43.4	14.5	135.9	87.0	13.5	0.8
1925	49.5	60.7	12.9	118.5	99.5	13.4	2.7
1926	50.1	65.7	15.5	140.1	105.2	20.8	0.9
1927	51.9	41.8	14.7	139.4	110.3	28.4	1.3
1928	58.0	74.1	23.6	125.1	157.0	39.3	0.5
1929	61.9	81.5	28.5	134.9	206.2	48.4	1.9
1930	53.8	69.1	23.9	97.7	175.9	53.3	1.8
1931	57.2	86.1	21.0	71.0	155.7	63.3	1.4
1932	41.8	86.0	16.7	39.5	175.2	67.9	2.1
1933	51.3	108.5	22.0	44.6	193.4	74.2	2.9
1934	26.8	93.5	21.2	48.7	238.2	91.3	2.5
1935	44.4	105.7	10.6	66.1	273.9	96.0	4.4
1936	28.3	142.7	11.0	51.8	309.5	104.0	5.2
1937	26.3	142.7	19.0	66.6	362.7	104.6	4.2
1938	42.4	120.3	10.1	52.2	411.9	134.9	3.7
1939	16.8	114.0	–	–	–	–	–

Table A4.3 Percentage Contributions to Exports

Year	Cocoa (%)	Sugar Products (%)	Petroleum Products (%)	Asphalt Products (%)	Coconut Products (%)	Others (%)	Total (%)
1919	51.2	20.6	16.7	2.7	7.1	1.7	100
1920	43.4	36.8	8.7	3.6	5.6	1.9	100
1921	33.3	37.1	17.7	5.8	4.2	1.9	100
1922	32.3	31.3	20.5	9.2	4.8	1.9	100
1923	29.9	26.1	28.7	8.8	4.6	1.9	100
1924	25.8	28.2	30.2	8.5	4.9	2.4	100
1925	26.9	24.1	33.4	7.7	4.0	3.9	100
1926	25.4	20.5	37.3	9.0	4.1	3.7	100
1927	29.9	14.0	41.6	8.3	3.4	2.8	100
1928	26.7	19.9	40.3	6.5	4.4	3.2	100
1929	22.1	16.5	46.7	6.6	4.3	3.8	100
1930	21.4	14.9	51.9	5.8	3.9	2.1	100
1931	19.8	22.4	46.7	5.7	2.8	2.6	100
1932	13.8	21.2	56.8	3.1	2.6	2.5	100
1933	12.9	26.8	52.1	3.5	2.5	2.2	100
1934	7.5	20.5	63.2	3.6	1.9	3.3	100
1935	11.1	20.5	58.5	4.8	1.1	3.9	100
1936	8.7	23.9	59.1	3.6	1.2	3.5	100
1937	9.8	20.4	59.9	3.8	2.1	4.0	100
1938	7.0	15.3	70.1	3.4	0.8	3.4	100
1939	3.3	–	72.6	3.3	–	–	100

Table A4.4 Imports of Flour

Year	Quantity (lb million)	Value ($M)	Average Price per lb (¢)	Index Quantity 1938 = 100	Index Price 1938 = 100	Imports/lb per Caput
1919	59.7	3.65	6.10	88	235	154.0
1920	52.9	3.62	6.80	78	262	
1921	50.5	2.77	5.50	74	211	
1922	57.8	2.23	3.86	85	149	
1923	60.1	2.07	3.40	88	130	160.0
1924	56.0	2.02	3.60	82	138	
1925	53.7	2.42	4.50	79	173	
1926	54.8	2.21	4.03	80	155	
1927	55.6	2.06	3.70	82	142	142.0
1928	60.6	2.15	3.55	89	137	
1929	63.5	2.15	3.39	93	130	
1930	59.3	1.94	3.30	87	127	
1931	64.5	1.45	2.25	95	87	156.0
1932	60.3	1.38	2.29	89	88	
1933	66.4	1.37	2.06	98	79	
1934	65.8	1.41	2.14	97	82	
1935	64.9	1.46	2.20	95	85	147.5
1936	68.1	1.61	2.35	100	90	
1937	66.2	2.06	3.10	97	119	
1938	68.1	1.78	2.60	100	100	
1939	75.3	1.56	2.08	111	80	160.0

Table A4.5 Imports of Rice

Year	Quantity (lb million)	Value ($M)	Average Price per lb (¢)	Index Quantity (1938 = 100)	Index Price (1938 = 100)	Imports/ per Caput lb
1919	15.4	1.09	7.10	36	310	40.0
1920	13.8	1.12	8.14	32	355	
1921	20.3	0.94	4.60	47	200	
1922	27.3	1.03	4.75	64	207	
1923	29.3	0.99	3.20	68	140	77.8
1924	25.7	0.94	3.66	60	160	
1925	25.8	1.04	4.03	60	176	
1926	26.6	1.12	4.21	62	184	
1927	27.3	0.96	3.53	64	154	70.6
1928	29.7	1.03	3.47	69	150	
1929	33.5	1.13	3.37	78	147	
1930	36.2	1.07	2.94	85	128	
1931	35.2	0.77	2.18	82	95	84.9
1932	35.0	0.77	2.20	82	96	
1933	37.8	0.72	1.90	88	83	
1934	42.5	0.79	1.85	99	81	
1935	40.5	0.81	2.00	95	87	92.0
1936	41.8	0.86	2.06	98	90	
1937	41.1	0.89	2.15	96	94	
1938	42.8	0.98	2.29	100	100	
1939	46.3	0.97	2.10	108	92	97.8

Table A4.6 Imports of Milk

Year	Quantity (lb million)	Value '000 $	Average Price per lb (¢)	Index Quantity (1938 = 100)	Index Price (1938 = 100)	Imports/lb per Caput
1919	1.27	244.3	19.20	14	231	3.3
1920	6.02	386.4	6.40	68	77	
1921	1.90	454.6	23.90	27	288	
1922	2.03	401.3	19.76	23	238	
1923	2.11	343.7	16.00	24	193	4.9
1924	2.05	348.9	17.10	23	206	
1925	2.25	366.7	16.39	25	197	
1926	2.73	380.6	14.14	31	170	
1927	3.03	468.9	15.50	34	187	7.5
1928	3.60	495.4	13.76	41	166	
1929	3.80	528.0	13.90	43	167	
1930	4.00	553.9	13.70	46	165	
1931	4.40	619.2	13.90	50	167	10.5
1932	4.10	489.6	11.94	46	144	
1933	4.60	390.2	8.50	52	102	10.9
1934	5.50	445.9	8.16	62	98	
1935	6.00	464.4	7.80	67	94	13.4
1936	7.40	546.9	6.77	83	82	
1937	8.40	568.5	6.80	94	82	
1938	8.90	739.9	8.30	100	100	
1939	9.40	858.0	9.20	105	111	19.7

Table A4.7 Imports of Fish

Year	Quantity (lb million)	Value $'000	Average Price per lb (¢)	Index Quantity (1938 = 100)	Index Price (1938 = 100)	Imports/lb per Caput
1919	5.01	634.1	12.6	73	200	13.0
1920	6.44	841.4	13.1	92	206	
1921	7.04	581.8	8.0	101	127	
1922	6.52	545.3	8.0	93	127	
1923	5.25	393.1	7.5	75	119	14.0
1924	4.93	468.0	9.5	70	151	
1925	4.74	438.2	9.0	68	143	
1926	5.33	424.8	8.0	76	127	
1927	6.44	435.8	6.7	92	106	16.4
1928	6.48	529.0	8.2	93	130	
1929	5.47	499.7	9.0	78	143	
1930	5.84	488.6	8.3	83	132	
1931	5.61	391.2	7.0	80	111	13.6
1932	5.84	374.4	6.4	83	101	
1933	6.15	432.7	5.7	88	90	
1934	6.03	348.1	5.8	86	92	
1935	5.94	353.3	6.0	85	95	13.5
1936	6.33	339.1	5.4	90	86	14.0
1937	6.43	403.6	6.3	92	100	
1938	7.00	439.7	6.3	100	100	
1939	6.81	439.5	6.5	97	103	14.4

Table A4.8 Imports of Textiles

Year	Cotton Piece Goods					Imports per Caput	All Silk Goods $'000	All Cottons ($M)	All Apparel $'000
	Gross Imports (Square Yards)	Value ($M)	Average Price per Yard (¢)	Index Quantity	Index Price (1938 = 100)				
1919	7.8	1.29	16.5	76	156	20.0	58.3	1.56	307.2
1920	9.6	2.71	28.0	94	264		197.2	3.64	613.3
1921	11.0	1.50	13.6	108	119		141.6	1.86	361.4
1922	9.5	1.25	13.0	93	123		149.8	1.67	334.7
1923	6.2	1.11	18.0	61	170	16.4	113.2	1.59	297.7
1924	8.9	1.24	14.0	87	132		92.3	1.69	230.0
1925	10.3	1.40	13.6	101	119		108.4	1.80	258.5
1926	8.9	1.15	13.0	87	123		90.6	1.52	200.6
1927	10.4	1.30	12.5	102	118	26.5	107.8	1.74	268.5
1928	11.0	1.35	12.3	108	116		126.5	1.81	296.4
1929	9.5	1.36	14.3	93	135		115.5	1.82	330.2
1930	9.1	1.02	11.2	89	106		330.7	1.35	309.8
1931	9.4	0.85	9.0	92	85	22.8	353.5	1.08	265.0
1932	9.3	0.81	8.7	91	82		395.7	1.06	274.8
1933	9.7	0.82	8.5	95	80		460.6	1.05	294.8
1934	7.5	0.69	9.2	74	87		273.8	0.90	298.3
1935	11.5	1.08	9.4	13	89	26.0	328.6	1.16	428.7
1936	9.6	0.95	9.9	94	93		403.1	1.03	571.8
1937	10.0	1.11	11.1	98	105		649.5	1.26	671.0
1938	10.2	1.08	10.6	100	100		591.0	1.22	587.0
1939	9.6	1.04	10.8	94	102	20.0	574.7	1.19	982.3

Table A4.9 Imports of Boots and Shoes

Year	Net Imports '000 Doz. Prs.	Value $'000	Average Price per Pair ($)	Index Quantity	(1938 = 100) Price	Imports per Caput
1919	14.3	283.2	1.70	23	215	0.4
1920	29.3	606.9	1.75	51	222	
1921	10.7	274.6	2.14	19	271	
1922	22.1	405.1	1.53	39	194	
1923	20.2	323.8	1.34	36	174	0.7
1924	20.4	319.6	1.31	36	166	
1925	23.3	328.3	1.17	41	148	
1926	22.9	328.4	1.19	40	151	
1927	34.0	471.0	1.15	60	146	1.0
1928	37.0	525.8	1.18	69	149	1.1
1929	44.5	581.4	1.09	78	138	1.3
1930	36.3	465.2	1.08	64	137	
1931	33.4	387.6	0.98	59	124	0.97
1932	46.6	455.9	0.81	82	103	
1933	37.1	369.6	0.83	65	105	
1934	43.5	377.1	0.81	76	103	
1935	43.1	373.6	0.72	76	91	1.2
1936	52.2	476.0	0.76	92	96	
1937	73.0	656.8	0.75	128	95	
1938	56.9	540.4	0.79	100	100	
1939	69.7	644.8	0.77	122	97	1.8

Table A4.10 Imports of Cement

Year	Quantity '000 Tons	Value $'000	Average Price per Ton ($)	Index Quantity (1938 = 100)	Index Price (1938 = 100)	Imports/ Tons per Caput
1919	5.09	126.7	24.9	11	160	0.26
1920	11.68	384.0	32.9	24	210	
1921	10.18	295.7	28.07	21	179	
1922	9.26	174.2	18.8	19	120	
1923	10.10	210.7	21.0	23	134	0.50
1924	9.25	144.0	1.6	19	99	
1925	9.08	141.1	15.5	19	99	
1926	13.05	175.2	13.4	27	85	
1927	12.01	192.5	16.0	25	102	0.60
1928	16.02	249.1	15.5	33	99	
1929	20.82	319.4	15.36	43	98	
1930	20.57	322.5	15.68	43	100	
1931	19.09	264.5	13.8	40	98	0.90
1932	13.35	202.6	15.2	28	97	
1933	18.83	267.4	14.3	39	91	
1934	20.59	261.3	12.7	43	81	
1935	26.54	332.8	12.5	55	80	1.20
1936	31.06	402.4	13.0	65	83	
1937	42.92	599.6	14.0	90	90	
1938	47.90	747.6	15.7	100	100	
1939	42.53	721.0	17.0	89	108	1.80

Notes

Chapter 1

1. It is interesting also to note that cocoa prices seemed to have suffered less than wheat prices in that period.
2. The expansion of world cocoa production in the late nineteenth and early twentieth centuries and that of certain producing countries is set out briefly in chapter 3 on the cocoa industry. See also FAQ Commodity Series, "Cacao" Bulletin No. 277, 27 November 1955.
3. In 1920 export prices had so outstripped production that Trinidad sugar producers yielded to the temptation of the high prices of sugar on the world market and tended to reduce their domestic sales. It was therefore necessary to introduce the Food and Fuel Ordinances, 1920 to curb the practice. Contrast that situation with the late 1920s and 1930s when decreases in price were considerably offset by an expansion of output and when also the local market price was kept artificially high so as to give a subsidy to the sugar industry.
4. The general short-term inelasticity of supply of cocoa is considered in chapter 3.
5. The tendency was for production to fall with price in the cocoa industry, while sugar production increase offset the fall in price.
6. See table 2 for a consideration of the distribution of export incomes between domestic and foreign income earners throughout the period.
7. See above, this page.
8. See Meyer, *Britain's Colonies in World Trade,* chapters 6 and 7.
9. Trinidad cocoa could not have benefited, as did sugar, from imperial preference since the competition was largely intra-empire and some of the most important markets were non-empire. The West Indies, however, had some

special arrangements with Canada, one of which was the Canadian guarantee under the terms of the 1925 agreement not to accord preference to British West African cocoa.

10. There are certain invisible items in the balance of payment about which there is very scanty data. It is therefore necessary to proceed carefully on this line. But in view of the size of the contribution of the petroleum industry to total exports and imports and the size of the dividends declared, this conclusion seems reasonable.
11. These statements were published as Council Papers for the years 1927–35. It was necessary to obtain data for the period 1936–39 direct from the Mines Department in Trinidad. See chapter 6 on the petroleum industry.
12. See chapter 6.
13. See lower section of table 1.
14 See chapter 3.
15. For a development of this point, see chapter 6 where the growth of Trinidad Leaseholds Ltd is discussed.
16. See chapter 9. From an employment and welfare point of view the new imbalance did have some ill effects, since petroleum was not labour intensive; but in most other respects (government revenue, stability of prices and so on) it was better than the first.

Chapter 2

1. Williams, *Capitalism and Slavery,* 110–11.
2. Director of Agriculture Report, 1931.
3. Since there are no precise data on income, it is necessary to use other factors, mainly export prices and values, as indicators of how domestic incomes have varied.
4. Rice was much more a basic food, much more sought after, in Trinidad than in many of the other islands where ground provisions, domestically produced, formed the base of the diet.
5. In addition a fair amount of rice was locally grown, mainly by the East Indians, for their own consumption. Per capita consumption would therefore have been somewhat higher.
6. Total export values, government revenue and expenditure and especially employment and the total wages bill in the petroleum industry increased rapidly in the period 1935–39.
7. The main source of the cheaper milk was Holland.
8. Williams, *Capitalism and Slavery*, 59.
9. Bauer, *West African Trade*, 48–49. For Trinidad and Tobago terms of trade analysis, see appendix 1.

10. The Legislative Council debates of the period show that the unofficial members were largely opposed to the higher tariffs. One member asked whether Canada was demanding such preferences from a barefooted country. It must be remembered also that hookworm disease was taking its toll on the population and that some sort of footwear was essential to safeguard against infection.
11. See chapter 7.
12. Kindleberger, *Terms of Trade: A European Case Study*, 358.
13. Ibid.
14. Trinidad Leasehold Ltd Report for 1919–20.
15. For a development of the point that such capital intensive industries as mining have to take a much longer term view of the price changes of their products; see Mikesell and Cheney, *Arabian Oil*.
16. In 1926, there were imports of refining plant, for example, the Dubbs cracking plant imported by TLL. In 1931 UBOT raised new capital for the purpose of constructing a new refinery and loading facilities at Point Fortin.
17. Romolini, *Evolution of the Sugar Economy*, 15.
18. Shephard, *Cacao Industry of Trinidad* part, 5.
19. See chapter 4, "The Sugar Industry" and especially the methods of determining the price of cane.
20. Beachey, *British West Indies Sugar Industry in the late 19th Century*, 123.
21. Romolini, *Evolution of the Sugar Economy*, 5–6.
22. It can also be argued that what Trinidad and Tobago should have done was to switch to dairy farming or some such new industry. The cost of switching from one industry to another is, however, very high and is difficult to meet, especially when trade generally is depressed.

Chapter 3

1. *Cocoa: A Crop with a Future*, 24.
2. Bareau, "Cacao: A Review of Current Trends in Production, Price and Consumption", FAO Commodity Series, Bulletin no. 27, November 1955, chapter 4.
3. For the development of this point, see Shephard, *Cacao Industry of Trinidad*, parts 2 and 5.
4. See ibid.; Peter Ady, "Trends in Cocoa Production (British West Africa)", *Institute of Statistics Bulletin* (1949): 389–404.
5. Braithwaite, "Social Stratification in Trinidad".
6. Matthews, *Crisis of the West Indian Family*, 14.
7. Shephard, *Cacao Industry of Trinidad*, part 4.

8. Although the contract system was useful in developing the industry it suffered from the following drawbacks: (1) there was no supervision by the owner (of the land) especially as to strains of plantings and pickets, (2) it facilitated expansion beyond the area that the owner could actually manage, (3) contractors from lack of capital were usually in debt to the village shopkeeper to whom they had to sell their produce at a price lower than that which they would have received at store in Port of Spain. See reports of the Imperial Economic Committee, no. 22, "Cocoa" BMSO London 1932.
9. For further development of the question of mortgages, see a later section of this chapter.
10. The inflow of indentured labour was about 134,900; see Roberts, *Population of Jamaica.*
11. See figure 1 in chapter 1.
12. Eric Williams, "Historical Background of British Guiana's Problems", *Journal of Negro History* 30 (1945).
13. FAO Bulletin on Cacao, 7, 9.
14. See Greaves, *Colonial Monetary Conditions*, 47, where the question of "creditworthiness" is discussed. Although the banking system would perhaps have considered real property as suitable collateral, it would hardly have financed the development of thousands of small farmers.
15. Shephard, *The Cocoa Industry*, part 4.
16. Greaves, *Colonial Monetary Conditions,* 47.
17. Theoretically he could have shifted to other crops, but chapter 5 on the "minor agricultural industries" shows that the outcome might have been the same.
18. See Report of the Imperial Economic Committee, para 217.
19. Trinidad Hansard, 9 Dec. 1921, 372.
20. Report of Imperial Economic Committee.
21. Bareau, *Cocoa: A Crop with a Future.*
22. Imperial Economic Committee, *op. cit.*
23. Ibid.
24. Ibid.
25. Trinidad Council Paper 61/1940.
26. Director of Agriculture's Report 1923.
27. Ibid., 1924.
28. Ibid., 1925.
29. Ibid., 1929.
30. Ibid., 1929, 32.
31. Ibid., 1931, 57.
32. Ibid., 1937, 12.

33. Ibid., 1925.
34. Ibid., 1928.
35. The effect of weather is discussed on p. 60.
36. Extract from mycologist's report in the Director of Agriculture's Report for 1936, 53.
37. Shephard, *Cacao Industry of Trinidad.*
38. Ibid. Here two most important points have been linked, the financial weakness of the industry and of the government, both brought about by adverse trading conditions.
39. Compare these yields with those in the Gold Coast. Shephard, "The Gold Coast Cacao Industry", found that the yield there was 500–600 pounds per acre. "This is at least twice as large as the yield obtained in Trinidad and equals that obtained by intensive methods in Grenada."
40. Short-term supply elasticity in cocoa is in any case very low but price increases can lead to more intensive cropping and greater care which can in turn increase output in the short run.
41. See Director of Agriculture's Report 1938, 8.
42. See chapter 9, "Public Finance".
43. Trinidad and Tobago Hansard, 9 December 1921, 327 ff.
44. Director of Agriculture's Report 1925, 7.
45. Ibid.,1931.
46. Trinidad and Tobago Council Paper 61/1940.
47. Compare Marper with Gold Coast production. See note 39.
48. Mortgages Extension Ordinance of 1921.
49. Trinidad and Tobago Hansard 1930, contribution by Hon. L.A.P. O'Reilly.
50. Shephard, *Cacao Industry of Trinidad*, part 5.
51. Trinidad and Tobago Disturbances 1937. Report of Committee, Cmd. 5641.
52. Newlyn and Rowan, *Money and Banking in British Colonial Africa*, 248.
53. Not only were the interest rates too high in view of the depressed condition of the industry, but it would appear that "the rate of interest to members of a society (agricultural) is decided by the society" up to a maximum of 12 per cent. "The interest of the Agricultural Bank was reduced in 1931 from 7% to 6% and it is at the latter rate that the Government makes loans to the Agricultural Credit Society." The higher rate (12 per cent) was charged to meet losses on loans, expenses and reserves, and to prevent further borrowing from government. The following is the history of one borrower:

Amount borrowed	$100.00 (August 1933)
Amount repaid	$64.00 (21.5.37)

But he is faced with an interest amounting to $54.71 besides a balance of $35.60 or a total of $90.31." (See Trinidad and Tobago Hansard, 21 May 1937.)

54. It provided, however, lessons for the future.
55. Special taxation was imposed in 1935 to subsidize the industry. See chapter 9, "Public Finance".
56. The Cocoa Planters' Association was established in the early twentieth century. That section of the industry which it embraces is run on much more businesslike lines than is the peasant sector. It encourages improved methods of cultivation and of preparation of the beans for export.
57. Report of Imperial Economic Committee, para 108.
58. A similar situation obtained in the Gold Coast and was one justification for the marketing boards.
59. Shephard, *Cacao Industry of Trinidad*, part 5.

Chapter 4

1. Pitman, *The Development of the British West Indies,* chapter 40.
2. Beachey, *British West Indies Sugar Industry*, 122.
3. See chapter 2, p. 29.
4. To encourage the mechanization of the industry, the government allowed the estates fuel free of excise duty for their tractors.
5. Lamont, *Problems of the Antilles*, 25.
6. Gilbert, *Notes on the Production of Sugar Canes.*
7. The yield is very largely dependent on water supply. In average West Indian conditions anything over 30 tons of cane to an acre is reckoned a good crop; but with irrigation in Hawaii over 100 tons per acre have been obtained. Cf. "An Economic Survey of the Colonial Empire" (1932), Co. No. 95, 440.
8. Ibid.
9. See later section concerning the quota system for supplying the domestic sugar market. It was argued that the smaller and more inefficient the factory the greater should be the proportion of its output it should be allowed to sell in the protected and subsidized local market.
10. It is realized that this argument savours of the "who should bell the cat" mentality; but since Trinidad production was but a small part of world output and her main agricultural industry had completely deteriorated she may be said to have had a good case – not that other small producers dependent only on sugar could not also claim to have a better one.
11. See Trinidad and Tobago Hansard, 3 September 1937, 313.

12. Woodford Lodge, chapter 3, 38–41.
13. Trinidad and Tobago Hansard, 1937.
14. Report on Cane Farming Industry 1932, Council Paper 84/1933.
15. Report Director of Agriculture, 1927, 7.
16. Trinidad and Tobago Council Paper 84/1933.
17. This question is further discussed in chapter 8, "Labour". It was one of the factors adversely affecting the supply of labour to sugar estates.
18. Cf. "An Economic Survey of the Colonial Empire", 441.
19. Lamont, *Problems of the Antilles*, 2
20. It should not be thought, however, that the declared price was legally binding. One of the conditions of granting a loan to the manufacturers was the maintenance of a minimum price for canes.
21. See motion proposed by the colonial secretary in the Legislative Council, 30 May 1930.
22. The premium on local sugar was decreased by 4¢ per ton for every 50¢ increase in the free-on-board price of exported sugar.
23. Cf. Trinidad and Tobago Council Paper, 119/1938.
24. Ibid.
25. Ibid.
26. Lamont, *Problems of the Antilles*, 18.
27. Gilbert, *Notes on the Production of Sugar Cane.*
28. *Economic Survey of the Colonial Empire.*
29. Lamont, *Problems of the Antilles*, 74.
30. Trinidad and Tobago Council Paper, no. 84/1933.
31. In some other cane producing countries the general practice is to burn the cane before reaping. This process requires immediate crushing as burnt canes deteriorate rapidly after 24 to 48 hours.
32. See Trinidad and Tobago Council Paper 84/1932. In the early twentieth century every effort was made to encourage cane farming: "Prizes given to the best cane farmers have stimulated the efforts of this industrious class." See Colonial Report 1908/9, 9.
33. Council Paper 84/1932. On this question, however, Mr Hosein said in the Legislative Council, 21 March 1930, during the debate on the bill to give financial assistance to the sugar industry, that one of the causes of the tension was that the sugar manufacturers had tried to collect all outstanding debts immediately the price of sugar fell.
34. It would appear (see Lamont, *Problems of the Antilles*) that on the whole cane farmers were better treated in his area in the south than in other cane farming areas. While his estate was able to obtain without difficulty the services of ex-indentured Indians the other estates had to replenish their labour supply by new immigration.

35. Dr McShine – contribution to the debate of 21 March 1930.
36. It is very interesting to compare the attitudes towards granting assistance to the two industries. The observations of the Hon. L.A.P. O'Reilly are here quoted again for ease of reference since they help to bring out clearly the change in attitudes, the lesson learned, since cocoa relief was given in the 1920s.
37. See table 22.
38. Trinidad and Tobago Hansard 1936: debate on the sugar quotas.
39. See chapter 3.
40. It has been argued by Prest in *War Economics of Primary Producing Countries*, 264, and others that American wartime spending in Trinidad was harmful to the sugar industry by robbing it of labour. This seems to be the result of looking at the problem too narrowly. The drift from the land had begun in the 1920s and 1930s. Wartime conditions only accelerated the trend. It is the opinion of the author that what happened to the sugar industry in 1941–43 was a blessing. It led to greater mechanization. It is conceivable that a break with the older, less efficient, systems of production could have been brought about only by such a shock as was administered by American spending. The latter reorganized the whole economic structure. Lamont had suggested that a cataclysm was required to save the Trinidad sugar industry from itself (*Problems of the Antilles,* 25); American spending provided this.

Chapter 5

1. Trinidad and Tobago Council Paper 1931.
2. Director of Agriculture Report 1931.
3. Cf. "An Economic Survey of the Colonial Empire", 1932.
4. Cf. Shephard, *Cacao Industry of Trinidad*, part 5: "The attitude of the planters towards subsidiary crops may be summarized briefly by stating that when cacao was profitable no other crop was allowed to compete for land."
5. Cf. Report of the Economic Committee (Trinidad and Tobago), 1949, 89, para. 70.
6. Ibid., 86, para. 62.
7. Ibid., 86, para. 64.
8. Note that war had affected the banana industry again in 1939.
9. Director of Agriculture Report 1934, 11.
10. Ibid., 1935, 48.
11. Ibid., 1936, 54.
12. Ibid., 1937, 7.
13. Ibid., 1935, 9.

14. Ibid., 1935, 9.
15. For the conversion ratio see Director of Agriculture Report 1919/20, 10.
16. Ibid., 1919/20, 10. It is interesting to note that at the same time as the "price of nuts and copra dropped heavily" local consumption of domestically produced coconut products increased "because of the high prices of imported oils and fats".
17. Hurricane damage was as follows:

Extent of Damage (Acres)

	Heavy	Medium	Light	Total
Coconuts	3,909	1,038	2,694	7,641
Cocoa	12,426	5,371	4,249	22,046

"The Icacos district was the finest coconut section in Trinidad and the damage in that area was particularly regrettable." Cf. Director of Agriculture Report 1933, 13.

18. See appendix 3.

Chapter 6

1. The first successful well had been sunk in this very area.
2. See *Trinidad Handbook*, 1924.
3. This company was immediately successful and paid very high dividends. See section on "Companies", and table 56.
4. This was the most prolific area in Trinidad. Its output as a percentage of total production is given in p. 145.
5. Sir Thomas H. Holland: Report on the Oil Industry of Trinidad. Trinidad and Tobago Council Paper 86/1928. The writer is indebted to Sir Thomas for much of the data in the early part of this chapter.
6. Trinidad and Tobago Hansard, "Debate on Hindu Marriages".
7. See Mines Department Report 1939.
8. One doubts whether the Trinidad administration of the early twentieth century would itself have been equal to the task.
9. See Mikesell and Chenery, *Arabian Oil*, chapter 4, 37–57.
10. Holland Report.
11. In the Middle East such problems rarely occurred as very often the whole of the area of the country or sheikdom was leased to one company. See Mikesell and Chenery, *Arabian Oil*, chapter 4.
12. See Holland Report.

13. Ibid.
14. Ibid.
15. Ibid.
16. Ibid.
17. Cf. Holland, *Mineral Resources of India.*
18. Holland Report.
19. See chapter 2 for imports of machinery and TLL Report 1920/21.
20. See Mines Department Report 1923.
21. See Mines Department Report 1926.
22. See chapter 1, "Exports". It should be noted, however, that production in India was already past its peak.
23. The period saw one of the great international price wars in oil.
24. There was also considerable expansion on the demand side, new domestic uses and vehicles especially in the United States were particularly responsible for the increase.
25. See Mines Department Report 1939.
26. Ibid.
27. Ibid.
28. Ibid.
29. See Economic Committee Report 1949.
30. Mines Department Report 1928.
31. See Gadgil, *The Industrial Revolution of India*, "Since 1924 there has been a steady falling off in production from this source."
32. See Mikesell and Chenery, *Arabian Oil*, for a similar motive in Middle East Oil Development, 41.
33. Holland Report.
34. As will be seen, however, Apex continued prosperous without entering the field of refining.
35. Mines Department Reports.
36. Ibid.
37. Ibid.
38. The two most important questions then stressed were ensuring employment and royalties from oil.
39. Government encouraged this action by allowing duty-free imports of crude oil.
40. See TLL Report quoted in the later section which deals with the companies engaged in the industry.
41. See Holland Report.
42. See Petroleum Information Bureau (Report 1955).
43. See Avendano, "Some Aspects of Petroleum Trade and Production in Venezuela", *Inter-American Economic Affairs* (1954).

44. Ibid.
45. Mines Department Report, 1929.
46. Mines Department Reports.
47. Mines Department Report, 1939.
48. The statements were issued annually as Council Papers 1927–35. The data were obtained for the period 1936–39 direct from the industry.
49. Chapter 9 gives an indication of the increases in revenue from this source.
50. Trinidad ranks among the highest importers of cinema films per head of population in the world.
51. Trinidad and Tobago Hansard, 23 February 1934.
52. See *Oil and Petroleum Year Book*, 1940.
53. Some of the information in this section came from *Oil and Petroleum Year Book*, 1940.
54. TLL was the chief operator in the field and formed various associations with firms that found themselves in difficulties. See note 62.
55. Most of the companies were incorporated in the United Kingdom.
56. See the Holland Report.
57. The most prolific area in Trinidad.
58. TLL Company Report, 1938.
59. Published in *Inter-American Economic Affairs*, 1954.
60. Ibid.
61. Ibid.
62. It was spreading both vertically and horizontally, sometimes offering to drill for oil on the lands of some smaller firms on the basis of a certain proportion of the profits after cost of drilling had been met.
63. Ibid.
64. Trinidad and Tobago Hansard, 1945.
65. The motion concerned the contribution of the oil industry to government revenue.

Chapter 7

1. The density problem was not as great as in, say, Barbados.
2. Since the whole population was increasing this increase in the number of the over 45s need not, by itself, cause alarm.
3. The diet of salted beef and fish and large quantities of carbohydrates would have hastened the deterioration. See also p. 111 of the Forster Report, Cmd. 5641.
4. See chapter 8, "Labour".
5. See Health Department Reports.
6. See chapter 9, "Public Finance".

7. The increase in immigration was once more evident in the early 1940s when American base construction was undertaken.
8. Lewis, on primary education.
9. Prest, *Fiscal Survey*, 264.
10. Census Report 1921.
11. West India Royal Commission Report, 1938–39, 242.
12. Forster Commission Report, 41. Cmd. 5641, 41.
13. Braithwaite, "Social Stratification in Trinidad", 7.
14. This was the opinion of an attorney general in Trinidad and Tobago.
15. The cost must be heavy especially if it involves technical training. The recurrent costs may be especially formidable since they are likely to increase steadily.
16. Human resources and poor soils are the only factors of production to be found in certain islands.

Chapter 8

1. Roberts, *Population of Jamaica*, 128.
2. See also chapters 3 and 4.
3. "In crop" means harvesting period; "out of crop" means growing period.
4. See chapter 4.
5. Shephard, *Cacao Industry of Trinidad* and *Agricultural Labour in Trinidad.*
6. Ibid.
7. Census Report 1921.
8. See chapter 7.
9. Ibid.
10. Shephard, *Cacao Industry of Trinidad.*
11. Ibid.
12. Trinidad and Tobago Council Paper 84/1933.
13. This did not happen in the post–World War II period, however. See Economic Committee Report 1949, table 5, 81.
14. See chapter 7.
15. See Trinidad Disturbances 1937, Forster Commission Report, Cmd. 5641, 14.
16. Reports of the Protector of Immigrants.
17. See Forster Commission Report, Cmd. 5641.
18. Relations were very cordial within the industry.
19. There was no labour department until after the riots of 1937.
20. See pp. 242–48.
21. See also appendix 2.
22. Shephard, *Agricultural Labour in Trinidad.*
23. There were constant complaints from the estates on this score.

24. West India Royal Commission Report, 1938–39, 195.
25. Herskovits and Herskovits, *Trinidad Village*, chapter 3, 60.
26. "Task" work corresponds to piece rates.
27. See report on the disturbances of 1937, published as a Council.
28. See table 73.
29. It is interesting that the riots and strikes should have occurred precisely at the time when onditions seemed to be improving. See in chapter 6 that the wages bill in petroleum had doubled in 1935–39. But the growth was unbalanced.
30. *Trinidad Handbook 1924.*
31. See tables 73 and 74.
32. See Lamont, *Problems of the Antilles*, 213 ff., for some interesting observations on this topic.
33. See table 73.
34. Council Paper 125 of 1920.
35. Trinidad and Tobago Hansard, 9 July 1937: Speech by the Hon. Colonial Secretary.
36. See chapter 6.
37. See the report published as Council Paper 88/1936. See also p. 116 of Forster Commission Report, Cmd. 5641.
38. Shephard, *Cacao Industry of Trinidad.*
39. See chapter 5.
40. The company paid a large percentage of the value of its exports as export duty. See p. 25 of Forster Commission Report, Cmd. 5641.
41. Ibid.
42. On the subject of the significance of increases in the number and proportion of persons engaged in tertiary categories of employment, see Bauer and Yamey, *Economics of Underdeveloped Countries*. See also Rottenberg, "Note on Economic Progress and Occupational Distribution", *Review of Economic and Statistics* (May 1953): 168.
43. Labour Conditions in the West Indies, Cmd. 6070.
44. The ordinances were largely ineffective in reducing hours of employment. Employees were threatened with dismissal if they did not work extra hours.
45. West India Royal Commission Report, 218.
46. Labour Conditions in the West Indies, Cmd. 6070.
47. See debate on Minimum Wages, Hansard, 5 March 1937.
48. Note the drop which was largely due to improved conditions of labour after American wartime spending.
49. The board's report on wages, Council Paper 88/1936, is discussed later.
50. See Forster Commission Report, Cmd. 5641, 52.
51. See appendix 1, "Terms of Trade".

52. See chapter 7.
53. The secretary of state showed greater interest in this question than did the Trinidad and Tobago government.
54. Minimum wages were fixed under similar conditions in India.
55. See Hansard, 1935.
56. This was left to the Minimum Wages Advisory Board.
57. This point was submitted by Captain Cipriani, the labour leader.
58. He did not elaborate on "man-day", however.
59. Cf. Forster Commission Report, Cmd. 5641, 16.
60. Shephard, *Agricultural Labour in Trinidad.*
61. This would most certainly have happened, but it would have intensified the imbalance discussed in chapter 1.
62. See pp. 108–9 of ILO Report: Basic Problems of Plantation Labour, Re-wage Legislation in India and Ceylon.
63. Ibid.
64. West India Royal Commission Report.
65. Forster Commission Report, Cmd. 5641, 75. See also Lamont, *Problems of the Antilles*, 23.
66. See chapter 4.
67. West India Royal Commission Report, 216.
68. Ibid.
69. See, for example, Vester, and Gardner, *Trade Unions and the Law.*
70. A reply to this effect was actually given to a question in the legislature on the subject; see debate 8 March 1935.
71. See debate in Trinidad and Tobago Hansard 1932.
72. For example, those embodied in the 1927 act.
73. It neither specifically allowed nor prohibited picketing.
74. See table 78.
75. See Labour Conditions in the West Indies, Cmd. 6070.
76. West India Royal Commission Report, 196–97.
77. See chapter 1.
78. Ibid. Note, however, that the wages bill in the oil industry was rapidly increasing.
79. Forster Commission Report, Cmd. 5641, 81, para. 277.
80. See Trinidad and Tobago Hansard, 1937.

Chapter 9

1. The failure of revenue to rise caused great inconvenience as reserves had to be used up.
2. That is to say, the purely internal economy should have begun to be more important.

3. The figures given for both revenue and expenditure are gross, that is, they include revenue and expenditure of railways and other government departments. It would have been better if such items could have been treated separately but the accounts of the Trinidad and Tobago government were so arranged in the inter-war period (and even in the 1950s as A.R. Prest found) that it was difficult to decide which items were purely current and which were capital. It has been decided, therefore, to proceed with the gross figures bearing in mind all the time that such supposedly self-balancing departments as the railways are included.
4. It would have been easier to cut expenditure on economic services than on most social services.
5. See chapter 3.
6. See figure 6.
7. This topic is discussed later.
8. It would have meant perhaps requesting "grants in aid" from the United Kingdom.
9. The recurrent costs of social services must always be carefully examined before the schemes are undertaken especially if revenue is likely to fluctuate violently.
10. Col. No. 298, para. 6.
11. MacDougall, *World Dollar Problem*, 52–54.
12. The former was sharper. On the latter, petroleum though also affected, was making a contribution to revenue.
13. It was once suggested that the man who carried his bottle in his pocket was supporting the country. The Economic Committee Report 1949, 79, praised the role played by rum in these terms: "The availability of rum in adequate quantities has helped to relieve the inflationary pressure on other commodities and in doing so has added 2½ million dollars a year to public revenue by way of excise duty."
14. See Banerjea, *Study of Indian Economics*, 208.
15. Prest, *Fiscal Survey,* chapter 3, section 2.
16. Whenever the question of the contribution of the petroleum industry to revenue was debated in the Legislative Council, the unyielding constant in the view of unofficial members was that, even if it were necessary to increase the revenue obtained from domestic consumption of petroleum products, the consumer should not be asked to bear any part of the tax.
17. Licences, and so on, are a composite item. A different classification could result in taxes on incomes taking second place as a source of revenue.
18. About 90 per cent of all customs and excise revenue was collected at the customs house in Port of Spain.
19. Trinidad and Tobago Hansard, 5 December 1919, 354.
20. Even in 1919 certain members of the Legislative Council attacked the tendency to depend for income tax revenue solely on those whose jobs made

it difficult for them to evade the tax. See Trinidad and Tobago Hansard, 28 November 1919, 3, 11 and references to "The Six Hundred", 354.

21. Income Tax Ordinance 1938; see Debate in Trinidad and Tobago Hansard, 9 December 1938, 604 f.
22. See thesis by J. O'Neil Lewis on the economic development of Puerto Rico, Trinidad and Jamaica.
23. See Laws of Trinidad and Tobago, revised 1925. Double taxation was later renegotiated and agreed with all relevant countries.
24. See chapter 6 for the companies operating in the industry.
25. Chapter 6.
26. Memorandum on the Sterling Assets of the Colonies, Col. 298.
27. This refers to gross expenditure. See note 1. On this question, compare Prest, *Fiscal Survey,* chapter 3, section 4, "Budgetary Procedure".
28. There was a greater emphasis on expenditure on social services.
29. Prest, *Fiscal Survey,* Table 333 found that in 1938 economic services accounted for only 15 per cent of expenditure. He does not say how this figure was arrived at. Even if he attempted, in spite of his warning in the section on budgetary procedure, to treat only current expenditure, this figure for economic services must be regarded as being somewhat low. Especially this is the case when it is seen that the largest item (31 per cent) in his table is "other".
30. See West India Royal Commission Report, chapter 6.
31. See pp. 274–76.
32. Tables 86 and 87.
33. See debate on the loan for the Harbour Scheme, Trinidad and Tobago Hansard, 1935.
34. Hansard, 22 May 1931, 367.
35. Ibid., 21 February 1936, 18. However, this system would have had the advantage of selecting the worst hit areas for relief.
36. Ibid., 28 November 1919.
37. See the various forms of financing development given in pp. 281–82.
38. Prest, *Fiscal Survey,* chapter 3, section 4.
39. Hansard, 21 November 1938, 334.

Appendix 1

1. Bauer, *West African Trade,* 410 ff.
2. Hicks and Hicks, *Report on Finance and Taxation in Jamaica,* 10.
3. Chapter 2 indicates the importance of these items in the consumption pattern of the population.
4. Even if account is taken of trading expenses, it would appear that the exporters, not the producers, were the real gainers from the cocoa trade.

Appendix 2

1. It is however possible that the farmer would have been no better off if he produced his own food. For one thing, his choice would have been restricted. He could not produce all of the full range of products needed.
2. Director of Agriculture Report, 1930.
3. Ibid., for 1931.
4. Williams, *Capitalism and Slavery,* 108.
5. See Prest, *War Economies of Primary Producing Countries,* 265 ff.
6. Woodford Lodge, chapter 3, 38–41.
7. Hansard, 21 October 1932, 403, Hon. L.A.P. O'Reilly: "The effect of this excessive duty is to shut out cheap watchekongs worn by the poorest people in this community and cotton socks which are now sold at 4d. per pair. Does Canada want that sort of preference from a barefoot community (because a great many people in this country are barefooted). It is not the cane farmer who buys the cheap article; it is the man whom the cane farmer employs. The cane farmer probably wears the better type of watchekong (Canadian). It is the next to the poorest section of the community that wears that article. The poorest wear none."
8. This preference on crude oil was of little use as Trinidad and Tobago exports of crude oil were very small. It was developing as a refining centre.

Appendix 3

1. Meyer, "Britain's Colonies in World Trade"; MacDougall, "Imperial Preference: A Quantitative Analysis".
2. See chapter 9.
3. See Hansard, 1931, 268–70.
4. It seems as though Jamaica did not try anything so ambitious.
5. See Hansard, 1930.
6. This information was obtained from a conversation with the man who was the then collector of customs in Trinidad and Tobago. Subsequent references to the Legislative Council debates confirmed it.
7. Hansard, 1930.
8. Coconuts and by-products have to meet the competition of many other crops from which vegetable oils are produced.

Selected Bibliography

Primary

Annual Report of the Department of Agriculture 1914–1940. Port of Spain: Government Printing Office, 1914–1940.

Annual Reports on the Colonies, Asia and the Pacific Basin 1908–1940. London: Colonial Office, HMSO, 1908–1940.

Basic Problems of Plantation Labour. Geneva: International Labour Office, International Labour Organisation, 1950.

British Parliamentary Debates and Council Papers 1918–1940. London: HMSO, 1918–1940.

Cacao: A Review of Current Trends in Production, Price and Consumption. Commodity Census Bulletin No. 27. Rome: Food and Agriculture Organization of the United Nations. 1955.

Census Reports for Trinidad and Tobago 1921. Port of Spain: Central Statistical Office, 1922.

Census Reports for Trinidad and Tobago 1931. Port of Spain: Central Statistical Office, 1932.

Census Reports for Trinidad and Tobago 1946. Port of Spain: Central Statistical Office, 1947.

Debates of the Legislative Council of Trinidad and Tobago 1912–1940. Port of Spain: Government Printers, 1912–40.

Forster, J. *Trinidad and Tobago Disturbances 1937: Report of the Forster Commission*. Cmd. 5641. London: HMSO, 1938.

Gilbert, M.S.M. *Notes on the Production of Sugar Cane, Trinidad: Council Paper No. 79 of 1932*. Port of Spain: Government Printers, 1932.

Hicks, U.K., and J.R. Hicks. *Report on Finance and Taxation in Jamaica*. Kingston: Government Printer, 1954; London: HMSO, 1955.

Holland, T. *Oil Industry of Trinidad Council Paper No. 86*. Port -of- Spain: Government Printing Office, 1928.

Imperial Economic Committee Reports 1928–1948. London: HMSO, 1929–49.

Legislative Council of Trinidad and Tobago. *Industrial Court Ordinance,* Council Paper No. 26 of 1920. Port of Spain: Government Printers, 1920.

———. *Labour (Minimum Wage) Ordinance No. 6 (1935)*. Port of Spain: Government Printers, 1935.

———. *Minimum Wage Fixing Machinery Council Paper No. 88 of 1936*. Port of Spain: Government Printers, 1936.

———. *Report of Labour Disturbances Commission 1934: Council Paper No. 109 of 1934*. Port of Spain: Government Printers, 1934.

———. *Report of Commission on the Trinidad and Tobago Disturbances, 1937. Council Paper No. 25 (Cmd. 5641) of 1937–38*. Port of Spain: Government Printers, 1938.

———. *Report of the Economics Committee of 1949: Council Paper No. 15 of 1949*. Port of Spain: Government Printers, 1949.

———. *Trade Union Ordinance No. 20 of 1932*. Port of Spain: Government Printers, 1932.

———. *Wages Committee Report Council Paper No. 125 of 1920*. Port of Spain: Government Printers, *1920*.

———. *Workmen's Compensation Ordinance No. 8 of 1926*. Port of Spain: Government Printers, 1926.

Mobilization of Domestic Capital: Reports and Documents of the *Second Working Party of Experts*. Bangkok: Department of Economic Affairs, Economic Commission for Asia and the Far East (ECAFE), 1953.

Olivier, S.H. *Report of the West Indian Sugar Commission*. Presented by the Secretary of State for the Colonies to Parliament by command of his Majesty, March 1930. London: HMSO, 1930.

Orde-Browne, G.St J. *Labour Conditions in the West Indies*. Presented by the Secretary of State for the Colonies to Parliament by command of His Majesty, July 1939. London: HMSO, 1939.

Relative Prices of Exports And Imports Of Under-Developed Countries. Lake Success, NY: United Nations, Department of Economic Affairs, 1949.

Reports of the Mines Department of Trinidad and Tobago for the Year 1912. Port of Spain: Government Printers, 1913.

Secretary of State for the Colonies. *The West India Royal Commission 1938–39: Report and Recommendations*. London: HMSO, 1945.

———. *West India Royal Commission, 1897: 5 Vol* C 8655, C 8656, C 8657, C 8669, C 8799. London: HMSO, 1898.

Statistical Abstract for the British Empire. London: Board of Trade, HMSO, 1939.

Shephard, C.Y. *The Cacao Industry of Trinidad.* Port of Spain: Government Printing Office, 1932.

———. *Agricultural Labour in Trinidad.* Port of Spain: Government Printing Office, 1926.

United Nations General Assembly. *Financing of Economic Development of Under-developed Countries. 622 (VII) Resolution.* 1952.

Secondary

Arndt, H.W. *Economic Lessons of the 1930s: A Report Issued under the Auspices of the Royal Institute of International Affairs.* Oxford: Oxford University Press, 1944.

Baran, P. *The Political Economy of Growth.* NewYork: Monthly Review Press, 1957.

Bareau, P. *Cocoa: A Crop with a Future.* Bournville, England: Cadbury Brothers, 1953.

Bauer, P.T. *West African Trade.* Cambridge: Cambridge University Press, 1954.

Bauer, P.T., and B.S. Yamey. *The Economics of Underdeveloped Countries.* London: Nisbet and Cambridge University Press, 1957.

Beachey, R.W. *The British West Indies Sugar Industry in the Late 19th Century.* Oxford: Blackwell, 1957.

Blanchard, P. *Democracy and Empire in the Caribbean: A Contemporary Review.* New York: Macmillan, 1947.

Dalley, F.W. *Trade Union Organisation and Industrial Relations in Trinidad No. 215: Economic Surveys of the Colonial Empire.* London: Colonial Office, HMSO, 1947.

Gadgil, D.R. *The Industrial Evolution of India in Recent Times.* Oxford: Oxford University Press, 1924.

Gabraith, J.K. *American Capitalism: The Concept of Countervailing Powers.* Boston: Houghton Mifflin, 1952.

Greaves, I.C. *Colonial Monetary Conditions: Colonial Research Studies,* No. 10. London: HMSO, 1953.

Herskovits, F.S., and M.J. Herskovits. *Trinidad Village.* New York: Alfred Knopf, 1947.

Kindleberger, C.P. *The Terms of Trade: A European Case Study.* Massachusetts: Technology Press of Massachusetts Institute of Technology and Wiley, 1956.

Lamont, N. *Problems of the Antilles: A Collection of Speeches and Writings on West Indian Questions.* Glasgow: J. Smith and Son, 1912.

Lewis W.A. *The Theory of Economic Growth.* London: George Allen and Unwin, 1955.

———. *Economic Survey: 1919–1939*. London: George Allen and Unwin, 1949.

MacDougall, Donald. *The world Dollar Problem: A Study in International Economics*. London: Macmillan, 1957.

Macmillan, W.M. *Warning from the West Indies: A Tract for Africa and the Empire*. Harmondsworth: Penguin, 1938.

Matthews, B. *Crisis of the West Indian Family: A Sample Study*. St Augustine: Extra Mural Department, University College of the West Indies, 1953.

Meyer, F.V. *Britain's Colonies in World Trade*. Oxford: Oxford University Press, 1948.

Mikesell, R.F., and H.B. Cheney. *Arabian Oil: America's Stake in the Middle East*. Chapel Hill, New York: University of North Carolina Press, 1949.

Myrdal, G. *An International Economy*. New York: Harper and Row. 1956.

Newlyn, W.T., and D.C. Rowan. *Money and Banking in British Colonial Africa*. Oxford: Oxford University Press, 1954.

Nurkes, R. *Problems of Capital Formation in Underdeveloped Countries*. New York: Basil Blackwell, 1953.

Pitman, F. *The Development of the British West Indies*. New Haven: Yale University Press, 1917.

Prest, A.R. *A Fiscal Survey of the British Caribbean*. London: HMSO, 1957.

Proudfoot, M. *Britain and the US in the Caribbean: A Comparative Study in Methods of Development*. London: Faber and Faber, 1954.

Romolini, E. *The Evolution of the Sugar Economy in the Interval between Two World Wars*. Rome: International Institute of Agriculture, 1944.

Rostow, W.W. *The British Economy in the 19th Century*. Oxford: Oxford University Press, 1948.

Simey, T.S. *Welfare and Planning in the West Indies*. Oxford: Clarendon Press, 1946.

Simkin, C.G.F. *The Instability of a Dependent Economy: Economic Fluctuations in New Zealand*. Oxford: Oxford University Press, 1951.

Skinner, W.R. *Oil and Petroleum Yearbooks 1912–1940*. California: University of California, 1913–1940.

Williams, E. *Capitalism and Slavery*. Chapel Hill: University of North Carolina Press, 1944.

Journals

Braithwaite, L. "Social Stratification in Trinidad". *Social and Economic Studies* 2.2–3 (1935): 5–175.

Lewis, W.A. "Economic Development with Unlimited Supplies of Labour". *Manchester School of Economic and Social Studies Publication* 22.2 (May 1954): 133–91.

MacDougall, D., and R. Hutt. "Imperial Preference: A Quantitative Analysis". *Economic Journal* 64.254 (1954): 5–175.

Pieris, W.V.D. "Coconut Cultivation in the Island of Trinidad". *Tropical Agriculturalist* (Ceylon) 96 (1946): 328–46.

Rippy, J.F. "Trinidad and Ceylon: Two Profitable British Colonies". *Inter-American Economic Affairs* 8.2 (1954): 82–93.

Shephard, C.Y. "The Gold Coast Cocoa Industry". *Tropical Agriculture* (Trinidad) 12.12 (1934): 311–12; 13.3 (1936): 59–6l; 13.9 (1936): 229–32.

Index

www.ingramcontent.com/pod-product-compliance
Lightning Source LLC
Chambersburg PA
CBHW031319230926
51848CB00001B/17
* 9 7 8 9 7 6 8 1 2 5 9 1 0 *